Sociolinguistics in England

Natalie Braber • Sandra Jansen
Editors

Sociolinguistics in England

palgrave
macmillan

Editors
Natalie Braber
School of Arts & Humanities
Nottingham Trent University
Nottingham, UK

Sandra Jansen
Department of English and American
Studies
University of Paderborn
Paderborn, Germany

ISBN 978-1-137-56287-6   ISBN 978-1-137-56288-3   (eBook)
DOI 10.1057/978-1-137-56288-3

Library of Congress Control Number: 2017962231

Cover illustration: © Jay's photo / Getty Images

Printed on acid-free paper

This Palgrave Macmillan imprint is published by Springer Nature
The registered company is Macmillan Publishers Ltd.
The registered company address is: The Campus, 4 Crinan Street, London, N1 9XW, United Kingdom

Map of England

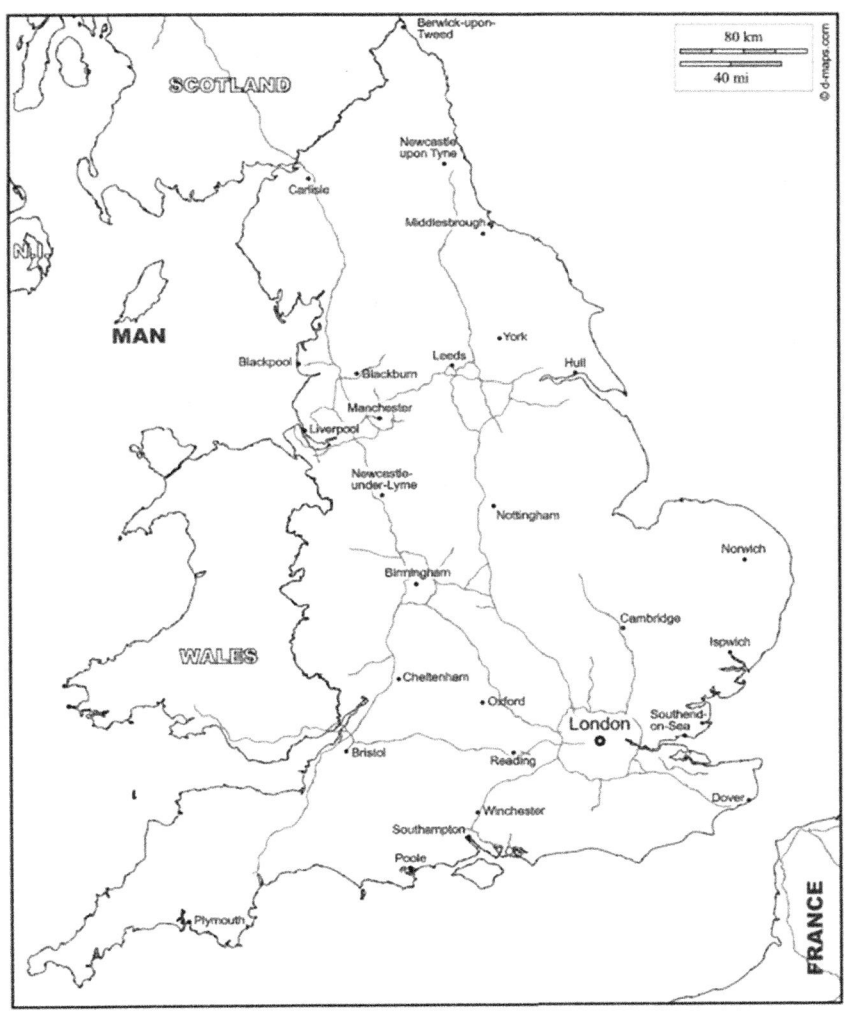

Acknowledgements

As with all projects of this kind, it has taken quite some time to complete! There are people who we would like to thank for their help in ensuring this book has made it to print.

First of all, we would like to thank the following colleagues for their time and expertise in providing detailed comments on the draft chapters: Anita Auer, David Britain, Thomas Devlin, Rob Drummond, Nicholas Flynn, Sue Fox, Sophie Holmes-Elliott, Sam Kirkham, Claire Nance, Dennis Preston, Tamara Rathcke, Devyani Sharma, Eivind Torgersen, Danielle Turton, Clive Upton and Kevin Watson. Special thanks go to Joan Beal who, in addition to reviewing a chapter, advised us on our introductory chapter.

We would also like to thank Rebecca Brennan, Chloe Fitzsimmons and Rebecca Wyde at Palgrave Macmillan for helping us throughout the publishing stages from proposal to final publication.

It goes without saying that we would like to thank all the contributors of this book who have been very patient with us and sent additional information when we have had to request this at short notice. It has been a pleasure to work with them.

Contents

Notes on Contributors

Anita Auer is Professor of English Linguistics at the University of Lausanne (Switzerland). As a historical (socio)linguist with a keen interest in interdisciplinary research, particularly the correlation between language variation and change and socio-economic history, she has carried out research and published widely on language standardization, corpus compilation, variation and change of different morpho-syntactic features, and historical sociolinguistics.

William Barras is Lecturer in Linguistics at the University of Aberdeen. He has research interests in dialectology, sociolinguistics and phonology. He completed a PhD in linguistics and English language at the University of Edinburgh in 2011. His thesis focused on rhoticity and intrusive-*r* in East Lancashire. He has also worked on the 'Fisherspeak' project at the University of Aberdeen, documenting loss of vocabulary in the fishing dialects of the East Coast of Scotland, and as a research associate at the University of Manchester on the project, 'Regional Identity and the Indexical Field'. He has taught at the universities of Edinburgh, York and Aberdeen. His publications include *Lexical Variation and Attrition in the Scottish Fishing Communities* with Robert McColl Millar and Lisa Bonnici, and a chapter in *The Archers in Fact and Fiction: Academic Analyses of Life in Rural Borsetshire.*

Natalie Braber is Reader in Linguistics at Nottingham Trent University. Her research concerns sociolinguistics and language variation, with a specific interest in the East Midlands, including language of coal miners in the region. Her articles have been published in *English Today*, *Journal of Pragmatics*, *Oral History* and *Identity,* and numerous book chapters in edited collections have also been published. She has also written *Nottinghamshire Dialect* (2015) and *Pit Talk* (confirm date) and was editor (alongside Liz Morrish and Louise Cummings) of *Exploring Language and Linguistics* (Cambridge University Press) in 2015.

Isabelle Buchstaller is Professor for Varieties of English at University of Duisburg-Essen. Her main research interests are language variation and change, including the role of contact in ongoing linguistic change. She has published widely on ongoing changes in the area of morpho-syntax, including her monograph *Quotative: New Trends and Sociolinguistic Implications* published by Wiley Blackwell in 2014. Her current ERC-funded research project (Buchstaller 2013–2017) investigates the mechanisms of intra-speaker instability with an eye on the range and the determinants of linguistic malleability across the lifespan of the individual.

Kearsy Cormier is Reader at University College London, and Director of the British Sign Language Corpus Project.

Rob Drummond is Senior Lecturer in Linguistics at Manchester Metropolitan University, working primarily within sociolinguistics. His main area of research interest is the role of language variation in the performance and perception of identities, especially in relation to urban youth language, Manchester accents and dialects, and non-native English.

Anne Fabricius is Associate Professor of English Language and a member of the LANGSOC research group at Roskilde University. She originally studied linguistics in Australia and then trained as a quantitative sociolinguist in Denmark, working on vocalic and consonantal variation and change in Received Pronunciation (RP) in England, and has worked on the sociolinguistics of RP since then. Her research interests also include language attitudes and ideologies, the English language in Danish Higher Education, and innovative methods for sociophonetic research, which she has published on together with Dominic Watt (University of York).

Jordan Fenlon is Lecturer in British Sign Language at Heriot-Watt University, and has worked on a number of studies drawing on the British Sign Language Corpus data.

Sue Fox is Lecturer in Modern English Linguistics at the University of Bern, Switzerland. She is a sociolinguist whose research interests are language variation and change, especially in urban multicultural contexts, multiethnolects, language and dialect contact, the impact of immigration on language change and the language of adolescents from a variationist perspective. Her research has mainly focused on the social and historical contexts that have led to the variety of English that is spoken today in London.

Eve Groarke is currently an MMedSci student in Clinical Communication Studies at the University of Sheffield, UK. She was formerly a research assistant at Lancaster University, UK.

Sandra Jansen is Senior Lecturer in English Linguistics at the University of Paderborn/Germany. Her research focuses on language variation and change, with a specific interest in Cumbrian dialects and L2 varieties of English. Jansen has published several journal articles and book chapters on language changes in the far north-west of England.

Sam Kirkham is Lecturer in Sociophonetics at Lancaster University, UK. His research interests include phonetics, sociolinguistics, bilingualism and contact varieties.

Adam Mearns has taught at the Universities of Sheffield and Leeds and at Northumbria University. He is currently Lecturer in the History of the English Language at Newcastle University. Recent publications have focused on the development of the *Diachronic Electronic Corpus of Tyneside English* (DECTE), the dialect of Tyneside and the concept of the supernatural in Old English.

Chris Montgomery is Senior Lecturer in Dialectology at the University of Sheffield. His research concerns Perceptual Dialectology, with a specific interest in methodological approaches to the study of non-linguists' perceptions. His articles have been published in the *Journal of Sociolinguistics,* the *Journal of Linguistic Geography,* and *Studies in Variation, Contacts and Change in English.* He was the editor (alongside Jennifer Cramer) of *Cityscapes and Perceptual Dialectology: Global Perspectives on Non-linguists' Knowledge of the Dialect Landscape* (Mouton de Gruyter), and with Karen Corrigan of a special issue of *English Language and Linguistics* on the role of place in historical linguistics. In addition, he has published numerous book chapters in other edited collections.

Claire Nance is Lecturer in Phonetics and Phonology at Lancaster University, UK. Her research interests include phonetics, laboratory phonology and socio-linguistics, with a particular focus on Scottish Gaelic and Celtic languages.

Ben Rampton is Professor of Applied and Sociolinguistics and Director of the Centre for Language Discourse and Communication at King's College London. He is the author of *Crossing: Language and Ethnicity among Adolescents* (Longman

1995) and *Language in Late Modernity: Interaction in an Urban School* (CUP 2006). He co-edited *The Language, Ethnicity and Race Reader* (Routledge 2003) and *Language and Superdiversity* (Routledge 2015), and he edits *Working Papers in Urban Language and Literacy*. He was founding convener of the UK Linguistic Ethnography Forum, and was the Director of the King's ESRC Interdisciplinary Social Science Doctoral Training Centre from 2011–2014.

Justyna A. Robinson is Senior Lecturer in English Language and Linguistics at the University of Sussex. Her research focuses on semantic variation and change, cognitive sociolinguistics, corpus linguistics and how these areas interact. Her recent publications include co-edited volumes on *Cognitive Sociolinguistics* (2014), *Corpus Methods for Semantics* (2014) and *Cognitive Perspectives on Bilingualism* (2016).

Rhys Sandow is a PhD student in Linguistics at the University of Sussex. His research interests include lexicography, lexical semantics and, primarily, sociolinguistics. His PhD research involves developing a lexis-oriented sociolinguistic framework. Consequently, Sandow works on sociolinguistic methodology and theory in order to explore the social function of the lexicon.

Adam Schembri is Lecturer in Sociolinguistics at the University of Birmingham, and co-editor (with Ceil Lucas) of *Sociolinguistics and Deaf Communities*, published with Cambridge University Press.

Rose Stamp is Postdoctoral Fellow at the University of Haifa, and has published research into variation and change in British Sign Language.

Eivind Torgersen is Professor of English Language in the Faculty of Teacher Education at the Norwegian University of Science and Technology in Trondheim, Norway. He has worked on projects on Multicultural London English and language change in London, in particular, modelling of phonological change and the use of spoken corpora in sociolinguistic research, and on multilingualism in the English language classroom in Norway. Other research interests are in experimental phonetics.

List of Figures

List of Tables

1

An Overview of Sociolinguistics in England

Sandra Jansen and Natalie Braber

Introduction

As we sat down for dinner at a conference in Rouen in May 2014, we got talking about the recent publication of *Sociolinguistics in Scotland*, edited by Robert Lawson. We were told that similar volumes were being planned for Ireland and Wales (they have since been published—in 2016 for Ireland, edited by Raymond Hickey, and in 2016 for Wales, edited by Mercedes Durham and Jonathan Morris). We were both working on sociolinguistic topics in England and therefore keen to complete the series, so we laid the plan for a similar publication. To our delight, Palgrave welcomed our proposal and you are now reading the fruit of what started as a dinner table chat.

S. Jansen
University of Paderborn, Paderborn, Germany

N. Braber (✉)
Nottingham Trent University, Nottingham, UK

© The Author(s) 2018
N. Braber, S. Jansen (eds.), *Sociolinguistics in England*,
DOI 10.1057/978-1-137-56288-3_1

This book, similar to its counterparts in Scotland, Ireland and Wales, encompasses a range of studies representative of the research conducted in the sociolinguistic field in England in the 2010s, notably on phonological, lexical, syntactic and intonational variation in English and British Sign Language. Set out over the next 13 chapters, they contribute to the development of sociolinguistic theory and suggest directions which may be fruitful for future studies. This introduction provides a short synopsis of the development of sociolinguistics as academic field in England. Finally, it considers directions which future research could, and perhaps should, take.

Previous Work on Sociolinguistics in England

Here we review previous dialectological and variationist work on varieties of English in England, outlining studies which encompass different aspects of the interplay between language and society. While this review presents a wide range of topics, we do not claim that this is a complete overview, but we aim to highlight important milestones in the development of sociolinguistics as academic field in England.

In the nineteenth and in the first half of the twentieth century regional variation was the main concern of linguists and philologists. A first large-scale dialectological survey was carried out by Alexander John Ellis in the middle of the nineteenth century. He used a dialect test in which people, usually from small villages, were asked to read a short passage of 76 words in their local dialect in order to identify dialect areas that were mainly based on vowel distributions. Some decades later, in the early twentieth century, Wright published his highly influential *English Dialect Dictionary*, a six-volume collection of dialect words, compiling 70,000 dialect words which is now available as digitised source.[1]

In the middle of the twentieth century, Harold Orton started work on the *Survey of English Dialects*, choosing the rural fieldwork sites. The aim of the project was to preserve a record of 'traditional vernacular, genuine and old' (Orton 1960: 332). Data were collected by fieldworkers who mainly interviewed non-mobile, older, rural males (cf. Chambers and Trudgill 1980) in these rural communities, that is, the least mobile, most static people in the fieldwork sites. Orton shared the sentiment on the need of recording traditional dialects before they are lost with Wright, who stated in the preface to the *English Dialect Grammar*: 'There can be no doubt that pure dialect speech is rapidly disappearing [...] The writing of this grammar was begun none too soon, for had it been delayed another twenty years, I believe it would by then be quite impossible to get together sufficient pure dialect material to enable anyone to give even a mere outline of the phonology of our dialects as they existed at the close of the nineteenth century' (Wright 1905: iv–v taken from Beal 2010: 3).

From the 1970s onwards, there was a notable shift away from dialectological topics towards variationist sociolinguistics with Peter Trudgill as the most influential representative of this approach in England. His work in Norwich mainly focused on external factors such as gender and social class in order to explain the present variation. Seminal works such as *Dialectology* (1980; with Jack Chambers), *Dialects in Contact* (1986) and *The Dialects of English* (1990) were based on his sociolinguistic and dialectological work in England and Norway. While Trudgill mainly focused on phonological variation of adult speech, in her playground study Cheshire (1982) explored grammatical variation in the speech of children and found that children already show language variation, and boys use more non-standard forms than girls. She concluded that language variation on the grammatical level is governed by social and linguistic factors.

In the 1990s, consequences of dialect contact were explored further and two seminal projects on dialect contact situations in England were conducted. Dialect levelling and diffusion were identified as driving forces in language change. Kerswill and Williams (e.g. 2000) picked up the idea of new dialect formation from Trudgill (1986) and investigated dialect levelling and the creation of a koine in Milton Keynes, a New Town west of London. Britain (1997) also investigated dialect contact scenarios in the Fens, a sparsely populated area in the east of England, where he showed the geographical proximity is not the only factor influencing language use in dialect contact situations and that we must also take into account the accessibility and psychological orientation of people. A question, which has sparked a lot of discussion in sociolinguistics in the last two decades, is whether local and/or regional varieties will be lost and a more general variety is the future of English in England or whether urban centres grow more apart in their use of language.

In the 1990s, a large project on *Phonological Variation and Change in Contemporary Spoken English (PVC)* investigated phonological variation and change in present-day urban dialects (cf. Milroy et al. 1999), focusing on Newcastle-upon-Tyne and Derby. The team around Lesley and James Milroy investigated variation and change processes in a considerable number of vowels and consonants. One of the outputs of this project was the edited volume *Urban Voices* (1999) by Foulkes and Docherty, in which phoneticians describe and discuss the variation in a number of urban varieties in the UK and Ireland. This book was highly influential for the research conducted in these areas in the first decade of the twenty-first century. It set the scene for investigating changes by diffusion, in particular of consonantal variables, such as Richards (2008), Jansen (2012) and Flynn (2012).

Research into the dialect use in the North East has a long tradition. The data of the PVC project were preceded by the *Tyneside Linguistic Survey* (TLS) in the 1960s, an investigation into the local dialect. In both projects, TLS and PVC, interview data were collected. Under the direction of Joan Beal, Karen Corrigan and Herman Moisl, the data of both projects were then amalgamated to what became the *Newcastle Electronic Corpus of Tyneside English* (NECTE, http://research.ncl.ac.uk/necte) in the early 2000s. This corpus was complemented by a corpus based on recordings conducted at the University of Newcastle since 2007, called NECTE 2. Both corpora were then combined to *The Diachronic Electronic Corpus of Tyneside English* (DECTE, http://research.ncl.ac.uk/decte/). The current website represents a unique example of a publicly available online corpus presenting dialect material spanning five decades. Various trend studies resulted from this corpus (e.g. Beal and Corrigan 2007; Barnfield and Buchstaller 2010). Isabelle Buchstaller's latest project involved panel studies where she traced some of the speakers from the TLS project and investigated their lifespan change (Buchstaller 2015). Buchstaller and Mearns report on some of these results in Chap. 9.

While dialect research in urban areas has been in focus since the early days of variationist sociolinguistics in the 1960s, Tagliamonte used a comparative sociolinguistic approach to study 'which changes are the legacy of its origins and which are the product of novel influences in the places to which it was transported' (Tagliamonte 2012: 1) by investigating morphosyntactic variation in peripheral areas of England, Scotland and Northern Ireland. The aim of this project was to study in how far the variation of certain forms provides a 'window to the past'. Jansen picks up this point in her study of vowel variation in West Cumbria in Chap. 12.

Although there has been a long history of migration to the UK and particularly England, people only started to focus on language contact situations due to ethnic migration in the middle of the 2000s. Jenny Cheshire, Paul Kerswill and their team studied the emergence of Multicultural London English in the two major projects *Linguistic Innovators: the English of Adolescents in London* and *Multicultural London English: the Emergence, Acquisition and Diffusion of a New Variety.* Torgersen and Fox provide an overview of findings from these projects in Chap. 8.

The third-wave approach to language variation (cf. Eckert 2012) has been applied and developed further by a number of researchers in the first decade of the 2000s. By employing ethnographic methods, Moore (2010) investigated how different groups of girls in a Bolton High School use language to create identity. She identified two groups of female teenagers on the basis of their different attitudes, behaviour and lifestyle choices and showed that these groups use language to create their identity. Sharma and Rampton investigated the use of style and dialect developments in ethnic groups from an interaction sociolinguistic point of view, and in Chap. 5 Rampton discusses the stylisation and dynamics of migration, ethnicity and class. Drummond reports on initial results from his UrBEn-ID project in Chap. 4. The project investigates ways in which young people in an urban environment use language in the construction, negotiation and performance of their identities.

While most of the studies mentioned above explore the production of language, studies on attitudes towards and perception of varieties have a fairly long tradition in Great Britain and Montgomery discusses this in more detail in Chap. 6. In recent years, the so-called north-south divide in England has sparked interest for linguists. This is a culturally engraved concept in England and linguists have been interested whether this can be delineated by language. This has resulted in the investigation of the linguistic markers separating the two regions (e.g. Wells 1986; Trudgill 1999). But it has been noted that this is not a straightforward division (e.g. Goodey et al. 1971; Wales 2002; Montgomery 2007; Beal 2008). There are clear stereotypes for the north and south, and they extend beyond language to political and socio-economic issues. The two main isoglosses which separate these two regions are the pronunciation of the STRUT and BATH vowels. These are very salient markers to people and can form important aspects of identity (e.g. Beal 2010: 14). However, Beal also comments that these particular examples of variation are relatively new and stem from the seventeenth century but since this time these distinctions have become very indicative of regional background.

There are problems with the north-south divide, for example, how areas like the East Midlands fit into the picture. The boundaries between north and south are defined in different ways. Beal's linguistic north does not include the East Midlands (Beal 2008: 124–5), neither does Wales' (2002: 48). Trudgill states that in traditional dialectology, the East Midlands area falls under *Central* dialects, which come under the *Southern* branch, but in modern dialectology, it falls in the *North* (Trudgill 1999: 35, 67). Hughes et al. (2012: 70) include a map which has the East Midlands in the north. Linguistically, the question has been raised whether there is a clear north-south boundary, see for example Upton (2012), where it is proposed that this region is a transition zone. There is other work on such transition zones, for example, Chambers and Trudgill (1998) and Britain (2003, 2013).

While Montgomery (2007) investigated the larger picture of this perceived border, Braber looked at the perceptions and attitudes in the East Midlands, a region where northern and southern features are used which resulted in the speakers not identifying strongly as being either from the north or the south but also from the Midlands (Braber 2014). Further study showed that the students were unlikely to name the East Midlands when mentioning dialect areas around the UK. They were also inaccurate when it came to labelling the East Midlands voices in dialect recognition tasks. The East Midlands may not have much cultural salience, and this could result in these students making errors in recognising and categorising the recorded voices. Pearce (2009) noted that cultural salience is an important aspect of identifying north-east varieties which could explain the problematic identification in the East Midlands. Another aspect of the issue of the inability to label local varieties was brought out by students rating them negatively when they discussed the mind maps, which can be linked to Montgomery and Beal (2011) who investigated claims and denials by speakers and their significance. What is also interesting is that the students in Braber's study did not comment on an east-west divide (see also Upton 2012: 267), although there is a West Midlands that they could differentiate themselves from. Wales has shown that the location of a division can depend on the background of the speaker with those coming from further south placing the divide further south and vice versa (2002). Montgomery (2007) examines this in more detail. This divide is particularly pertinent to the public and continues to be the focus of a heated discussion.

In recent years, two workshops focusing on the north and the south have been launched. For a decade now, the Northern Englishes Workshop has run biennially and two books investigating northern varieties have been published (Hickey 2015; Beal and Hancil 2017). In 2014, a Southern Englishes Workshop was started to give awareness to the fact that varieties in the south of England are understudied. This workshop has so far run three times and in 2017 a meeting focusing on language variation and change aspects of southern English varieties took place.

Current Volume

The present book completes a series of volumes on sociolinguistic research in the British Isles, namely *Sociolinguistics in Scotland* (Lawson 2014), *Sociolinguistics in Ireland* (Hickey 2016) and *Sociolinguistics in Wales* (Durham and Morris 2016). In all of them the increase of mobility and therefore the increase of diversity has been stressed and this theme continues in this book. In designing the volume, our aim was to present the wealth of sociolinguistic research currently taking place in England. We have included investigations into language variation and change (Jansen, Nance et al., Fabricius, Sandow and Robinson), lifespan change (Buchstaller and Mearns), perceptual dialectology (Montgomery), historical sociolinguistics (Auer), corpus investigation (Schembri), language contact (Torgersen and Fox), interaction sociolinguistics (Rampton), sociophonology (Barras), linguistic ethnography (Drummond) and semantic change (Braber, Sandow and Robinson). The structure of the volume is designed to reflect linguistic diversity in England.

In Chap. 2, Auer investigates the supraregionalisation processes behind the spread of the third-person singular –*s* form during the Early Modern English period in four locations. Fabricius discusses, in Chap. 3, changes in Received Pronunciation, the most prestigious accent in England. Drummond provides a pilot study on language use by urban youth in Manchester in Chap. 4. In Chap. 5, Rampton explores how practices like stylisation and language crossing fit into larger structures like migration, ethnicity and class. Montgomery, in Chap. 6, deals with the perception of the dialect landscape in England by non-linguists. Schembri et al. present variation and change results from their British Sign Language (BSL) corpus in Chap. 7. In Chap. 8, Fox and Torgersen provide an overview of results from the Multicultural London English projects. Buchstaller and Mearns investigate lifespan change in individuals in Tyneside in Chap. 9. Braber explores the lexical items present in 'pit talk' in the East Midlands in Chap. 10. Nance et al. explore intonational variation in Liverpool English in Chap. 11. In Chap. 12, Jansen discusses variation in the high back vowel in the peripheral area of West Cumbria. Sandow and Robinson present case studies of semantic changes in sociolinguistic contexts in Chap. 13. In the final Chap. 14, Barras conducts a comparative analysis of residual rhoticity and emergent *r*-sandhi in the north-west and south-west of England.

Future Direction

The sociolinguistic landscape in England is rapidly changing. As elsewhere, factors such as inward and outward migration and greater social mobility are leading to more diverse communities. Our aim with this volume is to show how current research on sociolinguistics in England highlights avenues for future research.

In addition to changing demographics, consequences of the political situation of the UK in this day and age will become more prominent in linguistics. At the time of writing (March 2017) the UK is leaving the European Union (EU), discussion of an independent Scotland is back on the cards and an exodus of EU citizens from Britain is possible. However, the linguistic consequences are not predictable. At the same time, heritage language transmission and preservation are of linguistic interest as these processes can provide us with more information about language contact.

Sociolinguistics mostly concentrates on smaller case studies as the funding of large-scale studies is often problematic. However, digital humanities may open the way for collecting large data sets from wide regional areas. The team around David Britain has shown with their dialect app how large data sets can be set up and analysed. The rapid advancement of technology will facilitate new paths for sociolinguistics and dialectological studies.

The chapter by Schembri et al. shows that more research in the sociolinguistics of BSL is needed. We are only starting to understand variation in this language and case studies complementing the available BSL corpus are necessary to deepen our understanding.

One last point is the underrepresentation of certain areas in sociolinguistic work in England. Regions like the East Midlands and the south of England have not been subject of much research but form unique social settings worth studying.

Notes

1. English Dialect Dictionary is available online: http://eddonline-proj.uibk.ac.at/edd/termsOfUse.jsp

References

Barnfield, K., & Buchstaller, I. (2010). Intensification on Tyneside: Longitudinal developments and new trends. *English World-Wide, 31*, 252–287.

Beal, J. (2008). English dialects in the North of England: Phonology. In B. Kortmann & C. Upton (Eds.), *Varieties of English 1: The British Isles* (pp. 122–144). Berlin: Mouton de Gruyter.

Beal, J. (2010). *An introduction to regional Englishes*. Edinburgh: Edinburgh University Press.

Beal, J. C., & Corrigan, K. P. (2007). 'Time and Tyne': A corpus-based study of variation and change relativization strategies in Tyneside English. In S. Elspaß, N. Langer, J. Scharloth, & W. Vandenbussche (Eds.), *Germanic language histories 'from Below' (1700–2000)* (pp. 99–114). Berlin/New York: Walter de Gruyter.

Beal, J., & Hancil, S. (2017). *Perspectives of Northern English*. Berlin: Mouton de Gruyter.

Braber, N. (2014). The concept of identity in the East Midlands of England. *English Today, 30*(2), 3–10.

Britain, D. (1997). Dialect contact and phonological reallocation: 'Canadian Raising' in the English Fens. *Language in Society, 26*, 15–46.

Britain, D. (2003). Welcome to East Anglia!: Two major dialect 'boundaries' in the Fens. In P. Trudgill & J. Fisiak (Eds.), *East Anglian English* (pp. 217–242). Woodbridge: Boydell and Brewer.

Britain, D. (2013). Space, diffusion and mobility. In J. Chambers & N. Schilling (Eds.), *Handbook of language variation and change* (2nd ed., pp. 471–500). Oxford: Wiley-Blackwell.

Buchstaller, I. (2015). Exploring linguistic malleability across the life-span: Age-specific patterns in quotative use. *Language in Society, 44*(4), 457–496.

Chambers, J. K., & Trudgill, P. (1980). *Dialectology*. Cambridge: Cambridge University Press.

Chambers, J. K., & Trudgill, P. (1998). *Dialectology* (2nd ed.). Cambridge: Cambridge University Press.

Cheshire, J. (1982). *Variation in an English dialect: A sociolinguistic study*. Cambridge/New York: Cambridge University Press.

Durham, M., & Morris, J. (Eds.). (2016). *Sociolinguistics in Wales*. Basingstoke: Palgrave Macmillan.

Eckert, P. (2012). Three waves of variation study: The emergence of meaning in the study of variation. *Annual Review of Anthropology, 41*, 87–100.

Flynn, N. (2012). *Levelling and diffusion at the North/South border: A sociophonetic study of Nottingham speakers*. Unpublished PhD thesis, University of York.

Foulkes, P., & Docherty, G. (Eds.). (1999). *Urban voices: Accent studies in the British Isles*. London: Edward Arnold.

Goodey, B., Gold, J., Duffett, A., & Spencer, D. (1971). *City scene. An exploration into the image of central Birmingham as seen by area residents*. Birmingham: Centre for Urban and Regional Studies, University of Birmingham.

Hickey, R. (Ed.). (2015). *Researching Northern English*. Amsterdam/New York: John Benjamins.

Hickey, R. (Ed.). (2016). *Sociolinguistics in Ireland*. Basingstoke: Palgrave Macmillan.

Hughes, A., Trudgill, P., & Watt, D. (2012). *English accents and dialects*. London: Hodder Arnold.

Jansen, S. (2012). *Variation and change in the Cumbrian city dialect of Carlisle*. Unpublished PhD thesis, University of Duisburg-Essen.

Kerswill, P., & Williams, A. (2000). Creating a new town koine: Children and language change in Milton Keynes. *Language in Society, 29*(1), 65–115.

Lawson, R. (Ed.). (2014). *Sociolinguistics in Scotland*. Basingstoke: Palgrave Macmillan.

Milroy, L., Milroy, J., Docherty, G. J., Foulkes, P., & Walshaw, D. (1999). Phonological variation and change in contemporary English: Evidence from Newcastle upon Tyne and Derby. *Cuadernos de Filologia Inglesa, 8*, 35–46.

Montgomery, C. (2007). *Northern English dialects: A perceptual approach*. Unpublished PhD thesis, University of Sheffield.

Montgomery, C., & Beal, J. (2011). Perceptual dialectology. In W. Maguire & A. MacMahon (Eds.), *Analysing variation and change* (pp. 121–148). Cambridge: Cambridge University Press.

Moore, E. (2010). The interaction between social category and social practice: Explaining was/were variation. *Language Variation and Change, 22*, 347–371.

Orton, H. (1960). An English dialect survey: Linguistic atlas of England. *Orbis: Bulletin international de documentation linguistique, IX*(2), 331–348.

Pearce, M. (2009). A perceptual dialect map of North East England. *Journal of English Linguistics, 39*(3), 162–192.

Richards, H. (2008). *Mechanisms, motivations and outcomes of change in Morley (Leeds) English*. Unpublished PhD thesis, University of York.

Tagliamonte, S. (2012). *The roots of English*. Cambridge: Cambridge University Press.

Trudgill, P. (1986). *Dialects in contact*. New York: Basil Blackwell.

Trudgill, P. (1999). *The dialects of England*. Oxford: Blackwell.

Upton, C. (2012). The importance of being Janus. In M. Markus, Y. Iyeiri, R. Henberger, & E. Chamson (Eds.), *Middle and modern English corpus linguistics* (pp. 257–268). Amsterdam: John Benjamins.

Wales, K. (2002). 'North of the Watford Gap'. A cultural history of Northern English (from 1700). In R. Watts & P. Trudgill (Eds.), *Alternative histories of English* (pp. 45–66). London: Routledge.

Wells, J. C. (1986). *Accents of English 2: The British Isles*. Cambridge: Cambridge University Press.

2

Urban Literacies and Processes of Supralocalisation: A Historical Sociolinguistic Perspective

Anita Auer

Introduction

The study of urban vernaculars has played and still does play a central role in the field of sociolinguistics in that it has significantly contributed to the advancement of sociolinguistic theories (cf. for instance Labov for New York City 1966; Trudgill for Norwich 1974; Kerswill and Williams for Milton Keynes 2000; Cheshire et al. 2011 for a selection of seminal studies in English linguistics). The language use in urban centres is of particular interest in that it brings people with different socio-economic backgrounds and different dialects, varieties and languages together, and it allows us to observe whether these dialects potentially have an influence on one another, that is, depending on the types of contact situations.

This chapter has been written in the context of the research project *Emerging Standards: Urbanisation and the Development of Standard English (c. 1400–1700)*.

A. Auer (✉)
University of Lausanne, Lausanne, Switzerland

N. Braber, S. Jansen (eds.), *Sociolinguistics in England*,
DOI 10.1057/978-1-137-56288-3_2

13

While the focus in synchronic linguistic studies on urban vernaculars is primarily on variation and change in spoken language, this type of data is not available for earlier stages of the English language history (and other language histories, cf. Deumert and Vandenbussche 2003). Instead, we have to rely on written documents in order to shed some light on the language situations in urban centres. The role of historical urban vernaculars, albeit only surviving as written materials, is of great importance for the study of standardisation processes in the history of the English language.

It is the aim of this chapter to shed some light on supralocalisation processes in the development of written Standard English by taking into consideration urban literacies in selected regional centres alongside London. More precisely, this chapter provides (a) some more information on written urban data that can be used by historical sociolinguistics, and (b) a case study based on *An Electronic Text Edition of Depositions 1560–1760 (ETED)* (edited by Kytö et al. 2011), which investigates the development of the present indicative third-person singular variable in depositions from the cities of Durham and Lancaster (north), Norwich (East Anglia) and London (south). Finally, the main findings and shortcomings, as well as future research directions, are discussed in the conclusion.

Historical Sociolinguistics, Urban Literacies and Language Standardisation

Within the framework of historical sociolinguistics, which 'draw[s] on insights and principles from modern-day sociolinguistics, on the working assumption that the fundamental principles and mechanisms of language variation and change are valid across time' (Auer et al. 2015: 4), in recent years, a twofold view has been taken on language histories, notably the 'language history from above' and the 'language history from below' (cf. Elspaß 2007: 3). With respect to studies on language standardisation processes, the focus on a uniform standard language and/or standard varieties, which pays much attention to the literate elite that provided language norms and that were considered *representatives of the language* as such would be regarded as an approach *from above* (cf. Milroy 1999, 2005; Trudgill and Watts 2002). As a complementary alternative to the latter approach, the concept of *language history from below* has been embraced by language historians working on a variety of languages. With regard to standardisation histories, this concept refers to (a) language varieties that deviate from the uniform standard, (b) texts that were untouched by editors and proof-readers, and may therefore be regarded as representative of authentic language, that is, the language below the surface of printed material, and (c) the language produced by the non-elite, which has hitherto largely been neglected. The view *from below* may therefore also be seen as an *alternative history* of a language. The current chapter also takes an alternative view on the English standardisation history in that the focus is on regional centres alongside the metropolis London, which allows us to shed light on the development of a *supra-local* linguistic feature.

Since the beginning of urbanisation in England in the later Middle Ages, urban communities have fulfilled many roles, for example, administrative and institutional functions, manufacturing and marketing, as well as being domestic and international trade hubs (Palliser 2000). Similar to today, but on a much smaller scale, people with different backgrounds and different dialects came together, that is, notably from a smaller radius as travel and migration was not as commonplace as it is today. Based on historical documents like letters of denisation[1] and protection, taxation records as well as grants and licences, it has been possible for historians and archaeologists to determine trade routes and therefore migration patterns and contact scenarios.[2]

Levels of literacy varied from place to place and from point in time to point in time. In any case, literacy rates in urban centres were significantly higher compared to small towns and rural areas, notably due to the many different roles (see above) that urban communities fulfilled (Palliser 2000). In fact, the rise of a monetary economy and the growth of towns also had an effect on the social order, namely occupational specialisation and the rise of guilds. Greater towns attracted ecclesiastical foundations and in addition had at least one school (Kermode 2000: 445). Between c. 1400 and the mid-sixteenth century in English towns, a shift can be observed in the provision of education from ecclesiastical to lay hands (Rosser 2000: 356, 361). As Orme (2014) notes with regard to fifteenth-century England and thereafter, what existed at the time were schools in religious houses such as monasteries, cathedrals, churches, nunneries as well as 'personal venture' schools in towns, which were supported by local patrons, for example, monasteries and bishops. Apart from these schooling options, private learning with the clergy or informal teachers, for example, when a merchant trained an apprentice, was also an option. This overview already shows that the training differed greatly, ranging from structured classical training to rather basic and informal learning. One may, thus, want to argue that the schooling before the 1st Education Act in 1870 led to different kinds of literacies. Literacy levels, which were socially stratified, thus, determine what written material was produced, and it is this type of material that serves as the basis for studies in historical sociolinguistics. In comparison to synchronic linguistic studies, historical sociolinguists are dealing with a so-called bad data-problem (cf. Nevalainen and Raumolin-Brunberg 2003; Auer et al. 2015), in that they have (a) to make the best use of written data that has survived and (b) to reconstruct socio-historical background information that is not always reliable, for example, determining the age, gender and economic background of a writer or scribe. According to Rees Jones (2014), literate behaviour is largely conditioned by the 'urban' way of life, that is, its complexity of social organisation and its occupations. Therefore, text types that we have at our disposal as historical linguists are letters (private and business), diaries, plays, wills, depositions, legal documents and civic records, such as accounts and ordinances. These range from ego-documents that can be rather informal in style to very formal text types. Also, some text types come with more extra-linguistic (social) information than others.

The available data is thus severely restricted and not necessarily representative of the make-up of the urban community, or of specific communicative situations. Written data merely represents those people who were literate at the time, or more precisely, those who were able to write (as opposed to other types of literacy such as reading). Until the 1st Education Act, only a selected part of the population would have had the prerogative of schooling and thus be literate before that landmark event.

The role of historical urban vernaculars, albeit only surviving as written materials, is of great importance for the study of standardisation processes in the history of the English language. More precisely, a *pre-standard* that constituted a linguistic norm for a written supra-regional variety emerged in England in the first half of the fifteenth century. Before the end of the fourteenth century, a more uniform variety of written English did not exist, and the language was characterised by local and regional dialects as writing systems, which by the beginning of the sixteenth century had largely disappeared (Benskin 1992: 71). By 1700, spelling and grammar books had been published that aimed at codifying/fixing and thus standardising the written English language. For a long time, there existed a general consensus that what became the written Standard English language developed from the Central Midland dialect, which was propagated by the Chancery clerks (based on Samuels 1963 who analysed the spelling of dialects in manuscripts from the south and Midlands; see also Ekwall 1956; Fisher 1977; Fisher and Richardson 1984). This view, which was based on the fact that the spelling used by Chancery clerks for official documents was more uniform in comparison to that found in other written documents, has been convincingly challenged in Benskin (2004). Along this line, the notion of a so-called single-ancestor theory, which can refer to a single dialect, text type, place or point in time, has also been challenged in Wright (2000).

The traditional account of the development of written Standard English attributes an important role to London in shaping the standard form, as this town was the national seat of government and justice. While London's eminent position[3] has undoubtedly played an important role in the standardisation of written English, for example, the impact that printing with movable type had on the uniformisation and distribution of written works, other regional centres also need to be taken into consideration when trying to shed some light on supralocalisation processes during the Late Medieval and Early Modern period. After all, some of the linguistic features which can be found in written Standard English today originated in regional dialects that are geographically far away from London, for example, the present indicative third-person singular suffix –*s* (*he goes*), which became the standard form, originated in the north and supplanted the southern form ending in –*th* (*he goeth*) (see for instance,

Holmqvist 1922; Schendl 1996). It is this particular linguistic feature that is investigated more closely in the following section.

The Third-Person Singular Present Indicative: Variation and Change in Urban Depositions

The development of the present indicative third-person singular suffix and in particular the replacement of the suffix *–th* by *–s* in the history of the English language has already drawn much scholarly attention (see for instance, Stein 1987; Lass 1992, 1999; Kytö 1993; Nevalainen 2000; Nevalainen and Raumolin-Brunberg 2003; Gries and Hilpert 2010; Evans 2015). This particular variable knows three variants, which are as follows:

(a) –s: *She walkes*
(b) –th: *She walketh*
(c) zero: *She walk*

As already indicated earlier, during the Middle English period (c. 1100–1500), when the written language was characterised by regional and local dialects, the northern present indicative third-person singular suffix was an *–s* (*he walk(e)s*), whereas the *–th* suffix (*he walketh*) was found in the south. According to Lass (1999: 163), the *–s* variant is present in London texts from the fourteenth century, followed by a gradual increase of this variant from this time onwards and with a particularly steep increase during the sixteenth and seventeenth centuries. The *–s* variant may be considered the norm around 1600; nevertheless, the *–th* suffix is also still found, notably in more formal text types (cf. Kytö 1993). Kytö (1993: 121) also observes that there is a difference in the transition from *–th* to *–s* between lexical verbs and the auxiliary verbs *do* and *have*. It is the auxiliary forms that resisted the shift to *–s* much longer than the lexical verbs. In their study of the present indicative third-person singular variable in the *Corpus of Early English Correspondence* (CEEC), which covers the period 1460–1681, Nevalainen and Raumolin-Brunberg (2003) find an interesting development of the *–s* variant. They observe a decrease of the –*s* variant in letters produced by northern writers, that is, the local form, between 1460 and 1539, notably at the expense of an increase of the –*th* variant (and originally the southern form) in the north. From 1539 onwards, a gradual increase of the –*s* variant can be observed in letter data from the north, London, the Court and East Anglia. It is striking that London data seems to lead the change, that is, the increase of the –*s* suffix, from 1580 onwards. Rather than spreading from the north, the originally northern variant has thus moved to the south and seems to move up north again from there. Similarly, Moore (2002), in her study of the Plumpton letters, observes this development, that is, a north-south movement of the –*s* variant first, which is followed by south-north movement. As these observations are based on a particular text type, notably letters, it will be interesting to see what development can be found in other text types like depositions, which were produced in different regional centres. Considering the particular geographical and urban focus and the fact that local and regional dialect features were still commonplace in texts during the later Middle English period, it will also be interesting to see for how long specific dialectal features can be found in local texts or whether we can already observe that supralocalisation and other changes have taken place.

As pointed out in the previous section, the corpus of written urban texts is fairly restricted during the Middle Ages and the Early Modern periods. In this case study, the data under investigation has been extracted from *An Electronic Text Edition of Depositions 1560–1760 (ETED)* (edited by Kytö et al. 2011). What makes depositions suitable for the current study is that they were recorded in a wide range of places in England, and that the depositions are localised, that is, when and where they were written down. In order to observe language change over time, the ETED data is subdivided into roughly 50-year time spans. Depositions may be described as 'oral testimonies taken down in writing by a scribe in connection with a legal case. They detail a person's experiences or actions in a particular context pertaining to the case' (Grund and Walker 2011: 15). These oral statements were made by witnesses, plaintiffs or defendants in relation to—criminal and ecclesiastical—court cases. While one may want to argue that we are not dealing with autograph language but scribal language here, we do still manage to catch a glimpse of language usage of the time, albeit possibly through a scribal filter. An important characteristic of depositions is that they are couched in the precise language of the law as exemplified in the deposition below (ETED F_1EC_NorwichA_035), where we encounter fixed phrases at the beginning and at the end of the deposition, for example, *Willm Prentys Servaunt to John ffawsett of Norwch Skynner abowt thage of xxij yerys sworne and exaied the Wednesdaye the xviijth of August Ao 1563 Sayeth* and *And further this deponent Sayeth not*. We can thus observe a fairly fixed structure that provides information about the deponent(s), notably expressed in a standard phrase, which is followed by the narrative(s) that records real speech events, that is, reported and direct speech. The deposition concludes with another fixed phrase.

The example below also provides some extra-linguistic information in the header. Even though we are in many cases able to retrieve information regarding the sex, age and occupation of the deponent, which is highly valuable background information for sociolinguists, the fact that a male scribe of unknown age has recorded the speech of the deponent(s) means that the social information may in fact not be reliable for sociolinguistic studies.

<Name of collection: Norwich 1560–1566>
<Period: 1 (1560–1599)>
<Decade: 1560–1569>
<Region: east>
<Type of court: criminal>
<Deposition date: 18 August 1563 (A)>
<Deponent sex: male>
<Deponent age: 22>
<Deponent occupation: servant>
<Manuscript reference: Norfolk Record Office, Norwich. Quarter Sessions (Interrogations and Depositions), MS NCR Case 12a/1c, f. 55r>
<Collection ID: F_1EC_NorwichA>
<Deposition ID: F_1EC_NorwichA_035>
<f. 55r> <Hand 1> Willm Prentys Servaunt to John ffawsett of Norwch Skynner abowt thage of xxij yerys sworne and exaied
the Wednesdaye the xviijth of August Ao 1563
Sayeth

That about vij wekes nowe last past one Thomas Eton
Skynner being at London at the Shoppwyndowe of the
John ffawsett Sayed that he wold go to Norwch And
then this deponent axed hym yf he wold go to Norwch and
was so lately in pryson there Then Sayed Eton I maye
thank Mr Willm ffarrour of yt lyke A pawnche as he
is and as for Mychell he was never pore mans frynd
but allweys A mortall foe to all poore men and hath the
good wyll of no pore man wthin Norwyche Then sayed Mr
ffawsett That is Thow sayest that because he ded set
you from the doble bere naye ^{sayed Eton} as for him he wyll be
as dronken as A beggar and as spackled as A Tode when
Mr Cobb and he mete together at Mr Hed Therfor yf ther
wer no man alyve but Mr Mychell I woold be his
could fynde in my hart to be his hangman / nowe is
Mr Davy Mayor he is somwhat my frynd but yet
he is as fowle A gutt as the rest Norwyche is
the moste cutthrote Cyttye that is in all the world
for yf A pore man owe but vjd he shalbe arrested
for yt And further this deponent **Sayeth** not /
by me Wyllyam prentes

In relation to the previously observed fixed phrases, it is striking that the above illustration of a deposition as well as most other depositions in ETED contains the verb *sayeth* (in variable spelling; my emphasis in the example above). Considering that the present indicative third-person singular suffix is under investigation here, this particular verb may behave differently from other verbs.

In this study, the focus is on depositions from the cities of Durham and Lancaster (north), as well as Norwich (East Anglia) and London (south). With regard to the linguistic variable under investigation, texts from these places would have been characterised by the –*s* suffix (north) and the –*th* suffix (East Anglia, south) during the Middle English period, respectively. The respective regional centres have been selected for geographical reasons, in that they lie in different Middle English dialect areas (in the broad sense; cf. Milroy 1992). As for including two cities from the north of England that are thus representative of the northern Middle

English dialect area, that is, Durham and Lancaster, this has to do with the fact that depositions from the respective centres do not exist for the entire period of 1560–1760, but Durham depositions cover the period 1560–1649, and Lancaster depositions cover the period 1650–1760. Similarly, Norwich deposition data is lacking for the intermediary period of 1600–1699; however, as early (1560–1599) and late data (1700–1760) is available, this allows us to make some observations and interpretations regarding supralocalisation processes over the entire period.

Considering Kytö's 1993 findings regarding the different behaviour of lexical verbs and auxiliary verbs, as well as the characteristic phrases containing *sayeth* (or other spelling variants) related to the text type of depositions, I decided to make a distinction between the different types of verbs when investigating the data, that is, the verb types *say, have, do* and *other* (lexical verbs) have been counted separately. As regards inflections, all three variants, notably *–s, –th* and *zero*, have been looked at. The raw frequencies have been normalised by 10,000 words so that they can be compared across the different regional centres and across sub-periods (where the data has differing word counts).[4] In the discussion below, I will only refer to normalised forms.

As already indicated above, the material in ETED is divided into four sub-periods, notably 1560–1599, 1600–1649, 1650–1699 and 1700–1760. This sub-division of the data allows us to trace the development of the linguistic variable over time. The results, which are presented in Tables 2.1 and 2.2, are discussed in the following order. First, the overall historical development of the linguistic variable under investigation is looked at (Table 2.1). The findings of the different regional centres are thus viewed together, that is, except for Norwich data between 1600 and 1699 that is lacking. Then, the findings according to regional area, notably the north (Durham, Lancaster), East Anglia (Norwich) and the south (London), which are presented in Table 2.2, are discussed. All of the different regional developments are compared and conclusions are drawn with regard to the supralocalisation process. In relation to previous findings, it is interesting to see whether the respective local Middle English variants, notably *–s* in the north and *–th* in the south, can be found in the depositions of the respective regions or whether *–th* forms are found in the north and *–s* forms in the south.

Table 2.1 Third-person singular forms in all investigated centres (normalised by 10,000 words)

Period	Verb types	Norm/raw		
		–th	–s	zero
		Total (36,157)		
1560–1599	SAY	60.60 (219)	0	0.28 (1)
	HAVE	26.27 (95)	0.28 (1)	3.32 (12)
	DO	3.87 (14)	0.28 (1)	0.28 (1)
	OTHER	25.44 (92)	2.50 (9)	0.83 (3)
		Total (22,336) (no Norwich data)		
1600–1649	SAY	74.32 (166)	0	0
	HAVE	52.83 (118)	0	0
	DO	3.58 (8)	0	0
	OTHER	77 (172)	0	2.69 (6)
		Total (22,336) (no Norwich data)		
1650–1699	SAY	20.15 (45)	2.24 (5)	0
	HAVE	6.27 (14)	0.90 (2)	0.90 (2)
	DO	1.79 (4)	0	0
	OTHER	11.20 (25)	12.98 (29)	0
		Total (36,157)		
1700–1760	SAY	32.36 (117)	9.13 (33)	0.28 (1)
	HAVE	16.32 (59)	6.64 (24)	0
	DO	7.19 (26)	1.66 (6)	1.94 (7)
	OTHER	4.98 (18)	39 (141)	7.47 (27)

During the sub-period 1560–1599, the –*th* suffix is clearly prevalent in all verb types, that is, in comparison to the competing forms –*s* and *zero*. It is worth pointing out that the occurrences of *say* (60.6) are much higher than the other lexical verbs (25.44), and *have* (26.27) is slightly higher than the latter verbs. This trend continues during the sub-period 1600–1649, where the –*th* suffix is almost exclusively used across the different verb types, that is, except for a few *zero* forms with lexical verbs. While the –*th* suffix continues to be predominantly found with the verbs *say, have* and *do* during the sub-period 1650–1699, we can observe a gradual shift in the lexical verbs from the –*th* suffix (11.2) to the –*s* suffix (12.98). This development continues during the period 1700–1760 where the distribution of the variants is 4.98 (–*th*), 39 (–*s*), and 7.47 (*zero*) in the lexical verbs. The –*s* suffix is thus clearly the prevalent form during that period in lexical verbs. We can also observe an increase of –s forms with the verbs *say, have* and *do*, but the –*th* form is still more frequent in comparison. This pattern confirms Kytö's 1993 observations that (a) the shift from –*s* to –*th* can first be observed in lexical verbs, while auxiliary verbs lag behind, and (b) the formality of the text type also has an effect on the choice of variant where fixed phrases as found in legal texts appear to preserve certain variants for a longer time, that is, –*th* in the verb *say* in this particular set of texts.

Considering that the depositions under investigation were written in different regional centres that were originally associated with different regional dialects, it will be interesting to see what the data provided in Table 2.2 reveals. Even though the numbers are rather low at times, the mere occurrence of selected variants is already considered valuable and useful information from a historical sociolinguistic perspective.

The findings in the northern centres—Durham and Lancaster—are of particular interest, in that the –*s* suffix is the local variant. However, this is not obvious in the results in the depositions. During the period 1560–1599 (Durham data), we can observe that the –*th* is by far the dominant suffix across all verb types, that is, particularly with regard to *say* and *have*. The –*s* suffix only occurs in lexical verbs and one *do* example, but it is lower in occurrence in comparison to the –*th* examples in those verb types, for example, 9.94 (–*th*) and 7.46 (–*s*) in lexical verbs. The 1600–1649 (Durham) results are even more clear-cut with regard to the distribution, in that they do not contain a single –*s* suffix. The –*th* variant is found in 20 different lexical verbs, of which *believeth* (in different spelling variations; 40 occurrences), *referreth* (21 occurrences), and *remembreth* (20 occurrences) are the most frequently used verbs. It is in any case striking that the originally southern –*th* form dominates in Durham petitions. The sub-period 1650–1699, which is based on Lancaster data, reveals slightly different findings. It looks like the –*th* form is still the prevailing suffix, with both *say* and lexical verbs; however, a closer look at the –*th* examples in lexical verbs reveal that all nine occurrences can be found in the word *informeth*, which in all of these instances makes up part of the fixed phrase *informeth and saith*. Apart from these examples, the –*s* suffix is found in lexical verbs and even in a few *say* examples. This trend continues into the sub-period 1700–1760 where the –*s* suffix becomes the dominant form with all types of verbs, that is,

Table 2.2 Third-person singular forms in different regional centres (normalised by 10,000 words)

Period	Verb types	Norm/raw			Norm/raw			Norm/raw		
		-th	-s	zero	-th	-s	zero	-th	-s	zero
1560–1599		**Durham (12,067)**			**Norwich (13,821)**			**London (10,269)**		
	SAY	85.36 (103)	0	0.83 (1)	60.78 (84)	0	0	31.16 (32)	0	0
	HAVE	53.04 (64)	0	2.49 (3)	7.24 (10)	0	5.79 (8)	20.45 (21)	0.97 (1)	0.97 (1)
	DO	8.29 (10)	0.83 (1)	0	0	0	0	3.9 (4)	0	0.72 (1)
	OTHER	9.94 (12)	7.46 (9)	1.66 (2)	24.60 (34)	0	—	44.8 (46)	0	0.72 (1)
1600–1649		**Durham (12,306)**						**London (8729)**		
	SAY	113.53 (117)	0	0	—			56.13 (49)	0	0
	HAVE	70.83 (73)	0	0				51.55 (45)	0	0
	DO	4.85 (5)	0	0				3.44 (3)	0	0
	OTHER	120.32 (124)	0	5.82 (6)				54.99 (48)	0	0
1650–1699		**Lancaster (3485)**						**London (8995)**		
	SAY	88.95 (31)	14.35 (5)	0	—			15.56 (14)	0	0
	HAVE	0	0	5.74 (2)				15.56 (14)	2.22 (2)	0
	DO	0	0	0				4.45 (4)	0	0
	OTHER	25.82 (9)	20.09 (7)	0				17.79 (16)	24.46 (22)	0

(continued)

Table 2.2 (continued)

Period	Verb types	Lancaster (4960)			Norwich (8705)			London (14,154)		
		Norm/raw			Norm/raw			Norm/raw		
		-th	-s	zero	-th	-s	zero	-th	-s	zero
1700–1760	SAY	38.31 (19)	62.5 (31)	0	43.65 (38)	2.3 (2)	1.15 (1)	42.39 (60)	0	0
	HAVE	0	18.15 (9)	0	0	14.93 (13)	0	41.68 (59)	1.41 (2)	0
	DO	0	0	0	0	0	8.04 (7)	18.37 (26)	4.24 (6)	0
	OTHER	20.16 (10)	34.27 (17)	0	9.19 (8)	10.34 (9)	2.3 (2)	0	81.25 (115)	17.66 (25)

say, have and lexical verbs, albeit *–th* forms still remaining in both lexical verbs and *say*. A closer look at the *–th* examples in lexical verbs reveals that two occurrences of *informeth* are specific to the phrase *informeth and saith* again and that the remaining eight instances are the verb *deposeth*, which is found in formal phrases such as the one given in example (1), thus also linked to the verb *say*.

1. Mary Smith (wife of Thomas Smith of Osbaldeston) being sworn **deposeth and saith** That the deceased Ann Duckworth on Sunday Morning last was taken very ill and Vomited a good deal of Matter,[…] (F_4NC_Lancaster_008)

All the *–th* forms in lexical verbs are thus used in very specific contexts again, which suggests that a shift to *–s* forms has already largely taken place with regard to lexical verbs. The northern data also contains a few *zero* forms in the different sub-periods, but the competition is mainly between the *–th* and the *–s* suffixes.[5] All in all, what can be observed with regard to the northern data is that the non-local form (*–th*) has been the dominant suffix from 1560 to 1699, with the local *–s* form gradually gaining ground from 1650 onwards and becoming the dominant form in 1700. This clearly shows that the scribes who recorded depositions in Durham and possibly also in Lancaster (at a later stage) will most likely have been trained in the south, or they followed a southern model. This is the only way in which we can explain the fact the *–s* form is barely (1560–1599) and not at all (1600–1649) found in the earlier data. Even though we do not have any early Lancaster data, one may assume that a similar pattern would have been found there, and that the increase of the *–s* form in the sub-periods 1650–1699 and 1700–1760 may, in fact, be a development that came from the south, that is, that the *–s* form was re-introduced from the south into the north. Even though depositions are regarded as a very formal and formulaic text type, the development pattern as described above is in line with the progression that Nevalainen and Raumolin-Brunberg (2003: 178) have observed with regard to letter data, that is, where the *–s* suffix decreases severely in the northern data during the period 1500–1539 (while the *–th* suffix increases), notably followed by a gradual increase of the *–s* form in the periods afterwards. Based on the

CEEC data, the increase of the *–s* suffix is driven by London letter writers (and closely followed by writers from the Court) during the period 1580–1681. Only then can we observe an increase of the *–s* form in northern and East Anglian letter data. Even though the timing with regard to the development of the linguistic variable differs in letters and depositions, the pattern appears to be the same from a northern perspective.

The findings in Norwich depositions during the sub-period 1560–1599 show that the *–th* form is clearly the dominant form in all verb types, with not a single *–s* suffix in the data, but a few *zero* forms. As the local dialect feature was a *–th* during the Middle English period, the lack of the *–s* suffix is not surprising. Similar to the northern data, during the sub-period 1700–1760, we can observe *–s* forms alongside *–th* forms. These are almost on an equal basis in the case of lexical verbs, the *–s* suffix is the only form with the verb *have* but with regard to *say*, the *–th* form (43.65) still clearly prevails over the *–s* form (2.3). A closer look at the *–th* examples in lexical verbs reveals that six of the eight occurrences can be found in the fixed phrase *maketh oath*, as exemplified in (2):

2. Alice the wife of Tho: Seaman Weaver **Maketh Oath** before us his Ma[=ties=] Justices of the peace That She lives in the Lane Called the Rising Sun-Lane And that last Night about Eight O' Clock Rob[=t=] Watson who is now pre^{se}nt and two other Men in Company with Ann Woollard Came up the Lane together And Watson Struck Ann Woollard Se[+v+][=[+ll+]=] times on the Side of her head and Knockt her down and[…](F_4EC_Norwich_033)

The majority of remaining *–th* forms in lexical verbs are thus fixed phrases. There are again a few *zero* forms in most verb types.[6] Even though 1600–1699 data is lacking, we can once again observe the existence (and possible increase) of the *–s* variant in the 1700–1760 sub-period, thus corroborating the findings by Moore (2002) and Nevalainen and Raumolin-Brunberg (2003).

As regards the London findings, they are very much in line (for as far as the data exist) with the Norwich results, in that the *–th* variant is the (almost) exclusive form in all verb types in the sub-periods 1560–1599 and 1600–1649, that is, except for one *–s* and one *zero* form with *have* in the first sub-period. During the sub-period 1650–1699, the *–s* variant has already become the prevailing form in lexical verbs (24.46 *–s* forms vs. 17.79 *–th* forms), while the *–th* variant is still dominant with *say, have* and *do*. The *–th* variant in lexical verbs occurs across six different verbs (*believeth, lodgeth, taketh, knoweth, conceiveth, followeth*), and any fixed phrases that explain the pattern cannot be found. The trends observed in the sub-period 1650–1699 continue in the 1700–1760 sub-period, where *–s* is mainly found in lexical verbs (81.25), that is, apart from a few *zero* forms (17.66). The *–th* variant is, however, still clearly prevailing with *say, have* and *do*. Once again, the London findings support the Nevalainen and Raumolin-Brunberg (2003) results as regards the gradual shift from *–th* to *–s*, particularly with regard to lexical verbs (see also Kytö 1993). What the data also clearly shows is that the London data is the most progressive with regard to the *–s* variant in lexical verbs, that is, no *–th* form any longer. The fact that the *–th* suffix is still found in the data may, in fact, be explained by the nature of the text type, that is, formal with formulaic language, as well as by the verb types affected (cf. Kytö 1993).

Concluding Remarks

In this chapter, I aimed to shed some light on the supralocalisation processes that took place during the time when the standardisation of written English took place. To this purpose, depositions from selected urban centres (retrieved from *An Electronic Text Edition of Depositions 1560–1760*), notably from Durham, Lancaster, London and Norwich, which represent different dialect regions, were used as the basis for a linguistic study. The linguistic variable under investigation was the present indicative third-person singular, that is, a feature that has already received a fair amount of scholarly attention due to the fact that a northern dialect feature (the suffix *–s*) entered the written Standard. The findings of the linguistic study which was based on deposition data confirmed the results of previous studies on letters (cf. Moore 2002; Nevalainen and Raumolin-Brunberg 2003), in that the *–th* variant was the dominant form in all urban centres—also the northern cities—until c. 1650–1699. From that point onwards, a shift to –s can be observed in the data of all urban centres. Also, in line with the previous study by Kytö (1993), the results show that lexical verbs adopt the –s suffix before auxiliary verbs and verbs that occur in fixed phrases, for example, *say*, as well as selected other verbs in combination with *say*. The *zero* variant can also be found in the data throughout the period under investigation, but it does not compete with the –*th* and –s suffixes in terms of frequency. The *zero* variant has therefore not received much attention in this chapter, but it should be looked at more closely elsewhere, especially in relation to the inflectional subjunctive and the Northern Subject rule. Finally, depositions produced in an urban context are merely one text type that allows us to make comparisons between different *written urban vernaculars* and to contribute to a better understanding of the standardisation processes. The study of more and different linguistic features in depositions as well as other urban text types will ultimately allow us to gain a better understanding of supralocalisation processes and the emergence of written Standard English.

Notes

1. Letters of denisation, which were issued by the Crown from the late fourteenth century onwards, would give the recipients the opportunity to 'pay a fee and take an oath of allegiance to the Crown and in return were to be treated and considered in the same way as any English subject born within the realm' (see website of the project *England's Immigrants 1330–1550*).
2. A recent and extremely valuable source that allows us to determine migration patterns and, therefore, potential language contact scenarios during the period 1330–1550 is the project database *England's Immigrants 1330–1550* that allows for full searches and is freely available: https://www.englandsimmigrants.com/
3. For a discussion of London's eminent role, as perceived by the sixteenth-century writer and literary critic George Puttenham in his *Arte of English Poesie* (1589), see Auer et al. (2016).
4. I have not used any linguistic tests on the data as the raw frequencies are rather low. In any case, it is still possible to observe when a shift from one variant to another takes place. This, in turn, allows us to interpret the processes that will most likely have taken place.

5. The zero form as variant of the present indicative third-person singular suffix and its relationship to the subjunctive mood and the Northern Subject Rule shall be discussed elsewhere.
6. While it may be tempting to link the *zero* forms to the third-person singular zero that can be found in the Norfolk dialect, a more thorough investigation of all *zero* forms as well as an exclusion of inflectional subjunctive forms and the Northern Subject Rule would be required.

References

Auer, A., Peersman, C., Pickl, S., Rutten, G., & Vosters, R. (2015). Historical sociolinguistics: The field and its future. *Journal of Historical Sociolinguistics, 1*(1), 1–2.

Auer, A., Gordon, M., & Olson, M. (2016). English urban vernaculars, 1400–1700: Digitizing text from manuscript. In M. J. López-Couso, B. Méndez-Naya, P. Núñez-Pertejo, & I. M. Palacios-Martínez (Eds.), *Corpus linguistics on the move: Exploring and understanding English through corpora* (pp. 21–40). Amsterdam: Brill/Rodopi.

Benskin, M. (1992). Some perspectives on the origins of standard written English. In J. A. van Leuvensteijn & J. B. Berns (Eds.), *Dialect and standard languages in the English, Dutch, German and Norwegian language areas* (pp. 71–105). Amsterdam: North Holland.

Benskin, M. (2004). Chancery standard. In C. Kay et al. (Eds.), *New perspectives on English historical linguistics* (pp. 1–40). Amsterdam: John Benjamins.

Cheshire, J., Kerswill, P., Fox, S., & Torgersen, E. (2011). Contact, the feature pool and the speech community: The emergence of multicultural London English. *Journal of SocioLinguistics, 15*(2), 151–196.

Deumert, A., & Vandenbussche, W. (Eds.). (2003). *Germanic standardizations. Past to present.* Amsterdam/Philadelphia: John Benjamins.

Ekwall, E. (1956). *Studies on the population of medieval London.* Stockholm: Almqvist and Wiksell.

Elspaß, S. (2007). A twofold view 'from below': New perspectives on language histories and language historiographies. In S. Elspaß, N. Langer, J. Scharloth, & W. Vandenbussche (Eds.), *Germanic language histories 'from below' (1700–2000)* (pp. 3–9). Berlin/New York: de Gruyter.

England's immigrants 1330–1550. Available online: https://www.englandsimmigrants.com/

Evans, M. (2015). 'The vsuall speach of the court'? Investigating language change in the Tudor family network (1544–1556). *Journal of Historical Sociolinguistics, 1*(2), 153–188.

Fisher, J. (1977). Chancery and the emergence of standard written English in the fifteenth century. Speculum. *A Journal of Medieval Studies, 52*, 870–899.

Fisher, J. H., & Richardson, M. (1984). *An anthology of chancery English.* Knoxville: University of Tennessee Press.

Gries, S., & Hilpert, M. (2010). Modeling diachronic change in the third person singular: A multifactorial, verb- and author-specific exploratory approach. *English Language and Linguistics, 14*(3), 293–320.

Grund, P. J., & Walker, T. (2011). Genre characteristics. In M. Kytö, P. J. Grund, & T. Walker (Eds.), *Testifying to language and life in early modern England. Including a CD-ROM containing an electronic text edition of depositions 1560–1760 (ETED)* (pp. 15–56). Amsterdam: John Benjamins.

Holmqvist, E. (1922). *On the history of the English present inflections, particularly –th and –s.* Heidelberg: Carl Winter Universitätsbuchhandlung.

Kermode, J. (2000). The greater towns 1300–1540. In D. M. Palliser (Ed.), *The Cambridge urban history of Britain. Volume I. 600–1540* (pp. 441–465). Cambridge: Cambridge University Press.

Kerswill, P., & Williams, A. (2000). Creating a new town koiné: Children and language change in Milton Keynes. *Language in Society, 29*, 65–115.

Kytö, M. (1993). Third-person present singular verb inflection in early British and American English. *Language Variation and Change, 5*, 113–139.

Kytö, M., Grund, P. J., & Walker, T. (2011). *Testifying to language and life in early modern England. Including a CD-ROM containing an electronic text edition of depositions 1560–1760 (ETED).* Amsterdam: John Benjamins.

Labov, W. (1966). *The social stratification of English in New York City.* Washington: Center for Applied Linguistics.

Lass, R. (1992). Phonology and morphology. In N. Blake (Ed.), *The Cambridge history of the English language. Volume 2: 1066–1476* (pp. 23–155). Cambridge: Cambridge University Press.

Lass, R. (1999). Phonology and morphology. In R. Lass (Ed.), *The Cambridge history of the English language. Volume 3: 1476–1776* (pp. 56–186). Cambridge: Cambridge University Press.

Milroy, J. (1992). Middle English dialectology. In N. Blake (Ed.), *The Cambridge history of the English language. Volume 2: 1066–1476* (pp. 156–206). Cambridge: Cambridge University Press.

Milroy, J. (1999). The consequences of standardisation in descriptive linguistics. In T. Bex & R. J. Watts (Eds.), *Standard English. The widening debate* (pp. 16–39). London/New York: Routledge.

Milroy, J. (2005). Some effects of purist ideologies on historical descriptions of English. In N. Langer & W. V. Davies (Eds.), *Linguistic purism in the Germanic languages* (pp. 324–342). Berlin/New York: de Gruyter.

Moore, C. (2002). Writing good southerne: Local and supralocal norms in the Plumpton letter collection. *Language Variation and Change, 14*, 1–17.

Nevalainen, T. (2000). Process of supralocalisation and the rise of standard English in the early modern period. In R. Bermúdez-Otero, D. Denison, R. M. Hogg, & C. B. McCully (Eds.), *Generative theory and corpus studies. A dialogue from 10 ICEHL* (pp. 329–371). Berlin/New York: Mouton de Gruyter.

Nevalainen, T., & Raumolin-Brunberg, H. (2003). *Historical sociolinguistics: Language change in Tudor and Stuart English*. London: Longman.

Orme, N. (2014). Schools and school-books. In L. Hellinga & J. B. Trapp (Eds.), *The Cambridge history of the book in Britain. Volume 3. 1400–1557* (pp. 449–469). Cambridge: Cambridge University Press.

Palliser, D. M. (Ed.). (2000). *The Cambridge urban history of Britain. Volume I. 600–1540*. Cambridge: Cambridge University Press.

Rees Jones, S. (2014). Civic literacy in later medieval England. In M. Mostert & A. Adamska (Eds.), *Writing and the administration of medieval towns: Medieval urban literacy I* (pp. 219–230). Turnhout: Brepols.

Rosser, G. (2000). Urban culture and the church 1300–1540. In D. M. Palliser (Ed.), *The Cambridge urban history of Britain. Volume I. 600–1540* (pp. 335–369). Cambridge: Cambridge University Press.

Samuels, M. L. (1963). Some applications of middle English dialectology. *English Studies, 44*, 81–94. revised by Margaret Laing (ed), *Middle English dialectology. Essays on some principles and problems*, 64–80. Aberdeen: Aberdeen University Press.

Schendl, H. (1996). The 3rd plural present indicative in early modern English: Variation and linguistic contact. In D. Britton (Ed.), *English historical linguistics 1994: Papers from the 8th international conference on English historical linguistics* (pp. 143–160). Amsterdam: Benjamins.

Stein, D. (1987). At the crossroads of philology, linguistics and semiotics: Notes on the replacement of th by s in the third person singular in English. *English Studies, 68*, 406–431.

Trudgill, P. (1974). *The social differentiation of English in Norwich*. Cambridge: Cambridge University Press.

Trudgill, P., & Watts, R. J. (2002). Introduction. In the year 2525. In R. J. Watts & P. Trudgill (Eds.), *Alternative histories of English* (pp. 1–3). London/New York: Routledge.

Wright, L. (2000). Introduction. In L. Wright (Ed.), *The development of standard English (1300–1800)* (pp. 1–8). Cambridge: Cambridge University Press.

3

Social Change, Linguistic Change and Sociolinguistic Change in Received Pronunciation

Anne H. Fabricius

Introduction

In this chapter, I examine one sociolinguistic niche that has been some-what downplayed in mainstream work, but as I will show below, it is one that has interesting ramifications for an understanding of the complexity of language in social life and the progression of linguistic change. The focus here is on the elite sociolect of the UK, the generational successor to Received Pronunciation (RP), also known as Standard Southern British English (SSBE). Taking a viewpoint that social class (admittedly a complex concept, as the debates in Skeggs 2015 show) continues to man-ifest in sociolinguistic life in the UK, I examine here a selected set of sociophonetic changes that characterise the history of the elite sociolect. It is trivially true that all language varieties change; the point of interest in this chapter is the sociolinguistic ramifications of the continued exis-tence of elite sociolects, and whether they continue to signal and con-struct social difference in the community. Our claim here is that, far from

A.H. Fabricius (✉)
Roskilde University, Roskilde, Denmark

© The Author(s) 2018
N. Braber, S. Jansen (eds.), *Sociolinguistics in England*,
DOI 10.1057/978-1-137-56288-3_3

being entirely levelled to other social varieties in the south of England, for example, these voices are still distinct and sociolinguistically significant.

Theoretical Preliminaries

Fifty years of sociolinguistic research have shown how we can see language practice, language ideology, social fabric and social practice as intertwined, mutually constitutive semiotic processes ebbing and flowing in the course of history (Labov 1994, 2001; Eckert 2008). Social processes such as large-scale urbanisation in the nineteenth and twentieth centuries, the upheavals of the Second World War and de-industrialisation in the late twentieth century had large impacts upon the human landscape of Britain, with waves of de-dialectalisation, dialect levelling and regionalisation as some of the sociolinguistic consequences (Trudgill 1986; Britain 2016; Coupland 2014, 2016). Multi-ethnic immigration is also presently bringing about linguistic transformations of many kinds (this is especially well researched in the UK: see e.g. Cheshire et al. 2011; Rampton 2011; Kerswill 2013). These large-scale social movements have had consequences for the entire sociolinguistic landscape of the UK.

As one case in point, on a political level in the UK at the moment, there seems to be a striking contrast to social class discourses of the late 1990s, when I began researching RP sociolinguistically. At that time, one dominant political current was encapsulated in the critiqued concept of the 'meritocratic society' (Adonis and Pollard 1997). Accompanying this was widespread talk in the media and among language experts of Estuary English as a levelled local replacement for RP in younger generations of speakers in London and the Home Counties (Kerswill 2001; Przedlacka 2002; Altendorf 2003). Writer India Knight in 2001 reported anecdotally that 'the only accent it is now actively all right to pillory is the so-called *posh*–the clear enunciation that comes from being privately educated or having upper-middle-class parents'.[1] At the time of writing this chapter, however, there has been something of a revival of interest in and a redefining of elite/establishment positioning in the public media sphere: television series such as *Life is Toff*, *You can't get the Staff* and *Posh People: Inside Tatler* have all been broadcast in recent years.[2] This is perhaps not coincidental, given the political context of the *neo-Thatcherite* premierships of old Etonian David Cameron from 2010–2015, and under a Conservative Party majority from May 2015 to July 2016. Class and class inequality are in the news again. At the same time, an academic sociological interest in elites and in class structure (Savage et al. 2013; Skeggs 2015) has intensified recently in the UK, alongside the Brexit vote of 23 June and the political upheaval it has caused so far, leading to Theresa May's premiership from July 2016.

What sociolinguistic implications and consequences can possibly be extrapolated from this history? What if, to paraphrase Coupland (2000: 264), where he writes: '(é)lites perpetuate élite society by being seen to be élites' (and contra to the Estuary English discourse of 20 years ago), élites still perpetuate elite society by being *heard* to be élites? Can sociolinguistic research identify continuing or renewed accent-stylistic dividing lines: clusters of phonetic features which alone or in combination as *posh styles* are enregistered in the UK, styles whose linguistic makeup certainly have changed from what they were in the first half of the twentieth century (e.g. Fabricius 2017), but whose distinctions function, if not as the reported accent-bar of the 1950s–1960s (Abercrombie 1965), at least as some sort of class-framing for speakers and listeners, as enregistered *construct resources* (Fabricius and Mortensen 2013)? Does class still resonate in the UK, and can sociolinguistics contribute to a nuanced understanding of new constellations of class and language?

In this chapter, then, I explore some of the quantitative research hitherto on this particular sociolinguistic niche. My summary of these findings look at changing sociophonetic features such as word-final /t/, weak vowels, the short vowel system and pre-vocalic, syllable-onset /r/, diphthong smoothing and yod coalescence. These socially distributed phonetic variations are of interest per se to linguists as sociophonetic changes with different trajectories in historical linguistic terms; their implications for wider social practice and the enactment of class remain unexplored, for instance by ethnographically oriented work, and this is a gap in the literature that I see as needing to be filled. The chapter also briefly discusses evidence of lifespan change in RP speakers, as well as recent language-attitudinal work on RP. What remains to be implemented is a wider agenda of theoretical research into elite sociolects, which will need to employ distinctions between social change, linguistic change and sociolinguistic change, the latter encapsulating changes in the sociolinguistic status and social implications of language forms (Coupland 2014). This is because the historical trajectory of an elite sociolect or an elite accent style is best understood through a wide linguistic anthropological and ethnographic lens, using a range of methods. I cannot do this research horizon full justice here, but I can outline some findings so far and suggest paths for future scholars to follow.

Standard Languages, Elite Sociolects and Language Change

Variationist sociolinguistics can be characterised as the linguistic study of variation and change in vernacular language varieties, understood as the systematic forms of language acquired by children as their first language(s) of socialisation. Pioneering survey-based studies such as Labov (1963, 2006), Trudgill (1972), and Macaulay (1977) concentrated on data from speakers in the middle of the social hierarchy. Upper-class speakers were often not included in survey samples, or were the subject of particularised studies (Kroch 1995), and as a result were regarded as much less interesting for mainstream variationist work for a long time, seen as being far from the locus of sociolinguistic change, conservative followers rather than first-movers. Similarly, Rampton (2009) discusses for instance a prevailing *romanticisation* of the working class in academic work of the time. Upper- and to some extent upper-middle-class speech also had a somewhat tenuous place within sociolinguistic thinking, because it was regarded as affected by conscious educational standardising processes that could modify the vernacular (understood here to mean the *first language of socialisation*).

This theoretical stance conflates two distinct sociolinguistic phenomena, however: the *standard language* and the *elite/establishment sociolect*. The tendency has been that upper-class groups' sociolect and *the standard language* were often assumed to be identical, and these speakers have been excluded as being *not vernacular* (where *vernacular* could also be understood to mean *non-standard*) (Bex and Watts 1999; Milroy and Milroy 1999; Kerswill 2006). 'The concept of the standard' was therefore for a long time, as Milroy (2004: 162) has pointed out, 'surprisingly underspecified and undertheorized' in variationist sociolinguistics, and standard variants were presented as self-evident counterpoints to the non-standard vernacular variants which dominated the sociolinguistics literature. This ignores the fact that, firstly, upper-class and upper-middle-class speakers, of course, do acquire their own *vernacular* (meaning primary language of socialisation), and that successive generations of such speakers exhibit vernacular variation and change over time. These sociolinguistically embedded changes have always provided a challenge for linguists aiming at describing a standard codified variety, often for foreign language teaching purposes (Wells 1990, 1994, 1997; the title of the latter is, revealingly, *Whatever Happened to Received Pronunciation?*; Upton 2012: 55–58).

In Fabricius (2000), the distinction between elite vernacular sociolect and standard language construct was captured under the terms *native-RP* and *construct-RP*, given the need to separate the vernacular aspect (phonetic features as part of a first language of socialisation), from the *standard language*, an abstract, explicitly codified and folk-linguistic model. Agha (2003, 2007) has since introduced the concept of *enregisterment* using RP as his canonical example. He claims that RP over time became enregistered as a folk concept, a recognised set of phonetic patterns, a certain type of *voice* in folk terms. The enregistered voice is indeed part of what construct-RP was intended to cover in Fabricius (2000, 2002a, b), but it also included codified manuals and dictionaries of the accent as explicit models, text-artifacts in Agha's terms (2003) which themselves also function as vehicles of enregisterment processes in the chains of transmission in which they participate historically.

As Agha (2003) describes it, the process of systematisation/codification of the accent and its characterisation as *received* or authorised by an external authority is part of an anthropological mechanism that produces a standard accent ideal that is external to any one speaker. This sense of distance between ideal and reality eventually makes it easier for claims to be made that *no one speaks RP any longer* if RP is solely understood as a construct model that comes up short against the forces of variationist linguistic change and no longer matches the way people are hearing language being spoken in their everyday lives. If the term *standard language/variety* is reserved for such a socially-generated and historically-sustained mental 'construct', it can be kept distinct from the concept of an *elite* (or even *establishment) sociolect*. This latter term can then be reserved to refer to linguistic patterns evidenced in the first language of socialisation (i.e. the vernacular in that particular sense) of a social group occupying a particular socio-economic niche within a socially stratified society. The term is, of course, also an idealisation, since no group contains completely homogeneous or identical speakers, enabling the identification of one single sociolect shared by all. Until sociolinguists appreciated this c-RP and n-RP distinction, there could not be progress in the empirical, variationist study of elite sociolect pronunciations as part of the sociolinguistic makeup of society, not solely as a model accent for foreign language teaching purposes, which was one of the major reasons for its continuation in books such as successive editions of Gimson's *Pronunciation of English* (in press continuously since 1962). This progress was needed: there is simply an acute empirical gap in understanding the sociolinguistic makeup of a class-stratified society if elite sociolect speakers are not represented. Debates within sociology about elites, class formation and social stratification in British society are particularly intense at the moment (Macionis and Plummer 2012; Lui 2015; Mills 2015; Savage 2015; Skeggs 2015; Wakeling and Savage 2015), and this renewed discussion of elite formation, the sociological perpetuation and reinforcement of class, and class disparities in Britain is prominently on the sociological agenda, and this should also inform British sociolinguistics in the future.

What's in a Name?

As I have pointed out above, while the study and description of n-RP features has not been a major concern of sociolinguists until fairly recently, c-RP has very much been the focus of mainstream phonetic research since the earliest days of the phonetic sciences in Britain and Daniel Jones' tenure at University College London. Cruttenden (2014: 77) writes that Jones' efforts at description and codification of the accent were spurred by 'increased interest in teaching English as a foreign language'. From the beginning, Jones' descriptive publications, such as Jones (1914, 1917), were based on his own variety and that of close associates, which he at the time labelled (PSP). The term RP replaced Public School Pronunciation (PSP) by the time of Jones (1926), and Gimson's *Pronunciation of English* from 1962 carried on this tradition. Under this name, the accent norm became well known in mainstream phonetics and in English-language teaching generally.

Wells (1990, 1994, 1997), acknowledging this tradition and heritage, discusses the implications for a pronunciation model of different ways of understanding the term RP: whether as a norm for foreign language teaching, as an ideal *Platonic* notion of correct speech or as a sociolinguistic concept, a function of a number of speaker characteristics centred on 'socioeconomic class, sex and age, perhaps with contextual style' (Wells 1994: 204). His clear preference was for a sociolinguistically-informed notion of RP, as this is the only one that could eventually incorporate changes (in many cases, originating from non-standard local varieties) in native-RP pronunciations, as they appear, disseminate and become established and standard, as t-glottalling has to some extent (Fabricius 2000). Wells (1990) recognised sociolinguistic continuity, as well as discontinuity, between speakers of RP in Daniel Jones's day and the present time, implying that a sociolinguistically sensitive methodology would enable the description and codification of an evolving accent (n-RP) for explicit teaching purposes (c-RP).

The term RP has by no means remained unchallenged. As a result of the advent of the *BBC* in 1922 and its decision to apply a unified pronunciation norm for broadcasting purposes, *BBC English* came over time to be added to the terminological battery (for a comprehensive history of the *BBC Advisory Committee on Spoken English*, see Schwyter 2016).[3] The *Oxford English Dictionary* lists the term RP as first occurring in 1928, followed by three mentions during the 1930s. The term is still used to denote the accent in the *Cambridge English Pronouncing Dictionary* (Jones et al. 2011). The first Head of the *BBC*, John Reith wrote that '[t]he policy might be described as that of seeking a common denominator of educated speech' (cited in Cruttenden 2014: 77).

Cruttenden (2014: 80) has recently argued in favour of Windsor Lewis' (1972) appellation *General British* (GB), not as a different accent of British English from RP, but as 'an evolved and evolving version of the same accent under a different name'. Cruttenden argues that the term RP is, in the public mind and for many linguists, a term used to refer to a particular sub-variety of RP: Wells' *U-RP* (Wells 1982), Upton's *trad-RP* (Upton 2012), the form spoken natively by an increasingly older population of aristocratic/upper-class origins, which Cruttenden himself labels Conspicuous GB.[4] Thus, he contends, the term RP is too restrictive and misleading (and age-based) to be of use for a more mainstream variety that is more widely socially based and more acceptable as a foreign language norm. In addition, the term *General British* parallels *General American* in the US, and Cruttenden argues that the two seem to serve somewhat similar social functions (although not everyone would agree with this point). Cruttenden (2014: 81) characterises Conspicuous GB (CGB) as 'that type of GB which is commonly considered to be "posh", to be associated with upper-class families, with public schools and with professions which have traditionally recruited from such families, e.g. officers in the navy and in some army regiments'. Note that the definition of CGB as being found *in certain families* allows for the implication that it is still a vernacular for a young group of speakers (the generational successors). But Cruttenden clearly has an old-fashioned form of pronunciation in mind, as he states that it is mainly limited to older speakers. He provides a list of characteristic pronunciation features that can be said to typify CGB. An empirical sociolinguist should regard such a list as a set of empirical hypotheses that can be tested on language data from such groups of speakers. To take one instance, very open NURSE vowels have recently been observed in a sociolinguistic interview of a female speaker born in 1990 and recorded in 2008 (Fabricius et al. 2012). This vowel quality is, therefore, not exclusively used by older speakers, although it is possibly more frequent there. The precise reach and quantitative distribution of such phonetic variants remain, however, subjects for future corpus-based research that is at present lacking.

These arguments for GB as a term for the codified norm notwithstanding, in this chapter, I regard the term *modern RP* as a more apt descriptive label for the evolving variable sociolinguistic phenomena represented by the speech of successive generations of sociologically identifiable speakers. This is precisely because the name makes an explicit link between present and previous distributions of accent features, the modern patterns being the historical, generational successors of the older patterns (in the same sense that modern speakers are descendants of older speakers). I leave aside the question as to whether these features form a consistently identifiable accent variety, since that question is perhaps more of an ideological one, a question of enregisterment (Agha 2003, 2007), and take the position here that I aim to simply describe elite sociolect features quantitatively and find out how they come together in sociolinguistic styles.

In addition, the issue of precise accent *labels* is something of a distraction, when the essential challenge of a sociolinguistic investigation could be said to be a secure sociological identification on criteria which keep it independent of linguistic form and thus avoid circularity. I argued in Fabricius (2000: 46–60) that socio-economic background and educational history would play a role here, but this is by no means uncontroversial, and I acknowledge it as a problem that needs to be tackled in more ethnographic depth. In operationalising this aspect for my original study, students at Cambridge University with independent school and upper-middle-class backgrounds (measured by examining parental occupations) made up the key set of speakers whose speech patterns (t-glottalling in particular) formed the basis of the quantitative investigation. Since these background factors were established independently, the task then became an empirical sociolinguistic one, and some of the findings that stem from this approach are detailed in the next section.

Quantitative Empirical Studies of Phonetic Variation in RP Speech

T-Glottalling

Fabricius (2000) provides an empirical study of variation in word-final /t/ in a single-age-cohort of speakers recorded in 1997 and 1998. As described above, these speakers had been educated at public and independent schools and were students at Cambridge University at the time of recording, aged between 18 and 30. Socio-economically, these speakers came from upper-middle-class family backgrounds: their parents (in the majority of cases, their fathers) had occupations at the upper levels of the Cambridge Scale for Occupations (Prandy, 1992), being for example barristers, solicitors, accountants, medical specialists and high-ranking civil servants (Fabricius 2000: 77–78, 163–164). Interview and reading passage data obtained from 12 male and 12 female speakers yielded 9888 tokens of word-final /t/, analysed auditorily. Analysis of variances (ANOVAs) explored social and linguistic factors that determined variation in rates of t-glottalling across groups of speakers. The results showed that the speakers in the 1997–1998 corpus used t-glottalling at a uniformly high rate pre-consonantally within interview style (60–70%). The utterance-final position (in the study, designated *pre-pausal*) showed greater variation between speakers, and this variation was shown to be regionally determined, with higher rates evident in speakers who had grown up closer to and in London. High rates of t-glottalling in the pre-vocalic environment in interview style were likewise restricted to speakers with London origins. In addition, pre-pausal and pre-vocalic (but not pre-consonantal) t-glottalling was widely avoided in reading passage style. The study concluded that there was support for the idea that the pre-pausal environment would stand to become the next widely acceptable environment for t-glottalling, perhaps within the next generation or two. In the study, however, pre-pausal and pre-vocalic t-glottalling were not in evidence in reading style. Moreover, since usage of pre-pausal t-glottalling in interview style did not show the same consistently high rates as the pre-consonantal environment, it was considered premature to accord pre-pausal t-glottalling the same sociolinguistic status as pre-consonantal t-glottalling.

Weak Vowel Variation

Fabricius (2002a) focused on the status of two ongoing processes of historical change within weak syllables that have been previously recognised in the literature on RP. The first was a change in the phonetic quality of the weak high front vowel within word-final V# syllables from [ɪ] towards [i], known as happy-tensing (Wells 1982). The second change, sometimes referred to as the drift from [ɪ] (also known as the KIT vowel in the British tradition following Wells 1982) to [ə] in closed weak syllables (Wells 1997: 18) is a change that has progressively affected a heterogeneous group of lexical words such as *item* and *civil* as well as certain derivational and inflectional affixes such as *-less*, *-ness*, *-ily*, *-ed*, and *-es*. Both of these changes have been reported as being generationally-based (e.g. Cruttenden 2001: 107). The data set consisted of four male and four female speakers, a subset of the interview corpus analysed in Fabricius (2000). Happy vowels in *-y* and *-ly* contexts, and variation between KIT and schwa in plural *-es* and past *-ed* were measured acoustically. First and second formants were measured at the midpoint of duration of the vowel for KIT, happy and schwa tokens and at the F1 maximum for FLEECE (following Labov et al. 1972; Labov 1994), which was used as a reference vowel for visual and statistical purposes. Comparisons were made in the data between values for F2-F1, as a reflection of the fact that more peripheral vowels have a higher F2 and lower F1, while more central vowels have a higher F1 and lower F2. F2-F1 thus gave a generalised measure of *peripherality*.

All speakers showed a tendency towards an intermediate or fronted value for the final vowel in -y words, either midway between the KIT and FLEECE ellipses or with the majority of tokens within the FLEECE area. Some tokens, however, appeared more conservative, being within the range of KIT. One male speaker's data, shown below, gives an example of this range: three tokens of #V are within the KIT area (indicated by + symbols), but the majority of tokens are either within the intermediate area, close to but slightly lower than FLEECE, or located within the hand-drawn ellipse for FLEECE (indicated by x). Similarly, the means and standard deviations data for this speaker show the #C environment as having the most advanced mean value for F2-F1, while the highest standard deviation and thus the greatest spread in these values is associated with the #V environment (Fig. 3.1; Table 3.1).

In the case of KIT→schwa drift, the data analysis demonstrated that there was no general evidence of drift towards schwa in the production of *-es* and *-ed* suffixes.

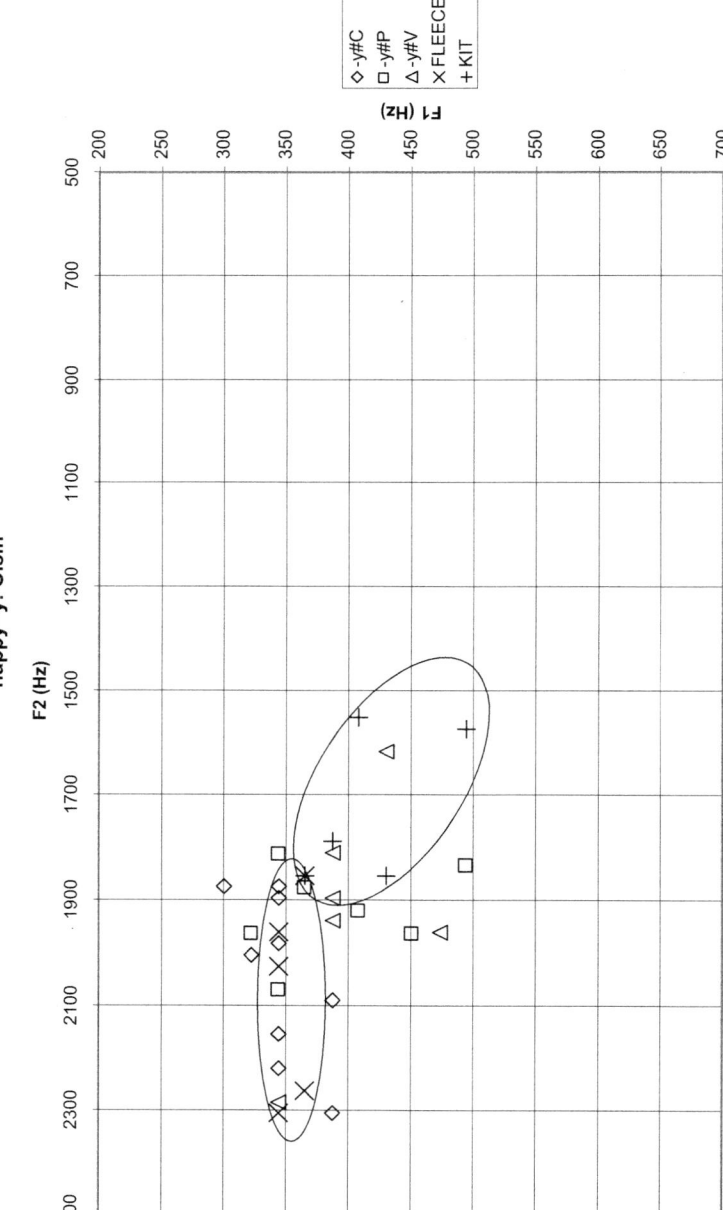

Fig. 3.1 Locations of ᴋɪᴛ, ꜰʟᴇᴇᴄᴇ and happʏ tokens, one male speaker (Reproduced from Fabricius 2002a: 228)

Table 3.1 Means and standard deviations in F2-F1, male speaker (Data from Fabricius 2002a: 228)

	M	SD	Max	Min	N
#C	1690	135	1916	1528	10
#P	1502	133	1722	1335	8
#V	1514	245	1938	1184	6
FLEECE	1727	197	1959	1486	5
KIT	1305	183	1486	1077	5

Table 3.2 Means and standard deviations for KIT/schwa, female speaker (Data from Fabricius 2002a: 222)

	M	SD	Max	Min	N
Past -ed	1409	101	1551	1292	7
Present -es	1410	62	1485	1335	4
KIT	1421	73	1507	1335	5
Schwa	1163	130	1314	991	5

The data for one female speaker are presented in Table 3.2 and Fig. 3.2. Comparison of the means and standard deviations shows the suffixes to be centred on the same F2-F1 values as KIT, in a pattern that corresponds to the six of the eight speakers in the corpus data, where the past and present/plural suffixes resemble each other. Two speakers, however, diverged slightly from this pattern and in a similar way. Both showed lower average F2-F1 values and greater standard deviations for the present/plural suffix than for the past suffix. The overall impression from the data was of a long-lasting process of change from KIT to schwa that had to some extent stalled or at least become sluggish as far as -ed and -es suffixes were concerned. Since KIT as opposed to schwa in such suffixes is a local British phenomenon that separates it from North American, Australian and New Zealand pronunciations, from a dialect contact point of view, maintenance of KIT in these suffixes may be playing a role as a salient British feature.

Changes in the RP Short Vowel System

Fabricius (2007) assembled a comparative corpus of formant measurements designed to give a real-time view of the changing short vowel

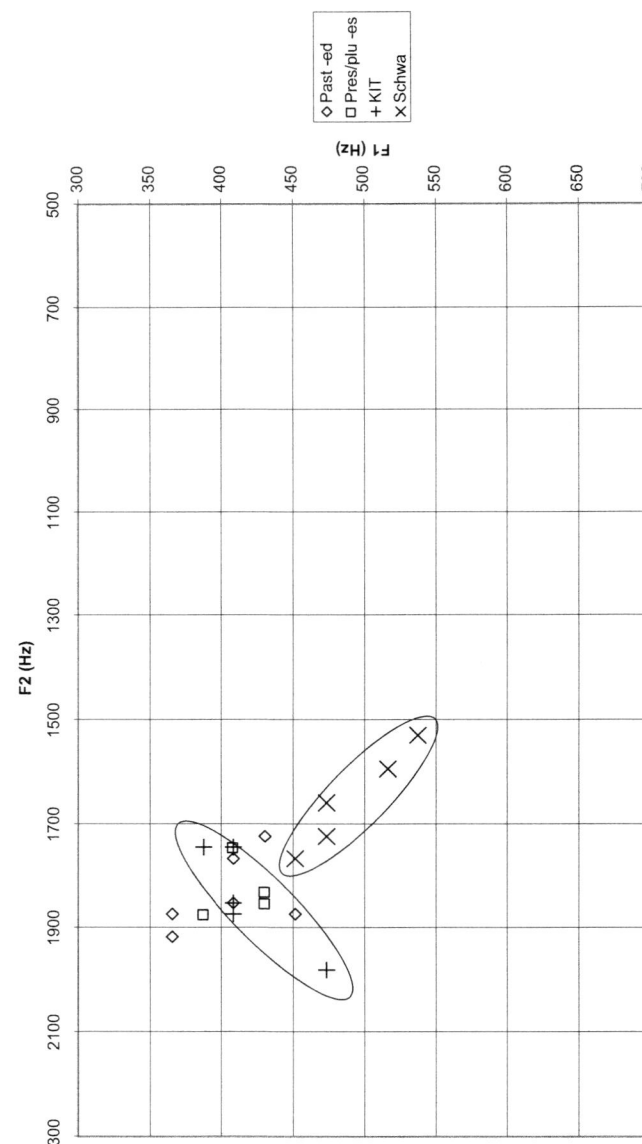

Fig. 3.2 Vowel plot, female speaker. Location of -es and -ed suffix vowels vis-à-vis KIT +, and schwa x (Reproduced from Fabricius 2002a: 222)

system of modern RP during the twentieth century. The data derived from instrumental acoustic measurements of vowel formants in speech were obtained from the following sources:

(a) Radio broadcasts by two male RP speakers from The Machine Readable Spoken English Corpus (MARSEC) corpus (Roach et al. 1993) analysed in Deterding (1997);
(b) Elicited citation forms spoken by a homogenous set of 25 male RP speakers born before 1945—representing average values for the 25 speakers in the corpus of Wells (1962);
(c) Elicited citation forms spoken by 20 male RP speakers in four age groups—representing individual values for citation forms (Hawkins and Midgley 2005);
(d) Broadcast speech tokens from Queen Elizabeth II's Christmas broadcasts over three decades: the 1950s, 1960s and 1980s (converted from Bark values given in Harrington et al. 2000);
(e) Sociolinguistic interview speech tokens from four male speakers of modern RP from the Cambridge corpus collected in 1997 and 1998 (discussed above and in Fabricius 2000).

Data were obtained as either Hertz values or Bark-transformed data (Harrington et al. 2000); the latter were transformed to Hertz using a conversion table between Hertz values and Bark values based on Zwicker (1961).

The chapter presented the first use of an innovative analytical procedure using angle and distance calculations to represent the geometric relationship between two vowel positions. This was a combinatory method which made the statistical comparisons typical of mainstream phonetics accessible to the two-dimensional vowel plots approach of Labovian sociolinguistics (taken further by Nycz and Hall-Lew 2014). The *visual comparison* method has been widely used for examining vowel variation (Labov et al. 1972; Labov 1994; Watt and Tillotson 2001; Fabricius 2002a; Torgersen and Kerswill 2004). The benefits of visual comparisons for understanding change in vowel systems are considerably enhanced by methodologies that also allow replicable statistical comparisons.

To turn to the results of the study, the combined data showed that the short vowel space of these speakers fitting the RP sociolinguistic profile had undergone a change from an early configuration (with the earliest speakers born before 1920) with STRUT as the lowest point, through a phase in the mid-twentieth century with TRAP and STRUT on a similar low level, to a late configuration, with TRAP lowest and STRUT centralised characteristic of speakers born late in the twentieth century. *TRAP/STRUT rotation* was proposed as a label for this trend as a shorthand term for the lowering and backing of TRAP and the backing and subsequent raising/centring of STRUT.

Smoothing and Yod Coalescence

Hannisdal (2006) is a quantitative analysis of British newsreaders' speech in broadcast situations, consisting of data from 30 speakers employed by three TV channels (*BBC, ITV, Sky*). Six phonetic variables were investigated in all; the present brief discussion limits itself to two: smoothing or monophthongisation of diphthongs, and yod coalescence.

Smoothing (discussed in Wells 1982: 238–242; as cited in Cruttenden (2014: 160), the term first used in Sweet (1888: 22)), is the phenomenon whereby the diphthongs PRICE and MOUTH, in combination with schwa, as in the words *fire* and *power*, respectively, undergo various degrees of monophthongisation to either a centring diphthong or monophthongal START /ɑː/. Hannisdal's quantitative analysis of 1339 potential smoothing items showed that 46.4% were realised overall as smoothed variants (Hannisdal 2006: 200–203), and moreover, FIRE-type words were slightly more likely to be smoothed (48.7%) than POWER-type items (43.5 %).

Hannisdal (2006: 200) also noted a certain amount of individual variation in rates of smoothing. The most striking of these results was the male dominance of rates of smoothing: male speakers used smoothing at an average rate of 59% and female speakers at an average rate of 33.5%, consistently across TV channels. Hannisdal argues that the sharply gender-differentiated pattern reflects a stance towards articulatory explicitness, with women preferring full forms rather than smoothed forms as part of a 'clarity of diction' ideology. At present, it is difficult to know how these speakers (aged as they were between 30 and 60 at the time of Hannisdal's data collection) fit into a larger diachronic picture of the fate of smoothing in modern RP, but the gender division does at least suggest that some sort of sociolinguistic dynamic is present.

The second of Hannisdal's phonological variables I will look at here is yod coalescence, which in her analysis encompasses the phonological variables (tj) (dj),[5] in words such as *tune* and *dune*, with their possible variants [tj] [tʃ] and [dj] [dʒ]. Hannisdal's corpus of 617 tokens showed coalescence occurring in 46.4% of these. Lexical considerations played a role, as the word *during* contributed almost half of the items showing coalescence, with coalescence in 83% of tokens. Hannisdal concludes that there is 'no doubt that yod coalescence in stressed syllables is becoming established in RP speech' (Hannisdal 2006: 213), and, indeed, she notes that yod coalescence was marked as *non-RP* in the second edition of Wells' *Longman Pronunciation Dictionary*, except for the case of the word *during* (Wells 2000).

/r/ Variation in RP

Fabricius (2017) reports on a quantitative study using *BBC* recordings from 14 English upper-class and upper-middle-class speakers born between 1880 and 1920. These recordings provided a corpus of tokens of syllable-initial /r/ ($N = 2511$). The results of an auditory analysis showed that two variants, in particular, tapped /r/ (including a small number of cases of trilled /r/) in medial and r-sandhi positions, and labialised /r/, mostly in word-initial position, had significantly different social and linguistic profiles. Tapped /r/s are now very rare in modern RP speech, while labialised /r/ now seems to be on the increase in many parts of British society (see Foulkes and Docherty 2000).

As Fig. 3.3 shows, cross-tabulations of the data showed decreasing tapped /r/ usage across the decades of the recordings. This decrease was found most starkly across medial (intervocalic) and linking /r/ contexts. The trend was independent of the speakers' dates of birth and suggested a changing *style of the time* whereby taps and trills became increasingly rarer in these *BBC* recordings.

The data were then modelled according to word position and decade of recording, with year of birth as a continuous factor and speaker as a

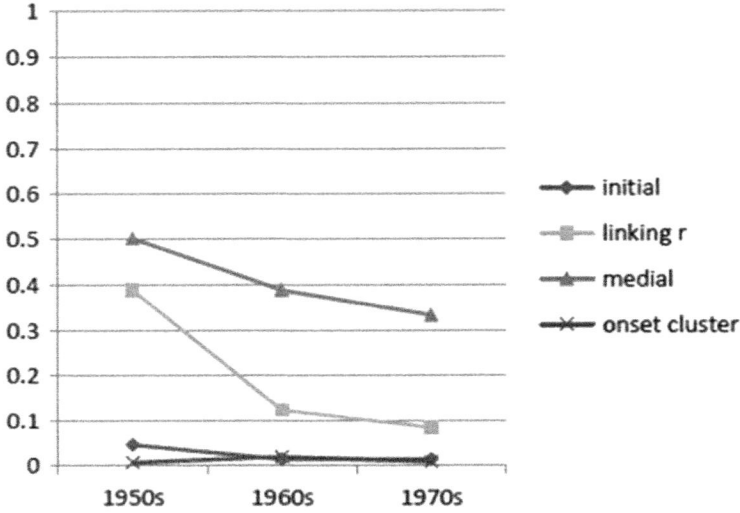

Fig. 3.3 Trends in rates of tapped and trilled /r/ by word position according to decade of recording (Reproduced from Fabricius 2017)

random factor. This model was highly significant, while factors such as gender and speech context (interview versus monologue) were not. Table 3.3 shows the results for 13 speakers and 2289 tokens (omitting OM4, as noted above) for tapped and trilled /r/, recoded and categorised together as *taps*. The three independent factors, in order from least to most significant effect, were position in the word (p = 6.26e-132), decade of recording (p = 157e-07) and year of birth, examined as a continuous variable (p = 0.000325).

While in the 1950s data the tapped/trilled /r/'s factor weight favoured taps and trills at 0.635, there is already a slight disfavouring of the feature in the 1960s and a further decrease in the 1970s. The significance of *Year of birth* as a continuous variable also showed that taps and trills steadily decreased with generation, following the *decade of recording* trend, while both are independently significant. Word-medial, intervocalic positions most highly favoured taps and trills (e.g. the common stereotypical pronunciation of *very*).

As Fig. 3.4 shows, labial variants (which included labiodentals and labialised alveolars) in the corpus were predominantly produced by three

Table 3.3 Mixed methods logistic regression modelling for tapped and trilled /r/, N = 2289 (excluding OM4; data from Fabricius 2017: 56)

Deviance				1283.101
Df				8
Grand mean				0.15
Factors	**Log odds**	**Tokens (N)**	**Proportion of application value**	**Centred factor weight**
Decade of recording				
1950s	0.556	1141	0.187	0.635
1960s	−0.033	823	0.119	0.492
1970s	−0.523	325	0.098	0.372
Year of birth (continuous)				
	0.025			
Position				
Medial	2.122	578	0.439	0.916
Linking r	1.234	260	0.250	0.775
Initial	−1.163	451	0.029	0.238
Onset cluster	−2.193	1000	0.011	0.1

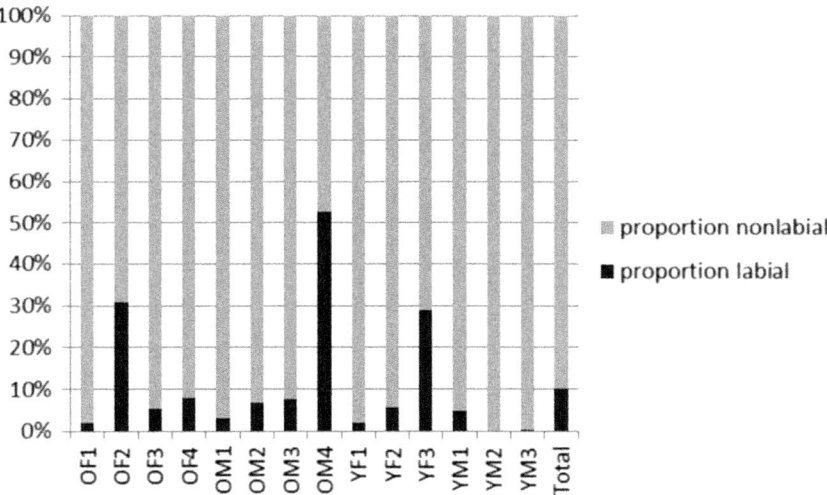

Fig. 3.4 Labial and non-labial /r/ in the corpus, by percentage (Reproduced from Fabricius 2017: 57)

individuals. OF2 (Baroness Stokes), OM4 (Lord Halifax) and YF3 (Daphne du Maurier) were the only three speakers whose production of labials was above the average for all speakers in the corpus of around 10%. OM4, Lord Halifax (with an aristocratic background) is by far the most prolific user of labials for /r/ at 52.7%. While he is the only speaker of this type in the corpus assembled for this study, the *BBC* archive potentially holds other examples of comparable recordings which could provide a firmer basis for future conclusions.

The logistic model showed that labials were most strongly favoured in initial position and medially. Decade of recording is strongly favoured only in the case of the 1930s, which isolates the single recording of OM4 referred to above. Other decades do not favour labial production, but as Table 3.4 shows, this is a result which is strongly affected by the dominance of a single speaker in this limited corpus. The result for speech type shows a strong factor weight favouring 'Interview' as speech context, which may seem anomalous, given that OM4's recording is a monologue, but Fig. 3.4 also shows that a large number of labial tokens also occur in the interviews recorded with YF3 (Daphne du Maurier) and OF3 (Baroness Stokes).

Table 3.4 Mixed methods logistic regression modelling for labiodental and labialised /r/, N = 2511 (including OM4; data from Fabricius 2017: 57)

Deviance				1118,775
Df				9
Grand mean				0.101
Factors	**Log odds**	**Tokens (N)**	**Proportion of application value**	**Centred factor weight**
Speech type				
Interview	1.012	1257	0.093	0.733
Monologue	−1.012	1254	0.108	0.267
Decade of recording				
1930s	3.449	222	0.527	0.969
1950s	−0.745	1141	0.035	0.322
1970s	−0.900	325	0.154	0.289
1960s	−1.803	823	0.056	0.141
Position				
Initial	1.062	498	0.189	0.743
Medial	0.266	624	0.093	0.566
Onset cluster	−0.076	1105	0.083	0.481
Linking r	−1.252	284	0.032	0.222

Although this small-scale study could not tell the definitive story of labial r in RP, there are indications that labial variants could be better characterised as idiosyncratic features in this corpus rather than a general sociolinguistic feature of the group, as tapped and trilled /r/s seem to be.

Variation and Change in RP Over the Lifespan

Studies of RP speakers have also contributed to an understanding of accent change over the lifespan post-adolescence. Harrington et al. (2000), Harrington (2006) and MacKenzie (2014) have employed close phonetic analyses of broadcast recordings to explore this, using Her Majesty (HM) Queen Elizabeth II's Christmas speeches and Sir David Attenborough's natural history programmes for the *BBC*.

Harrington et al. (2000) presented an analysis of vowel tokens gleaned from Queen Elizabeth II's Christmas broadcasts in three periods (the 1950s, the late 1960s/early 1970s, the 1980s). They demonstrated an expanded vowel space on the F1 dimension in the 1960s and 1980s data compared to data from the 1950s. These results were compared to the vowel positions of a set of 1980s Standard Southern British speakers from the MARSEC corpus, reported in Deterding (1997). The authors concluded that the Queen's vowels in the Christmas broadcasts had individually shifted in the direction of more mainstream forms of RP. However, Fabricius (2007) provides a comparison of the Queen's short vowel system with a set of vowel systems from contemporary and younger RP speakers, which shows that the Queen's short vowel system, even in the later recordings, if understood holistically as a geometrical configuration, is most closely aligned with speakers born in the same decade and consistently different from that of speakers born in subsequent decades.

In another study, MacKenzie (2014) conducted an analysis of Sir David Attenborough's broadcast speech, examining, in particular, the realisation of /r/ as taps intervocalically within lexical items and in cases of linking /r/. Data from two nature documentaries, *Zoo Quest* (1959) and *Planet Earth* (2006) provided tokens of /r/ for auditory coding. The results were modelled using logistic regression, and it was found that while overall rates of tapped r were not significantly different, the speaker had gone against community change over time in one particular detail. Sir David was found to use higher rates of tapped /r/ in linking /r/ contexts, and in 'voiceover' mode (which to some extent is equivalent to 'careful' speech in sociolinguistic work) but not in his onscreen, more 'casual' mode in the more recent recordings.

Attitudinal Studies of RP: Dialect-in-Discourse

Alongside a large body of literature on attitudinal studies of the reception of RP carried out in the 1970s (Giles et al. 1990), there is also a small amount of more recent literature on attitudinal studies of RP. The 'dialect-in-discourse' model of attitudinal analysis (Garrett et al. 2003) inspired a small-scale study of attitudes to modern RP in York in 2002 (published as Fabricius 2005, 2006). The study examined school students' attitudinal responses to recordings of the speech of upper-middle-class speakers born in the 1970s, with the recordings used being sourced from the set of sociolinguistic interviews conducted for Fabricius (2000). Sequences from sociolinguistic interviews were used to elicit responses. A total of 161 adolescents, aged 14 on average, from one independent and two comprehensive high schools in York took part in the study. Results comparing three of the six speakers made direct comparisons between responses to a male regional and a male non-regional speaker (Fabricius 2005), and to two non-regional speakers (one female, one male; Fabricius 2006).

The results showed that modern RP as a perceptual concept is to some extent hinged on gender: responses to the female modern RP speaker tended to be more positive than to the male modern RP speaker. Dynamism (encompassing independence and straightforwardness, Kristiansen 2001) distinguished the male regional speaker and the male non-regional, modern RP speaker, who was regarded as less dynamic. These two male speakers scored equally well on traits reflecting academic success (well educated, intelligent), differing somewhat from earlier evaluations of RP versus non-RP voices (Giles et al. 1990), where RP speakers were rated significantly higher than non-RP speakers. More in line with earlier results, the regional male speaker was graded more highly on interpersonal or social competence traits such as friendly, pleasant or trustworthy. The non-regional male speaker scored particularly badly relative to the female speaker in terms of what can be termed *social dynamism* (Kristiansen 2001), being enthusiastic and interesting. Fabricius (2006) ventured the conclusion that the male non-regional speaker's speech performance was particularly resonant with echoes of an older style of RP speech and an elitist discursive stance, and conjured up overt class differentiation, being redolent of the *male public school voice*.

To sum up then, with a long-term diachronic view of the transformation of RP into modern RP, it seems clear that there is evidence of generational change in vocalic realisations, in both stressed checked and free vowels, as well as weak vowels, alongside the persistence to some extent of diphthong smoothing. In the consonantal system, we can see changes in /t/, /r/ and /dj, tj/ realisations. In the attitudinal responses to gendered modern RP voices, we see indications that these sociolinguistic styles make coherent sense to listeners, and that the 'male public school voice' continues to conjure up overt class difference and distinction. The picture then is one of vigorous variation and change in native-RP alongside other elements of stability, as seen in the persistence of perceptions of *construct-RP*.

Sociolinguistic Change and Modern RP

In this concluding discussion, I take a step back from language variation and change, and bring issues of sociolinguistic change to the fore. Coupland (2014: 69) suggests that 'in its canonical form, variationism is not motivated to discover socially significant change, and it has no apparatus for gauging social impacts of change', although recent ethnographically inspired work (e.g. Snell 2010; Moore 2010; Kirkham 2015) and studies of sociolinguistic perception (e.g., Campbell-Kibler 2010; Drager 2011; Levon and Holmes-Elliot 2013; Pharao et al. 2014) have ameliorated this to a large extent. No matter the variationist details of language use that can be identified in one or another set of corpus recordings, and important as these patterns can be for understanding sound change trajectories as purely historical linguistic processes, we cannot evade the issue that the changing social context in which speech takes place over time remains to be addressed theoretically within sociolinguistics, and this is precisely where Coupland's important notion of *sociolinguistic change* is needed. Studies that embrace close ethnographic as well as close discursive analytical perspectives on this area are also needed.

Coupland presents an interesting and relevant (albeit, he demurs, tendentious) list of social changes in Britain between 1960 and 2009, 'some more material, some more ideological' (2009: 29–30). Those which seem at first glance most relevant to the topic at hand are: 'the decline of the Establishment[6]...Failing trust in professional authority...The growth of the middle class but the accentuation of the rich/poor divide', although others, such as 'massively increasing geographical mobility' and 'reframing and rescaling of local-global relationships' (Coupland 2009: 29–30) may also have a role to play. Further into the chapter, Coupland hypothesises the potential consequence for the standard language hegemony of a 'social change towards relative classlessness or towards more omnivorous cultural consumption' (Coupland 2009: 35):

> ...even where patterns of linguistic variation persist across class-indexed groups (as of course they do, despite degrees of linguistic levelling), we would expect the sociolinguistic indexicality of class – the value associations of 'standard' and 'non-standard' speech – to be weaker and less significant.

To re-phrase Coupland's quote, I would rather refer to 'the value associations of higher class and lower class speech' rather than 'standard and non-standard speech' in order to avoid the complicating factors of standardness and standardisation, as was discussed in the section on standardisation above.[7] Nonetheless, the distinction between n-RP and c-RP I have made there seems to enable us to specify the kind of difference Coupland is referring to: a weakening of the standard language hegemony would correspond to changes in c-RP whereby the import and authoritative position of an accent would be eroded, whereas (again, to quote Coupland 2009: 35) 'patterns of linguistic variation persisting [or changing – *my addition*] across class-indexed groups' (which I would define in terms of professional status, educational background, income and other sociological factors) would be matters of the description of changing patterns of sociolinguistically identifiable phonetic features, and thus changes in n-RP. The two types of change are closely related but also potentially independent sociolinguistic processes of considerable complexity.

Coupland further urges the consideration of a third type of change, sociolinguistic change, which is a complex of notions I will exemplify briefly with one case study below. In Coupland (2014: 69), sociolinguistic change is described as 'a broad set of language-implicating changes' within a society, and the study of sociolinguistic change involves 'discovering changing relationships between language and society and their instantiation at the level of practice' (Coupland 2014: 70). Coupland makes the case for an integrative sociolinguistic approach that can encompass a triad of types of change (social, linguistic, sociolinguistic), equally theoretically relevant and potentially empirically tractable in various ways.

One example of an integrative approach that illustrates how sociolinguistic changes over generations could be identified is in studies of metalinguistic discourses, as part of the study of 'discursive practices' in Coupland's exemplificatory Figure 1 (2014: 74). One such study is found in Fabricius and Mortensen (2013), where the authors examine the *construct resources* (understood as dynamic, socially situated and identifiable ideological elements of c-RP) in a metalinguistic discourse surrounding the concept of accent in the UK. The chapter examines a brief stretch of talk extracted from an interview recorded in 2008 with a student at Cambridge University, as a response to the question *Do you think that accents matter?* In this brief stretch of talk, the interviewee invokes a number of construct resources, such as the location of *posh accents* in the south of England, as well as other resources, such as the idea that accent prejudice is *off the record*. The latter compares with Abercrombie's assertion (1965, originally published in 1951) that the question of which side of the RP/non-RP accent-bar any speaker was placed on was never formulated explicitly at that time. The interviewee also performs hyperstylisations of the accent (in the word *posh* itself, for example) to get her message across. The authors argue that these findings give access to an emic perspective on the role of language variation in the community, and as such are a valuable supplement to more etic experimental approaches to language attitudes surrounding RP (such as Fabricius 2005, 2006 and their antecedents, discussed above). It is clear that we will need a battery of methods and approaches for the study of elite sociolects as dynamic and changing sociolinguistic phenomena in the future.

Conclusion

Our focus in this chapter has been to set out the state of the art for studies of the sociolinguistics and sociophonetics of the elite sociolects of the UK, known as they are under various labels that have been part of the linguistics and phonetics literature for a century. As I have shown, these forms of speech and their sociolinguistic profile within the setting of the south of England and beyond are a fruitful area of investigation. In order to tackle these phenomena, we need an arsenal of approaches encompassing many of the tools from all three waves of sociolinguistics (to use the label from Eckert 2012). I have set out to show historical trajectories and variations in consonantal and vocalic production, as well as attitudinal and language-ideological aspects of the elite sociolect.

In taking stock of the research that so far has been produced relating to the sociolinguistic study of elite sociolects in the UK, I have shown that this is a fruitful area that touches on many aspects of sociolinguistic theory, ranging from the more strictly linguistic understanding of variation and change to the more qualitative study of the attitudinal, ideological and meta-discursive space of an elite sociolect in the sociolinguistic landscape of Britain over time. Examination of what constitutes sociolinguistic change in this case can also be particularly rewarding, positioned, as these accent features and accent tropes are, at the nexus of a particular set of social, linguistic and historical circumstances, however, we may choose to name the variety or varieties, and whatever the future of its accent features may turn out to be.

Notes

1. https://www.phon.ucl.ac.uk/home/estuary/india.htm
2. All of which have in places somewhat ironic voiceovers, as a sign of a distancing 'semi-ethnographic gaze'.

3. As Schwyter (2016) demonstrates, the task of pinning down a spoken standard was fraught from its inception.
4. Note that these terms differ in the extent to which one could interpret them to allow for generational renewal.
5. /sj/ can also exhibit similar patterns of coalescence to /ʃ/.
6. Perhaps we would contend that this decline has resulted in a reframing and repositioning of the establishment rather than its demise, given the present political climate in the UK.
7. 'Standard', as Nikolas Coupland has also pointed out many times, is itself a troubled term (e.g. in Coupland 2000).

References

Abercrombie, D. (1965). *Studies in phonetics and linguistics*. London: Longman.

Adonis, A., & Pollard, S. (1997). *A class act: The myth of Britain's classless society*. London: Hamish Hamilton.

Agha, A. (2003). The social life of cultural value. *Language & Communication, 23*(3–4), 231–273.

Agha, A. (2007). *Language and social relations*. Cambridge: Cambridge University Press.

Altendorf, U. (2003). *Estuary English: Levelling at the interface of RP and South-Eastern British English*. Tübingen: Gunter Narr Verlag.

Bex, T., & Watts, R. (1999). *Standard English: The widening debate*. London/New York: Routledge.

Britain, D. (2016). Sedentarism and nomadism in the sociolinguistics of dialect. In N. Coupland (Ed.), *Sociolinguistics: Theoretical debates* (pp. 217–241). Cambridge: Cambridge University Press.

Campbell-Kibler, K. (2010). The sociolinguistic variant as a carrier of social meaning. *Language Variation and Change, 22*(3), 423–441.

Cheshire, J., Kerswill, P., Fox, S., & Torgersen, E. (2011). Contact, the feature pool and the speech community: The emergence of multicultural London English. *Journal of SocioLinguistics, 15*(2), 151–196.

Coupland, N. (2000). Sociolinguistic prevarication over standard English. Review of T. Bex & R. J. Watts (Eds.), (1999) Standard English: The widening debate. *Journal of Sociolinguistics, 4*(4): 630–642.

Coupland, N. (2009). Dialects, standards and social change. In M. Maegaard, F. Gregersen, P. Quist, & J. N. Jørgensen (Eds.), *Language attitudes, standardization and language change* (pp. 27–50). Oslo: Novus Forlag.

Coupland, N. (2014). Sociolinguistic change, vernacularization and broadcast British media. In J. Androutsopoulos (Ed.), *Mediatization and sociolinguistic change* (pp. 67–98). Freiburg: Linguae and litterae, Publications of the School of Language and Literature, Freiburg Institute for Advanced Studies.

Coupland, N. (Ed.). (2016). *Sociolinguistics: Theoretical debates*. Cambridge: Cambridge University Press.

Cruttenden, A. (2001). *Gimson's pronunciation of English* (6th ed.). London: Edward Arnold.

Cruttenden, A. (2014). *Gimson's pronunciation of English* (8th ed.). London: Edward Arnold.

Deterding, D. (1997). The formants of monophthong vowels in standard Southern British English pronunciation. *Journal of the International Phonetic Association, 27*, 47–55.

Drager, K. (2011). Speaker age and vowel perception. *Language and Speech, 54*(1), 99–121.

Eckert, P. (2008). Variation and the indexical field. *Journal of SocioLinguistics, 12*(4), 453–476.

Eckert, P. (2012). Three waves of variation study: The emergence of meaning in the study of sociolinguistic variation. *Annual Review of Anthropology, 41*(1), 87–100.

Fabricius, A. H. (2000). *T-glottalling between stigma and prestige: A sociolinguistic study of modern RP*. Unpublished PhD thesis, Copenhagen Business School.

Fabricius, A. H. (2002a). Weak vowels in modern RP: An acoustic study of happy-tensing and KIT/schwa shift. *Language Variation and Change, 14*(2), 211–237.

Fabricius, A. H. (2002b). Ongoing change in modern RP: Evidence for the disappearing stigma of t-glottalling. *English World-Wide, 23*(1), 115–136.

Fabricius, A. H. (2005). Investigating speech samples as 'dialect in discourse': Discourse analysis, phonetics and language attitudes. *Acta Linguistica Hafniensia, 37*, 81–99.

Fabricius, A. H. (2006). The 'vivid sociolinguistic profiling' of received pronunciation: Responses to gendered dialect in discourse. *Journal of SocioLinguistics, 10*(1), 111–122.

Fabricius, A. H. (2007). Variation and change in the TRAP and STRUT vowels of RP: A real time comparison of five acoustic data sets. *Journal of the International Phonetic Association, 37*(3), 293–320.

Fabricius, A. H. (2017). Twentieth-century received pronunciation: Prevocalic /r/. In R. Hickey (Ed.), *Listening to the past* (pp. 39–65). Cambridge: Cambridge University Press.

Fabricius, A. H., & Mortensen, J. (2013). Language ideology and the notion of 'construct resource': A case study of modern RP. In T. Kristiansen & S. Grondelaars (Eds.), *Language (de)standardisation in late modern Europe: Experimental studies* (pp. 375–402). Oslo: Novus Forlag.

Fabricius, A. H., Vaughn, C., & Kendall, T. (2012). Plotting speakers' vowel systems in "real-time" interaction. Paper presented at *advances in visual methods for linguistics* (AVML), University of York, UK, September 2012. Available online: http://avml-meeting.com/talks-at-avml-2012/

Foulkes, P., & Docherty, G. (2000). Another chapter in the story of /r/: 'labio-dental' variants in British English. *Journal of SocioLinguistics, 4*(1), 30–59.

Garrett, P., Coupland, N., & Williams, A. (2003). *Investigating language attitudes: Social meanings of dialect, ethnicity and performance.* Cardiff: University of Wales Press.

Giles, H., Coupland, N., Henwood, K., Harriman, J., & Coupland, J. (1990). The social meaning of RP: An intergenerational perspective. In S. Ramsaran (Ed.), *Studies in the pronunciation of English: A commemorative volume in honour of A.C. Gimson* (pp. 191–211). London: Routledge.

Gimson, A. (1962). *An introduction to the pronunciation of English.* London: Edward Arnold.

Hannisdal, B. R. (2006). *Variability and change in received pronunciation. A study of six phonological variables in the speech of television newsreaders.* Unpublished PhD thesis, University of Bergen. Available online: https://bora.uib.no/handle/1956/2335

Harrington, J. (2006). An acoustic analysis of 'happy-tensing' in the Queen's Christmas broadcasts. *Journal of Phonetics, 34*(4), 439–457.

Harrington, J., Palethorpe, S., & Watson, C. (2000). Monophthongal vowel changes in received pronunciation: An acoustic analysis of the Queen's Christmas broadcasts. *Journal of the International Phonetic Association, 30*(1–2), 63–78.

Hawkins, S., & Midgley, J. (2005). Formant frequencies of RP monophthongs in four age groups of speakers. *Journal of the International Phonetic Association, 35*(2), 183–199.

Jones, D. (1914). *The pronunciation of English* (2nd ed.). Cambridge: Cambridge University Press.

Jones, D. (1917). *An English pronouncing dictionary* (1st ed.). London: Dent.

Jones, D. (1926). *An English pronouncing dictionary* (2nd ed.). London: Dent.

Jones, D., Roach, P., Esling, J., & Setter, J. (2011). *Cambridge English pronouncing dictionary* (18th ed.). Cambridge: Cambridge University Press.

Kerswill, P. (2001). Mobility, meritocracy and dialect levelling: The fading (and phasing) out of received pronunciation. In P. Rajamäe & K. Vogelberg (Eds.), *British studies in the new millennium: The challenge of the grassroots* (pp. 45–58). Tartu: University of Tartu.

Kerswill, P. (2006). RP, standard English and the standard/non-standard relationship. In D. Britain (Ed.), *Language in the British Isles* (2nd ed., pp. 34–51). Cambridge: Cambridge University Press.

Kerswill, P. (2013). Identity, ethnicity and place: The construction of youth language in London. In P. Auer, M. Hilpert, A. Stukenbrock, & B. Szmrecsanyi (Eds.), *Space in language and linguistics: Geographical, interactional, and cognitive perspectives* (Vol. 24, pp. 128–164). Freiburg: Walter de Gruyter.

Kirkham, S. (2015). Intersectionality and the social meanings of variation: Class, ethnicity, and social practice. *Language in Society, 44*(5), 629–652.

Kristiansen, T. (2001). Two standards: One for the media and one for the school. *Language Awareness, 10*, 9–24.

Kroch, A. (1995). Dialect and style in the speech of upper class Philadelphia. In G. R. Guy, C. Feagin, D. Schiffrin, & J. Baugh (Eds.), *Towards a social science of language, Papers in Honour of William Labov* (Vol. 1, pp. 23–45). Amsterdam: John Benjamins.

Labov, W. (1963). The social motivation of a sound change. *Word, 19*, 273–309.

Labov, W. (1994). *Principles of linguistic change, Internal factors* (Vol. 1). Cambridge, MA: Blackwell.

Labov, W. (2001). *Principles of linguistic change, Social factors* (Vol. 2). Cambridge, MA: Blackwell.

Labov, W. (2006). *The social stratification of English in New York City*. Cambridge: Cambridge University Press.

Labov, W., Yaeger, M., & Steiner, R. (1972). *A quantitative study of sound change in progress* (2 vols). Philadelphia: U.S. Regional Survey.

Levon, E., & Holmes-Elliott, S. (2013). East end boys and West end girls: /s/− Fronting in Southeast England. *University of Pennsylvania working papers in Linguistics, 19*(2). Available online: http://repository.upenn.edu/pwpl/vol19/iss2/13

Lui, T.-L. (2015). GBCS: An answer in search of a question. *The Sociological Review, 63*(2), 480–492.

Macaulay, R. (1977). *Language, social class and education: A Glasgow study*. Edinburgh: Edinburgh University Press.

Macionis, J., & Plummer, K. (2012). *Sociology: A global introduction* (5th ed.). London: Pearson Education Limited.

MacKenzie, L. (2014). Testing the predictions of usage-based models on language change across the lifespan. Paper presented at *NWAV 43*, Chicago,

October 26, 2014. Available online: http://laurelmackenzie.com/presentations/MacKenzie_NWAV43_slides.pdf

Mills, C. (2015). The Great British class survey: Requiescat in pace. *The Sociological Review, 63*(2), 393–399.

Milroy, L. (2004). Language ideologies and linguistic change. In C. Fought (Ed.), *Sociolinguistic variation: Critical reflections* (pp. 161–177). Oxford: Oxford University Press.

Milroy, J., & Milroy, L. (1999). *Authority in language: Investigating standard English*. London: Routledge.

Moore, E. (2010). Interaction between social category and social practice: Explaining was/were variation. *Language Variation and Change, 22*(03), 347–371.

Nycz, J., & Hall-Lew, L. (2014). Best practices in measuring vowel merger. In *Proceedings of meetings on acoustics* (POMA) 20. http://dx.doi.org/10.1121/1.4894063

Pharao, N., Maegaard, M., Møller, J., & Kristiansen, T. (2014). Indexical meanings of [s+] among Copenhagen youth: Social perception of a phonetic variant in different prosodic contexts. *Language in Society, 43*(1), 1–31.

Prandy, K. (1992). *Cambridge scale scores for CASOC groupings*. Sociological Research Group, Social and Political Sciences, Cambridge. Working Paper 11.

Przedlacka, J. (2002). *Estuary English? A sociophonetic study of teenage speech in the Home Counties*. Bern: Peter Lang Publishing.

Rampton, B. (2009). Interaction ritual and not just artful performance in crossing and stylization. *Language in Society, 38*(2), 149–176.

Rampton, B. (2011). From 'multi-ethnic adolescent heteroglossia' to 'contemporary urban vernaculars'. *Language & Communication, 31*(4), 276–294.

Roach, P., Knowles, G., Varadi, T., & Arnfield, S. (1993). MARSEC: A machine-readable spoken English corpus. *Journal of the International Phonetic Association, 23*, 47–54.

Savage, M. (2015). Introduction to elites: From the 'problematic of the proletariat' to a class analysis of 'wealth elites'. *The Sociological Review, 63*(2), 223–239.

Savage, M., Devine, F., Cunningham, N., Taylor, M., Li, Y., Hjellbrekke, J., Roux, L., Brigitte, Friedman, S., & Miles, A. (2013). A new model of social class? Findings from the BBC's great British class survey experiment. *Sociology, 47*(2), 219–250.

Schwyter, J. (2016). *Dictating to the mob: The history of the BBC advisory committee on spoken English*. Oxford: Oxford University Press.

Skeggs, B. (2015). Introduction: Stratification or exploitation, domination, dispossession and devaluation? *The Sociological Review, 63*(2), 205–222.

Snell, J. (2010). From sociolinguistic variation to socially strategic stylisation. *Journal of SocioLinguistics, 14*(5), 630–656.

Sweet, H. (1888). *A history of English sounds* (2nd ed.). Oxford: Clarendon Press.

Torgersen, E., & Kerswill, P. (2004). Internal and external motivation in phonetic change: Dialect levelling outcomes for an English vowel shift. *Journal of SocioLinguistics, 8*, 23–53.

Trudgill, P. (1972). Sex, covert prestige and linguistic change in the urban British English of Norwich. *Language in Society, 1*, 179–196.

Trudgill, P. (1986). *Dialects in contact.* Oxford: Blackwell.

Upton, C. (2012). An evolving standard British English pronunciation model. In R. Hickey (Ed.), *Standards of English: Codified varieties around the world* (pp. 55–71). Cambridge: Cambridge University Press.

Wakeling, P., & Savage, M. (2015). Entry to elite positions and the stratification of higher education in Britain. *The Sociological Review, 63*(2), 290–320.

Watt, D., & Tillotson, J. (2001). A spectrographic analysis of vowel fronting in Bradford English. *English World-Wide, 22*(2), 269–303.

Wells, J. (1962). *A study of the formants of the pure vowels of British English.* Unpublished MA thesis, University of London. Available online: http://www.phon.ucl.ac.uk/home/wells/formants/index.htm

Wells, J. (1982). *Accents of English* (3 vols). Cambridge: Cambridge University Press.

Wells, J. (1990). A phonetic update on R.P. *Moderna Språk, 82*(1), 3–9.

Wells, J. (1994). The cockneyfication of R.P.? In G. Melchers & N.-L. Johannesson (Eds.), *Nonstandard varieties of language, Acta Universitatis Stockholmiensis* (pp. 198–205). Stockholm: Almqvist and Wiksell.

Wells, J. (1997). What's happening to received pronunciation? *English Phonetics* (English Phonetic Society of Japan), *1*, 13–23.

Wells, J. C. (2000). *Longman pronunciation dictionary* (2nd ed.). Harlow: Pearson Education Limited. ISBN 0 582 36468 X (cased edition), 0 582 36467 1 (paperback edition).

Windsor, L. J. (1972). *A concise pronouncing dictionary of British and American English.* London: Oxford University Press.

Zwicker, E. (1961). Subdivision of the audible frequency range into critical bands (Frequenzgruppen). *Journal of the Acoustical Society of America, 33*, 248.

4

The Changing Language of Urban Youth: A Pilot Study

Rob Drummond

Introduction

This chapter reports primarily on a pilot study[1] carried out in late 2013 into the speech of a group of young people (YP) aged 14–16 in Manchester, UK. The study took place in two learning centres within Manchester's Secondary Pupil Referral Unit (PRU)—a facility which caters for YP who have been excluded from mainstream school for discipline-related issues.[2] The pilot study had three main aims: to forge the relationships that would be needed in order to carry out a larger study, to test appropriate methods of data collection, and to identify some of the linguistic features and social factors that might warrant further investigation and analysis. This chapter reports primarily on the third of these aims.

The initial purpose of the project as a whole was to begin to explore the possibility of the emergence of an identifiable Multicultural Manchester English variety along the lines of what is known as Multicultural London English (MLE) (Cheshire et al. 2011) and to see how this might be used

R. Drummond (✉)
Manchester Metropolitan University, Manchester, UK

© The Author(s) 2018
N. Braber, S. Jansen (eds.), *Sociolinguistics in England*,
DOI 10.1057/978-1-137-56288-3_4

in the construction and negotiation of identities. One central idea was to see whether there was any value in looking for some kind of over-arching variety or repertoire, a possible Multicultural Urban British English (MUBE), with each city then having its own local version or sub-variety. In this approach, it is conceivable that within MUBE there exists an identifiable MLE, Manchester Multicultural English (MME), Multicultural Birmingham English (MBE) and so on. Clearly, in order to ascertain this, a lot more data is needed than can be provided by a pilot study, but I mention it here simply to give background as to the motivation behind the project. As a result, the research described here should be seen simply as a descriptive account of the speech of a selection of YP in a particular context, with some tentative suggestions as to the reasons behind the observed variation. Comparisons will be made to the London findings, but I fully acknowledge the differences in scope between the two projects at this stage. When reference is made to a possible MUBE variety, it is done so with the understanding that this concept remains, at present, un-theorised and underspecified. However, we have to start somewhere. This description should therefore be seen as taking some initial steps towards describing particular features in the speech of YP in Manchester which appear to differ from those found in a traditional Manchester accent. Time will tell if these features can indeed be seen as a constituting part of an identifiable MUBE variety.

Research on Youth Language

The initial influence and inspiration for the project was the work done on MLE by Paul Kerswill, Jenny Cheshire, Sue Fox and Eivind Torgersen (e.g. Cheshire et al. 2011), in which they describe how traditional East End London speech is changing, largely as a result of the various and numerous influences from the languages and cultures that make up the modern multicultural city. They conceptualise MLE as 'a repertoire of features' in which speakers select linguistic items from a 'feature pool' (Mufwene 2001: 4–6; Cheshire et al. 2011: 176) consisting of elements from the various input languages. The selection of features in any individual's (or group's) repertoire is determined by factors such as frequency and salience, the latter being affected by cultural influences. Friendship networks of the speakers were also found to be important, especially in terms of their ethnic diversity. MLE, along with similar emerging varieties of language around northern Europe [e.g. Germany (Wiese 2009), Denmark (Quist 2008) and Norway (Svendsen and Røyneland 2008)] is seen as an example of a multiethnolect, a variety/repertoire of language borne out of interaction within a multi-lingual/cultural/ethnic context, yet which remains itself ethnically neutral and available to be used by anyone (Cheshire et al. 2011: 2). Notable features of MLE include (Cheshire et al. 2011; Torgersen et al. 2011; Torgersen and Szakay 2012; Szakay and Torgersen 2015):

- Shorter trajectories for FACE, GOAT, MOUTH, PRICE
- FACE is a mid-high front vowel
- GOAT is a mid-high back vowel
- MOUTH and PRICE are lower than traditional London speech
- GOOSE is very front
- New quotative *this is* + *speaker*
- Simplification of article allomorphy ([ə] and [ðə] rather than [ən] and [ði] before word-initial vowels)
- Use of the pragmatic marker *you get me*
- Syllable-timed rhythm
- Breathy voice
- Low pitch

A selection of these features is presented in the description of the linguistic data later in the chapter.

Research on Manchester English

Manchester has traditionally been under-researched in terms of accent, although this is starting to change. The most recent edition of 'English Accents and Dialects' (Hughes et al. 2012) provides a description of Manchester English, and Baranowski and Turton (2015) describe some particular consonantal features in detail in addition to a more general overview of the sound system as a whole. There has also been recent focus on specific areas of accent and dialect in Manchester, such as the *happ*Y and *lett*ER vowels (Turton and Ramsammy 2012), ING (Schleef et al. 2015), and non-native Manchester speech (Drummond 2011, 2012, 2013; Howley 2016). Some of these sources will serve as reference points throughout the linguistic description below.

The Context

Data collection took place in two PRU learning centres in inner-city Manchester. Although the YP in the PRU follow a restricted version of the same curriculum as pupils in mainstream schools, the contexts are very different. PRU learning centres such as the two described here are often ex-youth club buildings which are not necessarily designed for classroom-based learning. The centres are small, each catering for school years 10 and 11 (aged 14–16) only and comprising no more than eight students from each year group at a time. Each centre has two centre coordinators, one permanent youth worker and peripatetic subject teaching staff. In a normal class session, there will be anywhere between one and seven YP, a subject teacher and one other adult (either the youth worker or one of the coordinators). In between classes, YP are generally free to play pool, table tennis, football (facilities and behaviour permitting), watch TV, listen to music or smoke outside.

The pilot study involved a data collection period of just over two months (September–November 2013), during which time I attended each centre once or twice a week. The study was ethnographically informed rather than ethnographic on the basis that while I did spend a great deal of my time observing, participating in and generally becoming part of the context, the vast majority of the data come from sitting down with the YP, usually in pairs or small groups, and recording our conversations. I therefore feel that my observations serve to inform this recorded data, but they do not in themselves constitute data for analysis. There are a few examples of self- or peer-recorded conversations which are also available for analysis, but these also tend to follow a more (informal) interview-type structure. This approach contrasts with the larger project, which is very much ethnographic, relying far more on recordings of spontaneous interaction in a variety of contexts, in addition to very detailed field-notes of observational data.

It should be pointed out, however, that in both this study and the follow-up study, it was vital for us as researchers to be accepted into the community. In many ways, this was a daunting task, given that we do not 'fit' into any existing categories of people usually found in the centres. 'University researcher' is not a role the YP are likely to have come across before nor is it one that carries much meaning for them. At one of the centres, one of my biggest problems was convincing the YP (especially boys) that I was not 'Fed' (police). In fact, one of the YP remained unconvinced throughout my whole time at the centre and only changed his mind when I happened to bump into him weeks later when I was walking from a university building; he looked me up and down, tutted and said 'I could have sworn you was Fed' before walking away, shaking his head. For most of the YP, I drifted somewhere between teacher, classroom assistant, youth worker and visitor, often depending on the individual and on the particular context. In reality, I was doing all I could to be friendly and approachable to the YP, and unobtrusive and helpful to the staff, while all the time trying to avoid all situations in which I might be called upon to act as an adult with any kind of authority.

During the pilot study, I collected recordings of varying lengths and of varying quality from 14 YP. Much of the variation stemmed from the fact that as a genuine pilot study, I was experimenting with different methods of data collection, so not everything was successful. The data presented here focus on four individuals: Damian, Ryan, Luke and Leah, two from each centre. These four have been deliberately chosen for this chapter purely due to the fact that between them, they offer a fair reflection of the variation within YP's language in this context. I am not claiming them to be a representative sample by any means, but neither is there anything to suggest they are unrepresentative of their peers. As will become clear in the following description, Luke and Leah tend to use features which align with a traditional variety of Manchester English, while Damian and Ryan exhibit some features which I would argue might represent an emerging MUBE variety of Manchester English due to their apparent similarity to MLE. I could have chosen several other individuals to illustrate the same point, but these four offered the clearest examples coupled with the best-quality audio recordings. Although the two pairs actually attended centres in different areas of the city (Damian and Ryan in centre A, Leah and Luke in centre B), this geographical fact is not thought to play a particular role in the language of the YP. It is the case that there is regional linguistic variation within Manchester, but this is tempered here both by the fact that YP do not always go to the learning centre that is nearest to where they live and also that they will have attended different mainstream schools, often moving location in the process. The conversational speech described in this chapter all comes from pair/group chats with me; however, the YP presented here were not recorded in the same conversations, that is, each was actually recorded with a different friend/group whose speech is not being discussed.

As a result of the approach taken, and the contextually limited nature of the data (albeit consistent with many studies into language variation), what is presented here can only offer a snapshot of each individual's spoken language. All I can say for sure is that what is presented here is a replicable and accurate analysis of the speech that was used in an informal conversation with me and one or more of each individual's peers. It might well be that this can be generalised to some extent across other linguistic interactions that these speakers engage in, or maybe even across other speakers. However, it is only right at this point to at least recognise the inherent flimsiness in this kind of generalising, despite it being an established part of much existing research into language variation.

A Description of the Language

The following description focuses on features that are deemed to be of interest or relevance in relation to either a typical Manchester variety or a possible emerging 'multicultural' variety along the lines of the aforementioned MUBE. Recordings were made on a Zoom H2 recorder placed unobtrusively on a surface near the participant. Recordings were stored as .wav files using a 44.1 kHz sampling rate with 16-bit precision, saved onto an SanDisk (SD) memory card then transferred onto a PC. Conversations were not planned or staged; they were the result of asking a YP if they could spare a few minutes for a chat as and when the opportunity arose. The content of the conversations generally revolved around life at the PRU, outside interests and language.

Vowels

Acoustic analysis of the vowels was carried out using *Praat* (Boersma and Weenink 2015). Tokens were identified and segmented manually, and a script was used to take F1 and F2 measurements at 20%, 50% and 80% of the vowel duration. These measurements were checked visually during the process. All raw Hz measurements were then normalised using the modified Watt and Fabricius method (Fabricius et al. 2009) and plotted onto charts. The 20% and 80% measurements were used for all vowels including monophthongs, in line with recent thinking in this area, suggesting that studying the trajectories of all vowels provides a more detailed picture of what is happening (see Watson and Harrington 1999 for a discussion of this point). Figures 4.1, 4.2, 4.3 and 4.4 show the complete normalised measurements for all four speakers and should be referred to throughout the following description. Measurements are based on 749 tokens overall, an average of 187 per speaker and just over 12 per vowel.

FOOT/STRUT

STRUT in all four speakers is entirely consistent with existing traditional accounts of Manchester English (e.g. Hughes et al. 2012; Drummond 2013; Baranowski and Turton 2015), in that the STRUT vowel is produced in the same area as FOOT,[3] with no apparent distinction between the two. This is an example then of a traditionally (supra)local feature potentially existing unchanged alongside possibly incoming MUBE features as there is no observable difference between the two pairs of speakers. However, perhaps this is unremarkable given the fact that there is nothing within what we know of multicultural varieties of English which would be working in opposition to a raised and backed STRUT. For example, if a particularly salient feature of MLE or a possible MUBE happened to be an especially lowered and/or fronted STRUT, it would be interesting to see how this was realised in a northern variety. But without such opposition, it remains unproblematic.

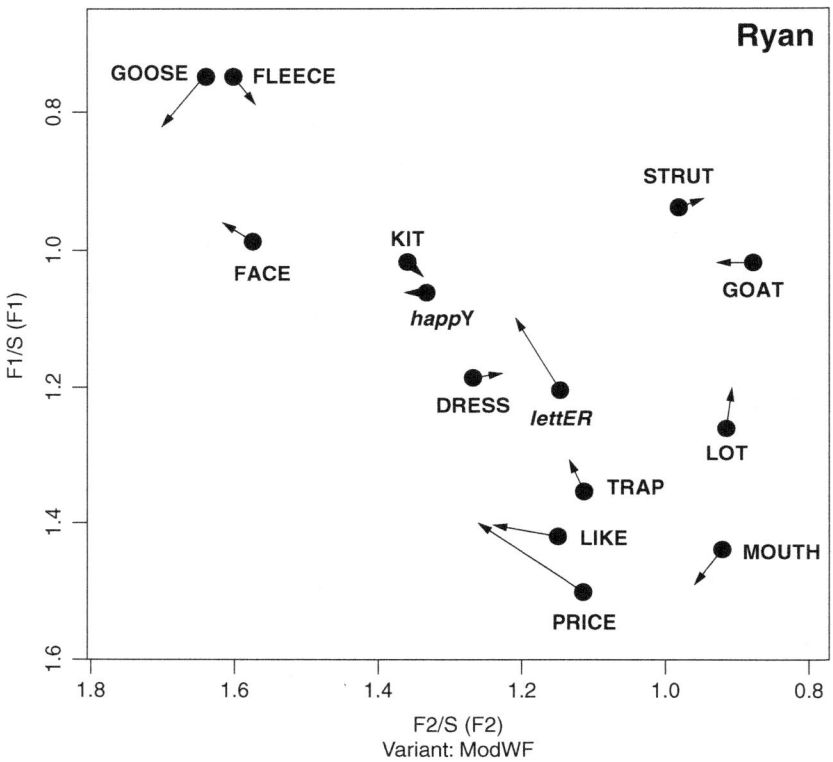

Fig. 4.1 Vowel chart showing the mean normalised (Watt and Fabricius modified method) F1 and F2 measurements for Ryan

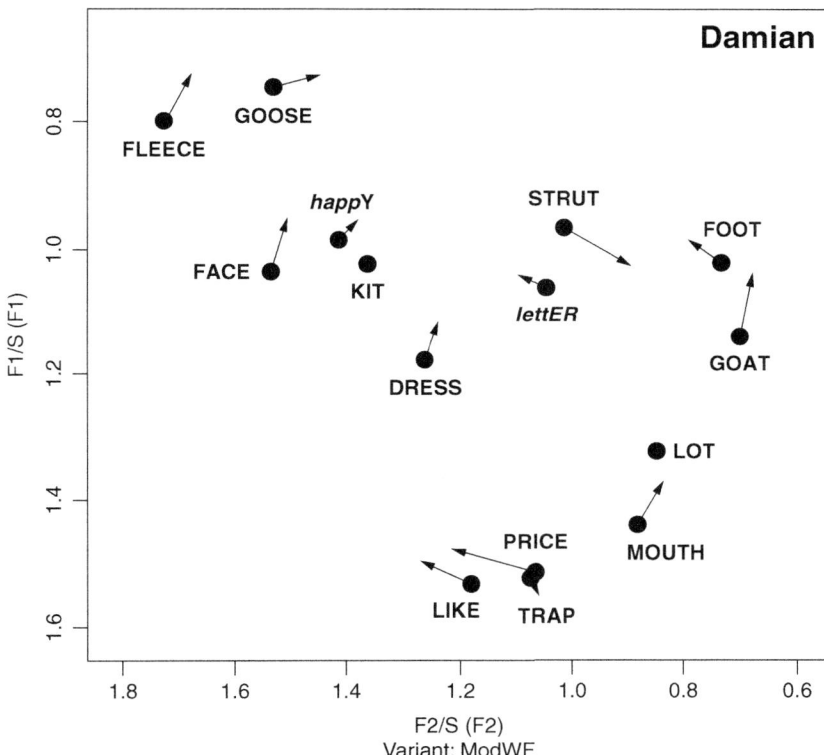

Fig. 4.2   Vowel chart showing the mean normalised (Watt and Fabricius modified method) F1 and F2 measurements for Damian

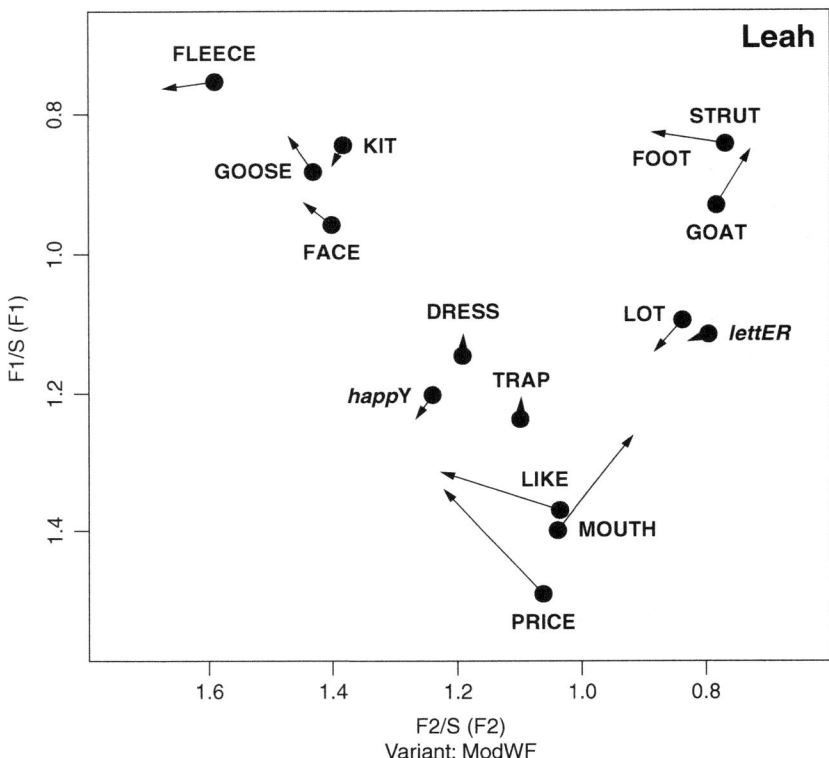

Fig. 4.3   Vowel chart showing the mean normalised (Watt and Fabricius modified method) F1 and F2 measurements for Leah

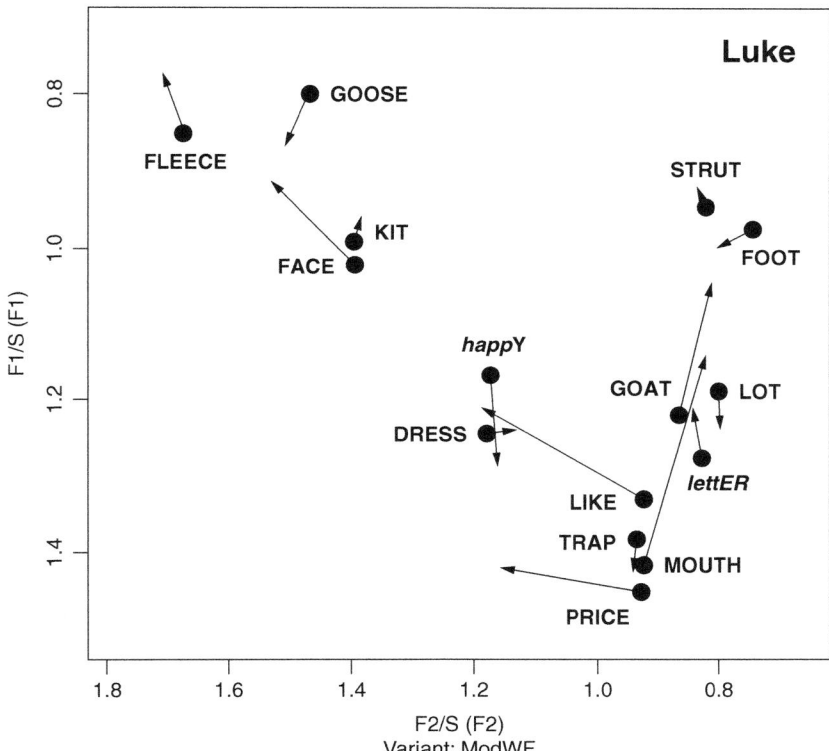

Fig. 4.4 Vowel chart showing the mean normalised (Watt and Fabricius modified method) F1 and F2 measurements for Luke

GOOSE

All four speakers have a very high and fronted GOOSE vowel, consistent with MLE (Cheshire et al. 2011: 158) but also with changes more generally in most varieties of English, including existing accounts of Manchester (e.g. Hughes et al. 2012; Baranowski and Turton 2015), especially with regard to younger speakers. The extent of some of the fronting, particularly in Ryan's speech, where it actually appears to be slightly more front than FLEECE, is indicative of the extreme fronting reported in MLE, but apart from this, there does not appear to be a significant difference between the two pairs of speakers as Luke and Leah both have vowels as fronted as Damian.

*happ*Y

The *happ*Y vowel is of interest as it represents a particularly Manchester feature, often being realised as a relatively open [ɛ] or [ɛ̈], especially in phrase-final position (Turton and Ramsammy 2012; Howley 2016). In fact, along with *lett*ER (see below), this lowered and centralised *happ*Y is often the source of stereotypical imitations of a Manchester accent (Howley 2016: 139). What is especially interesting here is the difference between the two pairs of speakers, with Luke and Leah showing considerably more open realisations of the vowel than Damian and Ryan. In fact, both Luke and Leah's *happ*Y vowels share the vowel space for DRESS, with Leah's even appearing to be more open. The apparent length and direction of Luke's *happ*Y trajectory is potentially interesting, possibly showing strong movement towards that more open variant even during the vowel; however, small token numbers mean this observation should be treated with caution. Despite the numbers, the position of the vowel is consistent with auditory analysis of other recordings of Luke and Leah. In contrast to this open variant, both Damian's and Ryan's *happ*Y vowels are realised in the same area as KIT, still suggesting a lack of *happ*Y-tensing (where *happ*Y would be closer to [i]), consistent with some other northern varieties (Beal 2008) but not typically 'Manchester'. There is nothing in a possible MUBE that would prohibit a more open realisation, but it is interesting that neither Damian nor Ryan tend to use the local variant.

*lett*ER

Similar to *happ*Y, but to a greater extent, the *lett*ER vowel represents a typically Manchester feature, often realised as a relatively open and backed [ʌ] rather than the more typical [ə] (Turton and Ramsammy 2012). Stereotypically, the variant is even more open in addition to being rounded (Howley 2016: 116), and the possibility of [ɒ] is mentioned in Hughes et al. (2012: 117), although Turton and Ramsammy suggest this is an exaggerated realisation. Baranowski and Turton (2015: 286) observe that the primary movement is backing along the F2 plane rather than lowering. Variability is constrained syntactically and morphologically, with a suffix such as plural 's' inhibiting movement and phrase finality encouraging it (Howley 2016: 114). Here, it is clear that both Luke's and Leah's realisations of *lett*ER are considerably more backed than Ryan's and Damian's, who both show a centralised schwa variant. As with *happ*Y above, this is arguably an example of possible MUBE-oriented speakers apparently rejecting the more localised variant, even though there is no obvious incoming variant to instigate this change.

PRICE

There is little difference between the four speakers' realisations of PRICE, and none differ from what would be expected from a typical Manchester realisation (Wells 1982). While nearby areas do have a monophthongal PRICE in traditional dialects (Beal 2008: 135), this is not the case for Manchester itself. Ryan's and Damian's appear slightly more open and with slightly shorter trajectories, but the difference is negligible. There is, however, a difference when we focus specifically on the vowel in the context of discourse marker or quotative 'like' (herein the LIKE vowel). Differences between PRICE and LIKE within an individual are to be expected, depending on the function of 'like' (e.g. Drager 2009; Schleef and Turton 2016), but what is interesting here are the differences between the pairs of speakers, both in terms of their LIKE vowels and their PRICE/LIKE contrast. Both Ryan and Damian produce a more open and more monophthongised LIKE compared to Luke and Leah, and there is little difference between the pairs' PRICE and LIKE in terms of position. Luke and Leah on the other hand have fully diphthongal LIKE which is slightly less open than their PRICE. Lowered and monoph-thongised PRICE is a feature of MLE (Cheshire et al. 2011: 163) and might therefore be a possible contender as a MUBE variant. Cheshire et al. do not separate *like* from other PRICE tokens, but it might be the case that it is discourse marker and quotative *like* that is pushing that process in their data. However, lowered and monophthongal PRICE is not unusual in southern England accents more generally (e.g. Tollfree 1999), so we should be cautious with this interpretation of it necessarily representing an incoming 'multicultural' variant as other factors might be at work.

FACE

All four speakers have a FACE vowel that is mid-high and front with a short trajectory. While it might be tempting to draw parallels with similar (and quite dramatic when compared to traditional London) realisations for FACE in the MLE data, in reality, the FACE vowel around Manchester generally has these features already (Hughes et al. 2012: 117), although Baranowski and Turton (2015: 285) stress that it is diphthongal in the city itself. Ryan and Damian's realisations are perhaps slightly more front than Luke and Leah's, but the difference is very small. This is not to say that the motivation between each pairs' realisations might not be the same, but when they overlap to such an extent, it is impossible to argue one way or another with the data available here.

MOUTH

MOUTH is interesting, in that Ryan and Damian both have very monophthongised realisations compared to Luke and Leah. This is similar to how this vowel is realised in MLE, with Cheshire et al. noting a lowered variant with a shorter trajectory (Cheshire et al. 2011: 158). Unlike FACE, there is no northern/Manchester pattern to this vowel with regard to monophthongisation, so I would argue that this could be viewed as a possible incoming MUBE feature. As with PRICE, it should be noted that monophthong MOUTH is a common feature in southern English accents more generally and not specifically 'multicultural'; however, I will put forward some arguments later in the chapter that support the MUBE interpretation.

Other Linguistic Features

Quotatives

An interesting comparison with the MLE data in terms of quotative forms is the complete absence of the innovative *this is* + *speaker* expression discussed in Cheshire et al. (2011: 172) in either the pilot study or in fact the follow-up study. Cheshire et al. do comment that it might be a transient phenomenon in London (and of course the data is almost ten years old), and that it is not used to a great extent, but they also make the point that it is used often enough to have been noticed by non-linguists, with British TV comedy actors such as Catherine Tate, Alexander Armstrong and Ben Miller using it in sketches portraying youth language (Cheshire et al. 2011: 173). Whatever the mechanisms for a possible spread of MLE/MUBE features (see later discussion), this is one feature that has apparently not been transferred into, or emerged in, a Manchester urban variety (Kerswill et al. 2008 also make the point that not all innovations in inner-city London are spreading). This might be due in part to differences in the linguistic backgrounds of some of the participants and families in the London and Manchester studies, with some caregivers in the London studies 'only just beginning to acquire English themselves' (Cheshire et al. 2011: 179), and a suggestion of 'interlanguage varieties' of English among the YP. They argue that this lack of fluency offers an environment in which *this is* + *speaker* can be utilised by younger speakers as a 'high-involvement deictic form used with gestures...to act out moments within a narrative as well as to quote speech' (Cheshire et al. 2011: 180) and is then later refined by 16- to 19-year-olds to be exclusively quotative in nature. Perhaps, then, its absence in the Manchester data is due to our speakers existing in different linguistic environments, where the overwhelming L1 English-speaking family contexts (albeit with a wide range of varieties, ethnicities, etc.) do not create that initial opening for the younger speakers to develop the expression in the first place. Clearly, further and more wide-ranging research in Manchester is needed in order to ascertain whether *this is* + *speaker* remains a uniquely London feature.

In terms of other quotative possibilities, it is hard to make meaningful comparisons with the data under investigation here as not all conversations included instances where they would be used. However, partial pictures from two of the speakers show something similar to the London data, at least in terms of there being a variety of quotatives in use. Small numbers make it hard to confirm, but there is a possibility that *be like* is perhaps not as frequent as it appears to be in London, an idea that is currently being followed up in the larger study. Extract 1 gives an example of the types of quotatives used by Damian.

Extract 1

Damian: I was- I was with my boy once and like (.) these two white police officers come over to us cos (.) we were just walkin' about (.) and then they come up to us and started- started saying sayin' bare like bare racist stuff to my mate and that(.) like sayin' erm (.) **they said** 'What you up to lads?' and I sai- **I said** 'nothin' we're just walkin' about' and **he goes** (.) 'well wha- wha- what's what's your black friend been doin'?' and I sai- so **I said** 'what do you mean?' **he goes like** and then **he starts goin' on like sayin'** (.) erm 'I'm sure I've seen him about an' all that selling drugs'.

Although the sample is small, both here and elsewhere in Damian's speech, straightforward *say* and *go* are by far his most frequent quotatives. What is missing here is *be like*, which does not occur at all in this recording, although he has been heard to use it in other situations.

Leah is more of a storyteller so provides more quotative data. In this recording, she uses *say*, *go* and *be like* in the proportions illustrated in Table 4.1.

Table 4.1 Leah's quotatives

Quotative	%	N
Go (go, goes, went, gone)	57	25
Say (say, says, said)	30	13
Be like	13	6

Again, the use of *be like* appears to be less frequent than perhaps expected, given that it is a feature that has been spreading rapidly through most English-speaking communities (see Buchstaller and D'Arcy 2009 for an overview).[4] What is interesting here is that when Leah does use *be like*, it is usually to convey an element of expressive or mimetic content rather than purely linguistic content. Compare, for example, the purely linguistic content of the examples in (1) with those in (2) below.

1.	a.	...and **she went** 'What you talking about you idiot?' and **I said** 'Oh my god!'
	b.	...and **I've gone** 'It's fucking roasting out here'
2.	a.	I bet you're gonna get home, play this in front of your wife and **she'll be like** '[gasps] Oh my god!'
	b.	...but you get them proper fucking girls ... proper bad yardie **they're like** '[imitates voice] yo what you on bro'
	c.	I phoned her the other day and **she was like** '[posh voice] hello'

In fact, five of the six uses of *be like* from Leah show some element of performance, be it through voice mimicry or action/gesture. This mimetic element is to be expected as mimetic re-enactment has been identified as one of three global constraints on *be like* (Buchstaller and D'Arcy 2009), but it will be interesting to see whether the strength of this constraint remains as consistent when the data set is enlarged.

Words and Phrases

At this point, it is difficult to identify particular words and phrases as being part of a possible MUBE repertoire or not. There are items that Ryan, Damian and their friends appear to be more likely to use than Leah, Luke and their friends, but more data is needed. For the purposes of this descriptive chapter, perhaps it is sufficient to detail some of the words and phrases encountered so far that are maybe not so widely known to everyone. Table 4.2 shows possible unknown words or words of interest that occurred in these conversations. Some emerged naturally, while others were in response to a question specifically about words they use that I might not know. Interestingly, when Luke was asked this question,

Table 4.2 Words and phrases of interest from the conversations

Man	Impersonal pronoun	Just a couple man innit	Ryan
Live /laɪv/	Adjective: cool, good	that's live that	Ryan
Spinning	Verb: lying	you're spinning you, G	Ryan
For time/time ago	Adverbial: for a long time / a long time ago	I haven't seen him for time. We used that time ago	Ryan
Peak	Adjective: negative, bad luck, embarrassing	[Someone trips over] yo that's peak man	Damian
Bare	Adjective: very	...started saying bare racist stuff	Damian
Hoodrat	Noun: person from the hood that thieves	People might say hoodrats yo	Damian
Bum	Adjective: good, nice	Oh it's bum that	Leah
Buttersket	Noun: derogatory name for girl (slag)	Fucking buttersket	Leah
Reef	Verb: batter (beat up)	[I'd] fucking reef em	Leah

he simply could not come up with anything other than very predictable and everyday terms such as 'mate', 'lad' or 'wanker'.

Awareness

One of the reasons these particular interactions were chosen to be studied here is that they all contain at least some discussion of the speech of the YP themselves as part of the conversation. During the chat with Leah, I asked if there were any words they use which I would not know, and Leah asked if I knew what 'breadbin' meant. I said I did not.

Extract 2

Leah: D'you know like, d'you know like you get boys that go 'what you on bredren [ˈbredrɪn]?' And they say bredren.
Rob: Yeah Yeah
Leah: Well you know to take the piss you say 'breadbin'.
Rob: Ah haa
Georgia: D'you get it?

Rob:	{Yeah yeah}
Leah:	{Thicko here} [referring to Georgia] didn't have a fuckin noggins what it {means.}
Georgia:	{I don't} get it.
Leah:	(unclear)
Georgia:	I really {don't get it}
Leah:	{D'you know} when boys say to each other 'yes what you on bredren?'
Georgia:	Yeah
Leah:	Like well you know breadbin (unclear)
Leah:	In other words, in say- instea- in-
Georgia:	Well why would you call someone a breadbin anyway?
Leah:	Fuck off Georgia.

My understanding of this and other similar exchanges is that the girls are aware of some kind of way of speaking that they are not part of, and they distance themselves from it by mocking those who do use its features. The extent to which this way of speaking can be interpreted as an identifiable variety with particular and regular features, or as a transient style, or as simply consisting of one or two specific items such as 'bredren', remains to be seen. However, the girls do appear to have a sense of something identifiable when they go on to say that it is mainly boys who speak like this and are clear in their own minds where it comes from.

Extract 3

Leah: …ever since fucking *Anuvahood*[5] and *Kidulthood*[6] started coming out…and they started watching too much soaps.

In the conversation with Damian, I had previously mentioned media stories in which young white men were portrayed as 'sounding black' (see Kerswill 2014 for a discussion on the use of 'Jafaican' in the media, also Drummond 2016). He returns to this idea with the following:

Extract 4

Damian: Nah but obviously though the accent…they – they they're trying to say that it's just black people that use it but it's white people as well. They're trying to like stereotype. Trying to say it's just…just black people that used to do it and all that but it's not though, it's like loads of people do it.

What is interesting is Damian's apparent understanding of what 'it' is when we had not actually discussed a particular way of speaking other than vague references to media stories. This is certainly suggestive of an identifiable 'accent' of some sort, and his comment about people 'using' it implies an element of choice.

That element of choice is also apparent in Ryan's views. Ryan has a very clear awareness of the way he speaks ('It's just a teenage accent innit, it's a standard teenage accent') and does not see it as permanent:

Extract 5

Ryan: When I'm like 40 yeah, I won't be speaking like this. But I will til I'm about 30 [or summat] innit. Cos the olders still speak like this innit (.) like set olders.

I again brought up the question of whether the way YP speak might relate to ethnicity, but this time, I consciously avoided talking about white kids 'sounding black'.

However, as I was in the process of relating this to Ryan, his friend interrupted:

Extract 6

Lee: They'll just say he [Ryan] thinks he wants to be black.
Rob: Exactly. And so people – but anyone who actually works with young people will say that's not true.
Lee: But that's just how he speaks cos of his area.

Rob: Exactly
Ryan: Yeah not cos of the colour and that, like so if they hear me speak-
          ing and they're gonna say that I think I'm black, why would I
          think I'm black? You get me?
Lee: [laughs]
Ryan: [laughing] You get me.

It is interesting that both Lee and Ryan focus on 'wanting to be black' rather than 'sounding black', suggesting a greater degree of agency. Ryan does not appear to see the connection between ethnicity and accent, and this is certainly a common view among other boys in the study. There is often an awareness of what other people may think about their speech in relation to ethnicity, but this view is then usually dismissed as inaccurate, at least among the boys who can be seen as using features linked to a possible MUBE. The extent to which the laughing at the end of the excerpt relates to the irony of ending a statement about not being black with a pragmatic marker 'you get me' that is strongly associated with non-Anglo aspects of MLE (Torgersen et al. 2011) is debatable, but it certainly is a possible interpretation.

Social Factors

Clearly, with only four speakers, it is difficult to discuss with much authority the social factors that might be at work in shaping the language of these YP, so in order to give a fuller picture, I will refer to some observations from the current larger study in addition to the pilot study in order to identify some emerging areas of interest.

Gender

At a superficial level, there is a difference between the way boys speak and the way the girls speak in both the pilot study and the follow-up study. Quantitatively, the boys are more likely to use non-traditional Manchester features, and the girls are more likely to use the traditional Manchester variants. That is not to say that several boys (including Luke above) do not use traditional variants; just that, of the speakers who do use possible MUBE variants, almost all are boys. There is also a potential gender difference in the use of phrases more associated with a MUBE repertoire such as *bredren, yo, bare, rass, mandem* and so on, which are used much more frequently by the boys than the girls. However, this gender difference remains superficial at present, in that it offers no kind of explanation—there is no reason why there should be such a pattern and observing it does not help us understand the variation. If we follow this route, we are in danger of falling foul of the 'correlation fallacy' (Cameron 2009), whereby we try to explain observed generalisations of language variation using the same identity categories that generated the observation in the first place.

Ethnicity

Equally superficial is a possible emerging pattern relating to the ethnicity of the speakers and the use of different features. Whatever pattern there appears to be would be problematic at best when explored a little further and, again, arguably holds no explanatory power even if it is shown to exist. From a purely quantitative perspective, it looks possible that those individuals who do not fall into a 'white British' census category (non-Anglos in the terminology of Cheshire et al.) are more likely to use non-traditional and potentially MUBE features. But it soon becomes clear again that using such macro social categories as ethnicity is not useful, as many of the differences between ethnicities are largely meaningless in the twenty-first-century urban Britain, certainly in this particular context. It is hard to see why the heritage of one grandparent, for example, should be given any sort of relevance in comparing the speech of two boys who have grown up side by side. Besides which, there are too many exceptions to any apparent ethnicity pattern to allow it much influence in our analysis, a point illustrated by the participants here, all of whom would be classified as white British Anglos, despite Ryan and Damian being two of the heaviest users of possible MUBE features.

In previous studies, ethnicity has been shown to have an effect on the use of variants from a distance, by way of friendship networks and their ethnic diversity (Cheshire et al. 2011), with speakers with more diverse networks favouring certain non-standard features. Friendship networks did not form part of the data collection for either the pilot or the follow-up study here beyond what was observed among the participants in the actual context. And while observed networks might be of interest in some ways, it would be wrong to interpret them in the same way as friendship networks in other studies, as here it is often the case that the YP in the centres do not see each other outside of the PRU context. Their real friendship networks exist outside the centres, a world to which we did not have access. Having said that, I was provided with one potentially useful insight when I happened to ask Ryan about the ethnic mix of his friends as part of a conversation:

Extract 7

Rob: And what sort of er is it a mix in terms of backgrounds?
Ryan: Nah, same background
Rob: White, black…
Ryan: White innit.
Rob: All white?
Ryan: Yeah, all white.

At present, I would argue that ethnicity does not appear to be playing a role in the language of these particular YP, at least in the traditional sense of externally defined macro categories, and certainly in the data from the pilot study. Whether ethnicity emerges as a meaningful explanation of variation in the larger study remains to be seen, although initial signs are doubtful (see Drummond and Dray 2015 in which we suggest social practices are a better predictor than ethnicity in the use of th-stopping).

Identity

It goes without saying that identity plays a crucial role in language variation (and vice versa) generally, and there is no reason to think that the relationship is any different here. If we apply current (third-wave) varia-tionist thinking to this data (see Drummond and Schleef 2016 for a dis-cussion), it would be interesting to explore the extent to which certain linguistic features are being used alongside non-linguistic semiotic prac-tices to possibly index or reflexively construct identities. Clearly, this is not possible in any meaningful way with the pilot data, but one of the purposes of this preliminary study was to identify potentially interesting areas to pursue. Certainly, an argument could be made that the *lett*ER vowel is worth investigating in relation to whether a backed variant is being used to signal a traditional Manchester identity, and a more cen-tralised realisation (clustered with other related features) is being used to align with a more current, multicultural youth identity. Similarly, the frequency and contextual use of some of the words and phrases in Table 4.2 might be a useful area to investigate in more depth. There is a sense that in addition to some of the words being used by some YP rather than others, there also exists an understanding that some of the words are not available to be used by everyone. This can only be addressed with the more ethnographic approach of the follow-up study.

However, even within third-wave thinking, there is sometimes a ten-dency to see identity as existing externally to the context in some way, so when we talk of linguistic features indexing aspects of identities, we are referring to something 'out there' that exists in a form in which it *can* be indexed by a particular clustering of features. More useful perhaps is viewing identity as not existing 'out there' at all but rather as something that is continually enacted and re-enacted within interaction (more along the lines of what is argued in Bucholtz and Hall 2005). Taking this approach, it becomes more important to identify what identity work (if any) a particular feature is doing within a particular space at a particular time rather than remove tokens of this feature from their context and impose a consistent meaning onto its repeated use and frequency.

Social Practices

Possibly, the most useful way in which to explore the variation that exists in the language of urban youth is to look at the practices which the YP value, participate in and identify with. This is an approach we have begun to use in relation to our analysis of th-stopping (Drummond and Dray 2015) by looking at how use of 'ting' for 'thing' patterns with those YP who are involved in the musical practices of grime/rap and/or dance hall. But this is not to suggest that using 'ting' (or any of the other features discussed above) always has that association, rather that by taking this approach we can attempt to identify within specific interactions what particular linguistic and non-linguistic features are 'doing' in terms of social meaning. So, going back to the gender and ethnicity points—yes, it might turn out to be the case that identifiable MUBE linguistic features tend to be used by boys more than girls and by YP with Jamaican, black British or black African heritage more than those with white British heritage. But this does not offer any kind of explanation as to why this tendency exists, unless we argue that the features are actively involved in the performance of masculinity, for example, which at the moment they do not appear to be. But taking a practice-based approach, we can begin to see how involvement in particular social practices and engaging in the linguistic requirements of those practices generate the use of particular variants in particular contexts, thus providing a clearer explanation of who is doing what and why.

A practice-based approach would also help to shed light on possible mechanisms for linguistic features to be shared between London and Manchester. In some ways, it makes sense that an MME (or a Manchester version of a possible MUBE) should emerge in the same way that MLE emerged in London as the social/linguistic conditions outlined in Cheshire et al. (2011) are not dissimilar in the two cities. But this does not explain why some traditionally Manchester features are apparently being rejected in an emerging Manchester variety of English, unless perhaps the new variants are spreading from London. However, if we start to look at social practices such as music as being part of the process of diffusion, things start to make a lot more sense. Following this idea might lead us to conclude that the incoming variants are not being imported from MLE; rather they are emerging in the realities surrounding certain practices in which the YP are taking part (and those practices happen to be similar, but not identical in London and Manchester). If the features 'belong' anywhere, they belong in the practices, not in any variety of English. Of course, the reality is that there are, as always, a combination of factors working together that are bringing about the current changes in the language of urban youth in Manchester, and many of these might be beyond our understanding until we dig deeper into the data. All we can ever do is use the evidence that we gather to piece together the bigger picture while remaining open to interpretations from related, if at times conflicting, areas of sociolinguistics.

Moving Forward

At the time of writing, the overall project is at an interesting stage. With the data collection period now over for the larger study also, we are starting to make sense of what is really happening linguistically and socially in this particular context. It has not always been easy, as the follow-up project has involved a collaboration between two people from different research backgrounds (a sociophonetician and an ethnographer/discourse analyst) which see language research and even the social world in often very different ways (see Dray and Drummond forthcoming for a discussion of the ups and downs of the process). However, the pilot study described here played a vital role in moving the project forward and preparing the way for the larger study. In addition to providing insights into the kinds of language features and social factors that might emerge as being of interest in a follow-up study, it also gave some idea as to the challenges involved in collecting data of this kind in such an unpredictable environment. While the data presented here is necessarily limited, the chapter represents only a fraction of the value of carrying out this kind of preparatory work. The relationships that were formed and developed, the techniques that were tried and the insights that were gained, all contributed to the next stage of the research. But perhaps, most importantly, the pilot study highlighted the need for a more flexible approach than traditional variationist-based techniques and approaches offer, especially with regard to the social meaning of the variation. I have hinted at this in the preliminary analysis above, but it is a theme that is continuing to be developed and will no doubt emerge more fully in future publications.

Notes

1. The subsequent larger study continued in the same sites and ran from 2014 to 2016. It was funded by The Leverhulme Trust—*Expressing inner-city youth identity through Multicultural Urban British English*. RPG 2015–059—and brought in Susan Dray, an ethnographer and discourse analyst. Although the main linguistic data presented here comes from the pilot study, reference will be made to the follow-up study where relevant in order to explore areas of explanatory or methodological interest.

2. The decision to focus the research on the PRU context was made for three main reasons. Firstly, from a practical perspective, it provided access to a relatively stable group of young people who, given their inner-city context, would serve as examples of current urban Manchester speech. Secondly, the Pupil Referral Unit (PRU) environment is one that lends itself to the ethnographically informed approach being aimed for, in that the learning centres exist as relatively closed groups of a small number of Young People (YP) in which there is flexibility in day-to-day activities and lessons (unlike the rigid nature of most mainstream school timetables). And thirdly and most importantly, the YP in the learning centres represented a group of potentially marginalised individuals who were in real danger of slipping through the cracks with regard to further education and employment prospects, and some of the marginalisation, arguably, could be seen as stemming from the general prejudice surrounding 'youth language' (e.g. West 2011; Johns 2012; Harding 2013).

3. There were no 'clean' tokens of FOOT in the recording of Ryan.

4. Perhaps the closet comparable Northern British English data comes from Buchstaller (2014) in which she shows that in the speech of her ten 19- to 21-year-olds (albeit middle class university students in Newcastle), *be like* is the most common form, followed by unframed quotatives, followed by *say* and then *go*.

5. A 2011 British comedy film about a young man in London http://www.imdb.com/title/tt1658797/

6. A 2006 British film about a group of 15-year-olds in London http://www.imdb.com/title/tt0435680/

References

Baranowski, M., & Turton, D. (2015). Manchester English. In R. Hickey (Ed.), *Researching Northern English* (pp. 293–316). Amsterdam: John Benjamins.

Beal, J. C. (2008). English dialects in the North of England: Phonology. In B. Kortmann & C. Upton (Eds.), *Varieties of English. Vol. 1: The British Isles* (pp. 122–144). Berlin: Mouton de Gruyter.

Boersma, P., & Weenink, D. (2015). *Praat: Doing phonetics by computer* [Computer program]. Version 5.4.18. Available online: http://www.praat.org/

Bucholtz, M., & Hall, K. (2005). Identity and interaction: A sociocultural linguistic approach. *Discourse Studies, 7*(4–5), 585–614.

Buchstaller, I. (2014). *Quotatives: New trends and sociolinguistic implications.* Oxford: Wiley-Blackwell.

Buchstaller, I., & D'Arcy, A. (2009). Localized globalization: A multi-local, multivariate investigation of quotative be like. *Journal of SocioLinguistics, 13*(3), 291–331.

Cameron, D. (2009). Demythologising sociolinguistics. In N. Coupland & A. Jaworski (Eds.), *The new sociolinguistics reader* (pp. 106–118). Basingstoke: Palgrave Macmillan.

Cheshire, J., Kerswill, P., Fox, S., & Torgersen, E. (2011). Contact, the feature pool and the speech community: The emergence of multicultural London English. *Journal of SocioLinguistics, 15*(2), 151–196.

Drager, K. (2009). *A sociophonetic ethnography of Selwyn Girls' High.* Unpublished PhD thesis, University of Canterbury.

Dray, S., & Drummond, R. (Forthcoming). Language variation-in-practice: Variationist and ethnographic research methods in collaboration. In K. Tustin (Ed.), *The Routledge handbook of linguistic ethnography.* London: Routledge.

Drummond, R. (2011). Glottal variation in /t/ in non-native English speech: Patterns of acquisition. *English World-Wide, 32*(3), 280–308.

Drummond, R. (2012). Aspects of identity in a second language: ING variation in the speech of polish migrants living in Manchester, UK. *Language Variation and Change, 24*, 107–133.

Drummond, R. (2013). The Manchester polish STRUT: Dialect acquisition in a second language. *Journal of English Linguistics, 41*(1), 65–93.

Drummond, R. (2016). (Mis)interpreting urban youth language: white kids sounding black? *Journal of Youth Studies,* 1–21. Available online: http://www.tandfonline.com/doi/full/10.1080/13676261.2016.1260692

Drummond, R., & Dray, S. (2015, October). 'Gimme dat ting': Word initial th-stopping among urban British youth. Paper presented at *NWAV 44*, University of Toronto, 22–25.

Drummond, R., & Schleef, E. (2016). Identity in variationist sociolinguistics. In S. Preece (Ed.), *The Routledge handbook of language and identity* (pp. 50–65). London: Routledge.

Fabricius, A., Watt, D., & Johnson, D. E. (2009). A comparison of three speaker-intrinsic vowel formant frequency normalization algorithms for sociophonetics. *Language Variation and Change, 21*(3), 413–435.

Harding, N. (2013). Why are so many middle-class children speaking in Jamaican patois? A father of an 11-year-old girl laments a baffling trend. *Daily Mail.* 11th October. Available online: http://www.dailymail.co.uk/femail/article-2453613/Why-middle-class-children-speaking-Jamaican-patois-A-father-11-year-old-girl-laments-baffling-trend.html

Howley, G. (2016). *The acquisition of Manchester dialect variants by adolescent Roma migrants.* Unpublished PhD thesis, University of Salford.

Hughes, A., Trudgill, P., & Watt, D. (2012). *English accents and dialects: An introduction to social and regional varieties of English in the British Isles.* London: Hodder Arnold.

Johns, L. (2012). Do we really need to listen more to young people? I'm, not so sure. *Mail Online.* 13th December. Available online: http://johnsblog.daily-mail.co.uk/2012/12/do-we-really-need-to-listen-more-to-young-people-im-not-so-sure.html

Kerswill, P. (2014). The objectification of 'Jafaican': The discoursal embedding of multicultural London English in the British media. In J. Androutsopoulos (Ed.), *Mediatization and sociolinguistic change* (pp. 428–455). Berlin: De Gruyter.

Kerswill, P., Torgersen, E., & Fox, S. (2008). Reversing 'drift': Innovation and diffusion in the London diphthong system. *Language Variation and Change, 20*, 451–491.

Mufwene, S. S. (2001). *The ecology of language evolution.* Cambridge: Cambridge University Press.

Quist, P. (2008). Sociolinguistic approaches to multiethnolect: Language variety and stylistic practice. *International Journal of Bilingualism, 12*, 43–61.

Schleef, E., & Turton, D. (2016). Sociophonetic variation of like in British dialects: effects of function, context and predictability. *English Language and Linguistics,* 1–41. Available online: https://doi.org/10.1017/S136067431600023X

Schleef, E., Flynn, N., & Ramsammy, M. (2015). Production and perception of (ing) in Manchester English. In E. Torgersen, S. Hårstad, B. Mæhlum, &

U. Røyneland (Eds.), *Language variation – European perspectives V* (pp. 197–209). Amsterdam: John Benjamins.

Svendsen, B. A., & Røyneland, U. (2008). Multiethnolectal facts and functions in Oslo, Norway. *International Journal of Bilingualism, 12*, 63–83.

Szakay, A., & Torgersen, E. (2015). An acoustic analysis of voice quality in London English: The effect of gender, ethnicity and f0. In The Scottish Consortium for ICPhS 2015 (Ed.), *Proceedings of the 18th international congress of phonetic sciences*. Glasgow: The University of Glasgow.

Tollfree, L. (1999). South East London English: Discrete versus continuous modelling of consonantal reduction. In P. Foulkes & G. Docherty (Eds.), *Urban voices: Accent studies in the British Isles* (pp. 163–184). London: Routledge.

Torgersen, E., & Szakay, A. (2012). An investigation of speech rhythm in London English. *Lingua, 122*(7), 822–840.

Torgersen, E., Gabrielatos, C., Hoffmann, S., & Fox, S. (2011). A corpus-based study of pragmatic markers in London English. *Corpus Linguistics and Linguistic Theory, 7*(1), 93–118.

Turton, D., & Ramsammy, M. (2012, May). /ɪ,ə/−lowering in Manchest[ʌ]: Contextual patterns of gradient variabilit[ɛ]. Paper given at the *20th Manchester phonology meeting,* University of Manchester, 24–26.

Watson, C., & Harrington, J. (1999). Acoustic evidence for dynamic formant trajectories in Australian English vowels. *Journal of the Acoustical Society of America, 106*, 458–468.

Wells, J. (1982). *Accents of English*. Cambridge: Cambridge University Press.

West, Ed. (2011). 'Jafaican' may be cool, but it sounds ridiculous. *The Telegraph.* 7th June. Available online: http://blogs.telegraph.co.uk/news/brenda-noneill2/100101050/starkey-racism-row-it-is-the-political-elites-ceaseless-denigration-of-white-working-class-culture-that-has-turned-kids-black/, http://blogs.telegraph.co.uk/news/edwest/100091088/jafaican-may-be-cool-but-it-sounds-ridiculous/

Wiese, H. (2009). Grammatical innovation in multiethnic urban Europe: New linguistic practices among adolescents. *Lingua, 119*, 782–806.

5

Stylisation and the Dynamics of Migration, Ethnicity and Class

Ben Rampton

Introduction[1]

Research on stylisation and language crossing often underlines the agency of speakers, but how do these practices fit into larger systems and structures? This chapter focuses on two pairs of contrasting styles—posh and Cockney, and Creole and Asian English—and it connects the ways that British adolescents engaged with these sociolinguistic contrasts to their experience of class, ethnicity and migration. Posh and Cockney were closely tied to class, and the Creole/Asian English binary was linked to ethnicity and migration. But the stylisation of Creole/Asian English was grounded in a shared working-class position and, so, although migration and ethnicity mattered a great deal, the structuring processes associated with class were more fundamental. This has wider implications for our understanding of contemporary multilingualisms.

B. Rampton (✉)
King's College London, London, UK

© The Author(s) 2018
N. Braber, S. Jansen (eds.), *Sociolinguistics in England*,
DOI 10.1057/978-1-137-56288-3_5

In recent years in the study of multilingualism and language style, as in the social sciences generally, there has been a major shift, away from the traditional emphasis on the conditioning of social structure towards an interest in the agency of speakers and recipients (Hill 2004: 193; Heller 2007: 341). Much of my own research has contributed to this emphasis on agency with its account of crossing and stylisation as practices in which people switch away from routine, unself-conscious ways of talking (e.g. Rampton 1999: 422–3). But where do *systems* feature in the crossing and stylisation that I have studied?

The Systems in Focus

There are, of course, many systems that ethnographic research can attend to, operating in many different macro/meso/micro linguistic, cultural and social processes (Rampton et al. 2014: 7–12). But in what follows, I try to examine the agency of British teenagers within two types of system: semiotic and socio-economic.

The *semiotic* systems I attend to are binary style contrasts of the kind described by Ferguson (1959), Irvine (2001) and many others. In the field-sites I researched, there were a large number of languages, dialects and speech styles. But from within this sociolinguistic diversity, particular varieties were highlighted and placed together in contrastive pairs, and these oppositional pairings were reproduced in public discourse, in the media, in education and in everyday practice. In the two settings that I discuss, posh and Cockney formed one contrastive pair, and Creole and Asian English formed another.

The *socio-economic* system is Britain in the late twentieth century—a stratified class society in which wealth and opportunity are unequally distributed, and where, among other things, post-war employers have relied on a continuing flow of immigrant labour to do low-paid work. This socio-economic system is obviously far more complex than just a style-contrast, involving all sorts of political, economic and institutional processes that I am hardly qualified to discuss. But plainly, semiotic representations play a central part in the ongoing construction and reproduction of this large-scale social system (e.g. Bourdieu 1991: 234 *et passim*) and, according to Parkin (1977), contrasts in style can themselves play a rather significant role (see also Irvine 2001: 22, 24). Studying urban multilingualism in newly independent Kenya, Parkin described how the values and connotations associated with different local, national and international languages converged in a complex system of symbolic oppositions. This system of contrasting varieties provided 'a framework for [the] expression of [both emergent and established] ideological differences,... a kind of template along the lines of which social groups [might] later become distinguished' (1977: 205, 187). Indeed, suggests Parkin, within polyethnic communities, 'diversity of speech... provides... the most readily available "raw" classificatory data for the differentiation of new social groups and the redefinition of old ones' (1977: 208).

But, if Parkin points to at least one potential connection between these two kinds of system, where does agency feature? For language users situated in the lower levels of a stratified society, the scope for agentively reshaping the social system as a whole is obviously limited. However, that does not mean that they have no scope at all for agentive engagement with the conditions shaping their lives and, in what follows, I describe adolescents positioning themselves in a multi-ethnic class society through their active involvement with the two binary style contrasts—posh and Cockney, Creole and Asian English.

The Argument

The chapter draws on two datasets, the first focusing on young people doing exaggerated posh and Cockney in a multi-ethnic secondary school in the 1990s, and the second involving stylised Creole and Indian English in multilingual friendship groups in the 1980s. With these data, I shall argue that:

- The posh/Cockney binary was intimately tied to social class, and it permeated the ordinary urban English habitually spoken by my

British-born informants. But when, agentively, they put on stylised posh and Cockney voices, adolescents *accentuated* and *denaturalised* class stratification.

- The Creole/Asian English binary was related to ethnicity and migration and, in their agentive stylisations of Creole and Asian English, youngsters actively *reworked* the ethno-linguistic imagery circulating in the dominant ideology, *adapting* it in ways that made much better sense of their multi-ethnic lives together.
- These reworkings of the Creole/Asian English binary were actually grounded in a shared working-class position, and the Creole/Asian English binary was also influenced by the high/low dualism central both to posh and Cockney and to social class. So, although migration and ethnicity certainly mattered a great deal, the structuring processes associated with class seemed to be more fundamental.
- In recent years, nation-states have been giving more recognition to minority bilingualism, but they base this on a model of monolingual standard languages. As standard language multilingualism becomes the new cosmopolitan posh, polylingual hybridity is positioned as a core characteristic of the multi-ethnic urban working classes.

In developing a relatively panoramic account like this, there are times when this chapter is unavoidably synoptic, leaving a lot of data, analysis and interpretation 'black-boxed', but I shall try to compensate for this by referring back to the two monographs where these datasets are treated in much more detail (Rampton 1995/2005; 2006).

We can start with the style-contrast tuned to traditional British social class stratification.

The Posh/Cockney Style Binary at Central High

In the 1990s, I studied a multi-ethnic secondary school in London that I called *Central High*.[2] Here, I found that on average about once every 45 minutes, adolescents spontaneously stylised posh and Cockney, and when they did so, they drew on a high/low, mind/body, reason-and-emotion dualism that is deeply embedded both in British class culture and in the schooling process (Cohen 1988). So, for example, in Extract 1 below involving two girls at the end of a tutor group lesson, Joanne's performance articulates quite a sharp contrast between the stances associated with standard and vernacular speech. Standard language gets linked to sceptical reasoning while Cockney is tied to passionate indignation.

Extract 1

During the tutor period while Mr Alcott is talking to the class, Joanne (wearing the radio-mic) has been telling Ninnette a bit about her parents and grandparents, and has just been talking about her mum's difficult pregnancy. (For a much fuller discussion, see Rampton 2006: 338–41):

1 Joanne:	(.)	
2	((*quietly:*)) she could have lost me ((*light laugh*))	
3	(3)	
4	((*with a hint of tearfulness in her voice:*))	
	n you'd all be sitting here today without me ((*laughs*))	
	[sɪtʔɪn hɪə]	
5 Tannoy:	((*eleven pips, followed by the din of chairs moving*))	
6 Jo:	((*louder, and in literate speech:*))	
	but you |wouldn't |care	
	[bt jə wʊdʰntʰ kɛə]	
7	**cos you |wouldn't ˋ know** ((*laughs*))	
	[kəz jə wʊdʰntʰ nǣu]	
8 ?N:	( )	
9 Jo:	nothing I'm just jok-)	
10	I'm being st-	
11	((*high-pitched*))ˋ**oooh::**	
	[u::]	
12	((*moving into broad Cockney:*) **Ninne::tte**	

13	you've	got	e͵nough		with	you	to͵day	

[ju   gɒt enʌf   wɪᶿ ju: tədẽɪ̃]

14	and	͵then	you	͵go	and		＼chee::k	＼me::

[æn   en   jə   gəʊ n   tʃi:k   mi:]

15	͵you	＼little::		͵bugg	͵aye	͵aye	͵aye	͵aye

[ju   lɪtʔʊ::ʔ   bʌg   ãɪ̃ jãɪ̃ jãɪ̃ jãɪ̃]

16   (15) ((the teacher is giving clearing up instructions))
17   ((Joanne leaves the classroom and then hums quietly to herself))

When Joanne shifts to careful 'literate' speech in lines 6 and 7 (Mugglestone 1995: 208), she uses logic to *undermine* sentiment, whereas in contrast, when she pretends to *intensify* the emotion in her speech in lines 12 to 15—when she abandons the apology she started in lines 9–10, and issues an indignant reprimand—her speech becomes markedly Cockney. Setting this episode next to many others where kids used exaggerated posh and Cockney in greetings, taunts, commands, rebukes, summonses and so on, or referred to physical prowess, social misdemeanours, sexuality and so forth, there was rather a consistent pattern (Rampton 2006: Ch. 9). In one way or another, Cockney evoked solidarity, vigour, passion and bodily laxity, whereas posh conjured social distance, superiority, constraint, physical weakness and sexual inhibition. And youngsters also positioned themselves around this ideological structure in a range of different ways—on some occasions, they put ironic distance between themselves and the image of, for example, an over-sexed low-life or a patronising snob, but on other occasions, they seemed to identify with the indexical possibilities, using Cockney to soften the boundary between sociability and work, or adding piquancy to sexual interest by introducing posh.

From the description so far, posh/Cockney stylisation certainly did seem to fit Hill's characterisation of agency as a 'capacity… to recruit [even]… unpromising semiotic materials for the construction of vivid and dynamic identities' (Hill 2004: 193). But the account becomes more complicated when it is remembered that this high/low contrast stretches back several centuries, and that there is a strong case for example, for seeing binaries like mind/body, reason/emotion and thought/action materialised in the institution of schooling itself. 'Mind over body' can be seen in the tight constraints on physical activity in classrooms; instead of humming, singing and the modalities of popular culture, the curriculum prioritises the production of lexico-grammatical propositions in thematically connected strings—a case, one might say, of reason over emotion; and, of course, high–low ranking is central to the whole organisation of education. Furthermore, when we recognise the high/low binary's extensive institutionalisation in schooling like this, the purchase offered, for example, by an 'acts of identity' idiom decreases (Le Page and Tabouret-Keller 1985). Instead of simply suggesting that these youngsters were 'projecting' a particular ideological imagery, it becomes more accurate to describe their stylisation as 'spotlighting' or 'illuminating' elements of a structure that they already inhabited. And this certainly fits much better with the fact that it was often at particular institutional and interactional moments that kids stylised posh and Cockney—they shifted into stylised posh and Cockney on occasions when they felt humiliated or offended by a teacher, when faced with separation from their pals, and at sharply felt states and changes in the structured flow of social relations. So here, for example, is Hanif's response to some patronising over-explanation from Mr A:

Extract 2
A Humanities class, working on how lawyers in an upcoming role-play will introduce their cases. (See Rampton 2006: 284–312 for more detailed discussion and other examples.)

```
1 Mr A:    how can y- (.) how can you introduce your speech
2          like writing an essay
3          you have t-
4 Rafiq:   I would like to bring up
5 Mr A:    I would like to::
6 Hanif:   bring forward
7 Masud:   bring forw[ard
8 Anon:              [(ex    )
```

```
 9 Mr A:   or even (.) I ₁in'te::nd ₍to
10 Anon:   pro[secute)
11 Hanif       [(((loudly, in a posh accent, stretched, with
               an exaggerated rise-fall: )) o:::h
                          [ əᴵʊ ]
```

But even this is not enough. Beyond the specific occasions in which youngsters put on exaggerated posh and Cockney voices, they continuously adjusted themselves to the high–low binary in their tacit speech practices, becoming more standard and less vernacular as the formality of the situation increased. In a small Labovian study of style-shifting among the four core informants (Labov 1972), I compared their use of standard and vernacular speech variants in *formal* and *informal* settings [reading aloud, speaking in front of the class etc., as opposed to arguing with friends or telling them a story (see Rampton 2006: Ch. 7.3)]. Table 5.1 presents the results for these students:

And Extract 3 shows this in action, with Ninnette, a black girl of mixed Caribbean/African descent, recoding her self-presentation in increasingly standard grammatical and phonological forms in an attempt to catch the teacher's attention:

Extract 3[3]

A drama class, where working in pairs, everyone has been told to prepare and rehearse a short role-play discussion involving one character who is going to have a baby. They will then be expected to perform in front of the rest of the group, but Ninnette and Joanne are fairly emphatic about not wanting to, and they have used their time joking around putting pillows up their jumpers. In the end, they successfully manage to avoid having to perform, but during the final moments allocated to preparation and rehearsal, just prior to their coming together to watch individual performances, Ninnette is recorded as follows (see Rampton 2006: 258–61):

1 Ninnette:	((calling out to the teacher, loudly:))
2	ˈMISS
3	(.)
4	MISS
5	WE ˈAINT ˈEVEN ˈDONE ˈNU IN
	[nʌʔĩŋ]
6	(.)
7	((even louder:))MISS WE ˈAINT ˈDONE ˈNOTHING
	[nʌfɪŋ]
8	(2)
9	((not so loud, as if Miss is in closer range:))
10	miss we lavent ldone anything
	[enɪθɪŋ]
11	(2)

Table 5.1 Percentage (and proportions) of STANDARD variants in four informants' production of 6 variables in formal and informal contexts

	Simon (white Anglo descent)		Hanif (Bangladeshi descent)		Ninnette (African Caribbean)		Joanne (white Anglo)	
	Formal	Informal	Formal	Informal	Formal	Informal	Formal	Informal
1. Word-medial voiced TH (other)	100% (9/9)	75% (3/4)	100% (6/6)	(1/1)	40% (4/10)	–	40% (2/5)	43% (3/7)
2. Word-initial voiced TH (the)	96% (27/28)	100% (35/35)	97% (32/33)	70% (35/50)	82% (40/49)	79% (34/43)	100% (37/37)	94% (16/17)
3. Word-initial H (not proforms)	(23/26)	(13/15)	100% (16/16)	86% (12/14)	100% (14/14)	79% (15/19)	86% (12/14)	44% (4/9)
4. Pre-consonantal, post-vocalic L (old)	89% (16/19)	50% (6/12)	66% (6/9)	64% (9/14)	42% (11/26)	23% (5/21)	47% (18/38)	66% (8/12)
5. Word-medial intervocalic T (butter)	87% (7/8)	0% (0/4)	66% (2/3)	20% (3/13)	70% (7/10)	0% (0/5)	14% (2/14)	0% (0/11)
6. -ING in participial suffixes (running)	86% (12/14)	40% (4/10)	100% (17/17)	33% (2/6)	66% (6/9)	0% (0/6)	61% (8/13)	22% (2/9)
Overall scores	90% 94/104	76% 61/80	94% 79/84	63% 62/98	69% 82/118	57% 54/94	65% 79/121	51% 33/65

These data show that my informants had absorbed the high/low posh and Cockney dichotomy into their ordinary, *non*-stylised speech (cf. Bourdieu 1991: Part 1; Stroud 2004: 198–9; Rampton 2006: 253, 258). Indeed, to push the 'luminescence' metaphor one step further, here one might say that these youngsters had been *irradiated* by the high/low posh/ Cockney binary – it was a fundamental structuring principle in their routine, everyday English speech.

To return to Hill and Heller, yes we *can* see agency in posh and Cockney stylisation (evidenced, for example, in the (more and less) artful stylisations in Extracts 1 and 2). But, agentive stylisation fits into a much more widespread and enduring system of social stratification and, in their routine Labovian style-shifting, these kids tacitly ratified and reproduced the semiotically marked distinctions and hierarchies that configure British social class. So amidst class structuring that was both institutionally entrenched and individually internalised like this, it makes most sense to see agentive posh and Cockney stylisation as practices of denaturalisation, throwing an ideological system into high relief that was otherwise hegemonic, omni-pervasive and taken-for-granted.

Denaturalisation like this certainly is not the only way in which stylisation operates as an agentive response to systemic conditions and, in the next section, I describe a rather different dynamic. But by way of introduction, there is one more point to make about posh, Cockney and social class at Central High. Even though they stylised posh and Cockney more than any other variety, and even though they displayed traditional British patterns of sociolinguistic stratification in their Labovian style-shifting, this was very much a multilingual, multi-ethnic school with a very high migrant and refugee population, and this makes it hard to explain the reproduction of classed speech simply in terms of inter-generational transmission within the family. Three of my four main informants lived in single-parent homes, but Ninnette's mum came from the French-speaking Caribbean and, when Hanif talked to his mum, he spoke Sylheti. So, instead of seeking an explanation in cultural inheritance and family reproduction, it is necessary to locate the development of a class sensibility in ongoing activity, in peer-group processes, in popular culture and school experience. In addition, it looks as though there could be a rather complicated relationship between class, migration and ethnicity, and this provides the cue for an overview of my second dataset, involving crossing and stylisation in Creole and Asian English in the 1980s.

The Creole/Asian English Style Contrast in Ashmead

In the 1980s, I researched multi-ethnic adolescent peer groups in Ashmead, a working-class neighbourhood in the south Midlands of England.[4] I looked at several speech varieties, and discovered that there was rather a sharp symbolic opposition between Creole and Asian English. There is a glimpse of this in Extract 4, which comes from a playback interview:

Extract 4

Participants: Asif (15 yrs old, male, Pakistani descent), Kazim (15, male, Pakistani descent), Alan (15, male, Anglo descent), Ben (the researcher, 30+, male, Anglo descent). *Setting:* An interview, in which Ben is struggling to elicit some retrospective participant commentary on extracts of recorded data, and is on the point of giving up. (See Rampton 2005: 123–4 and Harris and Rampton 2002: 39–44 for much fuller analysis.)

```
 1  Ben:                      right shall I- shall we stop there
 2  Kazim:                    no
 3  Alan:                     no come [ on carry on
 4  Asif:                             [ do another extract
 5  Ben:                      le- lets have (.) [ then you have to give me more=
 6  Alan:                                       [ carry on
 7  Ben:                      =attention gents
 8  Asif ((quieter)):         yeh [ alright
 9  Alan ((quieter)):             [      alright
10  Asif ((quieter)):             [      yeh
11  Ben:                      I need more attention
12  Kazim ((in Asian English)):   I   AM  VERY  SORRY  BEN  JAAD
                                [ɑɪ æm veɾi sɒɾi ben dʒɑːd]

13  Asif   ((in Asian English)):  ATTENTION     BENJAMIN
                                [əthenʃɑːn bendʒəmɪn]

14  :                        [((laughter))
15  Ben:                      [ right well you can- we cn-
16  Alan:                     [ BENJAADEMIN
17  Ben:                      we can continue but we er must concentrate a bit
18                            [more
19  Asif:                     [yeh
20  Alan:                     alright     [(go on) then
21  Asif((in Asian English)):             [concentrating       very        hard
                                [kɒnsestɾetɪn  veɾi  ɑɾ]

22  Ben:                      okay right
23  :                         ((giggles dying down))
```

24 Kazim((*in Asian English*)):   **what**   a   **stupid**   (   )
[vʌd ə stupɪd]

25 Ben ((*returning the microphone to what he considers to be a better position to catch all the speakers*)): concentrate a little bit-

26 Alan: alright then
27 Kazim ((*in Creole*)):   stop movin **dat**   **ting**   **aroun**
[dæʔ tɪŋ erɑʊn]

28 Ben: WELL YOU stop moving it around and then I'll won't need to
29   (.)   r[ight
30 Kazim ((*in Creole*)):   [stop moving **dat**   **ting**   **aroun**
[dæʔ tɪŋ erɑʊn]

31 Ben: right okay   [
32 Kazim: [BEN JAAD
33 Alan: ((*laughs*))
34 Ben: what are you doing
35 Alan: ben jaa[ad
36 Ben: [well leave ( ) alone
37 Kazim: IT'S HIM that ben jaad over there
38 Ben: right
((*Ben continues his efforts to reinstitute the listening activity*))

Things are not going quite as I had planned, and at the point where I threaten to stop the interview, Asif and Kazim switch into exaggerated Indian English in a sequence of mock apologies. Then a moment later in line 27, just as I seem to be signalling 'back-to-business' by repositioning the microphone, the boot moves to the other foot, Kazim switches into Creole and directs a 'prime' at me, this time constructing *my* activity as an impropriety. This difference in the way Asian English and Creole are used fitted with a very general pattern in my data. When adolescents used Asian English, there was nearly always a wide gap between self and voice, evident here in Asif and Kazim's feigned deference. In contrast, switches into Creole tended to lend emphasis to evaluations that synchronised with the identities that speakers maintained in their ordinary speech, and in line with this, Creole was often hard to distinguish from young people's ordinary vernacular English (cf. Rampton 2005: 215–219).

Away from stylised practices like this, Ashmead youngsters encountered many different uses of Asian and Creole English and, inside minority ethnic networks, the forms, functions and associations of Creole and Asian English were obviously much more complex and extensive. But in spite of this, the images evoked in stylisation were quite specific and, across a wide range of instances, there was a sharp polarisation. Creole indexed an excess of demeanour over deference, displaying qualities like assertiveness, verbal resourcefulness and opposition to authority, while Asian English stood for a surfeit of deference and dysfluency, typified in polite and uncomprehending phrases like 'jolly good', 'excuse me please' and 'I no understanding English'.

This contrast certainly was not just autonomously generated within Ashmead. Undoubtedly, there were a lot of local influences, experiences and histories that, in one way or another, could give this contrast a strong and complex emotional resonance, but it also tuned to a much more widely circulating imagery that polarised black and Asian people in threat/clown, 'problem/victim couplet[s]' (Gilroy 1987), echoing 'a common-sense racism that stereotypes Afro-Caribbean youth as violent criminals and all Asian people as the personification of victimage' (Paul and Lawrence 1988: 143). In the UK at the time, Asians were often stereotyped as compliant newcomers, ineptly oriented to bourgeois success, while Afro-Caribbeans were portrayed as troublemakers, ensconced in the working class and adept only in sports and entertainment (Hewitt 1986: 216). And within the education system itself, there was also some powerful contrastive stereotyping in institutional responses to the ethno-linguistic difference of Caribbean and Asian migrants—with the former seen as deserving pedagogies that responded to non-standard vernacular practices, while the latter needed English as a Second Language (ESL)(cf. Rampton 1988).

In Ashmead, awareness of racist imaging like this meant that, in the wrong mouth at the wrong time, stylised Creole or Asian English could certainly get very negatively sanctioned, and in the cross-ethnic production and reception of these expressive practices, local youngsters generally developed quite a reliable sense of what they could and could not do, where and with whom (Rampton 2005: 301–3 *et passim*). Even so, the public imagery was appropriated, reworked and recirculated at local level, so that crossing and stylisation became significant local currency.

Creole was clearly much more attractive to youngsters of all ethnic backgrounds, and it was often reported as part of the general local linguistic inheritance, particularly among Asian boys, who described it as something 'we been doing... for a long time' (Rampton 2005: Ch. 2.2). In the interpretation in my 1995/2005 book, I situated this sociosymbolic polarisation in the larger context of migration (Rampton 2005: 217). On the one hand, I suggested, *Creole* indexed an excitement and an excellence in youth culture that many adolescents aspired to, and it was even described as 'future language'. On the other, *Asian English* represented distance from the main currents of adolescent life, and it stood for a stage of historical transition that many youngsters felt they were leaving behind. In fact, though, this symbolisation of a large-scale historical trajectory, this 'weight[ing mediated] by the speaker[s'] social position and interest' (Irvine 2001: 24), went deeper. There was also a class dimension to the path indexed in the binary opposition of Creole and Asian English, and this showed up in at least four ways.

First and most notably among boys, crossing and stylisation themselves figured as something of a local class emblem, signifying the difference between Ashmead's mixed adolescent community and the wider Stoneford population. When my informants described the kinds of people who *would not* do crossing and stylisation, they referred to groups who were vertically placed at either end of a bipolar hierarchy of wealth and status—a hierarchy that matched the economic and demographic facts quite closely (Rampton 2005: Chs. 1.7 and 2). Up above, there were the 'posh wimpies' living in wealthier districts outside Ashmead, and down below, there were Bangladeshis living in the very poorest parts of town. So this, for example, is how Peter referred to youngsters from outside the neighbourhood:

Extract 5

'gorra' – 'white man' *((in Panjabi))*... always call the people who didn't go to [our school] gorras, yet I'm white myself... cos we reckon they're a bit you know upper class (most of them)... the gorra gang. (Peter, cited in Rampton 2005: 62)

A second reason for linking the Creole/Asian English contrast to social class lies in a significant overlap in the evaluation of Creole and local non-standard working-class English. When Asian and Anglo youngsters of both sexes described the efforts of their mums and dads to get them to speak properly, it was often the intrusion of swearwords, question tags and verb forms in Creole that were targeted (Rampton 2005: Ch. 5.6), and here is Ian (white), explaining how his American cousins were disappointed by his English:

Extract 6

they think we speak really upper class English in England...they they see on the... they say that Englishmen has got such beautiful voices, and they express themselves so well...((*shifting into an approximation to Creole:*)) **'eh what you talkin' abaat, wha' you chattin' about, you raas klaat'**, and they don't like it! They thought I was going to be posher

Indeed, beyond the confines of my own research, this broad functional equivalence of Creole and traditional non-standard British speech was widely celebrated (and extensively noted) during the 1980s in a code-switching record called 'Cockney Translation' by the black British MC Smiley Culture (see Gilroy 1987: 194–7).

Third, the Creole/Asian English contrast can itself be mapped into the high/low, mind/body, reason-and-emotion oppositions outlined in Section 1. According to Cohen, this dualistic high/low idiom was generated 'from within certain strategic discourses in British class society' from the seventeenth century onwards, and 'from the very outset [it was] applied across a range of sites of domination, both to the indigenous lower orders and ethnic minority settlers as well as to colonial populations overseas' (Cohen 1988: 63). In the light of the overlapping evaluation of Creole and working-class English identified immediately earlier, it is not difficult to see Creole linked to the low side of the traditional British class semiotic. But just as important, the high side of the class binary was linked to Asian English. English is a prestige variety in the Indian sub-continent, and when my informants compared themselves with relatives there, they saw their own varieties as inferior:

Extract 7

in India right, the people that I've seen that talk English… talk strict English, you know. Here, this is more of a slangish way… the English that people talk round here you know, they're not really talkin' proper English… if you go India right… they say it clear, in the proper words.

Extract 8

my cousin come ((*over from India*))… he's got a degree and everything, he speaks good English, but he didn't used to speak in English with us though, cos they sort of speak perfect English, innit. We sort of speak a bit slang, sort of innit – like we would say 'innit' and all that. He was scared we might laugh at this perfect sort of English… the good solid English that they teach 'em'

At the same time, there was very little evidence in any of these youngsters' stylised Asian English that this status carried over into Ashmead. Transposed to the UK and re-entextualised in stylisation, Ashmead kids depicted an Indian English orientation to the high, proper and polite as comical, its aspirations hopelessly marred by foreignness.

Lastly, there was little indication of a commitment to education in ethno-linguistic crossing and stylisation in Ashmead. Of course, schools were a vital meeting point for kids from different ethnic backgrounds, and the general pastoral and extracurricular ethos played a very significant part in promoting good interethnic relations. But Creole, which many admired, hardly featured at all on the curriculum and, rather than being tolerant of learners of English as a second language, or respecting them for their progress (as the teaching staff might hope), adolescents generally stigmatised pupils who had not yet been fully socialised into the vernacular ways of ordinary youth. Instead of curriculum learning, the activities and codes of conduct characteristic of playground recreation tended to be central to the cross-ethnic spread of minority languages and, if anything, this was easier if a style was used in opposition to school authority. Certainly, there were complex bodies of knowledge, skill and experience associated with different types of ethnically marked music and performance art, and there were, for example, white girls who were very interested in finding out more about reggae or bhangra. But a lot of this interest was embedded in heterosexual relations, and learning was much more a matter of legitimate peripheral participation than classroom study (cf. Rampton 2005: Part 3).

Putting all this together, there is a case for saying that the Creole/Asian English contrast oriented Ashmead adolescents to *two* major social processes. Not only did crossing and stylisation situate them at an endpoint in the migrant transition from outside into Britain, but then also once inside, the binary lined them up with values much more associated with the lower than the higher classes. Yes, iconically, Creole was first and foremost associated with Caribbeans, Asian English with Asians and local cross-ethnic respect for these ownership rights was evidenced in the way that, in some contexts, 'non-owners' either often avoided the use of these varieties and/or only invoked them in specially licensed interactional moments. But in the problems, pleasures and expectations of working-class adolescent life together, these kids experienced enough common ground to open up ethno-linguistic speech styles, realigning them with the high/low valuations hegemonic in British society, re-specifying their significance in crossing and stylisation practices which recognised and cultivated the shared social space that labour migration had now created.

It is worth now trying to pull the threads of this description together, first by discussing similarities, differences and the relationship between posh/Cockney, Creole and Asian English in England, and then by commenting on late modern multilingualism, ethnicity and social class more generally.

Comparing and Connecting Posh/Cockney and Creole/Asian English

High/low, mind/body and reason/emotion polarisation are central to English schooling and, at Central High, adolescents broadly ratified the institutional embodiment of this binary in their routine style-shifting. But posh and Cockney *stylisation* interrupted the routine patterning of everyday talk, exaggerating and elaborating evaluative differentiations that were otherwise normally treated as non-problematic in their practical activity. Stylisation made the sociolinguistic structuring of everyday life more conspicuous, and denaturalised a pervasive cultural hierarchy, disrupting its authority as an interpretive frame that might have otherwise been 'accepted undiscussed, unnamed, admitted without scrutiny' (Bourdieu 1977: 169–170).

In Ashmead, crossing and stylisation registered ethnicities in the first instance, recognising differences but integrating them in a repertoire of ethnically marked styles that adolescents could now more or less share (in speech reception, if not always in production). Partially reproducing but also appropriating and recasting racist imagery circulating more widely in public culture, peer-group crossing and stylisation figured Asian English as an emblem of ethnic difference rooted outside Britain and/or in older generations, and treated Creole as a powerful model of youth ethnicity grounded now in the UK. In addition, crossing and stylisation were reported as signs of mixed multi-ethnic community, and against a background of political agreement on ethnic groups getting along together, adolescents learnt—and got told—how and when to follow the lead of the owners of an ethnic speech variety in their crossing and stylisation, avoiding derogatory Creole, for example, and confining Asian English to particular interactional sites (Rampton 2005: Ch. 7.9). In short, Ashmead's active and explicit ideological commitment to multiculturalism produced significant levels of *normative standardisation* in local practices of crossing and stylisation (cf. Agha 2007), attested in rules of cross-ethnic avoidance and license of the kind documented in detail not only in Rampton (1995/2005) but also in Hewitt (1986).

There was nothing comparable to this in the stylisation of posh/ Cockney at Central High. Of course, there were plenty of representations of posh twats and vernacular slobs circulating in British public culture generally, but with nothing like anti-racism to challenge them, they were not particularly controversial. Kids did have a class-related sense of futures being potentially better and worse for them as individuals; they could be quite articulate in their images of lives to either aim for or avoid; there was a lot of very animated political debate focused on sexuality, race and ethnicity. But there was little evidence of any explicit, collectively mobilising, specific *class* consciousness among the youngsters at Central High (Rampton 2006: Ch. 7.2), and nothing to compare with the conditions that had produced the normative standardisation of Creole/Asian English stylisation in Ashmead. In Ashmead, you risked offending the putative owners if/when you did exaggerate Creole or Asian English, or were being seen to endorse racist representations. But at Central High, you could stylise posh and Cockney with much more freedom, relatively unconcerned about transgressing core codes of collective solidarity and, consistent with this, the patterns of alignment between self and voice in acts of stylisation were also much more varied (Rampton 2006: 366–7).

So overall, the social problematics that were thematised in these two sets of contrastive crossing and stylisation practices were very different and, in summarising this, we can return to the relationship between stylisation, structure and agency:

• At Central High, posh and Cockney stylisation seemed geared to the *deconstruction of a system of individual differentiation* that was very well established and that adolescents *already inhabited.* This system governed the vertical trajectory of individuals, elevating some and degrading others, and in school contexts, stylised posh and Cockney generally *denaturalised* this.

In rather stark opposition to this,

- In Ashmead, crossing and stylisation in Creole and Asian English oriented to the *collective construction of a shared habitation from group differences* which had only been encountered relatively recently and were represented in problematic ways in public culture generally. Crossing and stylisation 'domesticated' these differences—*made them orderly, familiar and acceptable*—by, among other things, articulating a contrast which depicted ethnic styles as different moments in group trajectories with a common destination in the British working class.

Viewed as simple but powerful semiotic systems like this, style polarities like posh/Cockney and Creole/Asian English allow people to plot positions and paths in the territory between, just as Parkin proposed and, in their exploitation of these contrasts, adolescents actively oriented themselves to two absolutely central axes in the organisation of British society—on a *horizontal* ethnic axis, the movement from outside Britain in and, then once inside, on a *vertical* class axis—up/down, high/low. So evidently, when seen as the agentive practice of historical actors engaging with the conditions where they find themselves, stylisation can support different ideological projects and, in Creole/Asian English stylisation, adolescents articulated collective commitments that were quite distinct from the kind of micro-political positionings entailed in stylised posh and Cockney. Whereas one, one might say, reinterpreted the dominant version of ethnicity and replaced it with the kinds of *new ethnicity* described by Stuart Hall (1988; Rampton 2005: Chs. 12.4 and 13.4), the other intimated the partial penetrations of class hegemony of the sort described by Paul Willis (1977; Rampton 2006: Ch. 9.6).

At the same time, these data also suggest that, underpinning the processes I have described, socio-economic class stratification was the most powerful systemic process, configuring the indexical ground from which adolescents spoke (Hanks 1996) and, in *both* of the datasets that have been discussed, it seemed to be an inter-ethnically shared experience of positioning within the British lower classes that gave crossing and stylisation so much of their shape, intelligibility, currency and resonance. Admittedly, my account has nothing to say about the dynamics within homes and intra-ethnic community settings, and further research could reveal much more about how the aspirations often associated with migration influence young people's sociolinguistic self-positioning within class structure. But in the account so far at least, it is hard to see posh and Cockney stylisation being shaped by ethnicity and migration, whereas in contrast, there was substantial evidence that the style polarisation of Creole and Asian English reflected class sensibilities in England. Of the two binaries that stylisation played on, the high/low contrast was omnipervasive, whereas the sense of collective trajectory from past to future was much more specific to the projection and recognition of ethnic and migrant identities.

With this view of working-class sensibilities influencing the stylisation of Creole and Asian English in Ashmead, as well as the stylisation of posh and Cockney at Central High, it is worth concluding with some general observations about recent developments in the political and institutional recognition of multilingualism.

Globalisation and Social Class: Standard Multilingualism and Vernacular Heteroglossia/ Polylingualism

As a number of recent commentators have noted, nation-states are often now significantly more proactive in promoting multilingualism:

> [p]olitical economic conditions are changing; the new economy places much greater emphasis on communicative skills in general, and multilingualism in particular, than did the old…; nation-states try to reposition themselves advantageously on the dynamic and increasingly globalised market…; labour migration takes new, mobile and transnational shapes. (Heller 2007: 15)

Influenced also by supra-national bodies and nongovernmental organisations, '[m]inority language education is now becoming the standard policy in the territories inhabited by linguistic groups other than that of the nation-state' (Pujolar 2007: 77). At the same time, however, the promotion of minority language bilingualism is often based on traditional monolingual models of literacy, schooling and language codification:

> the kind of public typically imagined within minority language revitalisation and/or ethnic nationalism movements... are typically bourgeois and universalistic in nature: the nation or linguistic community is imagined in the singular and envisioned primarily as a reading and writing public... [L]anguage politics tend to be oriented towards normalisation, expanding literacy, and gaining legitimacy within the terms of state hegemonic language hierarchies. (Urla 1995: 246)

Jaffe spells out the significance of this:

> [M]inority language movements like the Corsican one have often made monolingual minority language competence the centrepiece of their discourses about language and identity... *[This] makes the mixed cultural and linguistic practices and identities that are found in societies that have undergone language contact and shift 'matter out of place'.* (Jaffe 2007: 53, 60 [emphases added])

Influenced by a number of processes associated with globalisation, standard language multilingualism has become more respectable—positioning an expanded range of bilingual repertoires as (cosmopolitan) posh. But this accords little value to the kinds of mixed cultural and linguistic practices described in Ashmead and at Central High. In an emergent counterpart to the new multilingual posh, there is a good case for seeing this type of polylingual, heteroglossic hybridity as a key sociolinguistic dynamic within the globalised urban working classes.

This claim certainly fits with my reanalysis of the data from Ashmead, and there is broad support for it in a growing body of research which describes the hybrid language practices of young people in multi-ethnic working-class locations in European cities (e.g. Auer and Dirim 2003; Jaspers 2005; Madsen 2015). At the same time, if this claim is to be sustained, it needs to be nuanced, because heteroglossic multi-ethnic practices can also circulate beyond their territories of origin (Alim et al. 2009). Poly-lingual switching, mixing, crossing and stylisation may well thrive in demographic sites where there are migrant and minority populations in poorer housing and disadvantaged schools, but some of these practices get taken up by the popular media, relayed much more widely and subsequently reproduced by people in very different socio-economic locations. Androutsopoulos (2001) documents the process very clearly (cf. also Stroud 2004), and there is a vivid description in Cutler's account of how African American Vernacular English gets adopted by 'Mike', a very wealthy young white New Yorker (Cutler 1999). This kind of appropriation blurs a demographic view of the class distribution of this ethnically marked mixed speech and, with youngsters like Mike using it, maybe we should say that the associations of ethnically marked mixed speech are really just *non-work* rather than *working-class*. Indeed, if instead of economic subordination, it is actually more a matter of simply 'letting your hair down', recreation, informality or 'fun', then perhaps we ought to use a class-neutral label like *youth language* to characterise speech practices such as these.

There can be no doubt that, with global marketisation in late modernity, languages, dialects and styles are undergoing all sorts of complex revaluation. Still, there are two points to make in support of the identification of mixed speech with the working-class sites emerging with international migration.

First, media exposure is not simply a matter of status enhancement. Alongside the (selective) promotion of ethnically marked speech in popular culture, there is often very widespread denigration in, for example, political debates about nation and in-policy debates about education. Public discourses like these play a major role in official legitimation and the production of mainstream value (cf. Stroud 2004) and, indeed, it is often in counterpoint to these pejorative dominant representations that the hybrid language practices in popular culture gain their resonance (Urla 1995).

Closely linked to this, second, we have to retain a sense of the class-marking of hybrid polylingual speech practices when we consider how binary contrasts work in the subjective dynamics of social class. Sherry Ortner describes how class binaries get internalised, how class opposites affect individuals as an emotionally charged imagery of alternative pos-sibilities and how all of us live with 'fears, anxieties' and an insistent sense that people in higher and lower class positions mirror our 'pasts and pos-sible futures' (Ortner 1991: 177):

> we normally think of class relations as taking place *between* classes, [but] in fact each class contains the other(s) within itself, though in distorted and ambivalent forms… [E]ach class views the others not only… as antagonis-tic groups but as images of their hopes and fears for their own lives and futures… [M]uch of working class culture can be understood as a set of discourses and practices embodying the ambivalence of upward mobility, [and] much of middle-class culture can be seen as a set of discourses and practices embodying the terror of downward mobility. (Ortner 1991: 172, 175, 176)

Stallybrass and White provide valuable elaboration: this class-based self-other relationship is actually rather unstable and, mixed in with the bour-geois disgust and fear of the lower orders, there is also fascination and desire (Stallybrass and White 1996: 194). So when middle-class majority kids use speech forms historically associated with the urban ethnic lower class, this does not mean that class no longer matters. There is obviously a long tradition of young people temporarily 'slumming it', taking time off from the journey to middle-class futures and, with Ortner, Stallybrass and White, there is a stronger case for seeing the ethno-linguistic crossing and stylisation of middle-class teenagers as exactly the kind of exception which proves the rule—the rule being that ethnically marked mixed speech has a working-class base.

To say this is not to deny that the position and prestige of minority ethnicities and languages have improved in a number of places and, alongside minority movements and political campaigns, popular culture has played a very substantial part in this. But the de-stigmatisation of migrant ethnicities does not happen in a vacuum, and the central argu-ment in this chapter is that, in urban centres in the UK, as perhaps in many other places, ethno-linguistic emancipation actually means integra-tion into the stratified sociolinguistics of social class.

Notes

1. An earlier version of this paper was published in Journal of Pragmatics 43: 1236–1250.
2. This was part of a 28-month ESRC-funded project *Multilingualism and Heteroglossia In and Out of School* (1997–99), and data collection involved interviews, participant observation, radio-microphone recordings of everyday interaction and participant retrospection on extracts from the audio recordings. Analysis focused on four youngsters (two male, two female) in a tutor group of about 30 14-year-olds, and the account of posh and Cockney stylisation centred on c. 65 episodes identified in 37 hours of radio-mic audio data. At Central High itself, about a third of pupils were from refugee and asylum families, over half of the school's pupils received free school meals and almost a third were registered as having special educational needs.
3. The linguistic changes produced over this sequence of turns can be charted as follows:

Figure for Ben Rampton

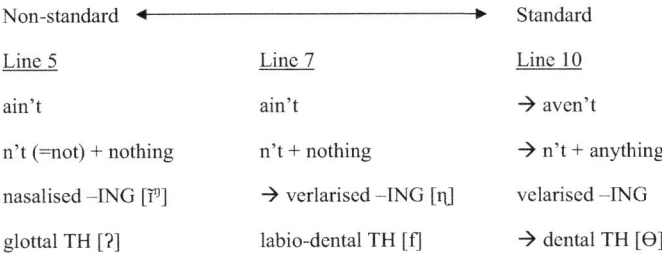

Non-standard ◄————————————►		Standard
Line 5	Line 7	Line 10
ain't	ain't	→ aven't
n't (=not) + nothing	n't + nothing	→ n't + anything
nasalised –ING [ĩⁿ]	→ verlarised –ING [ŋ]	velarised –ING
glottal TH [ʔ]	labio-dental TH [f]	→ dental TH [Θ]

[→ indicates the point where the variable becomes (more) standard]

4. This was an ESRC-funded project entitled *Language Use in the Multiracial Adolescent Peer Group*, and it involved two years of fieldwork with 23 11- to 13-year-olds of Indian, Pakistani, African Caribbean and Anglo descent in 1984, and approximately 64 14- to 16-year olds in 1987. Data-collection focused mainly on a youth club and on lunch and breaktime recreation at school, and included radio-microphone recording (approximately 145 hours), participant observation, interviewing and retrospective participant commentary on extracts of recorded interaction.

References

Agha, A. (2007). *Language and social relations*. Cambridge: Cambridge University Press.

Alim, S., Ibrahim, A., & Pennycook, A. (Eds.). (2009). *Global linguistic flows: Hip hop cultures, youth identities and the politics of language*. London: Routledge.

Androutsopoulos, J. (2001). From the streets to the screens and back again: On the mediated diffusion of ethnolectal patterns in contemporary German. *LAUD Linguistic Agency, Nr A522*, 1–24.

Auer, P., & Dirim, I. (2003). Sociocultural orientation, urban youth styles and the spontaneous acquisition of Turkish by non-Turkish adolescents in Germany. In J. Androutsopoulos & A. Georgakopoulou (Eds.), *Discourse constructions of youth identities* (pp. 223–246). Amsterdam: John Benjamins.

Bourdieu, P. (1977). *Outline of a theory of practice*. Cambridge: Cambridge University Press.

Bourdieu, P. (1991). *Language and symbolic power*. Oxford: Polity Press.

Cohen, P. (1988). Perversions of inheritance: Studies in the making of multiracist Britain. In P. Cohen & H. Bains (Eds.), *Multiracist Britain* (pp. 9–120). Basingstoke: Macmillan.

Cutler, C. A. (1999). Yorkville crossing: White teens, hip hop and African American English. *Journal of Sociolinguistics, 3*(4), 428–443.

Ferguson, C. (1959). Diglossia. *Word, 15*, 325–340.

Gilroy, P. (1987). *There ain't no black in the Union Jack*. London: Hutchinson.

Hall, S. (1988). New ethnicities. *ICA Documents, 7*, 27–31.

Hanks, W. (1996). *Language and communicative practices*. Colorado: Westview Press.

Harris, R., & Rampton, B. (2002). Creole metaphors in cultural analysis: On the limits and possibilities of (socio)linguistics. *Critique of Anthropology, 22*(1), 31–52.

Heller, M. (Ed.). (2007). *Bilingualism: A social approach*. Basingstoke: Palgrave.

Hewitt, R. (1986). *White talk black talk*. Cambridge: Cambridge University Press.

Hill, J. (2004). On where stereotypes come from so that kids can recruit them. *Pragmatics, 14*(2/3), 193–198.

Irvine, J. T. (2001). 'Style' as distinctiveness: The culture and ideology of linguistic differentiation. In P. Eckert & J. Rickford (Eds.), *Style and sociolinguistic variation* (pp. 21–43). Cambridge: Cambridge University Press.

Jaffe, A. (2007). Minority language movements. In M. Heller (Ed.), *Bilingualism. A social approach* (pp. 50–70). Basingstoke: Palgrave.

Jaspers, J. (2005). Linguistic sabotage in a context of monolingualism and standardisation. *Language & Communication, 25*(3), 279–298.

Labov, W. (1972). *Sociolinguistic patterns*. Oxford: Blackwell.

LePage, R. B., & Tabouret-Keller, A. (1985). *Acts of identity*. Cambridge: Cambridge University Press.

Madsen, L. (2015). *Fighters, girls and other identities: Interaction in a martial arts club*. Clevedon: Multilingual Matters.

Mugglestone, L. (1995). *Talking proper*. Oxford: Clarendon Press.

Ortner, S. (1991). Reading America: Preliminary notes on class and culture. In R. Fox (Ed.), *Recapturing anthropology: Working in the present* (pp. 164–189). Santa Fe: School of American Research Press.

Parkin, D. (1977). Emergent and stabilised multilingualism: Polyethnic peer groups in urban Kenya. In H. Giles (Ed.), *Language, ethnicity and intergroup relations* (pp. 185–210). New York: Academic Press.

Paul, G., & Lawrence, E. (1988). Two-tone Britain: White and black youth and the politics of anti-racism. In P. Cohen & H. Bains (Eds.), *Multiracist Britain* (pp. 121–155). Basingstoke: Macmillan.

Pujolar, J. (2007). Bilingualism and the nation state in the post-national era. In M. Heller (Ed.), *Bilingualism. A social approach* (pp. 71–95). Basingstoke: Palgrave.

Rampton, B. (1988). A non-educational view of ESL in Britain. *Journal of Multilingual and Multicultural Development, 9*(6), 503–529.

Rampton, B. (1995/2005). *Crossing: Language and ethnicity among adolescents* (2nd edn.). Manchester: St Jerome.

Rampton, B. (1999). Styling the other: Introduction. *Journal of Sociolinguistics, 3*(4), 421–427.

Rampton, B. (2005). *Language and ethnicity among adolescents*. Manchester/Northampton: St. Jerome Pub.

Rampton, B. (2006). *Language in late modernity: Interaction in an urban school*. Cambridge: Cambridge University Press.

Rampton, B., Maybin, J., & Roberts, C. (2014). Methodological foundations in linguistic ethnography. *Working papers in Urban language and literacies* 125. Available online: https://kcl.academia.edu/WorkingPapersinUrbanLanguage Literacies/Papers

Stallybrass, P., & White, A. (1996). *The politics and poetics of transgression*. London: Methuen.

Stroud, C. (2004). Rinkeby Swedish and semilingualism in language ideological debates: A Bourdieuean perspective. *Journal of SocioLinguistics, 8*(2), 196–214.

Urla, J. (1995). Outlaw language. *Pragmatics, 5*(2), 245–261.

Willis, P. (1977). *Learning to labour*. Farnborough: Saxon House.

6

The Perceptual Dialectology of England

Chris Montgomery

Introduction

This chapter examines the perceptual dialectology of England, that is, the perception of the dialect landscape in the country from the perspective of non-linguists. It is vital that we have as full a picture of the ways in which language users themselves think about language variation in order to understand the sociolinguistics of England. To this end, the chapter first deals with one of the traditional methods used to gain such a picture: research performed using the methods of language attitudes studies. After this, I move on to discuss perceptual dialectology research undertaken in various sites over the past 13 years, examining the main geographical patterns in non-linguists' perceptions. Qualitative data relating to perceptions of dialects and dialect areas is then considered, and compared to findings from language attitudes studies.

C. Montgomery (✉)
University of Sheffield, Sheffield, UK

© The Author(s) 2018
N. Braber, S. Jansen (eds.), *Sociolinguistics in England*,
DOI 10.1057/978-1-137-56288-3_6

Perceptual Dialectology and Language Regard

Research focusing on the perceptions of language from the perspective of non-linguists has a relatively long tradition in Great Britain (e.g. Giles 1970; Giles and Bourhis 1976; Giles et al. 1990; Coupland et al. 1994; Inoue 1996; Bishop et al. 2005; Coupland and Bishop 2007; Pearce 2009). These investigations have used two main techniques, either following the tradition of language attitudes study (i.e. Lambert et al. 1960) or using approaches associated with perceptual dialectology (e.g. Preston 1989)—a field of study which aims to address the following questions:

(a) How different from (or similar to) their own do respondents find the speech of other areas?
(b) What [i.e. where] do respondents believe the dialect areas of a region to be?
(c) What do respondents believe about the characteristics of regional speech?
(d) Where do respondent believe taped voices to be from?
(e) What anecdotal evidence do respondents provide concerning their perceptions of language variation? (Preston 1988: 475–476)

Although necessarily concerned with the attitudes towards regional speech held by non-linguists, perceptual dialectology has at its heart the investigation of the way in which lay people perceive the dialect landscape (either of a country, region or city). This introduces a dialect geography element to the field of study, and 'represents the dialectologist's-sociolinguist's-variationist's interest in folk linguistics' (Preston 1999a: xxv).

Indeed, a focus on lay people's perceptions of areal linguistics was a deliberate departure from the traditions of language attitudes study, which most typically asked respondents to react either to voice samples or concepts (dialect/sociolect labels) and indicate their attitudes to the stimuli. Such an approach to the study of dialect perceptions troubled Dennis Preston, who claimed that it did not assess whether informants had a 'mental construct of a "place"…[or]…their mental maps of regional speech areas' (Preston 2002: 51). Thus, as linguists examined non-linguists' evaluative responses to concepts or vocal stimuli, they did not examine where informants' thought voices came from, or if they knew the meaning of the concepts that they were presented with.

Although I have separated the language attitude and perceptual dialectology approaches above, developments in the methods and approaches to perceptual dialectology have made for a rapprochement between the two fields, with Preston stating that 'any study of responses to regional speech is an integral part of the perceptual dialectology enterprise' (Preston 1999a: xxxviii). As a result, clear dividing lines between the two fields are blurred to the extent that Garrett (2010) includes a chapter on perceptual dialectology in his book on language attitudes. In addition, Preston now uses the umbrella term 'language regard',[1] which covers:

> all approaches to the study of non-specialist belief about and reaction to language use, structure diversification, history, and status, and none of the various approaches that have concerned themselves directly with such matters - the ethnography of speaking and language (and various aspects of anthropological linguistics in general), language ideology, the social psychology of language, the sociology of language, and folk linguistics (including perceptual dialectology) - is excluded (Preston 2011: 10).

Accordingly, in this chapter, I will discuss research from the range of language regard studies relating to English dialects over the course of the last 45 years, examining perceptions of the dialect landscape along with perceptions of the characteristics and evaluations of dialect areas over time. The following section will introduce the major studies of language regard in England before I move on to discuss more recent perceptual dialectology research undertaken by myself.

Language Regard in England

As noted above, Great Britain has been well served in the field of language regard studies. Given the make-up of the country, however, few studies have focused exclusively on England. Most have investigated regard of language used in England as well as the other constituent countries of the nation. In this section I will discuss such studies, as well as those that have investigated perceptions of smaller regions, although I will only report results from England. I will commence with studies conducted within the language attitudes paradigm.

Language Attitudes Studies in England

An attitude is a disposition 'to react favourably or unfavourably to a class of objects' (Sarnoff 1970: 279). Language attitudes research investigates 'people's disposition to respond negatively or positively to a language (or language variety) and/or its speakers' (Smith 1998: 14). Garrett et al. (2003: 23) cite three main methods for obtaining language attitudes: *societal treatment* approaches, *direct* approaches and *indirect* approaches. The societal treatment and direct approaches will not be my concern here due to the fact that most language attitudes studies in England (and the ones most directly relevant to the data I will present later) have taken place using indirect approaches. Such approaches involve 'engaging in more subtle, and sometimes even deceptive, techniques than directly asking questions' (Garrett et al. 2003: 23).

The indirect approach is 'generally seen as synonymous with the matched-guise technique [MGT]' (Garrett et al. 2003: 23), which has been one of the most successful and enduring methodologies for investigating language attitudes. Stemming from studies performed by social psychologists (Lambert et al. 1960), the MGT involves listeners hearing samples of speech from a single speaker who has assumed multiple *guises* (dialects, accents or languages). From this, listeners are asked to rate each guise along evaluative scales. The use of only one speaker assuming guises allows controllability, ensuring that the researcher can eliminate any attitudes that the listener may have about voice quality or other variables inherent with different speakers.

Despite this, the MGT approach is problematic, not least because that in order for the technique to be successful, the speaker must be particularly competent in the guises they assume in order that the results are reliable. In addition, Preston has expressed reservations about the effectiveness of the MGT due to the 'gross, stereotypical imitations of varieties' used in such studies (1999b: 369). One way to overcome the problem of accent-authenticity is to use a verbal-guise approach, in which guises are spoken by different speakers but with the same content (Garrett 2010: 42), although this does not avoid other problems inherent with presenting numerous guises to listeners (discussed in Garrett et al. (2003: 59–61)). As a result, some studies have chosen to use conceptual approaches, which involve the use of dialect area labels as attitude objects and eliminate the need to play samples to respondents entirely, inviting 'people to explore the meaning associations of a simple (and arguably "pure") sociolinguistic concept[s]' (Coupland and Bishop 2007: 75).

Typically, respondents in indirect studies of language attitudes have been presented with a number of scales along which they are asked to provide ratings for stimuli to which they have been exposed. These scales vary from study to study, but largely map on to notions of prestige (or correctness) and pleasantness, which [along with dynamism (Kristiansen et al. 2005: 16)] previous research has found 'are highly productive and inclusive dimensions in the social evaluation of regional and social speech varieties' (Coupland and Bishop 2007: 77). Principal findings from the indirect approach to the study of language attitudes has found disparities between perceived 'standard' and 'non-standard' varieties, with an inverse relationship between the two. Therefore, there appears to be 'a general tendency to relate linguistic standardness with intelligence' (Clopper and Pisoni 2002: 273), in contrasts to evaluations of non-standard varieties which rate highly on social attractiveness scales (Paltridge and Giles 1984: 71).

The first language attitudes research undertaken in England was completed by Strongman and Woosley (1967), who undertook a MGT using *Yorkshire* and *Londoner* speakers speaking using their own accent and the accent of the other location (four samples in total). Listeners were split into two groups, northern and southern, and were asked to rate the samples. The Yorkshire samples were judged by both groups of respondents to be 'more honest and reliable than the London speakers and the London speakers to be more self-confident than the Yorkshire' (Strongman and Woosley 1967: 167). There were also some differences between the groups, with the Yorkshire samples judged more industrious by northerners and more serious by southerners. The northern raters 'also judged the Yorkshire speakers to be more generous, good-natured and kind-hearted than the London speakers, whom they rated as slightly more mean, irritable and hard' (Strongman and Woosley 1967: 167). A further study by Cheyne (1970) was also undertaken using a MGT approach, although this is less relevant as it looked only at differences in the perceptions of 'Scottish' and 'English' accents.

Giles (1970) undertook a more substantial piece of research using both MGT and conceptual methods to investigate attitudes to a number of regional and national varieties of English. This research used two groups of respondents—one of the mean age of 12 years 3 months and the other of 17 years 4 months. Respondents were presented with three seven-point rating scales (relating to prestige, pleasantness and dynamism) for both the MGT and conceptual components of the research. Most varieties were presented as both vocal and conceptual stimuli (vocal stimuli consisted of a voice sample, and conceptual stimuli consisted only of the dialect area label), although there were a greater number of conceptual stimuli.

Giles' findings (1970: 218) are shown (for English varieties) in Tables 6.1 (vocal stimuli) and 6.2 (conceptual stimuli). Giles found little disagreement between the two age groups in relation to their ratings of vocal stimuli (with the exception of ratings on the status dimension). There was also little difference in the rank ordering of the vocal and conceptual stimuli, with RP generally occupying the highest rank positions, and Birmingham the lowest.

Table 6.1 Giles' (1970: 218) results for English varieties, vocal stimuli (mean ratings shown in parentheses)

Rank	Aesthetic content	Rank	Communicative content	Rank	Status content
1	RP (2.9)	1	RP (3.1)	1	RP (3.1)
2	Northern English (4.0)	2	Northern English (4.3)	2	Affected RP (5.0)
3	Somerset (4.3)		Somerset (4.3)	3	Northern English (4.3)
4	Cockney (4.6)	4	Cockney (4.6)		Somerset (4.3)
5	Affected RP (4.8)	5	Affected RP (5.0)	5	Cockney (4.6)
6	Birmingham (5.1)	6	Birmingham (5.0)	6	Birmingham (5.0)

In Tables 6.1 and 6.2, lower scores equal more favourable ratings

Table 6.2 Giles' (1970: 218) results for English varieties, conceptual stimuli (mean ratings shown in parentheses)

Rank	Aesthetic content	Rank	Communicative content	Rank	Status content
1	RP (2.5)	1	'Accent identical to your own' (1.5)	1	RP (1.9)
2	'Accent identical to your own' (2.9)	2	RP (2.3)	2	'Accent identical to your own' (3.3)
3	Northern English (4.0)	3	Northern English (3.9)	3	Northern English (4.3)
	Somerset (4.0)	4	Somerset (4.0)		Somerset (4.3)
5	Birmingham (4.7)	5	Liverpool (4.4)	5	Liverpool (5.0)
	Liverpool (4.7)	6	Cockney (4.7)	6	Cockney (5.1)
7	Cockney (4.8)		Birmingham (4.7)		Birmingham (5.1)

After Giles, further research into the attitudes held about English varieties was undertaken by Trudgill (1983), who although not presenting numerical data relating to the ratings given for samples played to listeners in a verbal-guise study, does give a rank-order of the perceived pleasantness of the samples (RP>Bradford>Tyneside>Gloucestershire>Liverpool> West Midlands>London) (Trudgill 1983: 222).

It was not until 2004 that a further piece of research dealing with perceptions of numerous regional varieties of English in a similar fashion to Giles was conducted. This research, undertaken as part of the BBC Voices project, is reported in Bishop et al. (2005), and Coupland and Bishop (2007). BBC Voices was 'conceived in the British Broadcasting Corporation [BBC] to take a "snapshot" of the everyday speech and speech-attitudes... at the start of the twenty-first century' (Upton and Davies 2013: i). As part of the project, a conceptual study comprised of 34 varieties was administered by a market research company, gathering 5010 responses from individuals over the age of 15 (Bishop et al. 2005: 133). Respondents were asked to judge each concept using seven-point rating scales for a number of attitudinal dimensions, with those for prestige and social attractiveness reported in the two articles. Making comparisons with Giles' findings from over 30 years prior to the new research, Bishop et al. found small differences between the ratings of concepts common to both pieces of research. Overall, though, there is shown to be remarkable consistency, revealing 'relatively pure and pernicious ideologies' (Bishop et al. 2005: 152) towards varieties of English over time.

The attitudinal picture was updated nearly ten years after the BBC Voices research via data gathered by the political polling company ComRes (see http://www.comres.co.uk/) on behalf of ITV News; 4020 adults from across Great Britain were interviewed online between 2 and 11 August 2013 as part of the usual tracker poll for voting intention, along with other questions about stories in the news. Respondents were presented with ten varieties (seven of them from England) and asked to rate them along five-point scales of 'Friendliness' and 'Intelligence'. The data from the ComRes research are presented alongside the concept study results from Giles (1970) and the BBC Voices data (Bishop et al. 2005; Coupland and Bishop 2007) in Figs. 6.1 and 6.2 below.

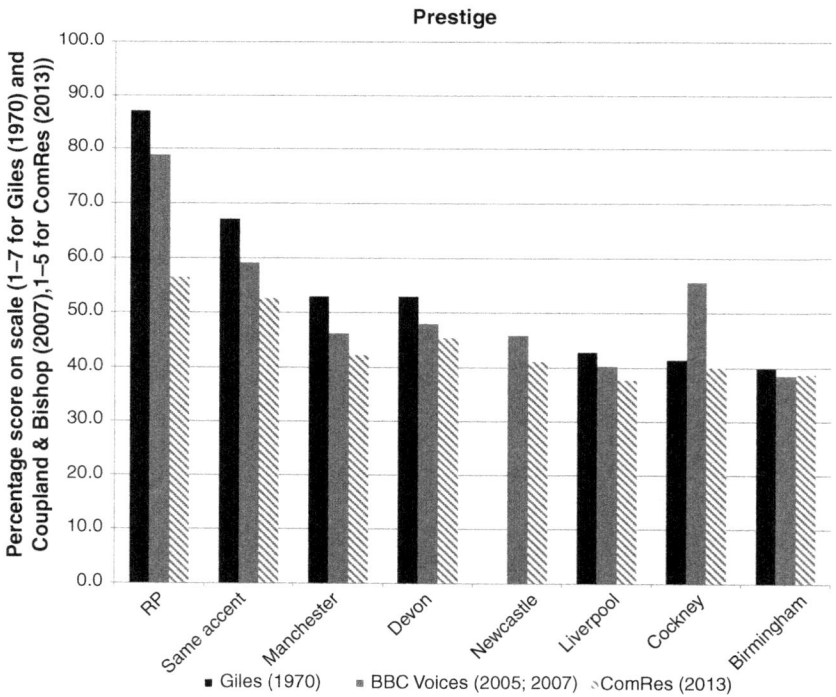

Fig. 6.1   Results for prestige from 43 years of language attitudes research in England

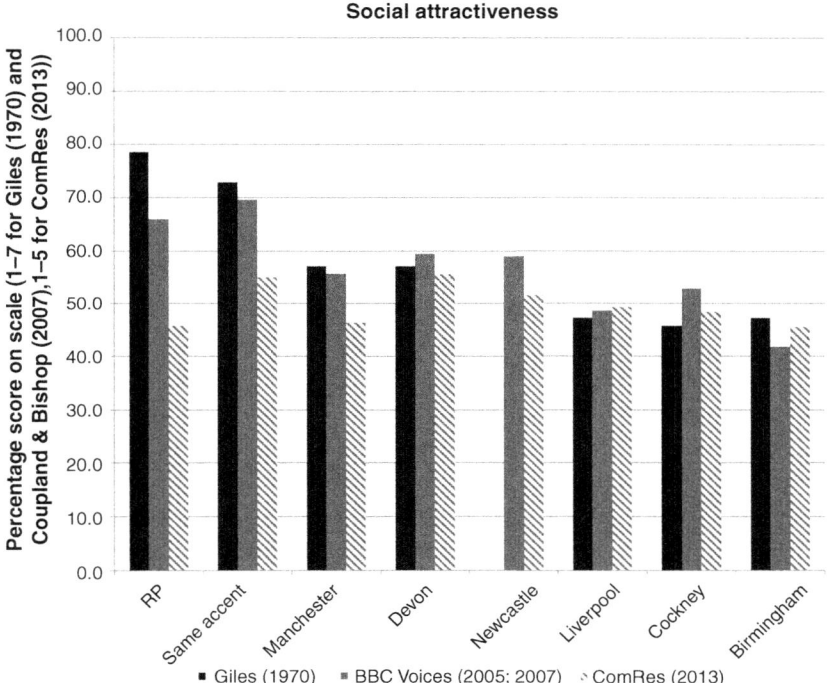

Fig. 6.2 Results for social attractiveness from 43 years of language attitudes research in England

For prestige, the ComRes data generally reveal a downward trend in the ratings, as Bishop et al. noted between Giles' data and the BBC Voices data (2005: 139). Despite this, the rank ordering of the concepts for prestige is very similar to that of both Giles and the BBC Voices survey. Ratings for social attractiveness are again generally lower than those in the previous research, although the differences between Giles' data and the BBC Voices data are amplified in the ComRes poll. RP, in particular, is dramatically downgraded for social attractiveness and is judged the least attractive of all of the English concepts. Other patterns are similar to those in previous research, although the position of the Manchester concept is notably lower than in earlier studies.

Taken together, the three main pieces of language attitudes research noted above reveal a particularly rigid set of attitudes towards the varieties that have been included in attitudes surveys. The latest data continue the trend of 'accent prejudice' noted in the title of Bishop et al.'s (2005) paper, and suggest that similar consistency would be exhibited in other studies of language regard. I deal with previous perceptual dialectology studies in the next section.

Perceptual Dialectology Studies in England

The field of perceptual dialectology has developed a number of methods, although the field is perhaps best known for its use of the *draw-a-map* task (Preston 1982). Such tasks involve respondents drawing lines on a blank or minimally detailed map indicating where they believe dialect areas to exist. Data are then processed by counting lines in order to assess the 'perceptual prominence' of dialect areas (e.g. Preston 1989), and by various compositing techniques which produce aggregate maps of dialect perceptions (see Montgomery and Stoeckle 2013 for an overview of these techniques).

It is not without reason that the draw-a-map task is most associated with perceptual dialectology, as it is this that has been most used in studies worldwide (e.g. Preston 1986; Inoue 1996; Long 1999a; Diercks 2002; Fought 2002; Bucholtz et al. 2007; Cramer 2010; Cukor-Avila et al. 2012; Montgomery 2012). Although I will concentrate my discussion below on the results of draw-a-map tasks, it is important to note that other methods are also part of the perceptual dialectology toolkit. These include ratings tasks similar to those used in language attitudes research (but focusing on 'cognitively real' (Preston 1999b: 368) dialect areas), research investigating the placement of voice samples (e.g. Preston 1996; Plichta and Preston 2005; Montgomery 2011) and qualitative techniques assessing interview data for anecdotal evidence of perceptions of dialect areas (e.g. Niedzielski and Preston 2003; Montgomery 2014). In addition, qualitative data from draw-a-map tasks have been analysed via various means (Coupland et al. 1994; Garrett et al. 1995; Williams et al. 1996; Long 1999b). I will discuss such qualitative data alongside the quantitative draw-a-map data in the following sections.

Other than my own research in England, there have been three other pieces of perceptual dialectology research dealing with the country (Inoue 1996; Pearce 2009; Braber 2015, 2016). Only one of these, conducted by Inoue (1996) in 1989, dealt with national perceptions as my research, described below, does. In order for it to remain proximal to my similar research, I will discuss Inoue's research at the end of this section.

The research conducted by Pearce took place in North East England— an area that has attracted considerable recent interest in production studies (see Watt and Milroy 1999; Beal and Corrigan 2000; Watt 2002; Beal and Corrigan 2005; Burbano-Elizondo 2006; Llamas 2007; Beal 2009; Beal et al. 2012) and is an important perceptual location for many respondents in national perception studies (see Inoue (1996), and below). Pearce's study was quite different to other perceptual dialectology studies that have conducted in England in that he used a method from earlier approaches to the study of dialect perception that used a questionnaire to directly assess respondents' perception of similarity and difference between themselves and others in their region (cf. Weijnen 1946). Participants in the study were asked to consider 51 locations and 'were invited to think about the speech of people in each of these places, assessing the extent of its similarity to or difference from the speech of people in their own hometown' (Pearce 2009: 5). Responses were scored on a one to six scale, with an option for respondents to state that they had not heard of a particular location or could not give a response.

Using the questionnaire data, Pearce adopted the *little arrow* method (Weijnen 1946), in which lines are drawn connecting locations that are perceived to be similar. Pearce was able to identify three perceptual *sectors* and seven *zones* subdividing these sectors, and was able to compare his data to production data to 'suggest that informants are potentially responding to "real" linguistic variation in their judgments of similarity and difference and not simply basing their assessments on broader non-linguistic perceptions' (Pearce 2009: 27). These findings underline the importance of scale in perceptual dialectology studies (where, as the research by Braber discussed below demonstrates, larger-scale maps will produce different results to small-scale ones), as well as pointing to the importance of using a range of techniques in order to uncover nuanced perceptions of dialect variation.

Braber's (2016) research focussed on the East Midlands region. This region is one 'not seen as being an obvious candidate for having regional variation' (Braber 2016: 218) amongst the wider population (cf. Inoue 1996 and my research discussed below). Using respondents from Nottingham, a large city in the East Midlands, Braber's research involved them conducting tasks including a draw-a-map task, a voice location task and an innovative *mind map* task (Braber 2016: 214–215). Braber's draw-a-map task requested respondents to add lines to a map of the British Isles, and saw familiar dialect areas drawn (e.g. Liverpool, Newcastle and Birmingham), as well as a Nottingham area drawn by 29% of her respondents, which represented the tenth most frequently recognised area. Although it might have been tempting to conclude from this result that the East Midlands region and other subdivisions within it were not perceptually salient, Braber's mind map task was able to shed more light on a more complex situation.

In the mind map task, a small number of respondents in groups of three were given a map of the East Midlands along with felt-tip pens. They were 'asked to talk about (and write down) language in their local and surrounding areas' (Braber 2016: 220), and specifically to reflect on where differences started to occur, and to provide examples of local lexis and pronunciation by writing on the maps. Six mind maps were completed, which revealed a much more detailed perceptual picture than that captured by the national draw-a-map task. As with Pearce's research discussed above, working at a smaller scale enabled Braber to understand the perception of variation in a more nuanced fashion than with a larger-scale map. This is the effect of proximity, which (as I discuss below) results in respondents being likely to know more about their local surroundings than those further afield. Such proximity effects can also be seen using large-scale maps that aim to gather the national picture of perception, which was the aim of the first perceptual dialectology study in England, undertaken by Inoue (1996).

Inoue's data were gathered in 1989 during a visit to Essex University and involved students completing a questionnaire which contained a draw-a-map task (Inoue 1996: 144), along with another listening task not relevant to this chapter. Inoue used a map that included county boundaries as his base map, which means that it differs from the maps used in my research. It seems from an example map included by Inoue in his paper (1996: 147) that the county lines were used to some extent as a guide to map completion but were not traced around by respondents. The county boundaries were, however, used by Inoue when calculating his composite map of his respondents' data, seen in Fig. 6.3.

Inoue gives little numerical data to accompany his map (although he does state that Scottish, Welsh and Irish were the most frequently drawn areas (1996: 151)); therefore, assessing the degree of perceptual prominence attached to each of the aggregate areas is not possible. More detail can be added to the map (although not in respect of the geographical boundaries of the areas) by combining the labels from Fig. 6.1 with those also included in Inoue's multivariate analysis of English dialects (1996: 153). Here, additional subdivisions of *Home Counties*, *Cockney* and *London* are given for the southern region; *Brummy* for the Midland region; and *Lancashire* for the northern region. This reveals a little more complexity in the perceptions of Inoue's respondents. Despite his method of data analysis and the lack of a full set of numerical data, Inoue's investigation sheds an important light on the perception of the dialect landscape from over 25 years ago. The next section will introduce my research, the results of which I will compare with the studies discussed above.

Studies, Respondents and Methods

The data presented in the remainder of this chapter are drawn from three perceptual dialectology studies undertaken over the last 13 years. All use the same method, outlined below, and involve respondents drawn from school and sixth-form colleges across the North and Midlands of England. The three projects all had slightly differing aims,[2] and survey locations were chosen accordingly. Despite this, the data are comparable and, when taken with Inoue's (1996) data, can be used to investigate stability and change in the geographical perceptions of English dialect areas over the last 25 years. Figure 6.4 shows the survey locations, along with other locations mentioned in this chapter, and Table 6.3 presents brief details of the respondents involved in each of the studies.

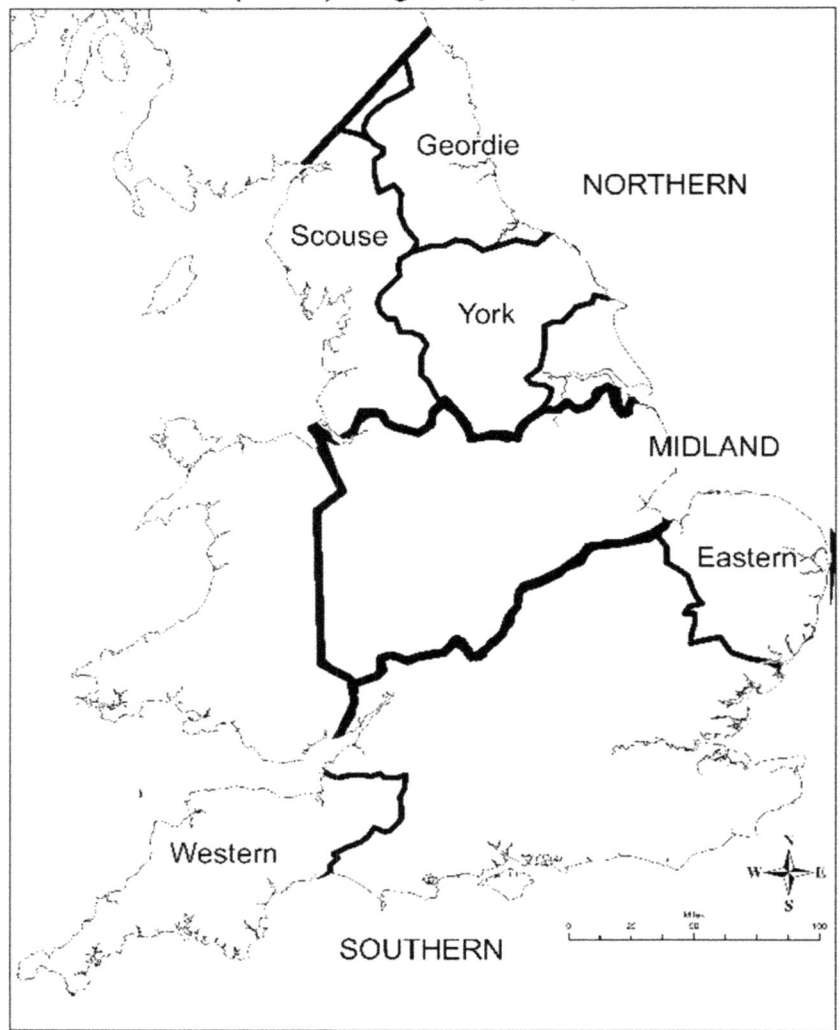

Fig. 6.3   Inoue's map of perceptual dialect areas in England (Redrawn from Inoue (1996: 149))

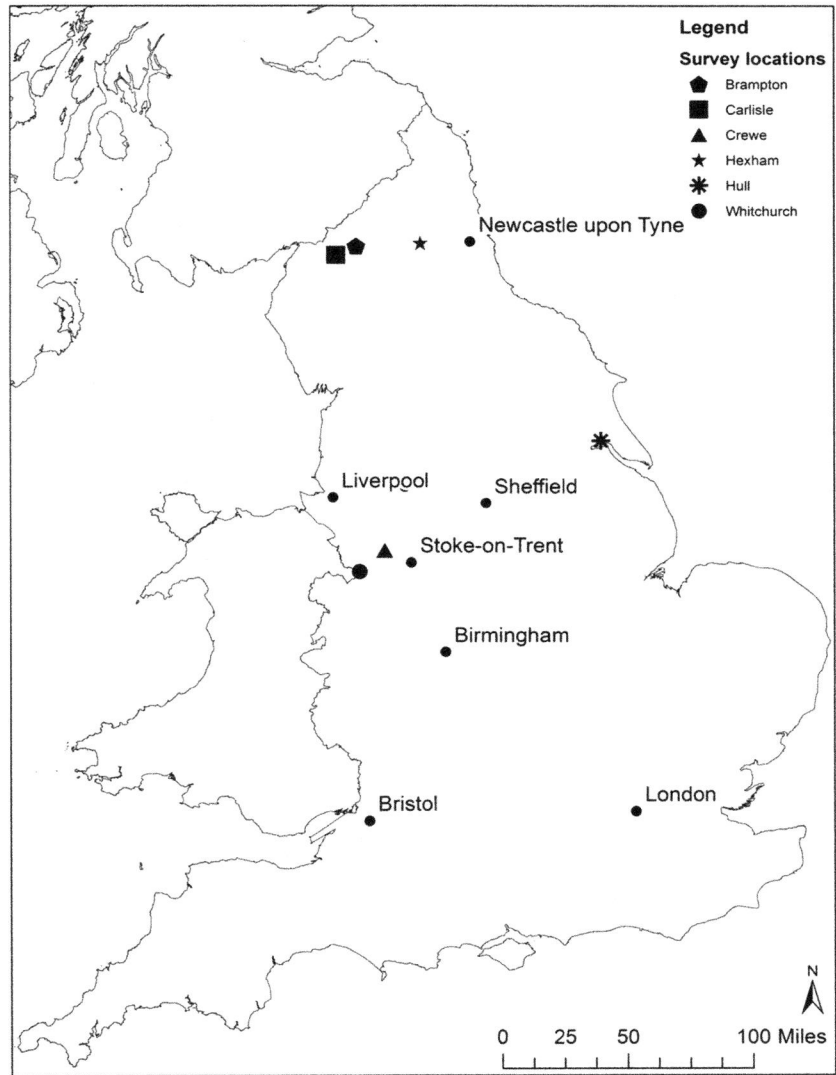

Fig. 6.4 Survey locations and other places mentioned in this chapter (This figure contains national statistics data, NISRA data, NRS data and Ordnance Survey data, all of which are © Crown copyright and database right 2013. Additional location data is © Crown Copyright and database rights 2016. Ordnance Survey (Digimap Licence))

Table 6.3 Respondent details for each survey

Study	Locations	Respondents		Total	Mean age
		Male	Female		
Study 1 (data	Carlisle	39	54	93	23.1
collected in 2004)	Crewe	21	64	85	16.5
	Hull	34	62	96	19
			Total	274	19
Study 2 (data	Galashiels	6	12	18	16.4
collected in 2008)	Moffat	19	19	38	16.2
	Langholm	6	14	20	16.5
	Hexham	9	11	20	16.5
	Brampton	17	38	55	17
			Total	151	16.5
Study 3 (data	Whitchurch	5	6	11	16.5
collected in 2014)					
			Total	11	16.5
			Grand total	436	

Respondents from each of the survey locations were given a minimally detailed map which contained information relating to country borders, along with city location dots[3] and were asked to add data to the map with a pen or pencil by responding to the following questions:

1. Label the nine well-known cites marked with a dot on the map.
2. Do you think that there is a north–south language divide in the country? If so, draw a line where you think this is.
3. Draw lines on the map where you think there are regional speech (dialect) areas.
4. Label the different areas that you have drawn on the map.
5. What do you think of the areas you've just drawn? How might you recognise people from these areas? Write some of these thoughts on the map if you have time.

In this chapter, I will focus on the data collected from parts 2–5 of the task. After their completion, maps in all studies were examined for geographical consistency, and any with incorrect city labels were discarded. Line data representing perceptual areas were counted in order to give a rank ordering of perceptual prominence, and to choose which areas to aggregate. Qualitative data from step 5 of the task was extracted from all maps in order to assess the attitudes held for the areas drawn on the maps.

At the aggregation stage, data collected in study 1 were processed using Onishi and Long's (1997) PDQ software, which produced basic aggregate area data. These data were later manipulated using Geographical Information Systems (GIS) software in order to facilitate comparisons with the data from the later studies. These data were processed using a GIS, following the methods outlined in Montgomery and Stoeckle (2013). The GIS processing method produces maps showing the extent of dialect areas as well as the level of informant agreement over their placement using gradient shading.

In the following sections of this chapter, I will first examine the numerical and aggregate dialect area data in order to understand the geographical perceptions of the dialect landscape of England, before moving on to consider what respondents say about these cognitively real areas.

Patterns in the Perception of English Dialect Areas

My research over the last 13 years, and that of Inoue's, points towards a relatively stable set of factors influencing the geographical perception of English dialect areas. I consider these factors—namely, *proximity*, *cultural prominence* and *claiming/denial*—after presenting the numerical data relating to the perceptual prominence of dialect areas over the three studies. These data can be found in Table 6.4, and show the number of lines drawn for each area by respondents in the studies. Figures in parentheses relate to the recognition rate for each area, which is the percentage of respondents who drew lines for the area.

Proximity

Following Tobler's (1970: 236) first law of geography, that 'everything is related to everything else, but near things are more related to each other',

Table 6.4 Numerical results from studies 1–3, showing 15 most frequently drawn areas across all studies

Overall rank	Dialect area	Study 1			Study 2		Study 3	Total
		Carlisle	Crewe	Hull	Hexham	Brampton	Whitchurch	
		(n = 92)	(n = 85)	(n = 96)	(n = 20)	(n = 55)	(n = 11)	(n = 359)
1	Scouse	55 (59.7)	67 (78.8)	46 (47.9)	10 (50)	43 (78.18)	9 (81.82)	230 (64.07)
2	Geordie	60 (65.2)	56 (65.8)	47 (48.9)	13 (65)	42 (76.36)	7 (63.64)	225 (62.67)
3	Brummie	43 (46.7)	65 (76.4)	45 (46.8)	9 (45)	32 (58.18)	10 (90.91)	204 (56.82)
4	Manc	38 (41.3)	48 (56.4)	26 (27.1)	10 (50)	30 (54.55)	7 (63.64)	159 (44.29)
5	Cockney	39 (42.3)	43 (50.5)	28 (29.1)	10 (50)	30 (54.55)	4 (36.36)	154 (42.9)
6	Yorkshire	10 (10.8)	12 (14.1)	34 (35.4)	6 (30)	17 (30.91)	1 (9.09)	80 (22.28)
7	Cumbrian	31 (33.7)	1 (1.2)	1 (1)	5 (25)	26 (47.27)	–	64 (17.83)
8	Cornwall	9 (9.7)	14 (16.5)	5 (5.2)	2 (10)	5 (9.09)	1 (9.09)	36 (10.03)
9	London	5 (5.4)	6 (7.1)	9 (9.4)	2 (10)	9 (16.36)	2 (18.18)	33 (9.19)
10	West Country	10 (10.8)	7 (8.2)	5 (5.2)	5 (25)	4 (7.27)	–	31 (8.64)
11	Bristol	–	4 (4.7)	4 (4.2)	2 (10)	6 (10.9)	5 (45.5)	21 (5.85)
12	Lancashire	8 (8.7)	–	5 (5.2)	–	3 (5.45)	–	16 (4.46)
13	Potteries	1 (1.1)	13 (15.3)	–	–	–	–	14 (3.9)
14	East Anglia	2 (2.2)	2 (2.4)	6 (6.25)	–	–	–	10 (2.79)
15	South West	–	–	10 (10.4)	–	–	–	10 (2.79)

The dialect area names reflect those most frequently provided by respondents and relate to the following locations: Scouse-Liverpool; Geordie-Newcastle upon Tyne; Brummie-Birmingham; Manc-Manchester; Cockney-East London; Potteries-Stoke-on-Trent proximity is one of the most important factors that conditions the way in which dialect areas are perceived. This was an initial finding of early perceptual dialectology research, and Preston found that (after drawing stigmatised areas), informants would add 'local areas more frequently' (1999b: xxxiv). Examination of Table 6.4 demonstrates the importance of proximity across all locations in all studies. This can most clearly be seen in the inclusion of *home* areas for each survey location, so a *Cumbria* area is drawn by respondents from Carlisle and Brampton,[4] and the *Yorkshire* area was added by the highest percentage of respondents from Hull. Not included in Table 6.4, due to its lack of prominence for other locations, is the *Shropshire* area, which was added by five respondents from Whitchurch. Near-to areas can also be seen to be important for respondents, with the *Potteries* area drawn by 13 respondents from Crewe (and no other respondents in other locations, with the exception of one person from Hull). The *Geordie* area is also most frequently drawn of all areas by respondents from Hexham, and the *Brummie* area by those from Whitchurch. Although this does not result in the most frequent perception for all local areas as Preston suggested was the case in earlier research outwith England, the increased likelihood of local areas' appearance in Table 6.4 is notable. What is perhaps more notable than this is the relative stability over the studies of the overall most frequently drawn areas. To understand this stability, I turn to the next factor in the perception of dialect areas in England: cultural prominence.

Cultural Prominence

The top five most frequently perceived dialect areas overall, *Scouse*, *Geordie*, *Brummie*, *Manc* and *Cockney*, lie in the top-ranking positions for all survey locations with the exception of Hull, where *Manc* and *Cockney* were less frequently drawn than *Yorkshire* (see Section 5.3 for a discussion of the 'claiming' of this area by Hull-based respondents). One might be tempted to draw the conclusion from this finding that, due to the city-focussed nature of the areas, respondents were simply noting large cities when drawing their areas. However, as I have demonstrated elsewhere (Montgomery and Beal 2011), there is no relationship between the population of cities and their recognition in the draw-a-map tasks.

Instead, I argue here (as I have elsewhere (Montgomery 2012, 2016)) that cultural prominence, or the prominence of the dialect area in the public consciousness via media exposure, results in the more frequent area drawing shown in Table 6.4. That the respondents in the three studies were drawing dialect areas, as opposed to cultural areas based on other considerations, is confirmed in the next section dealing with characteristics and evaluations of the areas, but why these areas were drawn and not others can be best explained via an understanding of the way in which areas can rise to prominence. Such a rise in cultural prominence can be observed by comparing numerical and map-based results from my research to those from Inoue's work. Figures 6.5 and 6.6 show composite map data from studies 1 and 2.[5]

Taken with the data in Table 6.4, the composite maps in Figs. 6.5 and 6.6 show a high level of consistency, not only in relation to the rank ordering of the dialect areas but also the placement and extent of the areas when drawn by respondents. Individual maps from study 3 also show similar patterns, the impact of local areas excepted. However, Inoue's aggregate map shown Fig. 6.3 differs in key respects to those based on my respondents' data. Starting in the North of England and working south, Inoue's map appears to be much more generalised than either Fig. 6.4 or 6.5. The major divisions of *Scouse* and *Geordie* appear, as does the *York(shire)* area. These areas mask others seen in my data, especially *Manc*, which I return to below. Further south, although Inoue's map does not show a *Brummie* area, this is one of the areas mentioned as being drawn by Inoue; so one must assume that a number of his respondents recognised it. East Anglia is subdivided by both Inoue's respondents and mine from study 1. By contrast, Inoue's South Western area generalises an area given numerous further divisions by respondents in all three of my studies (respondents draw a *West Country* area, as well as *Cornwall* and *Bristol*). There is less division of the South by respondents in my research, perhaps reflecting less recognition of dialect variation here due to the impact of proximity.

It is the finding in relation to *Manc* that I believe to be the most important here. This area goes from no recognition amongst Inoue's respondents to an overall rate of recognition of 44.3% amongst respondents in my studies. This suggests an important change in the perception of this area.

Montgomery's (2007) English perceptual areas

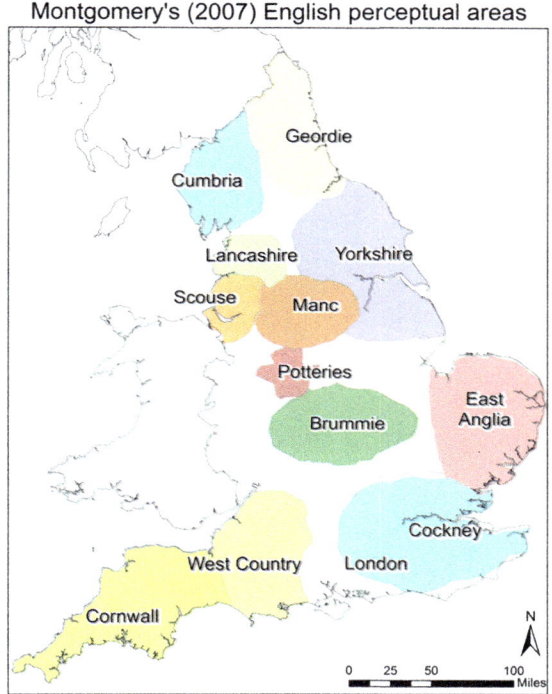

Fig. 6.5   Geographical results from study 1

I deal with this change much more extensively elsewhere (Montgomery 2016), and there is not space here to enter into too much detail, although I will briefly account for the increase in recognition. Based on analysis of newspaper coverage of Manchester, I have demonstrated a significant increase in the number of mentions of the city and the city-region since the time of Inoue's research. Important factors in this increased coverage included the Manchester music scene of the late 1980s and early 1990s, the IRA bombing of the city centre and its subsequent redevelopment, the city's hosting of the Commonwealth Games in 2002 and the founding of the Premier League, whose pre-eminent team until recent years was Manchester United. Coverage of these events, and others, led to a dramatic increase in media representations of Manchester which went hand in hand with the increased perception of a dialect area based on the city.

Montgomery's (2012) English perceptual areas

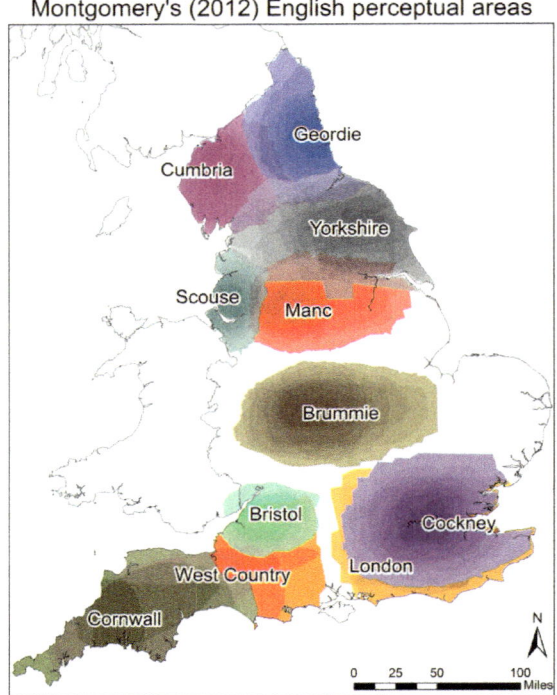

Fig. 6.6 Geographical results from study 2

This is the impact of cultural prominence, which serves to 'boost' some locations (and possibly suppress others) in the popular consciousness, resulting in a greater awareness of dialects based within them.

Claiming and Denial

The phenomena of *claiming* and *denial* have been discussed elsewhere in relation to the way in which voice samples might be (mis)recognised on the basis of the way in which they are perceived (Williams et al. 1999; Montgomery 2011). This phenomenon can also been seen in the way in which people perceive their linguistic landscape. Take the *Yorkshire* dialect area in study 1, noted above. Figure 6.7 shows this to be an area that it claimed by respondents from Hull as their own.

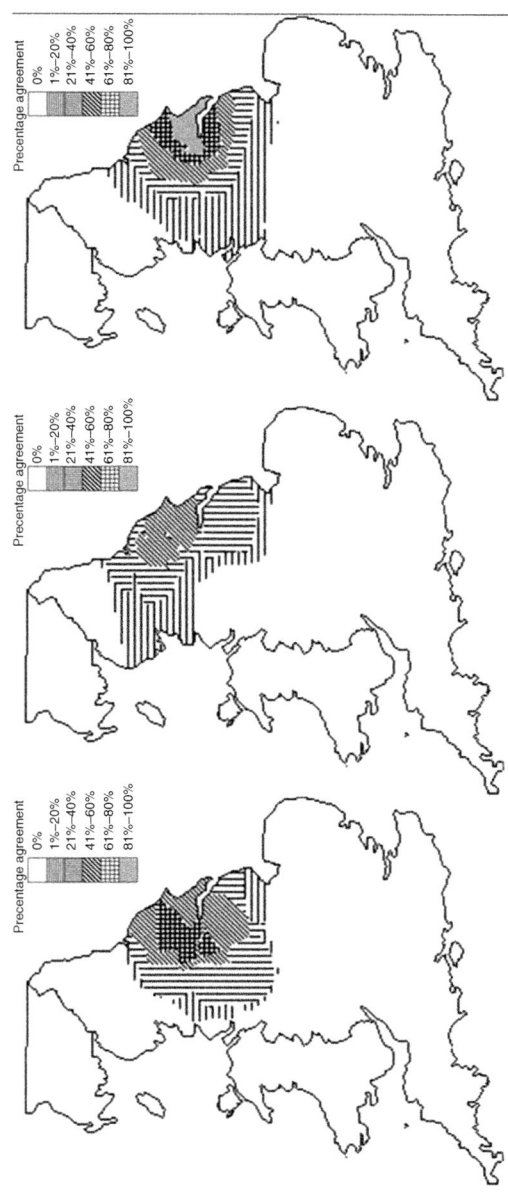

Fig. 6.7 Map-based perceptions of the Yorkshire dialect area by respondents from Carlisle (*left*), Crewe (*middle*) and Hull (*right*)

Rather than the slightly diffuse notion of the region drawn by Crewe- and Carlisle-based respondents, the Hull respondents draw the area centred very tightly on the city itself. This appears to send the message that 'Hull is Yorkshire', and effectively claims the wider county as belonging to the city.

A further instance of the way in which non-linguists position themselves in relation to dialect areas can be seen in the way in which respondents completed the north–south divide component of the draw-a-map task. As I discuss in more detail elsewhere (Montgomery 2015), respondents in Crewe, close to the generally agreed location of the north–south divide in England,[6] 'shift' the boundary further south so as to safeguard their status as 'northerners'. As the next section of this chapter demonstrates, qualitative data from draw-a-map tasks supports such a reading with comments classifying the South as 'posh', and the people across the divide being 'up themselves' indicating the importance of not being associated with the region. These comments relate to wider ideological factors which associate 'northern-ness' with positive values such as honesty, friendliness and trustworthiness. This contrasts with concepts of 'southern-ness', which is seen to be aloof and lacking in trustworthiness, and is associated with 'softness' (Beal 2009: endnote 4).

The ways in which the factors of *proximity*, *cultural prominence* and *claiming and denial* interact with each other produce overall perceptions of the dialect regions of England that are relatively similar, but which exhibit the importance of local circumstances on the way in which the dialect landscape is conceived. In particular though, the important factor of cultural prominence conditions, to a large extent, which areas are drawn on the map. The regard towards these areas, and in particular the characteristics and evaluations of them, will be discussed in the next section.

Characteristics and Evaluations of Dialect Areas

Investigating evaluation and characteristic data added to maps permits investigation of respondents' motivations for including the areas they drew. Comments have been classified following suggestions made by Long (1999b: 213), as below:

(i) Non-linguistic characteristics

    (a) Attributes (cold, crude, rough, farmer)
    (b) Comprehensibility (incomprehensible, hard to understand)
    (c) Classification/Comparison (standard, similar to x)

(ii) Linguistic characteristics

    (a) Paralinguistic (mumbling, fast-talking, nasal, loud)
    (b) Phonetic (excluding prosodic characteristics)
    (c) Prosodic (pitch accent of words, intonation of utterances)
    (d) Lexical/Morphemic (specific lexical or morphemic examples)

I have developed Long's classification in order to further enquire as the evaluation implicit in the comments made on the maps by splitting categories (i)a., (i)b., and (ii)a. into comments that had either positive or negative connotations.[7] Table 6.5 shows the numbers of comments for each dialect area classified according to the categories above.

There were local effects to be seen in the comments drawn on maps across the three studies, which mainly resulted in local areas being commented on more than further-away areas, in line with the impact of proximity discussed earlier. I will not discuss these local effects here, although a full account of such effects in relation to study 1 can be found in Montgomery (2007: 245–253). Instead, I will examine the main trends in the data across all studies and account for the way in which the dialect areas are generally characterised and regarded.

Table 6.5 demonstrates a clear preference for labelling dialect areas with non-linguistic characteristics, which is a departure from Long's findings in Japan where not only were data of this kind more abundant, but also the linguistic characteristics that were given far outweighed the non-linguistic characteristics (1999b: 213). In this way, respondents in England appear to be much more similar to Hartley and Preston's (1999) in their perceptual study of US English, where non-linguistic comments outweighed linguistic ones in respect of dialect area identification in draw-a-map tasks (1999: 228). In total, 86.2% comments were non-linguistic and 13.8% were linguistic. Of the non-linguistic

Table 6.5 Dialect area characteristics from draw-a-map tasks in all three studies

Rank	Dialect area	Non-linguistic characteristics					Linguistic characteristics					Totals	
		Attributes		Comprehensibility		Classification/ comparison	Paralinguistic		Phonetic	Prosodic	Lexical/ morphemic	Non-linguistic	Linguistic
		+	–	+	–		+	–					
1	Scouse	8	50	0	3	5	0	2	1	7	2	66	12
2	Geordie	28	18	0	4	2	0	5	2	0	5	52	12
3	Birmingham	11	42	2	1	0	0	6	0	3	1	56	10
4	Manchester	3	16	0	0	2	0	0	3	0	0	21	3
5	Cockney	7	13	0	1	0	0	1	1	0	4	21	6
6	Yorkshire	2	8	2	0	0	0	0	1	0	1	12	2
7	Cumbrian	4	4	0	0	2	0	0	0	0	0	10	0
8	Cornwall	2	5	0	0	0	0	0	0	0	0	7	0
9	London	10	34	0	0	0	0	0	2	1	1	44	4
10	West	0	11	0	0	0	0	0	0	0	1	11	1
	Country												
11	Bristol	6	10	0	1	2	0	0	0	0	0	19	0
12	Lancashire	0	0	0	0	1	0	0	0	0	0	1	0
13	Potteries	0	3	0	0	1	0	0	0	0	2	4	2
14	East Anglia	0	3	0	0	0	0	0	0	0	0	3	0
15	South West	0	4	0	0	0	0	0	1	0	0	4	1
	Totals	81	221	4	10	15	0	14	11	11	17	331	53

Only paralinguistic annotations generated positive and negative comments, with the other linguistic comments providing value-free descriptions of linguistic items

Classification and comparison comments were varied, with some comparisons made to standard English, and others to different dialects comments, 25.7% were positive, 69.8% negative and 4.5% related to classifications or comparisons. Of linguistic comments, there were no positive comments, and 26.4% negative comments, with the preponderance of comments (73.6%) relating to phonetic, prosodic and lexical or morphemic examples. The greater number of negative comments compared to positive again echoes the findings of Hartley and Preston (1999: 231–233), where, notwithstanding the largest category of comments being *neutral*, the number of negative comments outnumbered positive ones. In the remainder of this section, I will discuss the characteristics and evaluations given for the most commented on individual areas in my research, before examining the general patterns in relation to the less well-represented areas.

Scouse

The Liverpool dialect area is one that has been seen to be relatively poorly regarded in language attitudes research, and the relatively negative fashion in which this area is perceived is borne out in the characteristics data from the three studies. The *Scouse* area attracted the greatest number of comments (78 in total), the majority of which were negative. Taking the non-linguistic comments first, eight related to positive characteristics (e.g. 'Good'; 'Friendly'; 'Lovely'), with 50 comments dealing with various negative perceptions of the variety. Many of these dealt with perceptions of criminality in relation to the city (e.g. 'Scallies'; 'Criminals'; 'Not to be trusted'), with a number more from various survey locations claiming that the variety was 'Annoying'. Other negative comments related to perceptions of class, claiming the dialect to be 'Common', 'Lower Class' and 'Chavvy'. Negative comprehension characteristics related to difficulties in understanding the variety, without any specifics given, although the linguistic characteristics perhaps shed some light on these difficulties. In this subgroup of comments, the variety was characterised as having a 'sing song', 'high-pitched', 'choking' and 'nasal' quality, with specific examples of lexical/morphological features given ('calm down', and 'errm').

Geordie

The only specific dialect area which has an overall positive attributes balance is the 'Geordie' area, reflecting the positive evaluations of the variety seen above in relation to social attractiveness. Such social attractiveness is seen in the positive attribute comments, a number of which related to the friendliness of the dialect, as well as other positive attributes (e.g. 'Funny'; 'Sexy'; 'Kind'; 'Good'; 'Party Animals'). Unlike the case of Scouse, above, the negative attributes could not be easily grouped and are, instead, more disparate (e.g. 'Rough'; 'Nutters'; 'Aggressive'; 'Gangs'). This said, there were a number of comments relating to class and education (e.g. 'Uneducated'; 'Unintelligent'; 'Poor'), reflecting the negative status ratings shown in language attitudes research. The preponderance of positive attributes given for the area is despite the negative comprehension comments (e.g. 'Hard to understand'/'Can't understand them'; 'Fast'). There were 12 linguistic characteristics given for the area, with two respondents claiming that the dialect is 'loud', and a further claiming it to be a 'deep' variety. Numerous mentions of stereotypical lexical items associated with the variety were also given ('why-aye', and 'pet').

Brummie

This dialect area is one which has consistently demonstrated poor ratings over the course of language attitudes study in England (cf. Bishop et al. 2005: 141), and this pattern remains in Table 6.5. The area attracts a good number of negative evaluations across all categories, not least in the 'Attributes' column. As with the *Scouse* area discussed above, it is possible to group these comments. Comments largely fall into three types, those to do with intelligence, others to do with social class, and miscellaneous other comments (e.g. 'Rough'; 'Annoying'; 'Ugly'). Of these, the comments relating to the perceived lack of intelligence of *Brummie* speakers are the most prevalent, followed by the common second groups of comments relating to the perception of lower-class speech. That there is such a tightly focussed evaluation of this dialect area might be one of the reasons for its consistently poor showing in language attitudes research. The linguistic comments also point towards a motivation for such non-linguistic attitudes, with numerous negative paralinguistic comments claiming the variety 'sounds like they [the speakers] are complaining', and that speakers appear 'sad' and 'dull'.

Manc

There were fewer comments relating to this dialect area, which given its status as a newly recognised variety is perhaps not unexpected. If, as I have argued elsewhere and above, the variety is being added to maps due to its burgeoning cultural prominence, one would expect there to be a less well-focussed dialect image than other more well-recognised areas. I would therefore hypothesise that, as this dialect image becomes more established, the number of characteristics given for the area would increase. Again, as with all areas other than *Geordie*, negative comments outweighed positive ones. Negative attributes can be grouped, with the majority referring to the 'Rough' nature of the dialect, and others relating to perceptions of (lower) social class, as for other areas. Two respondents noted the presence of /t/ to /k/ in the variety.

Cockney and London

Geographically, it is sometimes difficult to disambiguate these two dialect areas, as Figures 6.4 and 6.5 show, and Bishop et al. found in the BBC Voices conceptual study (2005: 151). In addition, it was sometimes the case that respondents added comments that could be applicable to either area. Both *Cockney* and *London* attracted a large number of labels claiming the varieties to be 'Common' [echoing the 'fusing stereotypes of vernacular working class speech with very different stereotypes linked to a busy and dynamic metropolis' seen in Bishop et al. (2005: 139)], but only the *London* area had labels indicating that it was perceived to be 'Posh' (mentioned by 16 respondents). This demonstrates the same pattern as found by Bishop et al., and points towards the association of the 'traditional working class connotations' (2005: 139) of *Cockney*, and a view of *London* as largely oppositional to this. Cockney rhyming slang was mentioned by four respondents, and only in relation to Cockney (not unsurprisingly), with few linguistic features noted for London, with the exception of comments relating to 'stretching out vowels', presumably in response to BATH broadening.

Characteristics of Rural Areas

Although other areas listed in Table 6.5 had fewer characteristics noted by respondents, there was one further pattern that I wish to discuss here. This is the treatment of areas which were perceived to be rural in some fashion. This relates to *Bristol, Cornwall, Cumbrian, South West, Yorkshire* and *West Country*, all of which had comments relating to rurality. One of the most common labels applied to many of these areas was 'Farmer', which is assumed to be pejorative (and, perhaps, also jocular), and carrying negative urban stereotypes. This term is used alongside others such as 'Country' (in the *West Country* area), 'Very Broad' (for *Yorkshire*) and 'Weird' (attached to *Cornwall*). Areas in the South West of England are also discussed in terms of rhoticity, with some respondents using an extra <r> in 'Farmer' (i.e. 'Farmerr') to indicate this. This appears to demonstrate a link between rhoticity, farming and rural locations (indeed, one respondent labelled the *East Anglia* area using a similar 'double r' technique, despite rhoticity being absent from this area for a good length of time).

In this section, I have discussed the main characteristics given for the dialect areas drawn across the three studies. These characteristics in many cases support the findings of language attitudes research discussed above. In some instances, they provide a glimpse of possible motivations for the ratings that are given in such attitudes work and indicate that non-linguistic judgements are sometimes more important than linguistic ones when non-linguists think about dialect areas.

Of course, there is only so much that the researcher is able to glean from comments from draw-a-map tasks (although Braber's collaborative *mind maps* add a new dimension to the data that can be obtained via map-drawing methods). As such, there is a great need to gather further qualitative data from folk linguistic interviews, as in Niedzielski and Preston (2003). Although I have gathered a limited amount of this type of interview data in relation to the Scottish–English border zone (see Montgomery 2014), this has not been a central tenet of my field-work thus far, and I have no such data relating to the perceptions of English dialects. I hope to rectify this in future work, and urge others to do so in theirs, as in many of the chapters collected in Cramer and Montgomery (2016).

Summary and Conclusions

In this chapter, I have described the main patterns in non-linguists' per-ceptions of the English dialect landscape. Language attitudes research has demonstrated relatively robust patterns in respect of English dialects over the last 45 years, and whilst there has been some similar stability in the geographical patterns of perception, there has been a shift in the last 25 years. My research into the national perceptual landscape has shown the importance of three factors: proximity, cultural prominence and claiming and denial. All of these factors interact on the local level to pro-duce maps that show the relative importance of different areas depending on survey location. Despite this, cultural prominence is particularly important as it allows far-away areas to become more proximal, resulting in areas such as *Scouse*, *Geordie*, *Brummie* and *Manc* reliably being drawn by the greatest number of respondents in all survey locations. The effects of cultural prominence can be seen in the rise of the *Manc* area over the last 25 years.

Although the Manc area has fewer characteristics noted by respon-dents, I would expect this to change as the concept becomes more embed-ded in the national consciousness. Other areas have many more characteristics attached to them by non-linguists, with an overwhelming number of these relating to non-linguistic attributes. This underlines the importance of such factors when respondents make judgements about dialect areas, and permits understanding of the stable picture in relation to the attitudes held towards them.

It will not have escaped anyone's notice that this chapter has only dealt with locations in the North of England (with one, Whitchurch, in the Midlands). As such, the results are biased in favour of northern dialect areas. There is much need for further research to take place in the Midlands and the South of the country, investigating both local and national perceptions, and it is my hope that this will soon commence.

Notes

1. Preston uses the term 'regard' instead of 'attitude' 'since some folk linguistic beliefs are not necessarily evaluative and evaluation is taken to be a necessary component of attitude' (Preston 2011: 10).
2. The first project's aim was to investigate perceptions of the north-south divide, and the second and third projects' aims were to uncover perceptions along the Scottish–English and Welsh-English borders, respectively.
3. The decision to include these city location dots was made to ensure that respondents' geographical knowledge was consistent and the spatial data they provided could be treated as accurate (cf. Preston 1993:335). Further details relating to this methodological decision can be found in Montgomery (2007).
4. With small numbers of respondents further subdividing the county, although in insufficient numbers to be included in Table 6.4.
5. I have not included a composite map of data from study 3, due to the small numbers of respondents from this survey location.
6. A phenomenon of longstanding interest in England (see, e.g., Meegan 1985; Green and Elizabeth 1988; Wales 2000, 2006; Russell 2004; Montgomery 2007).
7. Of course, it was sometimes difficult to ascertain exactly how a certain comment was intended. Where this could not be determined, comments were not counted under either heading. However, some comments or labels that I assumed to have a pejorative tone (e.g. 'Posh') have been included under the negative heading.

References

Beal, J. C. (2009). Enregisterment, commodification, and historical context: 'Geordie' versus 'Sheffieldish'. *American Speech, 84*(2), 138–156.

Beal, J. C., & Corrigan, K. (2000). Comparing the present with the past to predict the future for Tyneside English. *Newcastle and Durham Working Papers in Linguistics, 6*, 13–30.

Beal, J. C., & Corrigan, K. (2005). A tale of two dialects: Relativization in Newcastle and Sheffield. In M. Filppula, J. Klemola, M. Palander, & E. Penttila (Eds.), *Dialects across borders: Selected papers from the 11th international conference on methods in dialectology* (pp. 211–229). Amsterdam: John Benjamins.

Beal, J. C., Burbano-Elizondo, L., & Llamas, C. (2012). *Urban North-Eastern English: Tyneside to Teesside.* Edinburgh: Edinburgh University Press.

Bishop, H., Coupland, N., & Garrett, P. (2005). Conceptual accent evaluation: Thirty years of accent prejudice in the UK. *Acta Linguistica Hafniensia, 37*, 131–154.

Braber, N. (2015). Language perception in the East Midlands in England. *English Today, 31*(1), 16–26.

Braber, N. (2016). Dialect perception and identification in Nottingham. In J. Cramer & C. Montgomery (Eds.), *Cityscapes and perceptual dialectology: Global perspectives on non-linguists knowledge of the dialect landscape* (pp. 209–231). Berlin: Walter de Gruyter.

Bucholtz, M., Bermudez, N., Fung, V., Edwards, L., & Vargas, R. (2007). Hella nor cal or totally so cal? The perceptual dialectology of California. *Journal of English Linguistics, 35*(4), 325–352.

Burbano-Elizondo, L. (2006). Regional variation and identity in Sunderland. In T. Omoniyi & G. White (Eds.), *The sociolinguistics of identity* (pp. 113–128). London: Continuum.

Cheyne, W. M. (1970). Stereotyped reactions to speakers with Scottish and English regional accents. *British Journal of Social and Clinical Psychology, 9*(1), 77–79.

Clopper, C. G., & Pisoni, D. B. (2002). *Perception of dialect variation: Some implications for current research and theory in speech perception.* Indiana: Indiana University.

Coupland, N., & Bishop, H. (2007). Ideologised values for British accents. *Journal of SocioLinguistics, 11*(1), 74–103.

Coupland, N., Williams, A., & Garrett, P. (1994). The social meanings of Welsh English: Teachers' stereotyped judgements. *Journal of Multilingual and Multicultural Development, 15*(6), 471–489.

Cramer, J. (2010). *The effect of borders on the linguistic production and perception of regional Identity in Louisville, Kentucky.* Unpublished PhD thesis, University of Illinois at Urbana-Champaign. Available online: https://www.ideals. illinois.edu/bitstream/handle/2142/18426/Cramer_Jennifer.pdf?sequence=1

Cramer, J., & Montgomery, C. (Eds.). (2016). *Cityscapes and perceptual dialectology: Global perspectives on non-linguists knowledge of the dialect landscape.* Boston: De Gruyter Mouton.

Cukor-Avila, P., Jeon, L., Rector, P. C., Tiwari, C., & Shelton, Z. (2012). 'Texas – It's like a whole nuther country': Mapping Texans' perceptions of dialect variation in the Lone Star state. *Proceedings of the twentieth annual symposium about language and society* (vol. 55), Austin, 10–19.

Diercks, W. (2002). Mental maps: Linguistic geographic concepts. In D. Long & D. R. Preston (Eds.), *Handbook of perceptual dialectology* (pp. 51–70). Amsterdam: John Benjamins.

Fought, C. (2002). Californian students' perceptions of, you know, regions and dialects? In D. Long & D. R. Preston (Eds.), *Handbook of perceptual dialectology* (pp. 113–134). Amsterdam: John Benjamins.

Garrett, P. (2010). *Attitudes to language.* Cambridge: Cambridge University Press.

Garrett, P., Coupland, N., & Williams, A. (1995). 'City harsh' and 'the Welsh version of RP': Some ways in which teachers view dialects of welsh English. *Language Awareness, 4*(2), 99–107.

Garrett, P., Coupland, N., & Williams, A. (2003). *Investigating language attitudes: Social meanings of dialect, ethnicity and performance.* Cardiff: University of Wales Press.

Giles, H. (1970). Evaluative reactions to accents. *Educational Review, 22*, 211–227.

Giles, H., & Bourhis, R. Y. (1976). Voice and racial categorisation in Britain. *Communication Monographs, 43*, 108–114.

Giles, H., Coupland, N., Henwood, K., Harriman, J., & Coupland, J. (1990). The social meaning of RP: An intergenerational perspective. In S. Ramgaran (Ed.), *Studies in the pronunciation of English: A commemorative volume in honor of A. C. Gimson* (pp. 191–211). New York: Routledge.

Green, A. E., & Elizabeth, A. (1988). North–south divide in great Britain: An examination of the evidence. *Transactions of the Institute of British Geographers, 13*, 179–198.

Hartley, L., & Preston, D. R. (1999). The names of US English: Valley girl, cowboy, yankee, normal, nasal, and ignorant. In T. Bex & R. J. Watts (Eds.), *Standard English: The widening debate* (pp. 207–238). London: Routledge.

Inoue, F. (1996). Subjective dialect division in great Britain. *American Speech, 71*(2), 142–161.

Kristiansen, T., Garrett, P., & Coupland, N. (2005). Introducing subjectivities in language. *Acta Linguistica Hafniensia, 37*, 9–35.

Lambert, W. E., Hodgson, E. R., Gardner, R. C., & Fillenbaum, S. (1960). Evaluation reactions to spoken languages. *Journal of Abnormal and Social Psychology, 60*(1), 44–51.

Llamas, C. (2007). 'A place between places': Language and identities in a border town. *Language in Society, 36*(4), 579–604.

Long, D. (1999a). Geographical perception of Japanese dialect regions. In D. R. Preston (Ed.), *Handbook of perceptual dialectology* (pp. 177–198). Amsterdam: John Benjamins.

Long, D. (1999b). Mapping nonlinguists' evaluations of Japanese language variation. In D. R. Preston (Ed.), *Handbook of perceptual dialectology* (pp. 199–226). Amsterdam: John Benjamins.

Meegan, R. (1985). Are there two Britains? The North–south divide. In *Changing Britain, changing world: Geographical perspectives*. Milton Keynes: Open University Press.

Montgomery, C. (2007). *Northern English dialects: A perceptual approach*, Unpublished PhD thesis, University of Sheffield. Available online: http://etheses.whiterose.ac.uk/1203/

Montgomery, C. (2011). Starburst charts: Methods for investigating the geographical perception of and attitudes towards speech samples. *Studies in variation, contacts and change in English, 7*. Available online: http://www.helsinki.fi/varieng/journal/volumes/07/montgomery/index.html

Montgomery, C. (2012). The effect of proximity in perceptual dialectology. *Journal of SocioLinguistics, 16*(5), 638–668.

Montgomery, C. (2014). Perceptual ideology across the Scottish–English border. In D. Watt & C. Llamas (Eds.), *Language, borders and identities* (pp. 118–136). Edinburgh: Edinburgh University Press.

Montgomery, C. (2015). Borders and boundaries in the North of England. In R. Hickey (Ed.), *Researching northern English* (pp. 345–368). Amsterdam: John Benjamins.

Montgomery, C. (2016). Perceptual prominence of city-based dialect areas in Great Britain. In J. Cramer & C. Montgomery (Eds.), *Cityscapes and perceptual dialectology: Global perspectives on non-linguists knowledge of the dialect landscape* (pp. 185–207). Boston: Walter de Gruyter.

Montgomery, C., & Beal, J. C. (2011). Perceptual dialectology. In W. Maguire & A. McMahon (Eds.), *Analysing variation in English* (pp. 121–148). Cambridge: Cambridge University Press.

Montgomery, C., & Stoeckle, P. (2013). Geographic information systems and perceptual dialectology: A method for processing draw-a-map data. *Journal of Linguistic Geography, 1*(1), 52–85.

Niedzielski, N., & Preston, D. R. (2003). *Folk linguistics*. Berlin: Mouton de Gruyter.

Onishi, I., & Long, D. (1997). *Perceptual dialectology quantifier (PDQ) for Windows*. Available online: http://nihongo.hum.tmu.ac.jp/~long/maps/perceptmaps.htm

Paltridge, J., & Giles, H. (1984). Attitudes towards speakers of regional accents of French: Effects of rationality, age and sex of listeners. *Linguistische Berichte, 90*, 71–85.

Pearce, M. (2009). A perceptual dialect map of North East England. *Journal of English Linguistics, 37*, 162–192.

Plichta, B., & Preston, D. R. (2005). The /ay/s have it: The perception of /ay/ as a north–south stereotype in United States English. *Acta Linguistica Hafniensia, 37*(1), 107–130.

Preston, D. R. (1982). Perceptual dialectology: Mental maps of United States dialects from a Hawaiian perspective. *Hawaii Working Papers in Linguistics, 14*(2), 5–49.

Preston, D. R. (1986). Five visions of America. *Language in Society, 15*, 221–240.

Preston, D. R. (1988). Change in the perception of language varieties. In J. Fisiak (Ed.), *Historical dialectology: Regional and social* (pp. 475–504). Berlin: Mouton de Gruyter.

Preston, D. R. (1989). *Perceptual dialectology: Non-linguists' view of aerial linguistics*. Dordrecht: Foris.

Preston, D. R. (1993). Folk dialectology. In D. R. Preston (Ed.), *American dialect research* (pp. 333–377). Amsterdam: John Benjamins.

Preston, D. R. (1996). Where the worst English is spoken. In E. W. Schneider (Ed.), *Focus on the USA* (pp. 297–360). Amsterdam: Benjamins.

Preston, D. R. (1999a). Introduction. In D. R. Preston (Ed.), *Handbook of perceptual dialectology* (pp. xxiii–xxxix). Amsterdam: John Benjamins.

Preston, D. R. (1999b). A language attitude approach to the perception of regional variety. In D. R. Preston (Ed.), *Handbook of perceptual dialectology* (pp. 359–375). Amsterdam: John Benjamins.

Preston, D. R. (2002). Language with an attitude. In J. K. Chambers, P. Trudgill, & N. Schilling-Estes (Eds.), *The handbook of language variation and change* (pp. 40–66). Oxford: Blackwell.

Preston, D. R. (2011). The power of language regard: discrimination, classification, comprehension and production. *Dialectologia,* (Special Issue 2), 9–33.

Russell, D. (2004). *Looking north: Northern England and the national imagination.* Manchester: Manchester University Press.

Sarnoff, I. (1970). Social attitudes and the resolution of motivational conflict. In M. Jahoda & N. Warren (Eds.), *Attitudes* (pp. 279–284). Harmondsworth: Penguin.

Smith, P. L. (1998). *Language attitudes, choice and use in pedagogy: A case study of primary teachers in the Gokana area of southern Nigeria.* Surrey: University of Surrey.

Strongman, K. T., & Woosley, J. (1967). Stereotyped reactions to regional accents. *British Journal of Social and Clinical Psychology, 6*(3), 164–167.

Tobler, W. (1970). A computer movie simulating urban growth in the Detroit region. *Economic Geography, 46*(2), 234–240.

Trudgill, P. (1983). Sociolinguistics and linguistic value judgements. In *On dialect: Social and geographical perspectives* (pp. 201–225). New York: New York University Press.

Upton, C., & Davies, B. (2013). Preface. In C. Upton & B. Davies (Eds.), *Analysing 21st century British English: Conceptual and methodological aspects of the 'Voices' project.* London: Routledge.

Wales, K. (2000). North and south: An English linguistic divide? *English Today, 61*(1), 4–15.

Wales, K. (2006). *Northern English: A social and cultural history.* Cambridge: Cambridge University Press.

Watt, D. (2002). 'I don't speak with a Geordie accent, I speak, like, the northern accent': Contact-induced levelling in the Tyneside vowel system. *Journal of SocioLinguistics, 6*(1), 44–63.

Watt, D., & Milroy, L. (1999). Patterns of variation and change in three Newcastle vowels: Is this dialect levelling? In P. Foulkes & G. J. Docherty (Eds.), *Urban voices: Accent studies in the British Isles* (pp. 25–46). London: Arnold.

Weijnen, A. A. (1946). De grenzen tussen de Oost-Noordbrabantse dialecten onderin [The borders between the dialects of eastern North Brabant]. In A. A. Weijnen, M. Renders, & J. van Guineken (Eds.), *Oost-Noordbrabantse dialectproblemen [Eastern North Brabant dialect problems]* (Vol. 8, pp. 1–15). Amsterdam: Bijdragen en Mededelingen der Dialectencommissie van de Koningklijke Nederlandse Akademie van Wetenschappen te Amsterdam.

Williams, A., Garrett, P., & Coupland, N. (1996). Perceptual dialectology, folklinguistics, and regional stereotypes: Teachers' perceptions of variation in Welsh English. *Multilingua, 15*(2), 171–199.

Williams, A., Garrett, P., & Coupland, N. (1999). Dialect recognition. In D. R. Preston (Ed.), *Handbook of perceptual dialectology* (pp. 345–358). Amsterdam: Benjamins.

7

Variation and Change in Varieties of British Sign Language in England

Adam Schembri, Rose Stamp, Jordan Fenlon, and Kearsy Cormier

Introduction

British Sign Language (BSL) is the language used by the deaf community in the UK. In this chapter, we describe sociolinguistic variation and change in BSL varieties in England. This will show how factors that drive sociolinguistic variation and change in both spoken and signed

Sections of this chapter have been adapted from the following two publications: Schembri and Johnston (2013) and Schembri et al. (2010).

A. Schembri (✉)
University of Birmingham, Birmingham, UK

R. Stamp
University of Haifa, Haifa, Israel

J. Fenlon
Heriot-Watt University, Edinburgh, UK

K. Cormier
University College London, London, UK

© The Author(s) 2018
N. Braber, S. Jansen (eds.), *Sociolinguistics in England*,
DOI 10.1057/978-1-137-56288-3_7

language communities are broadly similar. Social factors include, for example, a signer's age group, region of origin, gender, ethnicity and socio-economic status (e.g., Lucas et al. 2001). Linguistic factors include assimilation and co-articulation effects (e.g., Schembri et al. 2010; Fenlon et al. 2013a).

It should be noted, however, that some factors involved in sociolinguistic variation in sign languages are distinctive. For example, phonological variation includes features, such as whether a sign is produced with one or two hands, which have no direct parallel in spoken language phonology. In addition, deaf signing communities are invariably minority communities embedded within larger majority communities whose languages are in an entirely different modality and which may have written systems, unlike sign languages. Some of the linguistic outcomes of this contact situation (e.g. the use of individual signs for letters to spell out written words on the hands, known as fingerspelling) are unique to such communities (Lucas and Valli 1992). This picture is further complicated by patterns of language transmission which see many deaf individuals acquiring sign languages as first languages at a much later age than hearing individuals (e.g., Cormier et al. 2012).

The Deaf Community in England

The prevalence of deafness in developed societies has long been estimated to be approximately 0.1% of the population (i.e. 1 in a 1000 people) (Schein 1968). If this were the case, one would expect the deaf community in England to number approximately 50,000 people. The 2011 Census for England and Wales[1] reported 22,000 sign language users, but with some 70% of these (i.e. 15,000) explicitly identifying BSL as their primary sign language. These figures have been disputed, however, because it is not clear how many deaf people with lower levels of literacy would have answered these questions accurately. As a result, the British Deaf Association's website gives an estimate of 73,000 deaf BSL users in England alone (https://www.bda.org.uk/bsl-statistics). Some research indicates that there may be fewer people with severe and profound deafness in the populations of developed nations than has previously been assumed (e.g., Johnston 2004); therefore, it may be that the Census figures are reasonably accurate after all.

Regardless of the varying estimates of its size, the signing deaf population in England forms a thriving, cohesive community (Ladd 2003). National and local deaf social and sporting clubs and associations are active in all the major urban centres, along with a range of welfare organisations specifically offering services to signing deaf people.

The History of BSL

The origins of BSL are unknown, as there are relatively few early records of sign language use in England (although many in comparison with other sign languages). BSL, nevertheless, may be assumed to be a relatively 'old' language when compared to many of the sign languages that have been identified in other parts of the world. For example, Taiwan Sign Language dates back to only the late nineteenth century (Smith 1989), and Israeli Sign Language from the early twentieth century (Aronoff et al. 2003). In contrast, there is some evidence of links between BSL and varieties of signing used in England during the seventeenth century, as we explain below.

The earliest references to sign language use in England date from the sixteenth century, although there is no evidence to link these with BSL as it subsequently developed (Jackson 1990). These include a report of signed communication used between deaf friends Edward Bone and John Kempe in Richard Carew's *History of Cornwall* (Carew 1602). None of these early references, however, provide any formational descriptions of signs or of sign language grammar.

Amongst the earliest records which describe the sign language(s) in use in seventeenth-century England are two books by John Bulwer, *Chirologia* and *Philocophus*, published in 1644 and 1648, respectively (Bulwer 1644, 1648). The latter book was dedicated to a baronet and his brother, both of whom were deaf. Bulwer provided mostly written descriptions of the signs used by the deaf brothers, and some seem to closely resemble signs with a related form and meaning used in BSL today, such as GOOD, BAD, WONDERFUL, SHAME, CONGRATULATE and JEALOUS[2] (see Fig. 7.1).

CONGRATULATE   BAD

Fig. 7.1 Two signs described by Bulwer (1648) that are still used in BSL today

A number of other written sources make it clear that some deaf people were using forms of sign language before the first schools and institutions for the deaf opened in England. In the novel *The Life and Adventures of Mr. Duncan Campbell, Deaf Mute*, Daniel Defoe mentioned that signs and fingerspelling (the use of a manual alphabet to spell out English words on the hands) were widely used by deaf people in the early eighteenth century (Woll 1987). The famous diarist, Samuel Pepys, described an encounter with a deaf servant who reported to his master, George Downing, of the Great Fire of London in 1666 using signing (Stone and Woll 2008).

The more widespread use of signed communication among English deaf people, however, most certainly began during the industrial revolution starting around the 1750s. The resulting population explosion and the mass migration to cities led to a significant increase in the number of deaf children in urban centres, and this seems to have played a significant role in the introduction of public education for deaf children (Johnston 1989). The first British school for deaf children (and perhaps the first school of its kind in the world) was opened in 1760 by Thomas Braidwood in Edinburgh, in the same year that Abbe Charles-Michel de l'Épée (widely considered the father of deaf education) established his institution in Paris (Jackson 1990). It is likely, in a similar way to recent reports of the impact of the establishment of deaf education on deaf people in Nicaragua (Kegl et al. 1999), that these educational institutions created the first environment for a deaf community and BSL to develop in England.

By 1870, some 22 schools for the deaf had been established in the UK (Kyle and Woll 1985). Most of these were residential. The existence of these schools supported the creation and consolidation of the deaf community in England and of modern BSL. Many schools were set up by former pupils and teachers (who were themselves deaf) who graduated from other previously established schools.

BSL in the Twentieth Century

The use of signs and fingerspelling continued to varying degrees in English schools for deaf children into the twentieth century, but there was also an increased emphasis on teaching students to speak and lip-read (Kyle and Woll 1985). This was increasingly true after the Milan International Congress of Educators of the Deaf in 1880 where the majority of teachers called for a ban on the use of signed communication in the classroom and demanded purely oral methods of instruction. School records from this period show falling numbers of deaf teachers of the deaf, and a decreasing reliance on signs in teaching (Brennan 1992). Sign language, however, certainly continued to be used in dormitories and playgrounds.

In the early to mid-twentieth century, educational methodologies in England became increasingly focused on the sole use of spoken English as a medium of instruction. Following changes in educational philosophies in the 1960s, the emphasis shifted to normalising the education of deaf children as much as possible, and residential schools began to scale down or close. By the 1980s, deaf children were increasingly integrated into classes with hearing children or attended classes in small units attached to regular schools. The increase in mainstreaming and closure of centralised, residential schools for deaf children meant that many deaf children did not have children from deaf families or deaf ancillary staff as linguistic role models (Ladd 2003).

Despite the many changes in approaches to the education of deaf children over the last two centuries, it seems that BSL has remained the primary or preferred language of the deaf community in England throughout much of that time. There can be little doubt, however, that the various educational philosophies which dominated deaf education over the last century—all of which have variously emphasised skills in signed, spoken, fingerspelled and written English (with different degrees of success) rather than the use of natural sign languages—have had considerable impact on the transmission of BSL varieties within England.

Sociolinguistic Variation and Change in English Varieties of BSL

The socio-historical circumstances of BSL varieties contribute to variation in usage, and this has served as the focus of a number of past and current studies of sociolinguistic variation in BSL (Deuchar 1981; Woll et al. 1991; Stamp et al. 2015). Each of these projects has focused on specific phonological, lexical and syntactic variables that will be explored in the following sections. Variations in these linguistic features have been correlated to social characteristics, such as region, age and gender.

BSL Corpus Project

Recent and on-going work on the sociolinguistics of BSL has drawn on data from the BSL Corpus Project[3]; therefore, we describe it here in some detail. The BSL Corpus Project, which began in 2008, is the first large-scale sociolinguistically informed corpus project to be undertaken for BSL. The aim of the project is to create a corpus of elicited and spontaneous BSL digital video data from deaf native, near-native and early learners of BSL. The project has established an online, open-access video dataset available for researchers and the sign language community (Schembri et al. 2013), and has provided data for a number of studies investigating sociolinguistic variation and change and language contact that will be explored in this chapter.

Sites

In order to obtain samples of regional variation, data were collected from eight sites across the UK: Belfast, Birmingham, Bristol, Cardiff, Glasgow, London, Manchester and Newcastle. These sites were selected because they are, or were previously, locations of a centralised school for deaf children, and because, as relatively large urban centres, it was assumed that they would provide a sufficiently large deaf community from which to recruit.

Participants

Thirty participants were filmed at most sites, although slightly larger samples were collected in Bristol and London, with 32 and 37 participants, respectively. In total, 249 deaf individuals were filmed. We attempted to recruit native and near-native signers, as well as early learners of BSL (cf., Lucas et al. 2001) who were representative of the dialect used in their particular region. Target participants were those who were British-born, exposed to BSL before age seven and have lived in the region where they were filmed for the last ten years. A small number of people who did not fit these criteria were included: five individuals were not British-born and 12 reported learning BSL after age seven (all but one, however, learned BSL before age 12). Deaf participants were recruited by deaf community fieldworkers who were themselves native or fluent BSL signers and familiar with the local deaf community. Fieldworkers recruited local deaf people who they knew personally (e.g., friends, family, work colleagues) and who matched the project criteria. In recruitment, we attempted to balance the sample for age groups, gender and social class and to represent deaf individuals from both deaf and hearing family backgrounds.

Data Collection

The methodology for the BSL Corpus Project was based on two similar large-scale sociolinguistic investigations of ASL (Lucas et al. 2001) and Auslan (Schembri et al. 2010), with some key differences. Unlike the other projects where groups of several participants were included, all British participants were filmed in pairs with another person from the same region and of a similar age (in London, one participant requested to be filmed a second time with a different partner). Four types of data were collected: a personal experience narrative, a free conversation of 30 minutes, responses to interview questions and to a lexical elicitation task.

Lexical Variation and Change

Lexical variation is significant in BSL varieties within England (with considerable variation in some core aspects of the lexicon), and was the focus of one of the first studies to emerge from the BSL Corpus project; therefore, we discuss it here.

Region

Some of the existing regional variation in BSL lexis has been documented in the *Dictionary of British Sign Language/English* (Brien 1992) and in other publications (e.g. a book by Elton and Squelch (2009) on regional signs from London and the South-East), but compared to the lexicographic projects undertaken on closely related varieties of sign language, for example, in Australia (Johnston 1998), lexical variation and its relation to region in BSL remains relatively poorly described. We do not yet have complete documentation of all existing regional vocabulary variants in the language, neither across the whole UK nor in England itself.

The research design of the BSL Corpus Project was influenced by the first research on regional variation in BSL, which was carried out at the University of Bristol by Woll et al. (1991). This involved the collection of lexical variants from deaf BSL signers living in Glasgow, Newcastle, Manchester, London and Bristol. Flashcards with written English equivalents of the images displayed were used to elicit a set of signs from specific semantic fields including signs for colour terms, days of the week and numbers. Signs for these concepts were known to vary greatly and in fact, the study showed that signs used in Glasgow for the days of the week MONDAY to SATURDAY are all completely different from signs used in the

English cities. In England, these same signs are all lexicalised fingerspelled loans whereas, in Glasgow, signs completely unrelated to fingerspelling are used. Words from English can be borrowed into BSL through fingerspelling as it allows for the manual spelling of English words. In the varieties of BSL in England (as opposed to Scotland), the fingerspelled sequence -M-M- is used for MONDAY, -T-T- for TUESDAY, T-H for THURSDAY and so on.

In attempting to account for regional lexical variation within BSL, it should not be assumed that there was a single homogeneous sign language (an '*Old BSL*') from which the current lexical variants in England and other British varieties are historically derived. The variation is much more likely to be due to the fact that residential deaf schools were set up independently from each other in different parts of the UK during the nineteenth century. When these schools were established, there was no single, centralised training programme for teachers who wanted to use sign language in the classroom; thus, the signs used (by the teachers and by the students) must have varied from school to school. Furthermore, in many schools from the late nineteenth century, signed communication was forbidden in the classroom. This meant that there were no adult language models for those deaf children with hearing parents who did not sign; therefore, this led to the creation of new signs by deaf children outside the classroom. Because sign languages must be used face to face, and because opportunities for travel were few, each variant tended to be passed down from one generation to the next without spreading to other regions. In a 1980 survey (Kyle and Allsop 1982), for example, 40% of people surveyed in the Bristol deaf community claimed that they had rarely met a deaf person from farther than 125 miles away. Around half of the individuals in this study suggested that they could not understand the varieties of BSL used in areas in the UK beyond this distance.

Of course, the situation is very different today. Travel within England is much easier, and so signers more commonly come in contact with other regional variants. There is also regular signing on broadcast television in England, and regular interaction in BSL on the internet and using smartphones. Thus, deaf people are now exposed to many more lexical variants of BSL than they once were. It appears that this may be the reason deaf people now report much less trouble communicating with those from distant regions of the country (Woll 1994). This greater contact between regional varieties appears to be leading to dialect levelling (Woll 1987; Stamp et al. 2014, 2015). There is, in fact, much controversy amongst sign language teachers surrounding the issue of dialect levelling and standardisation, with conflict arising between preserving traditional diversity within BSL and the notion of standardising signs for teaching purposes.

The single largest investigation into BSL regional lexical variation drew on the BSL Corpus dataset (Schembri et al. 2013) using the lexical elicitation task data (which involved the elicitation of signs for 102 concepts from all 249 participants, using slides with an illustration and an English word equivalent). The study by Rose Stamp and colleagues (Stamp et al. 2015) analysed variation and change in 41 lexical items in the following semantic domains: colours (*brown, green, grey, purple and yellow*), countries (*America, Britain, China, France, Germany, India, Ireland and Italy*), number signs for 1 to 20 and UK place-names (*Belfast, Birmingham, Bristol, Cardiff, Glasgow, London, Manchester* and *Newcastle*).[4] These specific concepts were selected on the basis of the earlier work into variation described above (Woll et al. 1991), existing lexicographical information, as well as through consultations with native signers. The study produced a complex dataset, with considerable regional variation identified for almost all the signs elicited.

The UK place-name data were analysed to investigate anecdotal claims about their usage (Stamp et al. 2015). Such claims suggest that place-name signs may work to index local, in-group versus non-local or out-group identity. For example, it is claimed that Bristol signers use a different lexical variant for 'Bristol' than those living elsewhere. A total of 1992 tokens were classified as either local or non-local for the particular place-name analysed. The results revealed that, with the exception of signs meaning *Glasgow, London* and *Manchester*, the use of the local place-name variant significantly correlated with residency in that location. This means that residents of some cities were found to strongly favour the use of a local variant that was different to signs used to refer to that city by people from outside the community. For the English data, the effect was strongest in Newcastle, followed by Bristol and Birmingham.

It is not known to what extent BSL signers understand all the existing lexical variants, and how they respond to the signing produced by someone from a different region than their own. A follow-up study by Stamp et al. (2016)

is the first of its kind on a sign language which aimed to investigate if regional differences led to some degree of lexical accommodation when BSL signers interact with signers from a different region. Twenty-five deaf participants in total were recruited from Belfast, Glasgow, Manchester and Newcastle and paired with the same deaf conversational partner (who was from Bristol). Participants completed a 'spot-the-difference' task which was specifically designed to elicit regional variants. During the task, younger signers tended to accommodate more than older signers, by incorporating the regional sign used by their interlocutor in their own signing, but overall rates of accommodation were not high (around 14% of all responses items exhibited some degree of lexical accommodation).

An interesting observation from this study was the fact that participants had few problems understanding one another during the task, despite the lexical differences. In a follow-up study (Stamp 2016), the same participants took part in a computer-based lexical recognition task in which they had to identify the meaning of 47 colour signs from various regions across the UK. The results indicate that signers had a poor knowledge of regional signs for colours when signs were presented in isolation and without mouthing (which involve the silent articulation of spoken language words while producing a lexically equivalent sign) of the equivalent English colour word. Signers with deaf parents performed better in the recognition task than signers with hearing parents, however, and the results indicate that varieties from London and Birmingham were easiest to recognise. The author suggests that this reflects the fact these signs are from two of the largest urban centres in England and are, therefore, the most widely known—and that signers who have been exposed to older varieties used by their deaf parents have enhanced knowledge of regional variation.

Age

The vast majority of deaf people are born into hearing families and the age at which they acquire sign language may be delayed relative to hearing children's acquisition of spoken language. Thus, the intergenerational transmission of BSL varieties is often disrupted. This can result in cross-generational differences, such that younger BSL signers sometimes report difficulty in understanding older signers. A study reported by Woll

(1994), for example, showed that younger signers (i.e. those under 45 years of age) recognised significantly fewer lexical variants in BSL than older signers. An earlier study showed that the BSL colour signs BROWN, GREEN, PURPLE and YELLOW and numbers HUNDRED and THOUSAND used by older deaf people were not used by younger deaf people from hearing families in Bristol (Woll 1983). New signs had replaced these older forms, with the colour signs having an identical manual form that was differentiated solely by mouthing the equivalent English words for 'brown', 'green' and so on.

Sutton-Spence et al. (1990) conducted a major investigation of sociolinguistic variation in BSL fingerspelling, using a dataset of 19,450 fingerspelled items collected from 485 interviews with BSL signers on the deaf television programme *See Hear*. They analysed the use of the British manual alphabet in relation to four social factors: sex, region, age and communication mode used. There were no significant effects due to gender on the use of fingerspelling, but age was significant. In the data from those aged 45 years or older, Sutton-Spence and her colleagues found that over 80% of all clauses included a fingerspelled element. In comparison, fingerspelling was used in fewer than 40% of clauses in the data from participants under 45. Region was also an important variable: most fingerspelling was found in the signing of individuals from Scotland, Northern Ireland, Wales and the Midlands, with the least used by signers from Southwest England. Deaf individuals who used simultaneous communication (i.e. speaking and signing at the same time) also used significantly more fingerspelling than those who used signed communication alone.

In BSL, these age-related differences in fingerspelling usage undoubtedly reflect the educational experiences of older deaf people, many of whom were instructed using approaches that emphasised the use of fingerspelling. Language attitudes may also play a role here, with older people possibly also retaining stronger negative attitudes towards sign language use, although this has not yet been the focus of any specific empirical study.

The sociolinguistic variation study as part of the BSL Corpus Project revealed that variation in the BSL lexical variants for colours, countries and numbers is systematically conditioned by social characteristics, especially age (Stamp et al. 2015). Figure 7.2 below, for example, shows the

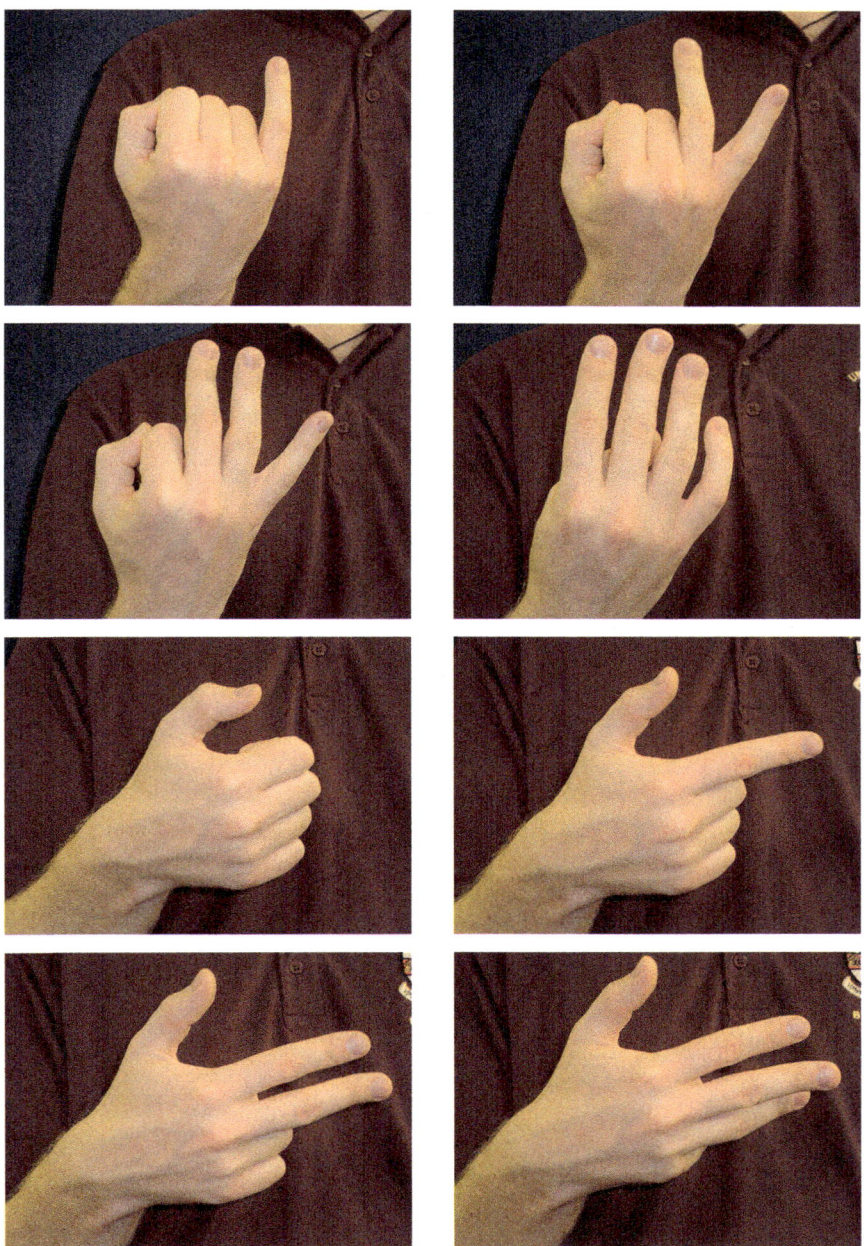

Fig. 7.2 Birmingham and London number signs

signs six to nine that represent the most common variants in two English cities: Birmingham and London.

Multivariate analyses of this data revealed that age has the strongest effect on variation in colour, number and country signs, with older signers strongly favouring the use of traditional regional variants compared to younger signers. Further analysis revealed a significant difference between the younger and middle-aged groups in the use of number signs, indicating a dramatic change between these generations in the use of traditional variants. Moreover, school location (whether they attended a local school or one from another part of the UK) and language background (whether participants had deaf signing parents or not) were significant. Those who were educated locally favoured the use of traditional signs compared to those who were educated outside of the region where they reside. Participants with hearing parents disfavoured the use of traditional signs, while those with deaf parents favoured the use of traditional signs.

A recent project drawing on data from six of the cities in the BSL Corpus investigated age and regional differences in fingerspelling patterns in both non-nativised fuller fingerspellings (which involve fully spelling out English borrowings using the manual alphabet) and nativised fingerspelling-based signs (which involve abbreviations and other modifications of fingerspelled words so that these more closely fit into the phonology of BSL) (Brown and Cormier 2017). This study showed that English signers differed in fingerspelling patterns compared to those from Scotland and Northern Ireland. Glasgow and Belfast residents favoured non-nativised fingerspelling production compared to signers in London, Birmingham, Manchester and Bristol. In addition, for Glasgow and Belfast, age is also a significant predictor for favouring non-nativised fuller fingerspellings, particularly for those over age 60. This suggests a language change in progress in the use of fingerspelling. In London and, to a lesser extent, Birmingham, there is a marked preference for using single manual letter fingerspelled signs. In future, it would be interesting to conduct ethnographic investigations to find out which of these fingerspelling patterns signers are aware of, their attitudes towards fingerspelling, and how these relate to social factors.

Gender

There have not yet been any empirical studies demonstrating systematic lexical variation in any BSL variety due to gender. There have, however, been studies reporting the existence of other types of gender variation. In terms of conversational interaction, for example, Coates and Sutton-Spence (2001) claimed that female BSL signers in their dataset tended to set up a collaborative conversational floor, while male signers generally took control of the floor one at a time and use fewer supportive back-channelling strategies.

In a follow-up study, however, Fenlon et al. (2013b) failed to find any gender differences. They looked at 28 dyads, balanced for gender and age, taken from the BSL Corpus conversational data. Fenlon and his colleagues coded which signer had the floor and any manual and non-manual (i.e. head-nods) back-channel strategies used. In an analysis of the duration and frequency of turns and manual back-channels, age, but not gender, was significant, with older signers taking longer turns and using manual back-channels with greater duration. Neither gender nor age were significant for non-manual back-channels.

Ethnicity and Religion

Generally, there are no clearly identifiable distinctions in the sign language used by various ethnic groups in England, unlike what has been identified in deaf communities elsewhere (e.g. lexical variants used predominantly or exclusively by deaf African-American signers of ASL, see McCaskill et al. 2016), partly because the education of deaf children in England has, for the most part, never been fully segregated by ethnicity or religion. Some older members of this community were educated in a separate Jewish deaf school that existed in London from 1866 to 1965 (Jackson 1990). A book of BSL signs used to represent key elements of Judaism was published in 2003 (Jewish Deaf Association 2003). Catholic schools for deaf children were also established in England, such as St John's school in Leeds, and anecdotal reports suggest that the signing used in this school was quite distinct, but it is yet to be the focus of any detailed investigation.

Many deaf people in England from other minority ethnic backgrounds are increasingly forming social groupings which combine their deaf and ethnic identity (e.g., social groups formed by deaf people with south Asian backgrounds) and, thus, we might expect some sociolinguistic variation reflecting these identities to develop over time.

Language Contact and the Lexicon

A recent study using the BSL Corpus data investigated mouthings in conversation and spontaneous narratives in 1781 tokens of verb signs, collected from 100 participants in Glasgow, Belfast, London and Bristol (Proctor 2016). Mouth actions form a key component of all sign languages, and fall into two categories: 'mouthings' and 'mouth gestures' which involve mouth actions unrelated to spoken language words. The study found gender and region to be significant, though the effects were not strong: female participants and signers from the English cities in the study produced more mouthing than males and signers from outside England. The regional differences support anecdotal observations about the relatively greater prevalence of mouthing in English varieties of BSL (compared to the data from Scotland, Northern Ireland and Wales), and may be partly due to relatively more emphasis on speech skills in English schools for deaf children. The gender difference may also reflect wider sociolinguistic trends in the English-speaking world, where women are more likely to use more prestige variants (Labov 2001). The influence of English and educational methods, however, remained to be explored in a more detailed ethnographic study.

Phonological Variation and Change

There has been only a little work on phonological variation in BSL varieties. Deuchar (1981) noted that phonological deletion of the non-dominant hand in two-handed signs was possible in BSL (sometimes known as 'weak drop', e.g. Brentari 1998). Deuchar claimed the deletion of the non-dominant hand in symmetrical two-handed signs, such as GIVE and HOSPITAL, was frequent, as in ASL (Battison 1974). She also suggested that weak drop in asymmetrical two-handed signs appeared most likely in such signs where the handshape was a relatively unmarked configuration, such as B handshape (in which all the fingers are extended and held together flat) or S handshape (a fist). Thus, variants without the subordinate hand seemed more common in her data in signs such as RIGHT (with subordinate B) than in FATHER (subordinate H—in which only the index and middle fingers are extended from the fist handshape). Furthermore, she undertook a pilot study to investigate what social factors might affect the frequency of weak drop. Deuchar predicted that signers might use more deletion in less formal situations. She compared 30 minutes of BSL data collected under two situations: one at a deaf club social event and another in a church service. Based on a small dataset of 201 tokens, she found that only 6% of two-handed signs occurred with weak drop in the formal situation, whereas 50% exhibited deletion of the non-dominant hand in the informal setting. She also suggested that weak drop variation may also reflect language change in progress, based on Woll's (1981) claim that certain signs (e.g. AGAIN) which appear to be now primarily one-handed in modern BSL were formerly two-handed.

Glimpses of diachronic change in phonological structure emerged in the study of BSL numeral signs discussed above. Stamp et al. (2015) found that older people made significantly greater use of two-handed variants of number signs compared to younger signers. Language background was also important with signers from deaf families using more two-handed number signs compared to those from hearing families. Finally, gender was also found to be a significant factor, with male signers favouring the use of two-handed number signs and female signers favouring the use of one-handed number signs. Stamp et al. (2015) suggest that this is indicative of a language change in progress. This finding adds to the growing observation across unrelated sign languages that there is a shift from two- to one-handed signs (e.g., McKee et al. 2011). Furthermore, the study revealed that women are using more one-handed forms than men. If we regard the shift from two- to one-handed forms as a language change in process, then we might conclude that women are leading this change in accordance with Labov's *change from below* principle II (Labov 2001).

The BSL Corpus Project team also conducted an investigation into phonetic variation in BSL signs produced with a '1' handshape—a hand configuration in which only the index finger is extended from the fist (Fenlon et al. 2013a). Using 2110 tokens collected from spontaneous signed discourse involving 211 signers from 7 urban centres across the UK, multivariate analyses revealed that handshape variation in these signs is constrained by linguistic factors such as the handshape of the preceding and following sign (i.e., there was evidence of assimilation/co-articulation of handshape), the grammatical category of the sign (with pronominal signs showing the most variation) and lexical frequency (with the highest frequency signs showing the most variation in handshape). Only one social factor appeared to be significant: region. Within England, participants from Bristol appeared to make relatively greater use of variation in the 1 handshape, compared to participants from London and Birmingham. Manchester signers were least likely to display variation in the 1 handshape. These results were surprising, as they seem to suggest subtle differences in the phonetics of handshape variation in different regions across England. Regionally based phonetic differences like these have not been reported for BSL before, and more work is needed to understand if we have any evidence here for the emergence of regional accents in BSL.

Syntactic Variation and Change

There has been little research into syntactic variation in BSL varieties, and there have not yet been studies demonstrating whether there are grammatical differences between individual signers due to gender, age, social class or region (though differences due to age of acquisition have been investigated, see Cormier et al. 2012).

There has been some speculation that increased access to English (e.g., in the provision of captioned television) and growing influence from hearing, non-native signers in the British deaf community may, for example, be leading to an attrition of heritage BSL signing (Turner 1995), but no work has as yet been conducted on syntactic change in any BSL variety. Many authors have, however, noted the existence of English-influenced varieties of signed communication in the BSL community (e.g., Sutton-Spence and Woll 1999). Deuchar (1984) suggested that BSL and signed English varieties exist in a diglossic relationship, building on a similar account first proposed by William Stokoe (1969) for ASL, with signed English as the high prestige variety used in formal situations. As explained earlier, Deuchar's research involved the collection of data both from hearing and deaf participants, as well as native and non-native signers. She identified a more English-like variety of signing used in church services, primarily found in the signing of the hearing missioners but also among some deaf individuals. This variety incorporated a lot of fingerspelling, and lexical items followed English word order. Moreover, it lacked what Deuchar claimed were typical BSL morphosyntactic patterns, such as topicalisation, non-manual marking of negation and interrogatives and spatial modifications of signs. While recognising that such variation exists and that it may be partly situational in nature, there has been some debate about whether it is best characterised as a diglossic situation and, indeed, whether this model is at all appropriate for the current social situation in deaf communities (e.g., Lee 1982; Deuchar 1984; Lucas and Valli 1992). English is no longer tied exclusively to some social situations—BSL has become the language of instruction in some schools for deaf children (whereas English remains the language of instruction in most schools), for example, and is used in nationally broadcast television programmes. Woll et al.'s (1991) work showed a dramatic shift away from simultaneous communication (spoken English together with sign) to BSL varieties among deaf people appearing on the *See Hear* programme during the 1980s: from 52% of all communication in 1981 to only 12% in 1987. More formal varieties of BSL appear to exist, although how they structurally differ from more informal varieties has not yet been the subject of any specific research.

The BSL Corpus Project team investigated variation and change in a subset of BSL verbs, known as indicating verbs (Fenlon et al. (forthcoming)). These verbs can be directed towards locations in space associated with their arguments, and the focus of the study was to investigate under what circumstances this directionality was used. Their findings suggest that modification of indicating verbs in BSL is a pointing-based reference-tracking system with a number of linguistic factors predicting whether or not signs are modified directionally. There was, however, no evidence of an interaction with social factors in the data and they concluded that there is little to suggest that the use of space is becoming grammaticalised in BSL as part of an on-going change in progress (unlike what has been reported for other sign languages, e.g., Padden et al. 2010).

Conclusion

In this chapter, we have explored some of the research conducted in the past few decades on sociolinguistic variation in BSL varieties in England. We have shown how, just as the *first wave* of sociolinguistic research on spoken language communities has also demonstrated (Eckert 2012), variation is often not random, but is conditioned by linguistic and social factors. Although our understanding has grown since the beginning of the BSL Corpus Project, much work remains to be done. The major sociolinguistic studies of BSL to date have covered a number of different regions in each country, but have not yet examined any particular region's deaf community to the same depth that is common in sociolinguistic studies of spoken languages. Moreover, many urban centres were not included in these studies (e.g., Liverpool, Sheffield and Leeds) and no rural sites were visited in England, for example, as part of the BSL Corpus Project. Other sociolinguistic variables need to be investigated (e.g., the influence of English language contact on word order, for example), and stylistic factors need to be more fully explored. The influence of immigrant communities and the impact of the many late learners and second-language users on BSL is also important. All of this work could contribute to a *second* and *third wave* of sign language sociolinguistics, in which the social meaning of variation and change, and its relationship to identity, could be explored more fully. Pursuing such research questions will increase our knowledge about the sociolinguistics of sign languages, as well as broaden our understanding of variation and change in language generally.

Notes

1. https://www.ons.gov.uk/peoplepopulationandcommunity/population-andmigration/populationestimates/bulletins/2011censusquickstatisticsfo renglandandwales/2013-01-30
2. Glosses of signs are generally represented with the use of upper-case letters in the sign language linguistics literature.
3. http://www.bslcorpusproject.org
4. Video clips of the regional variants for all of these 41 items can be found on the BSL Signbank website: http://bslsignbank.ucl.ac.uk/regional/

References

Aronoff, M., Meir, I., Padden, C. A., & Sandler, W. (2003). Classifier constructions and morphology in two sign languages. In K. Emmorey (Ed.), *Perspectives on classifier constructions in sign languages* (pp. 53–84). Mahwah: Lawrence Erlbaum Associates.

Battison, R. (1974). Phonological deletion in American Sign Language. *Sign Language Studies, 5*, 1–19.

Brennan, M. (1992). The visual world of BSL: An introduction. In D. Brien (Ed.), *Dictionary of British Sign Language/English* (pp. 1–133). London: Faber and Faber.

Brentari, D. (1998). *A prosodic model of sign language phonology*. Cambridge, MA: MIT Press.

Brien, D. (Ed.). (1992). *Dictionary of British Sign Language/English*. London: Faber and Faber.

Brown, M., & Cormier, K. (2017). Sociolinguistic variation in the nativisation of BSL fingerspelling. *Open Linguistics* 3, 115–144.

Bulwer, J. (1644). *Chirologia: Or the natural language of the hand*. London: R. Whitaker.

Bulwer, J. (1648). *Philocophus: Or the deafe and dumbe man's friend*. London: Humphrey Moseley.

Carew, R. (1602). *Survey of Cornwall*. London: John Jaggard.

Coates, J., & Sutton-Spence, R. (2001). Turn taking patterns in deaf conversation. *Journal of SocioLinguistics, 2*, 2–34.

Cormier, K., Schembri, A., Vinson, D., & Orfanidou, E. (2012). First language acquisition differs from second language acquisition in prelingually deaf signers: Evidence from sensitivity to grammaticality judgement in British Sign Language. *Cognition, 124*(1), 50–65.

Deuchar, M. (1981). Variation in British Sign Language. In B. Woll, J. G. Kyle, & M. Deuchar (Eds.), *Perspectives on British Sign Language and deafness* (pp. 109–119). London: Croom Helm.

Deuchar, M. (1984). *British Sign Language*. London: Routledge and Kegan Paul.

Eckert, P. (2012). Three waves of variation study: The emergence of meaning in the study of sociolinguistic variation. *Annual Review of Anthropology, 41*, 87–100.

Elton, F., & Squelch, L. (2009). *British Sign Language: London and South-East signs*. London: Lexisigns.

Fenlon, J., Schembri, A., & Cormier, K. (forthcoming). Modification of indicating verbs in British Sign Language: A corpus-based study. *Language*.

Fenlon, J., Schembri, A., Rentelis, R., & Cormier, K. (2013a). Variation in handshape and orientation in British Sign Language: The case of the '1' hand configuration. *Language & Communication, 33*(1), 69–91.

Fenlon, J., Schembri, A., & Sutton-Spence, R. (2013b, July). Turn-taking and backchannel behaviour in BSL conversations. Poster presented at the *11th theoretical issues in sign language research conference*, University College London, 10–13.

Jackson, P. W. (1990). *Britain's deaf heritage*. Edinburgh: Pentland.

Jewish Deaf Association. (2003). *Sign language in Judaism*. London: Jewish Deaf Association.

Johnston, T. (1989). *Auslan: The sign language of the Australian deaf community*. Unpublished PhD thesis, University of Sydney.

Johnston, T. (Ed.). (1998). *Signs of Australia: A new dictionary of Auslan*. Sydney: North Rocks Press.

Johnston, T. (2004). W(h)ither the deaf community? Population, genetics, and the future of Australian Sign Language. *American Annals of Deaf, 148*(5), 358–375.

Kegl, J., Senghas, A., & Coppola, M. (1999). Creation through contact: Sign language emergence and sign language change in Nicaragua. In M. DeGraff (Ed.), *Language creation and language change: Creolization, diachrony and development* (pp. 179–237). Cambridge, MA: MIT Press.

Kyle, J., & Allsop, L. (1982). *Deaf people and the community*. Bristol: University of Bristol, School for Education: Centre for Deaf Studies.

Kyle, J. G., & Woll, B. (1985). *Sign language: The study of deaf people and their language*. Cambridge: Cambridge University Press.

Labov, W. (2001). *Principles of linguistic change: Social factors*. Oxford: Blackwell.

Ladd, P. (2003). *Understanding deaf culture: In search of Deafhood*. London: Multilingual Matters.

Lee, D. M. (1982). Are there really signs of diglossia? Re-examining the situation. *Sign Language Studies, 35*, 127–152.

Lucas, C., & Valli, C. (1992). *Language contact in the American deaf community*. San Diego: Academic Press.

Lucas, C., Bayley, R., & Valli, C. (2001). *Sociolinguistic variation in American Sign Language*. Washington, DC: Gallaudet University Press.

McCaskill, C., Lucas, C., Bayley, R., & Hill, J. C. (2016). *The hidden treasure of Black ASL: Its history and structure*. Washington, DC: Gallaudet University Press.

McKee, D., McKee, R., & Major, G. (2011). Numeral variation in New Zealand Sign Language. *Sign Language Studies, 11*(5), 72–97.

Padden, C., Meir, I., Sandler, W., & Aronoff, M. (2010). The grammar of space in two new sign languages. In D. Brentari (Ed.), *Sign languages* (pp. 570–592). New York: Cambridge University Press.

Proctor, H. (2016). *Sociolinguistic variation in mouthings in the BSL Corpus*. Unpublished MSc thesis, University College London.

Schein, J. D. (1968). *The deaf community: Studies in the social psychology of deafness*. Washington, DC: Gallaudet College Press.

Schembri, A., & Johnston, T. (2013). Sociolinguistic variation and change in sign languages. In R. Bayley, R. Cameron, & C. Lucas (Eds.), *Oxford handbook of sociolinguistics* (pp. 503–524). Oxford: Oxford University Press.

Schembri, A., Cormier, K., Johnston, T., McKee, D., McKee, R., & Woll, B. (2010). Sociolinguistic variation in British, Australian and New Zealand Sign Languages. In D. Brentari (Ed.), *Sign languages* (pp. 479–501). Cambridge: Cambridge University Press.

Schembri, A., Fenlon, J., Rentelis, R., Reynolds, S., & Cormier, K. (2013). Building the British Sign Language corpus. *Language Documentation and Conservation, 7*, 136–154.

Smith, W. H. (1989). *The morphological characteristics of verbs in Taiwan Sign Language*. Unpublished PhD thesis, Indiana University.

Stamp, R. (2016). Do signers understand regional varieties of a sign language? A lexical recognition experiment. *Journal of Deaf Studies and Deaf Education, 21*(1), 83–93.

Stamp, R., Schembri, A., Fenlon, J., Rentelis, R., Woll, B., & Cormier, K. (2014). Lexical variation and change in British Sign Language. *PloS One, 9*(4), e94053.

Stamp, R., Schembri, A., Fenlon, J., & Rentelis, R. (2015). Variation and change in British Sign Language number signs. *Sign Language Studies, 15*(2), 151–181.

Stamp, R., Schembri, A., Evans, B., & Cormier, K. (2016). British Sign Language (BSL) regional varieties in contact: Investigating the patterns of accommodation and language change. *Journal of Deaf Studies and Deaf Education, 21*(1), 70–82.

Stokoe, W. C. (1969). Sign language diglossia. *Studies in Linguistics, 21*, 27–41.

Stone, C., & Woll, B. (2008). Dumb O Jemmy and others: Deaf people, interpreters and the London courts in the 18th and 19th centuries. *Sign Language Studies, 8*(3), 226–240.

Sutton-Spence, R., & Woll, B. (1999). *The linguistics of British Sign Language: An introduction*. Cambridge: Cambridge University Press.

Sutton-Spence, R., Woll, B., & Allsop, L. (1990). Variation and recent change in fingerspelling in British Sign Language. *Language Variation and Change, 2*, 313–330.

Turner, G. H. (1995). Contact signing and language shift. In H. Bos & G. M. Schermer (Eds.), *Sign language research 1994: Proceedings of the fourth European congress on sign language research, Munich, September 1–3, 1994* (pp. 211–230). Hamburg: Signum Press.

Woll, B. (1981). Borrowing and change in BSL. Paper presented at the *Linguistics association of Great Britain autumn meeting*, University of York.

Woll, B. (1983). *Historical change in British Sign Language*. Bristol: University of Bristol.

Woll, B. (1987). Historical and comparative aspects of BSL. In J. G. Kyle (Ed.), *Sign and school* (pp. 12–34). Clevedon: Multilingual Matters.

Woll, B. (1994). The influence of television on the deaf community in Britain. In I. Ahlgren, B. Bergman, & M. Brennan (Eds.), *Perspectives on sign language usage: Papers from the fifth international symposium on sign language research* (pp. 293–301). Durham: International Sign Linguistics Association.

Woll, B., Allsop, L., & Sutton-Spence, R. (1991). *Variation and recent change in British Sign Language: Final report to the ESRC*. Bristol: University of Bristol.

8

Language Change and Innovation in London: Multicultural London English

Sue Fox and Eivind Torgersen

Introduction

London is one of Europe's largest cities: 8.6 million people live within the Greater London Authority and about 21 million live within the larger metropolitan region. In general, capital cities have a major influence on national languages due to their position as *standard* and *reference* varieties; it is therefore no surprise that London has been regarded as the centre of linguistic innovation in British English. Wells (1982: 301) states that 'in view of its position in England as the political capital and the largest city, it is not surprising that London is also its linguistic centre of gravity', and, further, he claimed that '[London's] working class accent is today the most influential source of innovation in England and perhaps the whole English-speaking world'. This claim has remained untested for 34 years.

S. Fox (✉)
University of Bern, Bern, Switzerland

E. Torgersen
Norwegian University of Science and Technology, Trondheim,
Norway

© The Author(s) 2018
N. Braber, S. Jansen (eds.), *Sociolinguistics in England*,
DOI 10.1057/978-1-137-56288-3_8

189

There had been no large-scale sociolinguistic investigations of London English, mainly due to the potential problems of carrying out a project, including issues such as population size, demographic complexity and selection of localities. Whatever was taking place in London was only speculation from findings of studies of change processes in south-east England. Torgersen and Kerswill (2004) investigated converging short vowel systems in Reading and Ashford and assumed that what they found were the London vowel features that had diffused and influenced the local accents in the London periphery. Studies in Milton Keynes and Reading found an increase in T-glottaling, H-reinstatement, TH-fronting and RP-like diphthong qualities, and it was suggested that these were the results of diffusion and regional dialect levelling (Kerswill and Williams 2000; Cheshire et al. 2005). The features were hypothesised to originate in London and then spread out following a gravity model (Britain 2002a).

In addition, the few existing studies of London English were old or small scale (Sivertsen 1960; Tollfree 1999) or only included single families (Hurford 1967) or groups of schoolchildren (Beaken 1971). These studies also concentrated on a limited number of linguistic features, but they did demonstrate differentiation according to social class and gender, though almost exclusively for phonological features.

Language Contact in London English, Ethnicity and Immigration

None of the existing studies had considered ethnicity as a social variable. This is a critical limitation as there have been high levels of immigration to London for a long time, and a particularly large increase over the last 60 years. Do immigrant speakers simply adopt existing language usage or are they innovators of new forms of language use? Beaken (1971) indeed argued that school students with immigrant backgrounds spoke Cockney, the traditional London working-class accent, no different from anyone else. However, some speakers were reported to code-switch between Cockney and London Jamaican (Sebba 1993), and Hewitt (1986) observed *crossing* within established friendship groups, an acceptable practice among friends where speakers use elements of the speech of someone with a different ethnic background.

The level of immigration to London has been high for hundreds of years: people have moved there from Scotland, Ireland and the rest of the UK, western and eastern Europe, Empire and Commonwealth countries and more recently countries such as Poland and Turkey. According to Nevalainen and Raumolin-Brunberg (2003: 162), waves of migration have had a significant impact on the language of London. Indeed, in the sixteenth and seventeenth centuries, no more than 15% of Londoners had been born there (Nevalainen and Raumolin-Brunberg 2003: 164). In 2013, more than a third of the foreign-born population in the UK were living in London and about 1.3 million foreign-born people were living in inner London, representing an increase of 50%, from just over 800,000 in 1995 (The Migration Observatory 2013). Inner and outer London boroughs have the highest number of immigrants in terms of percentage of the whole population in the UK. Over half of inner London schoolchildren are known or believed to have a first language other than English (Department for Education 2015). It seems almost inconceivable that the presence of such a large immigrant community would not have had an impact on the language. Kerswill and Torgersen (2017) in fact argue that there are early signs of effects of ethnicity on London English, that is, before the large-scale waves of immigration from the 1950s onwards. In recordings of speakers born between 1870 and 1890, they found support of this view in that a speaker who had links with the Jewish community had more *modern* vowel features and more Yiddish-like voice onset time (VOT) values than a speaker without such links.

Continued Effects of Language Contact and Non-UK Varieties of English and the Role of Friendship Networks in the Propagation of Linguistic Changes and Innovations

Fox (2015) also argues for the continued effects of language contact and the impact of non-UK varieties on the language of London. In her study of Bangladeshi adolescent males and white British adolescents attending a youth club in the traditional East End of London, she found that the

Bangladeshi males had not acquired the traditional Cockney variety of London English and were leading in innovative variants of FACE and PRICE vowels not previously documented for London. They were also leading in changes in the allomorphy system of the definite and indefinite articles. Furthermore, she found that friendship networks provide fertile ground for the diffusion of innovations. Figure 8.1 is a representation of the youth club members' friendship groups and shows the distribution of the [æ] variant of PRICE among the participants in the study. It can clearly be seen that the Bangladeshi males are the most frequent users of this innovative variant but that it is also used by the younger and older white British males to some extent, seemingly reflecting the fact that these groups engage in some of the same social practices. Interestingly, the non-use of this variant by the white British girls appears to correlate with the fact that they did not interact socially with the Bangladeshi males at all. The same pattern was observed for the innovations found for the FACE vowel and also for the changes occurring in the article system (see Fox 2015 for more details).

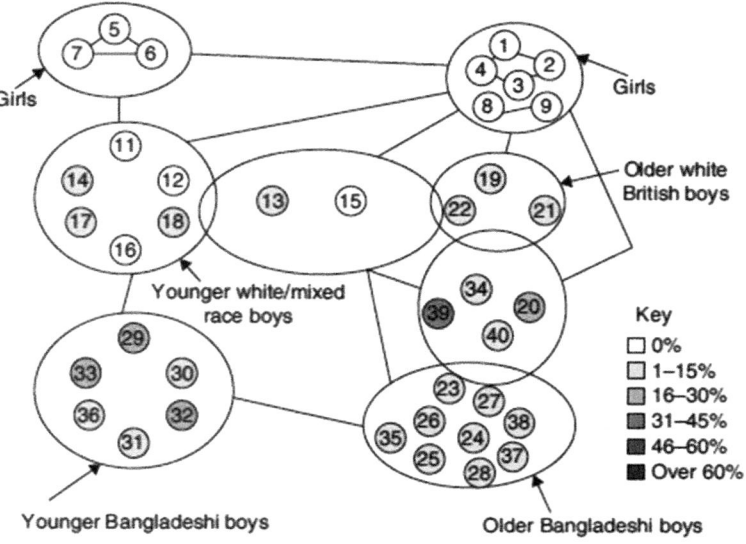

Fig. 8.1   Distribution of the PRICE variant [æ] among different friendship groups

The link between innovation, diffusion and friendship networks was also examined in the Linguistic Innovators study (Kerswill et al. 2007). To analyse speakers' friendship networks in the Linguistics Innovators study, each speaker was asked to name their closest friends and to provide their ethnic background, a task that the speakers found straightforward. The informants were then given a score of 1–5 depending on the ethnic makeup of the friendship network:

1 = all friends of the same ethnicity as self
2 = up to 20% of a different ethnicity
3 = up to 40% of a different ethnicity
4 = up to 60% of a different ethnicity
5 = up to 80% of a different ethnicity

The results (discussed further below) showed that the speakers with the highest friendship network scores had the highest proportion of innovative variants.

It would appear, then, that friendship networks could provide the key to the diffusion of linguistic innovations and that particular speakers could be the innovators responsible for the spread of innovations to other friendship groups and ultimately to the wider community.

The Linguistic Innovators Study

The rationale for this study was to investigate the claim/hypothesis that London is the centre of linguistic innovation in Britain and to investigate the effect of ethnicity on language change and innovation in London. As innovations are hypothesised to be more advanced in the inner city than in the outer city, potentially diffusing outwards, an inner city location, Hackney in the traditional East End, and an outer city location, Havering in the east, were chosen. The locations are shown in Fig. 8.2.

The two boroughs have a very different demographic setup, albeit they are similar in population size. Data from the 2011 Census, shown in Table 8.1, demonstrate that Hackney has a much more diverse population that Havering. While Havering is predominantly white British, in

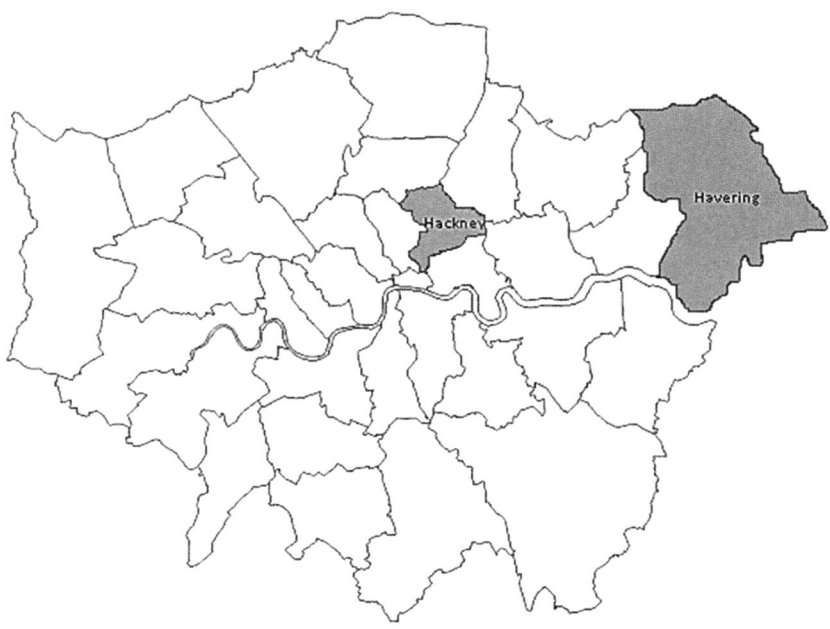

Fig. 8.2   Localities in the Linguistic Innovators project

Table 8.1   Population mix in Hackney and Havering

	Hackney	Havering
White British	89,030	197,615
White Other	39,897	7185
Mixed/multiple ethnic group	15,869	4473
Asian/Asian British	25,867	4933
Black/African/Caribbean/British	56,858	11,545
Other	13,059	11,481
Total population	246,270	237,232

Hackney less than half of the population is white British with the other ethnic groups being fairly equal in terms of size. We would therefore expect a high degree of dialect/language mixing in Hackney, while less so in Havering.

Two age groups of speakers were interviewed. The young speakers were hypothesised to have more advanced or innovative forms than the old speakers, who represented a traditional Cockney baseline. The young speakers were 16–19 years old, while the old speakers were 70–80 years old. Forty-nine young speakers were interviewed in both Hackney and Havering, giving a total of 98. Eight old speakers were interviewed in both localities, 16 in total. All speakers had a broadly working-class background in terms of their place of residence, low level of education and their relatively unskilled occupations before retirement.

As stated above, the older speakers represented a traditional Anglo Cockney baseline; thus, ethnicity was only a social variable for the young speakers. Two groups of speakers were targeted: Anglos and non-Anglos. The Anglos were those whose families had lived in the area for three generations or longer. The non-Anglo speakers, although mostly born in London, had a more recent immigrant background, with one or both parents being first or second-generation immigrants to the city. It turned out to be impossible to find enough non-Anglo speakers in Havering; hence a small number of *commuters*, who attended local colleges but lived outside the borough and who commuted from areas closer to inner London, were added to the sample. The sample of young speakers is shown in Table 8.2.

The Hackney Anglo adolescents can be divided into two groups: those with a low friendship network score (3) and those with a high score (4–5). In Havering, however, the Anglo speakers in the most diverse networks only reached a score of 3. This clearly describes the large difference in ethnic composition of friendship networks for Anglo speakers in the two boroughs. Thus, much of the linguistic difference between the boroughs can be linked to the ethnic composition of friendship networks among the Anglo speakers. The non-Anglo speakers were all in diverse friendship networks (network score 4 and 5), and the non-Anglo group was much more ethnically heterogeneous with 11 different self-defined ethnicities.

Table 8.2 Sample of young speakers

	Anglo girls	Non-Anglo girls	Anglo boys	Non-Anglo boys	Total
Hackney	10	12	12	15	49
Havering	14 (+ 2 commuters)	3(+ 3 commuters)	20 (+ 2 commuters)	1(+ 6 commuters)	49

The data consist of sociolinguistic interviews with pairs of friends or small groups of friends, chosen by the participants themselves. The same female fieldworker conducted all interviews. All interviews were transcribed in full to allow for analyses of grammatical and discourse variables. The transcriptions were transformed into the Linguistic Innovators Corpus and used for corpus linguistic analyses of grammatical and discourse variables (e.g. Gabrielatos et al. 2010; Torgersen et al. 2011). In total, the dataset consists of 1,079,845 words, excluding the fieldworkers' contributions. There are in total 110 hours of recordings.

Results

Several phonological, morphological, syntactical and discourse variables have been examined to date and we will present an overview of the main findings. We have examined the effects of geographical location, age, gender, ethnicity and friendship network on the realisation of linguistic variables. For phonological variables, monophthongs demonstrated differentiation between inner and outer city. A number of the short vowels appear to be undergoing an anti-clockwise chain shift when we compare the old speakers to the young speakers.

As shown in Fig. 8.3, there is lowering and centralisation of TRAP, raising and backing of STRUT and fronting of FOOT, while there are only small changes for KIT, DRESS and LOT. The shifting of TRAP, STRUT and FOOT are part of the south-eastern short vowel shift (Torgersen and Kerswill 2004). There is also a large difference between young and old speakers for GOOSE, with extreme GOOSE-fronting particularly for non-Anglos and Anglos in dense multicultural friendship networks (Cheshire et al. 2008). In Havering, the young speakers have a less lowered and backed TRAP, suggesting conservatism in outer London, which puts them more in line with the elderly speakers and shows them as having qualities that more resemble the levelled diphthongs observed in the rest of south-east England (Kerswill and Williams 2005; Kerswill et al. 2008). This is shown in Fig. 8.4.

For diphthongs, we have documented diphthong shift reversal. It involves the backing of MOUTH where the non-Anglos are in the lead and a more raised onset for FACE, where non-Anglos have a more raised

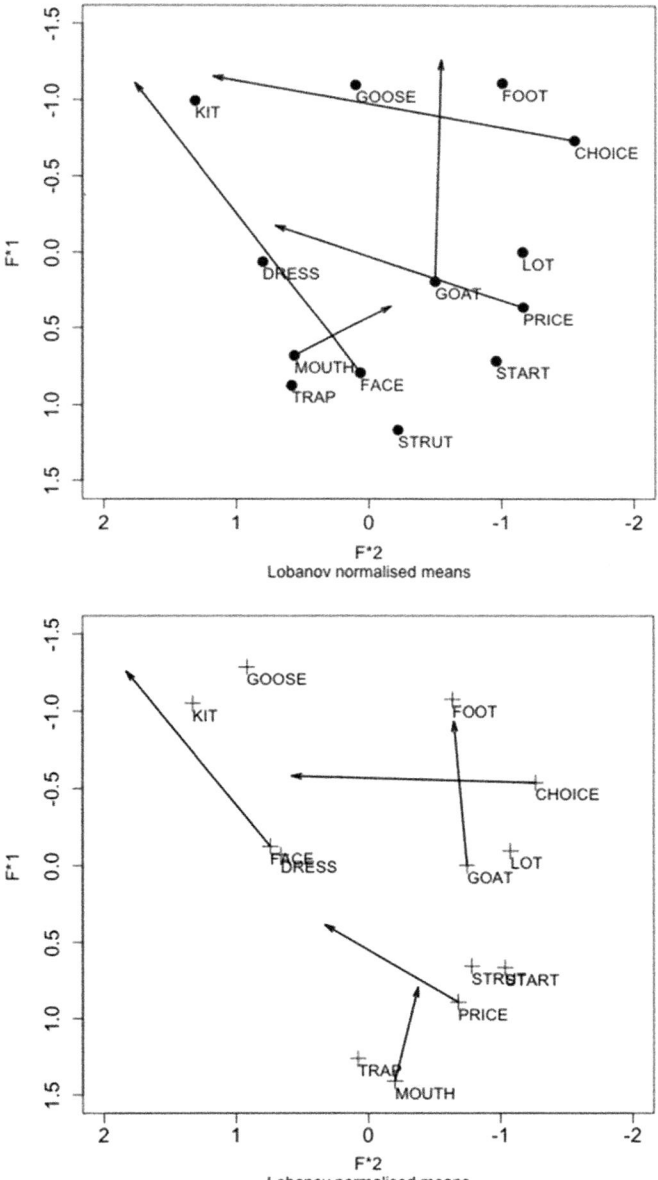

Fig. 8.3 Vowel system in Hackney, old speakers (filled circle) and young speakers (cross)

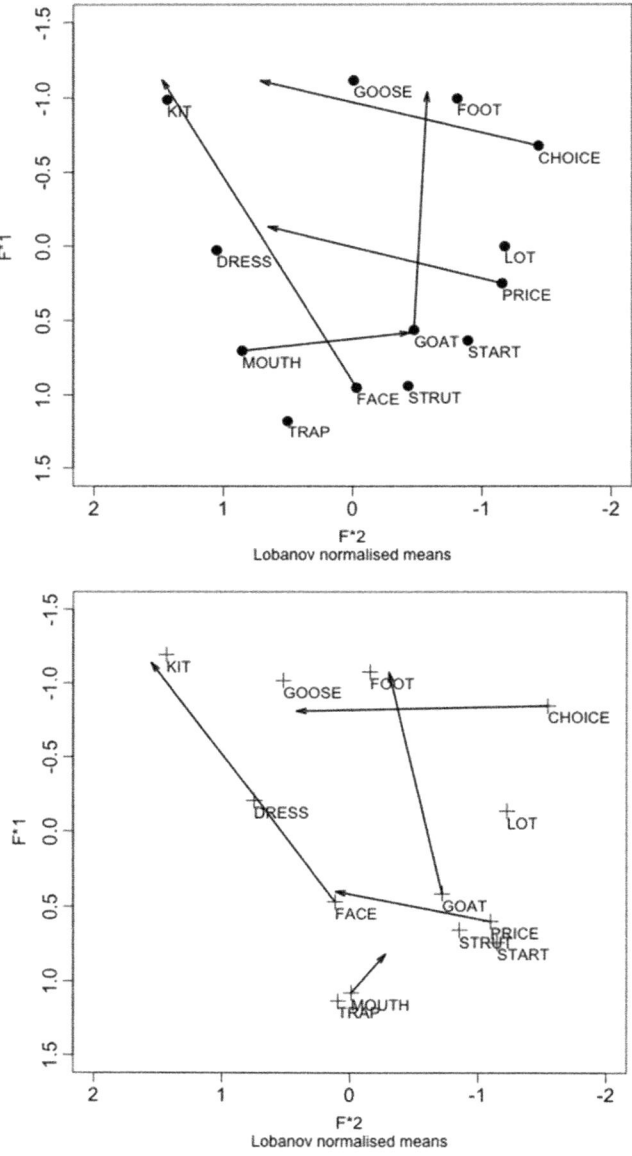

Fig. 8.4 Vowel system in Havering, old speakers (filled circle) and young speakers (cross)

FACE compared to Anglos. For this vowel, the friendship network exerts an additional effect: Anglos in dense networks have a more raised FACE compared to Anglos who are not in such networks. Two other diphthongs display ethnic differentiation. The non-Anglos in Hackney, shown in Fig. 8.5, are in the lead in fronting and lowering for PRICE and they have a more raised GOAT compared to Anglo speakers.

Taken together, the findings indicate that non-Anglos are innovative when it comes to vowel change processes. As the Anglo speakers in dense multicultural friendship networks have intermediate qualities for some vowels, the results document and support the findings of Fox (2015) regarding the role that friendship networks play in the adoption of innovative vowel variants.

A number of consonantal features were also examined auditorily. These features were analysed in word-initial position. For H-dropping, the young speakers have less H-dropping than the elderly speakers: 20.8% vs. 44.4%. This is part of a general process of H-reinstatement in south-eastern British English (Cheshire et al. 2005). In addition, the non-Anglo speakers in Hackney have less H-dropping than the Anglos, 18.0 vs. 3.9%. There were no gender and friendship network effects (Cheshire et al. 2008). In Havering, the young speakers have slightly more H-dropping than the elderly speakers. DH-stopping, [d] in words like *this* and *that*, which is a traditional Cockney feature (Wells 1982), appears to have been reallocated as an ethnic marker. There is more DH-stopping in Hackney than Havering, and there is more DH-stopping among the non-Anglos than the Anglo speakers. However, the Anglos in largely Anglo networks had more DH-stopping than the Anglos in multicultural networks, demonstrating that it is a traditional Cockney feature as well. As DH-stopping is additionally found in contact varieties of English such as African American Vernacular English (AAVE) and Jamaican English, the reason for its reallocation to an ethnic marker may be found there. A feature that has previously not been documented is the backing of /k/ (*K-backing*) word-initially in front of non-high stressed back vowels (STRUT, START, LOT and THOUGHT). The backed /k/ is found in both Hackney and Havering, but more so in Hackney than in Havering. There are small differences between ethnic groups, but the most backed variant [q] was found less often among

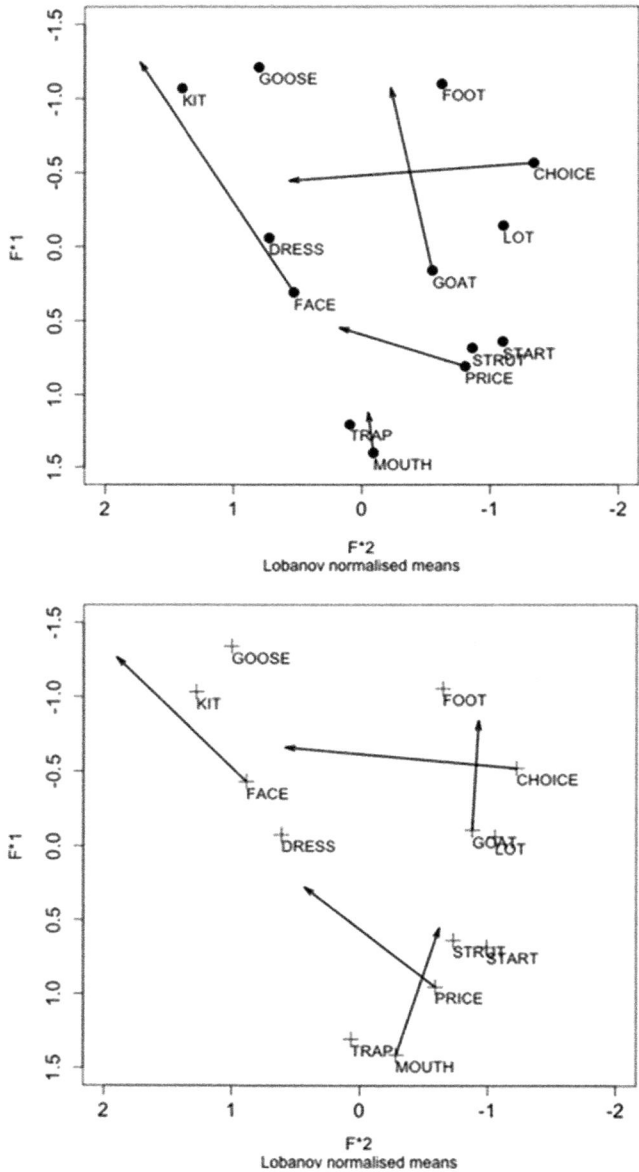

Fig. 8.5 Hackney Anglo (filled circle) and non-Anglo speakers (cross)

the female speakers and the Anglo speakers who were not in dense multicultural friendship network (Cheshire et al. 2008).

For morphological and syntactic variables, we observed processes of levelling as well as innovation. The process of reallocation in the use of indefinite articles is similar to that observed for H-reinstatement, which in turn leads to levelling of the paradigm. The use of *a* instead of *an* in front of vowel sounds is a traditional dialect form in British English, but is also found in contact varieties like AAVE. Age, ethnicity and friendship network had effects on levelling of the indefinite article paradigm. Non-Anglo speakers, male speakers and speakers in Hackney, including Anglos in multicultural friendship groups, used more *a* in front of vowel sounds. There was little use of *a* in front of vowel sounds in Havering (Gabrielatos et al. 2010). For past tense BE, there is both levelling and innovation. Britain (2002b) identifies two broad patterns of non-standard past BE. The first is variable levelling to *was* across person, number and polarity, for example *you **was** a defender* or *we **wasn't** allowed to wear hats*. The second pattern is variable levelling to *was* in clauses with positive contexts, as in *you **was** a defender*, but variable levelling to *weren't* in clauses with negative contexts, as in *I **weren't** talking to you*. In Havering we find levelling to a *was/weren't* system in line with many other urban accents in the UK, but in Hackney, we find the *was/wasn't* pattern competing with the *was/weren't* pattern. Specifically, it is the speakers of black and Afro-Caribbean background who lead in levelling to *wasn't* in negative polarity, which means they could be following the *was/wasn't* system in line with many other contact varieties around the world, a system which Chambers (1995: 242) calls a 'vernacular primitive'. This leads to Hackney diverging from the rest of the south east. There was also an effect of friendship network on past tense BE: speakers in multi-ethnic networks, including Anglo speakers, tended to favour levelling to *was* in positive polarity and levelling to *wasn't* in negative polarity contexts. This pattern was most frequent with non-Anglo speakers in Hackney (Cheshire and Fox 2009; Cheshire et al. 2011: 182), which means that speakers in multicultural friendship networks are in the lead in innovation of the past tense BE paradigm (Cheshire and Fox 2009).

For discourse markers, there is considerably more variation in the use of quotatives among young speakers than among old speakers. While the old speakers overwhelmingly use *say* and the zero quotative to introduce reported speech, the young speakers use *say*, *go*, *be like*, the zero quotative and others. In Hackney there is also a new quotative *this is + speaker*. Examples are: *this is them 'what area are you from what part'?* and *this is my mum 'what are you doing? I was in the queue before you'*. The source of the expression is unknown and cannot be traced to a particular language, but it is likely that the form originated due to language contact since it occurs among *ethnic minority* speakers in the Bergen Corpus of London Teenage Language (COLT) and also in the speech of London Jamaicans in the 1980s (see Fox 2012: 246 for further details). It is used more often by female speakers, favoured in first person contexts and also favoured in the conversational historical present tense, and in these respects, it runs parallel with *be like* in its earliest forms. An examination of the contexts in which it occurs shows that *this is + speaker* is used in narratives of personal experience which are *performed* (Wolfson 1978). Furthermore, it appears to fulfil the function of highlighting a particularly dramatic peak in the performing of a story (Fox 2012).

A similar functional innovation is seen for the use of pragmatic markers. While there are some differences in frequency of use of particular pragmatic markers between male and female speakers, the raw frequencies vary little between inner and outer city and between ethnic groups. Male speakers regardless of ethnicity appear to prefer the pragmatic markers with the overall highest frequencies, *innit* and *yeah*, while the female speakers show more variation (Torgersen et al. 2011). However, *innit* in Hackney is being used in a way that is not observed in Havering, such as outside of the canonical tag position of negative tags (Pichler 2016: 60), and it is the female speakers who are in the lead in this functional innovation (Pichler 2013: 207). A differentiation between Hackney and Havering is observed for the emerging pragmatic marker *you get me* in Hackney. It is found among male speakers, non-Anglos and Anglos in multicultural friendship networks. Specifically, the non-use of *you get me* is predicted by a low friendship network score for Anglos (Torgersen et al. 2011).

Functional innovation was documented also for relative pronouns. As seen for pragmatic markers, there is similar overall frequency of *who* in Hackney and Havering; however, it has taken on a new function in

Hackney. In one particular group (the young speakers in Hackney), a new pattern emerges that connects the use of the relativiser *who* to topicality in restrictive relative clauses, such as *my medium brother who moved to Antigua* (Cheshire et al. 2013a: 64). The results show that the use of topic marker *who* is led by the non-Anglo speakers, like other innovative forms in Multicultural London English (MLE) (Cheshire et al. 2011). There is a clear correlation between using *who* as a topic marker and speaking a language other than English (Cheshire et al. 2013a: 72).

There were some social effects on prosody documented for speech timing and voice quality. A so-called *syllable-timed rhythm* is a feature of contact varieties of English such as Singapore English (Deterding 2001) and AAVE (Thomas and Carter 2006). The term *syllable-timed rhythm* is controversial (Arvaniti 2009), but what we can observe is a reduced difference in duration between long and short vowels and stressed and unstressed vowels which in turn has an effect on the durational relationship between types of vowels. In Hackney, monophthongal diphthongs (in particular FACE and GOAT) are shorter and schwa is longer (Torgersen and Szakay 2012). The monophthongal diphthongs are also found in other (contact) varieties of English, such as Jamaican English (Wassink 2001) and African English (Hoffmann 2011). The result is a more *syllable-timed rhythm* as measured by nPVI, which is a formula for calculating the relationship between pairs of segments, such as vowels, in adjacent syllables (Grabe and Low 2002). Non-Anglo speakers are more syllable timed than Anglo speakers and male speakers are more syllable timed than female speakers. In Havering a more *stress-timed rhythm* in line with British English was found (Torgersen and Szakay 2012).

Sociolinguistic effects have also been found for voice quality, namely fundamental frequency, creakiness and breathiness. Szakay and Torgersen (2015) found that phonation and fundamental frequency differed significantly between Hackney and Havering, where Hackney speech is lower in fundamental frequency, yet more breathy. A low fundamental frequency is also reported to be a feature of AAVE, together with more breathiness for male speakers (Thomas 2007). Overall, the Hackney males are breathier than the Hackney female speakers. In particular, the female Anglo speakers in Hackney exhibited the creakiest phonation of all the speaker groups. The Havering results show a more traditional pattern, with female speech being more breathy, and male speech being more creaky (Szakay and Torgersen 2015).

In a perception test, listeners in London correctly identified inner and outer city London English speakers (Torgersen 2012). An important finding is that speakers' ethnic background as Anglo or non-Anglo does not appear to have an impact on the identification of speakers' geographical location: inner city voices might therefore be more ethnically neutral than outer city speakers. Conversely, Havering Anglo voices were correctly identified as *white* and these voices had a strong geographical marking. *Multicultural voices*, including speakers from Birmingham with Afro-Caribbean background, were identified as coming from London, which means that such voices are associated with well-known multicultural areas. For the listeners, Birmingham may not have been such an area.

To sum up, changes in inner London English are more advanced than those for the same linguistic features in outer London. Examples are the short vowel TRAP and STRUT and long vowel GOOSE. The diphthong shift reversal is also more advanced, but must be seen together with the monophthongal qualities. H-reinstatement is near-categorical. Other changes show that inner London is diverging from outer London. These include past tense BE levelling to a *was/wasn't* system, indefinite article paradigm levelling, having the most extreme variant for K-backing, DH-stopping, use of the *this is me* quotative and the *you get me* pragmatic marker. There is also functional innovation in inner London: *who* as topic marker and functional innovation for *innit*. In terms of suprasegmentals/prosody, there is more *syllable-timed* rhythm in inner London, and phonation in inner London also differs from the traditional British pattern. Overall, the findings for inner London show similarities with other contact varieties of English.

The innovations discussed in this section constitute what we have called Multicultural London English. We found that there were differences between the inner and outer city in the use of these innovations, they were restricted to inner London and that membership in a multicultural friendship network was central to the use of these innovations. However, it is difficult to generalise these results to other areas of London, bearing in mind that only one part of inner London was investigated and the study was also limited to one age group of young speakers. The second project, *Multicultural London English* (MLE), therefore aimed to address these limitations.

The Multicultural London English Study

The objective for this study was to investigate acquisition of MLE by younger children and to investigate whether the variety is spoken outside of Hackney by speakers of different ethnicities than those recorded for the Linguistic Innovators study. Data came from different age groups, from four-year-olds to speakers in their mid-20s, where the latter group was interviewed to examine if MLE features are maintained into adulthood. In addition, the parents of the youngest children were recorded to examine linguistic transmission, the passing-on of linguistic features from one generation to the next. Again, speakers were divided into two broad ethnic groups, Anglos and non-Anglos. The data collection was carried out in 2008 and, in total, 127 speakers were interviewed. The dataset consisted of 726,240 words in total, excluding the fieldworkers' contributions. The localities are shown in Fig. 8.6.

For vowels, a comparison of vowel qualities of children and caregivers (Cheshire et al. 2011) show that even the youngest children had different vowel qualities than their parents, suggesting that MLE features are acquired early. The process of incrementation, where children advance the variants produced by their caregivers (Labov 2007), was documented for only one vowel feature: GOOSE-fronting. The teenagers had the most fronted qualities, which suggests that MLE is acquired in full only in teenage years. The speakers in their 20s did not have a full set of MLE vowel features. It might be that some of the features are diffusing more quickly than others and that the teenagers are the earliest adopters of linguistic innovations. Adult speakers have either traditional Cockney vowel qualities, such as shifted diphthongs, or qualities typical of varieties from outside the UK, such as a back GOOSE vowel (Cheshire et al. 2011).

While the Linguistic Innovators project only included two age groups, the sample in the MLE project allowed for investigation of changes in apparent time across several age groups. We will now examine whether there is more evidence of incrementation in our MLE data other than for

Fig. 8.6 Localities in the MLE project

fronting of the GOOSE vowel (Cheshire et al. 2011). Previously, incrementation has, for example, been shown for the *be like* quotative in data from
Toronto, as there was an increased frequency in the use of *be like* across
apparent time (Tagliamonte and D'Arcy 2009).

Grammatical variables show similar findings as in the Linguistic
Innovators study. For past tense BE, there is levelling of the paradigm in
positive polarity to *was,* and for indefinite and definite articles, a reduction of paradigm to *a* and /ðə/ in front of both vowel and consonant
sounds. Such simplification is observed in creole and learner varieties of
English (Cheshire et al. 2013b). The quotative *be like* is used more often
by the younger speakers than the caregivers, (Cheshire et al. 2011). This
is another example of incrementation, and the frequency distribution of
be like has an *adolescent peak* with the teenagers being the highest users of
this feature, just as we noted for GOOSE-fronting. The dataset also reveal
further developments. A new pronoun, *man,* used by male teenagers of

mainly, but not exclusively, non-Anglo background has been documented and it is used for a variety of rhetorical functions such as distance and reduction of confrontation and face threat (Cheshire 2013). The new quotative *this is + speaker* is also used by all young speaker groups, but with functional innovation. In addition to its quotative use, it is also used for non-quotative functions among the youngest speakers to indicate reported actions, gestures and feelings (Cheshire et al. 2011; Kerswill et al. 2013), such as *this is her she get in trouble she get in trouble*, *this is him in the water <sound effect>* and *this is me I'm scared I'm like this*. The speakers in these examples are eight-year-old boys with non-Anglo background.

The Linguistic Innovators data revealed a reduction in H-dropping when we compared the young speakers to the old speakers. In the MLE dataset as a whole, we had similar results, but the overall differences between the different ages and also between ethnic groups were small. However, while there are only minor differences between Anglo and non-Anglo speakers within the young age groups, the difference between the Anglo caregivers, with 37.5% H-dropping, and non-Anglo caregivers, with 6.7% H-dropping, is large. If we consider all the young speakers, the Anglo speakers had 7.6% and non-Anglo speakers 5.2% H-dropping. Overall, though, including the caregivers, there is 8.5% H-dropping for Anglo speakers and 5.6% for non-Anglo speakers. Although not significant, there are differences between all young speakers (four-year-olds to young adults) with 5.8% H-dropping compared to caregivers with 18.2% and an increase in H-dropping in the expected direction from the youngest to the oldest speakers. The differentiation according to age is shown in Table 8.3.

Table 8.3 H-dropping across age groups

	[0] in %	[h] in %
4-year-olds	3.6	96.4
8-year-olds	3.2	96.8
12-year-olds	6.6	93.4
Teenagers	7.3	92.7
Young adults	10.5	89.5
Caregivers	18.2	81.2

The Linguistic Innovators data also revealed a new variant, backed /k/, which was only used by the young speakers. We here present the results for the most backed variant [q], a uvular stop. In the MLE data-set as a whole, there is 7.5% K-backing for Anglo speakers and 19.6% for non-Anglo speakers, demonstrating an ethnic differentiation for this consonant variable, a clearer differentiation than in the Linguistic Innovators study. In the Linguistic Innovators study, we showed that K-backing was a feature of young people's speech only. However, even though there are again large differences between age groups with a sig-nificant effect of age, the four-year-olds only have a very small amount of K-backing. Older age groups have more K-backing than the young-est speakers, but the young adults have less K-backing than the teenag-ers. This is a process of incrementation, but it also resembles the adolescent peak discussed by, for example, Tagliamonte and D'Arcy (2009) for *be like*, where they argue that the peak they observe (the adolescent speakers have a higher frequency of *be like* than the young-est speakers) supports Labov's (2001) claim that such a peak is a requirement of a change in progress. However, because the youngest children aged four have less K-backing than the caregivers, transmis-sion from parents/caregivers resulting in incrementation is unlikely. A more likely explanation is a change in progress with diffusion through dialect contact. Labov (2007) has argued that transmission of linguis-tic features from parents to children is completely separate from diffu-sion of features through language and dialect contact. Table 8.4 presents the increase in K-backing with increased age. It is possible that children encounter the backed /k/ variants in peer groups and then the variants increase in frequency as friendship networks become

Table 8.4 K-backing across age groups

	[q] in %	[k] in %
4-year-olds	1.0	99.0
8-year-olds	7.2	92.8
12-year-olds	18.0	82.0
Teenagers	40.2	59.8
Young adults	24.0	76.0
Caregivers	8.3	91.7

Table 8.5 K-backing across ethnic groups and age

	[q] in %	[q] in %
	Anglo	Non-Anglo
4-year-olds	0	1.0
8-year-olds	1.6	9.1
12-year-olds	13.4	21.8
Teenagers	9.5	47.8
Young adults	1.2	36.2
Caregivers	5.7	9.3

more diverse in teenage years, or just that the teenagers are faster in taking up this innovation, as we have suggested for the MLE vowel features.

For the non-Anglo speakers this is even more so, and as we have shown earlier, the non-Anglo speakers have a higher proportion of MLE variants than the Anglo speakers. The ethnic differentiation together with more K-backing with increased age is shown in Table 8.5.

The non-Anglo speakers have more K-backing in all age groups. Cheshire et al. (2008) list K-backing as one of the innovative features in MLE, and the MLE study shows that this is one of the features the speakers acquire early. To our knowledge, the use of backed /k/ has not previously been reported in other varieties of English. It is therefore difficult to explain its existence in London English. It may be that it is a feature of language contact that has lain dormant in the *feature pool* (Mufwene 2001) and has subsequently been picked up initially by non-Anglos during a process of group second language learning (Winford 2003). However, we cannot discount the possibility that this is simply an innovation that has arisen in inner London and which is diffusing to outer London areas.

Conclusion

In the Linguistic Innovators study, we found that it was particular types of speakers who had the full set of MLE features. These speakers represented different ethnicities, but they were all members of high-density multicultural friendship networks, and they were subsequently identified as being the linguistic innovators (Cheshire et al. 2008). The MLE project did not explicitly seek to identify linguistic innovators, but we have documented that the highest users of MLE features, for example extreme GOOSE-fronting, backed /k/, the pronoun *man* and levelling to *was/wasn't*, are among the teenage non-Anglo speakers (Cheshire et al. 2011; Cheshire 2013). It seems likely, then, that the innovations arise among speakers in the teenage non-Anglo group and that the innovative features then spread to other members of the friendship networks and into the wider community. The fact that we find these innovations among younger speakers may also indicate that they are transmitted from older to younger siblings and through peer interactions rather than from their caregivers, many of who do not have English as their first language and, in many cases, are not proficient in English. In other words, the teenagers become the linguistic role models for the younger generations.

We have shown that the local innovative features in London, unlike the global innovations such as GOOSE-fronting and the quotative *be like*, have other frequency distributions than those predicted by a model of incrementation. To fully understand the complex processes of language variation and change in London (and indeed other multicultural metropolises), we need to take into account the sociohistorical context in which a variety occurs, changes in demography and effects of immigration and other social variables like composition of friendship network and degree of social interaction among different ethnic groups and individual speakers, in addition to the usual social variables such as speaker ethnicity and age.

Acknowledgements This chapter contains Ordnance Survey data © Crown copyright and database rights.

References

Arvaniti, A. (2009). Rhythm, timing and the timing of rhythm. *Phonetica, 66*(1-2), 46–63.

Beaken, M. (1971). *A study of phonological development in a primary school population of East London*. Unpublished PhD thesis, University College London.

Britain, D. (2002a). Space and spatial diffusion. In J. K. Chambers, P. Trudgill, & N. Schilling-Estes (Eds.), *The handbook of language variation and change* (pp. 603–637). Oxford: Blackwell.

Britain, D. (2002b). Diffusion, levelling, simplification and reallocation in past tense BE in the English Fens. *Journal of Sociolinguistics, 6*(1), 16–43.

Chambers, J. K. (1995). *Sociolinguistic theory: Linguistic variation and its social significance.* Oxford: Blackwell.

Cheshire, J. (2013). Grammaticalisation in social context: The emergence of a new English pronoun. *Journal of Sociolinguistics, 17*(5), 608–633.

Cheshire, J., & Fox, S. (2009). Was/were variation: A perspective from London. *Language Variation and Change, 21*(1), 1–23.

Cheshire, J., Kerswill, P., & Williams, A. (2005). Phonology, grammar and discourse in dialect convergence. In P. Auer, F. Hinskens, & P. Kerswill (Eds.), *Dialect change: The convergence and divergence of dialects in contemporary societies* (pp. 135–167). Cambridge: Cambridge University Press.

Cheshire, J., Fox, S., Kerswill, P., & Torgersen, E. (2008). Ethnicity, friendship network and social practices as the motor of dialect change: Linguistic innovation in London. *Sociolinguistica, 22*, 1–23.

Cheshire, J., Kerswill, P., Fox, S., & Torgersen, E. (2011). Contact, the feature pool and the speech community: The emergence of multicultural London English. *Journal of Sociolinguistics, 15*(2), 151–196.

Cheshire, J., Adger, D., & Fox, S. (2013a). Relative who and the actuation problem. *Lingua, 126*, 51–77.

Cheshire, J., Fox, S., Kerswill, P., & Torgersen, E. (2013b). Language contact and language change in the multicultural metropolis. *Revue Française De Linguistique Appliquée, 18*, 63–76.

Department for Education. (2015). *Statistics: Schools, pupils and their characteristics: January 2015.* Available online: https://www.gov.uk/government/collections/statistics-school-and-pupil-numbers

Deterding, D. (2001). The measurement of rhythm: A comparison of Singapore and British English. *Journal of Phonetics, 29*(2), 217–230.

Fox, S. (2012). Performed narrative: The pragmatic function of this is + speaker and other quotatives in London adolescent speech. In I. van Alphen & I. Buchstaller (Eds.), *Quotatives: Cross-linguistic and cross-disciplinary perspectives* (pp. 231–257). Amsterdam: Benjamins.

Fox, S. (2015). *The New Cockney: New ethnicities and adolescent speech in the traditional East End of London.* Basingstoke: Palgrave Macmillan.

Gabrielatos, C., Torgersen, E., Hoffmann, S., & Fox, S. (2010). A corpus-based sociolinguistic study of indefinite article forms in London English. *Journal of English Linguistics, 38*(4), 297–334.

Grabe, E., & Low, E. L. (2002). Durational variability in speech and the rhythm class hypothesis. In C. Gussenhoven & N. Warner (Eds.), *Papers in laboratory phonology* (Vol. 7, pp. 515–546). Berlin: Mouton de Gruyter.

Hewitt, R. (1986). *White talk, black talk*. Cambridge: Cambridge University Press.

Hoffmann, T. (2011). The black Kenyan English vowel system. *English World-Wide, 32*(2), 147–173.

Hurford, J. (1967). *The speech of one family: A phonetic comparison of the speech of three generations in a family in East London*. Unpublished PhD thesis, University College London.

Kerswill, P., & Torgersen, E. (2017). London's Cockney in the twentieth century: Stability or cycles of contact-driven change? In R. Hickey (Ed.), *Listening to the past* (pp. 85–113). Cambridge: Cambridge University Press.

Kerswill, P., & Williams, A. (2000). Creating a new town koine: Children and language change in Milton Keynes. *Language in Society, 29*(1), 65–115.

Kerswill, P., & Williams, A. (2005). New towns and koineisation: Linguistic and social correlates. *Linguistics, 43*(5), 1023–1048.

Kerswill, P., Cheshire, J., Fox, S., & Torgersen, E. (2007). *Linguistic innovators: The English of adolescents in London*. Final report on ESRC grant.

Kerswill, P., Torgersen, E., & Fox, S. (2008). Reversing 'drift': Innovation and diffusion in the London diphthong system. *Language Variation and Change, 20*(3), 451–491.

Kerswill, P., Cheshire, J., Fox, S., & Torgersen, E. (2013). English as a contact language: The role of children and adolescents. In D. Schreier & M. Hundt (Eds.), *English as a contact language* (pp. 258–282). Cambridge: Cambridge University Press.

Labov, W. (2001). *Principles of linguistic change, vol. 2: Social factors*. Oxford: Blackwell.

Labov, W. (2007). Transmission and diffusion. *Language, 83*(2), 344–387.

Mufwene, S. (2001). *The ecology of language evolution*. Cambridge: Cambridge University Press.

Nevalainen, T., & Raumolin-Brunberg, H. (2003). *Historical sociolinguistics: Language change in Tudor and Stuart England*. Harlow: Longman.

Pichler, H. (2013). *The structure of discourse-pragmatic variation*. Amsterdam: Benjamins.

Pichler, H. (2016). Uncovering discourse-pragmatic innovations: *Innit* in multicultural London English. In H. Pichler (Ed.), *Discourse-pragmatic variation and change in English: New methods and insights* (pp. 59–84). Cambridge: Cambridge University Press.

Sebba, M. (1993). *London Jamaican*. London: Longman.

Sivertsen, E. (1960). *Cockney phonology*. Oslo: Oslo University Press.

Szakay, A., & Torgersen, E. (2015). An acoustic analysis of voice quality in London English: The effect of gender, ethnicity and F0. *Proceedings from the 18th international congress of phonetic sciences,* Glasgow.

Tagliamonte, S., & D'Arcy, A. (2009). Peaks beyond phonology: Adolescence, incrementation and language change. *Language, 85*(1), 58–108.

The Migration Observatory. (2013). *London: Census profile.* Available online: http://www.migrationobservatory.ox.ac.uk/briefings/london-census-profile

Thomas, E. R. (2007). Phonological and phonetic characteristics of African American vernacular English. *Language and Linguistics Compass, 1*(5), 450–475.

Thomas, E. R., & Carter, P. M. (2006). Prosodic rhythm and African American English. *English World-Wide, 27*(3), 331–355.

Tollfree, L. (1999). South East London English: Discrete versus continuous modelling of consonantal reduction. In P. Foulkes & G. Docherty (Eds.), *Urban voices. Accent studies in the British Isles* (pp. 163–184). London: Arnold.

Torgersen, E. (2012). A perceptual study of ethnicity and geographical location in London and Birmingham. In S. Hansen, C. Schwartz, P. Stoeckle, & T. Streck (Eds.), *Dialectological and folk dialectological concepts of space* (pp. 75–95). Berlin: Mouton de Gruyter.

Torgersen, E., & Kerswill, P. (2004). Internal and external motivation in phonetic change: Dialect levelling outcomes for an English vowel shift. *Journal of SocioLinguistics, 8*(1), 23–53.

Torgersen, E., & Szakay, A. (2012). An investigation of speech rhythm in London English. *Lingua, 122*(7), 822–840.

Torgersen, E., Gabrielatos, C., Hoffmann, S., & Fox, S. (2011). A corpus-based study of pragmatic markers in London English. *Corpus Linguistics and Linguistic Theory, 7*(1), 93–118.

Wassink, A. B. (2001). Theme and variation in Jamaican vowels. *Language Variation and Change, 13*(2), 135–159.

Wells, J. (1982). *Accents of English.* Cambridge: Cambridge University Press.

Winford, D. (2003). *An introduction to contact linguistics.* Oxford: Blackwell.

Wolfson, N. (1978). A feature of performed narrative: The conversational historic present. *Language in Society, 7*(2), 215–237.

9

The Effect of Economic Trajectory and Speaker Profile on Lifespan Change: Evidence from Stative Possessives on Tyneside

Isabelle Buchstaller and Adam Mearns

Introduction

This chapter focuses on longitudinal change in a dialect called *Geordie*, spoken in the North East of England,[1] in the city of Newcastle and town of Gateshead, which are located on the north and south banks of the River Tyne. While, to the outsider, Geordie has become a general label for the North East (Wales 2006; Pearce 2011; Beal et al. 2012), amongst the people of the North East the term has a much more specific meaning.[2] Beal (2004b: 34) states that, in addition to Newcastle, the 'heart of the "Geordie Nation" [...] those who would consider themselves as Geordies can be found throughout Northumberland and even in the northern part of the old County Durham, at least in Gateshead and South Shields' (see Fig. 9.1).

The heartland of the Geordie dialect was traditionally associated with the heavy industries characteristic of many Northern industrial cities in

I. Buchstaller (✉)
University of Duisburg-Essen, North Rhine-Westphalia, Germany

A. Mearns
Newcastle University, Newcastle, UK

© The Author(s) 2018
N. Braber, S. Jansen (eds.), *Sociolinguistics in England*,
DOI 10.1057/978-1-137-56288-3_9

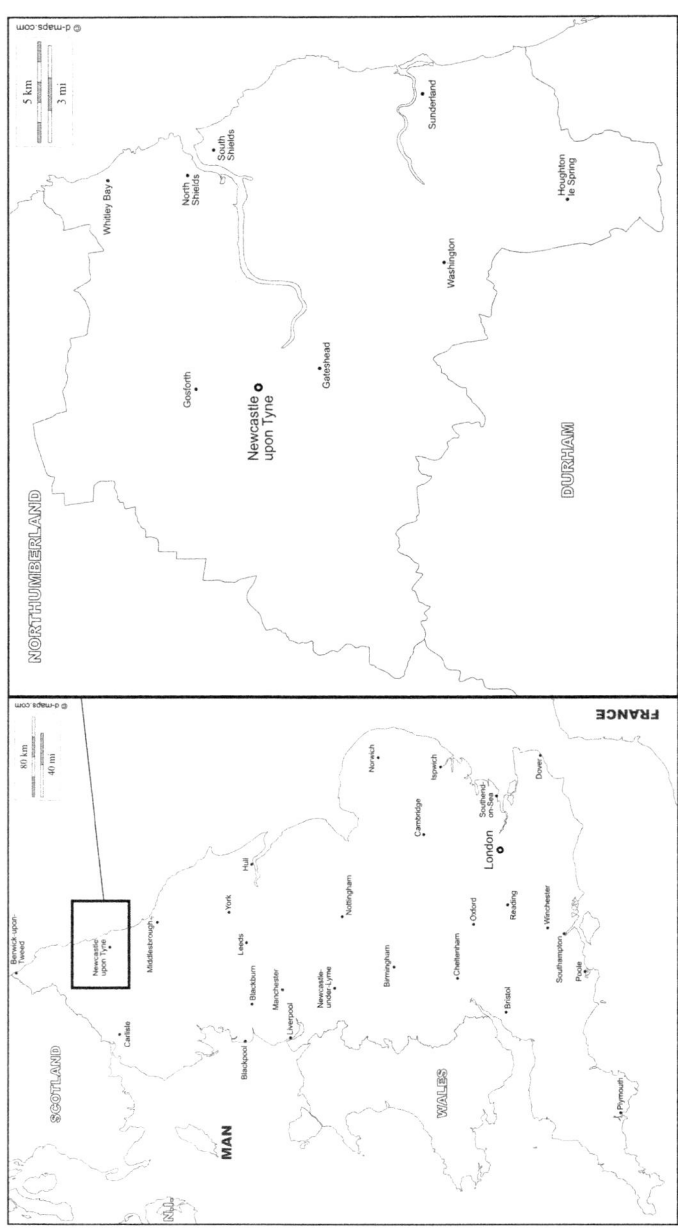

Fig. 9.1 Map of Tyneside

the British Isles (see the papers in Colls and Lancaster 2001; Beal et al. 2012). Since the 1950s, however, the Tyneside community has undergone dramatic socio-economic changes. Traditional economies, which had provided mass employment in the North East region, such as shipbuilding, mining, steel and glass manufacture, declined sharply, resulting in large-scale unemployment (see Figs. 9.2 and 9.3). As exemplified in (1), the economic downturn had traumatic consequences for many people living in the North East.

(1) ... that was around the eighties especially with the shipyards closing, the mines closing, steelworks you know (...) ehm when they've lost their job through no fault of their own and then they can't get a job because there's none to be had ... [Rob]

Since this economic depression, Tyneside has successfully reinvented itself as the retail, cultural and educational centre of the North of England (see OECD 2006; Vall 2007; Beal et al. 2012).[3] Not everyone has been able to benefit from this socio-economic recovery, however, and the

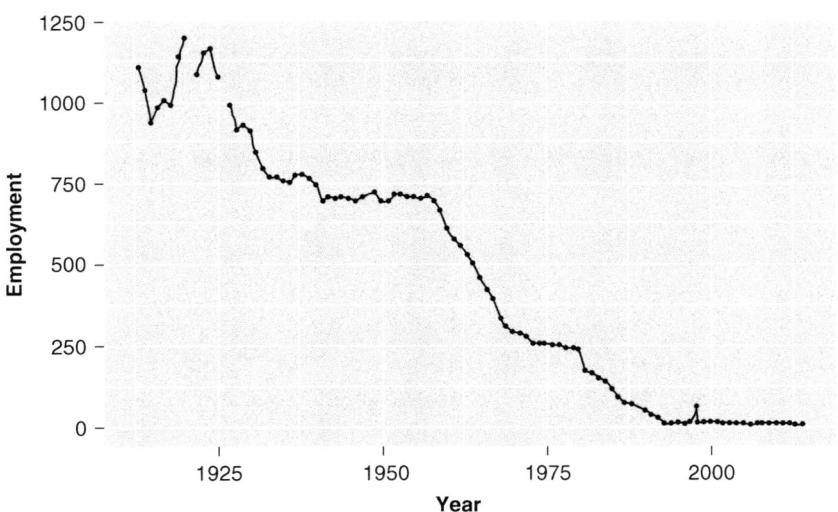

Fig. 9.2 Coal mining employment in the UK 1913–2014 (Source: Department of Energy & Climate Change 2015)

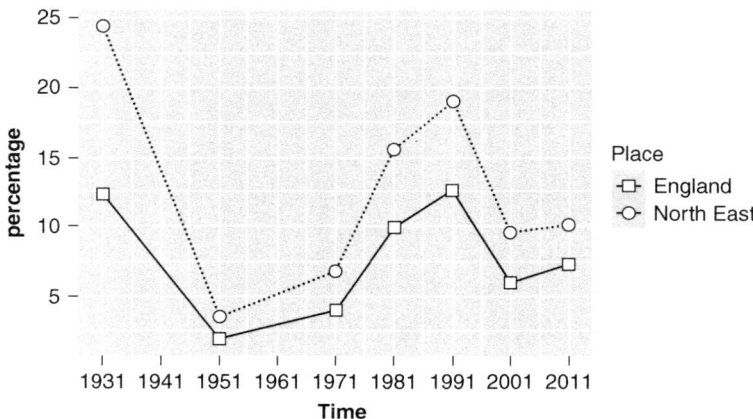

Fig. 9.3 Male unemployment rate (Data: Office for National Statistics)

region has still some of the highest indices of deprivation and unemployment of the UK.[4]

Social changes of the kind described for the Tyneside community present sociolinguists with a challenge. Labov (1994: 76) famously claimed that 'for a trend survey to yield a meaningful portrait of linguistic development, it is essential that the community have remained in a more or less stable state in the intervening period. If drastic changes in its demographic make-up have taken place, the changes we observe in language may have little to do with the logic of linguistic change in progress'.[5] In this chapter, we argue that sociolinguistic research can contribute vital information on the ways in which large-scale societal changes have impacted on the language use of socio-economically unstable populations, including, on a micro-level, the individuals who live in and, thus, form these communities. We will illustrate how comprehensive ethnographic research not only allows us to understand the effect that changes in social structure can have on linguistic change, but also—and more importantly—how it allows us to assess the extent to which individual speakers are representative of the community in the sense that they are typical of the time and place in which they were recorded.

The chapter explores the participation of Tyneside speakers in changes in the system of stative possessives, an ongoing morphosyntactic change that has been playing out in the English language for centuries (see Tagliamonte et al. 2010; Tagliamonte 2012). In our study, we illustrate the gradual increase of two incoming forms, *have got* and *got* on the basis of trend time data. We then report on a panel sample of six speakers recorded first in 1971 and then again in 2013, whose socio-economic trajectories epitomise the complex impact which the recent socio-economic upheaval has had on people's lives. Tracing language change across the lifespan of the individual allows us to investigate the effect of speaker-based factors, such as their personalities (Denis 2011), their contact with children (Buchstaller 2016) and the socio-economic trajectory of the individual speaker on their participation in ongoing longitudinal change (Wagner 2008; Bigham 2010; Sankoff and Wagner 2011; Rickford and Price 2013; Buchstaller 2016; Buchstaller et al. 2017). The present study, thus, contributes to our understanding of the extent to which older speakers past critical age go along with changes that sweep through the community around them (Sankoff 2004, 2005).

Data and Methods

Large-scale data collection efforts on Tyneside date back to the late 1960s/early 1970s, when the *Tyneside Linguistic Survey* (TLS) gathered a sample of about 180 recordings in Gateshead and Newcastle.[6] In 1994, the *Phonological Variation and Change in Contemporary Spoken British English* (PVC) project recorded a second data-set on the Newcastle side of the river (Milroy et al. 1997, 1999). The corpus consists of 18 recordings with speakers from two neighbouring parts of the city which differ in terms of their socio-economic profiles, roughly corresponding to working-class and middle-class areas. Between 2000 and 2005, these two legacy corpora were combined to form the *Newcastle Electronic Corpus of Tyneside English* (NECTE) held at Newcastle University (Corrigan et al. 2005).

The most recent data collection project—the *Diachronic Electronic Corpus of Tyneside English* (DECTE, Corrigan et al. 2012; Mearns et al. 2016)—has added another layer to our growing repository of Tyneside speech. It combines the NECTE data-sets with a new monitor corpus, NECTE2, which was begun in 2007 at Newcastle University and has since yielded an average of 65 recordings per year. The creation of this third sub-corpus, therefore, expands the coverage of the Tyneside community from 1891, when the oldest TLS speaker was born, to 1996, the birth year of our youngest DECTE speaker. The combined data-sets, thus, cover over 100 years of speech from local people in the North East, which is—to our knowledge—the longest time span of any corpus of spoken English. Crucially, they allow us to trace longitudinal linguistic variation and language change during a time when the Tyneside community underwent radical social and economic changes.

Sociolinguistic research recommends trend studies as the most reliable method for studying ongoing change across the community (Trudgill 1988; Labov 1994). In this chapter, we investigate longitudinal change in the Tyneside area on the basis of a balanced sample of 16 speakers from the TLS data-set recorded in the early 1970s and a similar sample of 16 speakers from the part of the NECTE2 corpus collected in 2007–2008. We will compare and contrast the findings from this trend data-set with a small panel sample collected during an FP7 European Commission funded project (Buchstaller 2013–2017). For this panel data-set, we traced and re-recorded six of the original TLS speakers who were first interviewed in 1971 (see Table 9.1).

The analysis of longitudinal trend and panel data gives us the opportunity to study the linguistic malleability which individual speakers exhibit during their lifespan by comparison to the community trend (Sankoff 2004; Wagner 2008; Bigham 2010; Prichard and Tamminga 2012). Note that the 2013 re-interviews carefully replicated two aspects of the original interview situation: (i) the interactional setting (see Gregersen and Barner-Rasmussen 2011) and (ii) the interlocutor (Rickford and McNair-Knox 1994). In 2013, as previously in 1971, informants were recorded in their homes (with the exception of a former teacher who preferred to be interviewed at the university). Also, the 2013 fieldworker very closely matches the sociolinguistic characteristics of the 1971 interviewer. Both

Table 9.1 Sampling frame for the diachronic investigation of language change across longitudinal time as well as across the lifespan of the individual speaker

Trend sample				Panel sample	
1960s–1970s		2000s		1960s–1970s (ages 21–32)	Change across the life-span
Older (35+)	Younger (18–22)	Older (35+)	Younger (18–22)	6	
				2013 (ages 63–74)	
8	8	8	8	6	

Change across time in the community

were male Newcastle University employees from the North East and both have a general Northern accent, which the informants were unable to localise when they were asked where they thought the interviewer was from.

The 1971 interviews asked a range of diagnostic questions regarding informants' tastes, values and lifestyle choices[7] and enquired about their general socio-economic situation. Our 2013 re-interviews aimed to find out about informants' lives since the initial interviews. Ethnographic questions tailored towards the individual speaker (based on what we knew about them from their first interview) provided us with important insights into their life-course during this time of economic upheaval and the way in which they position themselves towards these socio-demographic changes. Crucially, the rich personal data gleaned from the two interviews allowed us to situate the individuals within the overall Tyneside community in which they are embedded.

Table 9.2 briefly introduces our panel speakers, focusing on their socio-economic trajectories. Below, we give more information about these six individuals, especially regarding their personality and the type and intensity of their contact with children and younger speakers (see Labov 2001; Denis 2011).

Given what we know about the socio-economic development of the area in the past century, we would like to argue that these six speakers are representative of the time and place in which they were recorded. Their socio-economic trajectories span the gamut of life histories that characterise the complex development which the North East has undergone in

Table 9.2 Speaker profiles

	1971		2013	
	Age	Profession	Age	Profession
Upwardly mobile				
Fred	21	Clerk, student teacher	63	Retired religious education teacher
Aidan	25	Welder, starting lecturer	66	Retired college lecturer
Consistently middle class				
Nelly	29	Nursery nurse / kindergarten teacher	71	Retired housewife
Consistently working class				
Rob	23	Engraver	64	Engraver
Anne	23	Seamstress	64	Retired seamstress
Edith	32	Co-op salesperson, home-help	74	Retired home-help

the 42 years covered by our data. The upwards trajectory of two speakers, Fred and Aidan, epitomises the drastic changes from heavy industry to a post-industrial cultural and educational economy. Rob, Anne and Edith remained consistently working class, epitomising the large chunk of Tyneside which is economically classified largely as *traditional manufacturing* and *industrial hinterland* (Buchstaller and Alvanides 2013). Nelly, finally, remained at an economically stable middle-class position (as measured by aspirations, attitudes and housing).

In the following sections, we will assess the linguistic behaviour of our six panel speakers in the light of the ongoing longitudinal changes affecting the system of stative possessives in the Tyneside community.

The Change Under Investigation: Stative Possessives

In contrast to other ongoing linguistic changes described for the Tyneside community, such as the loss of traditional local features (Watt and Milroy 1999; Watt 2000; Beal 2004a) or the sudden influx of innovations in the system of quotation and intensification (Barnfield and Buchstaller 2010; Buchstaller 2014), the competition in the system of stative possession is characterised by a gradual turnover. The resulting layering within the linguistic variable has played out since Early Modern English (Tagliamonte et al. 2010).

As a primary verb, *have* has expressed static ownership since the 10th century (see 2a).[8] In the late 16th century 'the idiom *have got,* [which] derives historically from a perfect construction' (Huddleston and Pullum 2002: 112) developed stative possessive function, especially in the British Isles (as in 2b). In line with grammaticalisation predictions, the phonetic substance of *have got* has eroded over time, resulting in the contracted forms *'ve/'s got* typical of spoken language or spontaneous registers (see 2c). This reduction process has been brought to completion in some varieties of English, leading to the complete elision of *have* and the concomitant expression of stative ownership via *got* (2d).

(2)   Development of stative possession (Tagliamonte et al. 2010; see also Crowell 1959; Jespersen 1961; Visser 1963–1978, examples from the OED, except for 2d).

		Stative possessive verbal complex	Example
a.	Late 10th century	*Have*	*He..hæfde blæc feax (he had black hair)*
b.	Late 16th century	Addition of *got*	*What a beard hast thou got*
c.		Contraction of *have*	*She's got plenty of money*
d.	Early ModE	Elision of contracted *have*	*You got a light (T8_1971)*

In contemporary British Englishes, the competition in the system of stative possession plays out principally between two variants—*have* and *have got* (and its phonetically reduced forms). The latter has been steadily increasing in frequency throughout the last century (see Kroch 1989; Huddleston and Pullum 2002).[9] Whereas the newest variant, *got*, is generally considered US English and still rare in British Englishes (Jespersen 1961: 53; Tagliamonte 2012), recent research suggests that UK speakers have started to use *got* as a minority form (see Tagliamonte et al. 2010; Tagliamonte 2012; Buchstaller 2016).

Following the precedent set in the literature, our analysis examines the variability in the system of stative possessives by setting up a ternary variable which consists of the oldest form *have*, the bourgeoning variant (reduced or full) *have got*, as well as incipient *got* (see Tagliamonte et al. 2010). We will follow Tagliamonte and her collaborators in restricting the variable context to present (i.e. non-past tense) forms that are not modified by modal auxiliaries (see also Buchstaller 2016).

Changes in the Community and Across the Lifespan

We first consider the community trend before examining the behaviour of the individual panel speakers. Table 9.3 demonstrates that, by the early 1970s, when the TLS corpus was collected, *have got* had already made substantial inroads into the system of stative possession (50% *have* versus 49% *have got*). This result corroborates apparent time results on the basis of data collected in the late 1990s/early 2000s in Wheatley Hill—a locality approximately 20 miles (32 km) from Gateshead—where older speakers use *have got* in slightly less than 60% of all stative possessive contexts (Tagliamonte 2012). The trend data from our DECTE corpus extends the time-frame over which the variable can be explored into the 21st century and allows us to trace the incursion of *have got* into the system of stative possession in real time. As Table 9.4 reveals, by 2007, *have got* ratios have increased to 63%, an increment of 14% since the 1970s (compare Table 9.3). At the same time, the speakers of the recent time slice produce lower frequencies of *have*, which merely accounts for 31% in 2007, a reduction of 9%. The totality of our findings, therefore, supports the contention that Tyneside is part of a larger supra-local trend

Table 9.3 The system of stative possession in the 1970s

	N	%
Have got	64	49
Have	65	50
Got	2	2
Total	131	100

Table 9.4 The system of stative possession in 2007

	N	%
Have got	159	63
Have	77	31
Got	16	6
Total	252	100

Table 9.5 The system of stative possession amongst the older panel speakers on Tyneside recorded in 1971

	N	%
Have got	49	66
Have	24	32
Got	1	1
Total	74	100

towards increasing rates of *have got* (see also the results for speakers in Buckie and York, in Tagliamonte 2012). These findings place the North East of England fully in line with the development of the variable reported in the literature (see also Kroch 1989; Tagliamonte et al. 2010). A comparison between Tables 9.3 and 9.4 also reveals that *got*—the most recent incursion into the British system of stative possessives—is on the rise across real time.[10] The variant edges its way into the system with 2% frequency in the 1970s compared to 6% in 2007. We will revisit this issue below.

Let us now explore the sociolinguistic reality of this ongoing change in the panel data. Table 9.5 illustrates the system of stative possessives amongst our six panel speakers in 1971. Table 9.6 plots the same speakers 42 years later.

While the increase in stative possessive *got* is immediately noticeable (frequencies rose from 1% in 1971 to 8% in 2013), our panel speakers do not mirror the community-wide incrementation of *have got*: usage rates drop somewhat from 66% in 1971 to 61% in 2013. Hence, while the individuals constituting our panel corpus slightly surpass the community average of *have got* in 1971, by the time of their 2013 re-interviews, they have fallen behind the mean use of the form in the rest of the community. One possible reason for the patterning in Table 9.6 might be that the change in progress towards increasing rates of *have got* is arrested in the North East. Tagliamonte's (2012) apparent time data from

Table 9.6 The system of stative possession amongst the older panel speakers on Tyneside recorded in 2013

	N	%
Have got	115	61
Have	59	31
Got	16	8
Total	190	100

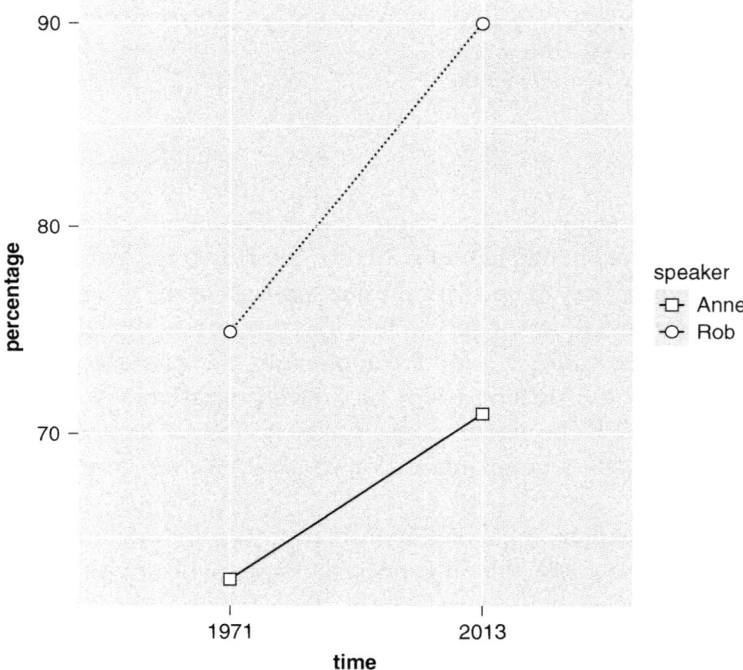

Fig. 9.4 *Have got* use amongst the panel speakers on Tyneside recorded in 1971 and 2013, socially stable working-class speakers

Wheatley Hill suggests that this might be the case since speakers in the youngest age bracket (ages 36 and below) seem to have retreated from *have got*. But the question remains why this would be the case. Historical sociolinguistics has revealed a number of cases where ongoing linguistic changes are arrested, often due to speakers' hyper-attentiveness of the form (Nevalainen and Raumolin-Brunberg 2003). However, as Figs. 9.4 and 9.5 suggest, this seems not to be the case in the Tyneside community.

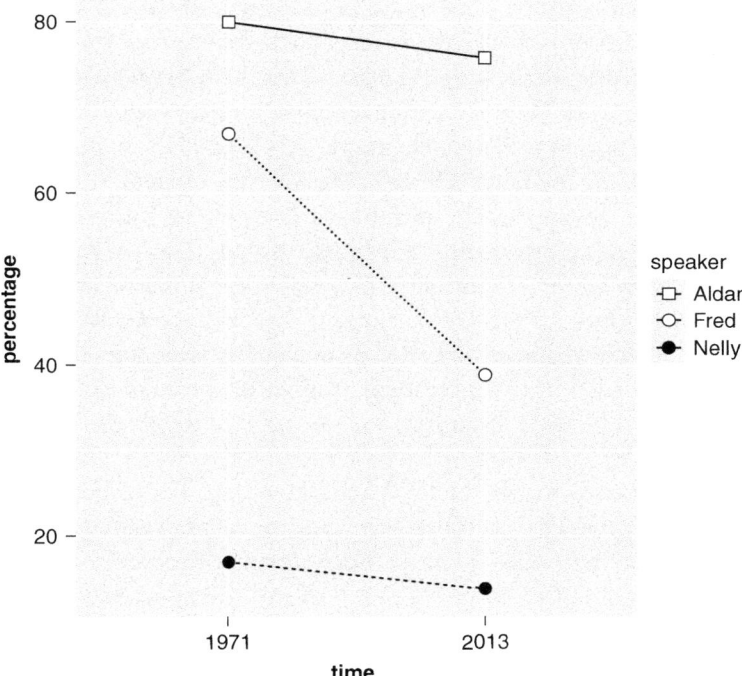

Fig. 9.5 *Have got* use amongst the panel speakers on Tyneside recorded in 1971 and 2013, socially upwardly mobile speakers (Fred, Aidan) and the stably middle-class speaker (Nelly)

In the following, we examine the stative possessive choices of five of our panel speakers across their life-course.[11] As we will see below, a detailed ethnographic analysis which considers speakers' socio-economic trajectory, their personality and their type and amount of contact with children can provide explanatory parameters for the different linguistic trajectories in our speaker pool.

When we split up the results for *have got* by the individual speakers—as Figs. 9.4 and 9.5 do—it becomes immediately obvious that two broad trends lie behind the aggregate numbers displayed in Tables 9.5 and 9.6: two speakers follow the overall community trend towards increasing ratios of *have got*. The three others show a falling trajectory across their lifespan. Fred, in particular, exhibits a drastic drop in the use of *have got* across the 42 years covered by the data.

The two speakers who participate in the ongoing change in the community are those individuals whose socio-economic trajectory has remained relatively stably working class across the 42 years covered by the data. This applies to Rob, the engraver, who increases his *have got* ratios from 75% to 90%, as well as to the upper-working-class seamstress Anne, whose frequencies rise from 63% to 71%. Recent research in variationist sociolinguistics has reported a number of cases where individuals follow community-wide trends during the course of their lives—a phenomenon termed *lifespan change* (Sankoff 2006; see also Thibault and Daveluy 1989; Yaeger-Dror 1994, 1996; Sankoff and Blondeau 2007; Wagner 2012a, 2012b; Buchstaller 2015). Our two stably working-class speakers can, thus, be added to the increasing number of speakers who have been shown to modify their linguistic system after critical age (Lenneberg 1967).[12]

Three other individuals, Nelly, Fred and Aidan, fail to go along with the community-wide trend towards increasing ratios of *have got*. All three speakers reduce their *have got* frequencies during the course of their lives, slightly in the case of Nelly (17% to 14%) and Aidan (80% to 76%) and rather more drastically in the case of Fred (67% to 39%). Sankoff and Wagner (2011: 206) have termed this behaviour, where speakers retreat from ongoing community-wide change, a 'retrograde change' (see also Buchstaller 2015). Notably, Sankoff and Wagner (2006: 10) found that the speakers who withdrew from incoming variants towards older, more conservative forms in their Canadian French sample were those individuals situated 'highest on the job scale'. Similarly, in our Tyneside community, Nelly, the middle-class speaker, not only produces the lowest frequency of *have got* in the sample, she also retracts from this incoming form during her lifespan. Also, note that Fred and Aidan, who do not participate in the ongoing change towards increased ratios of *have got,* were at the beginning of their upward socio-economic trajectory when they were first recorded in 1971. Speakers' ascent up the social ladder, therefore, seems to be marked linguistically by increasingly conservative language choices.

Let us now move on to examine an aspect of the ongoing change in the system of stative possessives which the speakers' socio-economic trajectory alone is unable to explain: the use of the most innovative (and low-

Table 9.7 Use of stative possessive *got* per speaker in the 2013 panel sample

	N	%
Aidan	5	10
Anne	3	9.7
Nelly	4	9.5
Rob	2	6.7
Fred	0	0

frequency) stative possessive form *got*. Table 9.7 plots the use of *got* across all speakers in the 2013 data (the 1971 data contained only one token of *got*, produced by Rob). While overall numbers are small and need to be supported by further evidence, it is obvious that, with the exception of Fred, all our panel speakers have taken on board the newest arrival in the system.

The two stably working-class speakers, Rob and Anne, who participate in the trend towards increasing use of *have got,* also pick up incoming *got* (*N* = 2 and *N* = 3). These two individuals are, thus, 'swept along with historical language change[s in the system of stative possessives which occur] in the wider community' during their life-course—the epitome of lifespan change (Sankoff and Blondeau 2007: 562).

In contrast, the speakers who exhibit retrograde change in their use of *have got* do not pattern in unison in terms of the adoption of innovative *got*. Fred, who drastically reduced his *have got* levels in opposition to the community-wide trend, also eschews innovative *got*. We interpret this finding to mean that Fred remains staunchly conservative with respect to incoming linguistic innovations—an observation that is supported by his behaviour with respect to a range of changes in progress (Buchstaller 2016; Buchstaller et al. 2017). Aidan and Nelly, on the other hand, who exhibit diminishing frequencies of *have got*, go along with the ongoing community-wide change towards the newest innovation—stative possessive *got*. Indeed, Aidan is the most prolific user of stative possessive *got* in the 2013 panel recordings (*N* = 5, 10%). In the following, we will draw on the ethnographic information gleaned from our in-depth conversations to help us interpret the linguistic trajectories of these speakers.

First, let us consider Nelly. How can we consolidate her linguistic conservatism towards the slow incoming change towards *have got* with her adoption of the newest form in the system of stative possession? Nelly's professional choices and personal trajectory have meant that she has had regular and close contact with children and young people. She worked as a nursery nurse and kindergarten/preparatory school teacher until the age of 28, when she quit her job to care for her own children. Since becoming a grandmother, Nelly has been closely involved in the upbringing of her grandchildren (ages 9, 15 and 16), two of whom live nearby and whom she sees regularly (see example 3).

(3) We [Nelly and her grandson] sit at the table. And we just sit and chat and you can't shut him up. And then his parents come downstairs and they'll say 'just listen to you two'. But it's amazing what I can find out about him and he finds out all sorts of things you know.

Maybe due to her lifelong regular interaction with young people, Nelly displays very positive attitudes towards innovation and change in general. At 71 years of age, she is the only woman in the sample who reports using a mobile phone. As she discusses in (4), she has also embraced internet-based technology, even more so than her husband.

(4) The mobile phone it's very handy when you have your grandchildren there you know and they want picking up or anything like that. But otherwise, well my husband he can hardly text … I've had to program my name in it so that he can just press the button and we speak … We do have the internet. We only go on it really if we want to find something out. And e-mails that's — I very seldom do it that's why I don't have an e-mail address. It's my husband's. Just occasionally I'll say 'can I just borrow it a minute'

Nelly's adoption of the most recent newcomer in the system of stative possessives might, thus, be explained by her regular interaction with young people of all ages in combination with her positive attitude towards innovations and change more generally. Indeed, Buchstaller (2015) has shown that Nelly also takes on board *be like*, another fast-spreading linguistic form that indexes [+youth].[13] She, thus, fits Chambers' (2003: 95) speaker type of the hip 'insider, …who [orients to or] is more similar to the people in the next generation … linguistically' (see also Labov 2001).

What this effectively means is that Nelly picks up on highly salient youth trends (*be like, got*), but she does not necessarily go along with slowly progressing longitudinal changes (see Buchstaller 2015).

Finally, let us consider Aidan, who enthusiastically adopted stative possessive *got* without participating in the ongoing trend towards increasing ratios of *have got*. We will discuss Aidan in contrast to Fred, since both speakers underwent a rather meteoric social ascent into a position in the educational sector. Both Fred and Aidan mention the linguistic scrutiny under which they found themselves and Fred in particular comments on the degree to which he has changed his accent as a consequence of normative pressures (see 5, consider also Chambers 2003). But as we will see below, in spite of their parallel socio-economic trajectories, Aidan and Fred assume almost diametrically opposite stances in their 2013 interview, including their tastes, political persuasions and views of the world (see Buchstaller 2015, 2016; Buchstaller et al. 2017). Fred is not only staunchly conservative in his language use, he also revels in 'old-fashioned' pastimes, such as playing the flugelhorn (in 6a), and he regrets throwing away his Bakelite music records. Indeed, in our 2013 interview, Fred repeatedly describes himself as a 'nerd [who] … doesn't like modern stuff' (see also 6a and b). While we would rather characterise Fred as a geek, that is 'someone who has odd interests, and … who can be themselves and not care what anyone thinks' (Urban Dictionary), he certainly fits Roger's (2003: 284) adopter type of the 'laggard', which describes someone whose 'point of reference … is the past and [who is] suspicious of innovation and change'.

(5) *Interviewer*: Has your accent changed?

Fred: It certainly has changed. It changed because of grammar school ehm passing the Eleven Plus and going to grammar school. Being you know one of the one of the kids from the rough end of Gateshead you know you try to fit in with the middle-class kids … I find it difficult to classify myself. I'm obviously I would say I'm from working-class origins … I think I'm probably lower middle-class I would say. I don't have a posh accent but I don't have a broad Geordie accent which of course has changed anyway since the since the sixties and seventies.

(6) a. I learned to play the cornet or the flugelhorn … I enjoy playing the classical guitar which again is a typical nerd's instrument really ehm

  b. I don't know yes it may be nostalgia yeah it may be it may be yeah no when I started it wasn't vinyl it was *(pause)* Bakelite. I should have kept those as well. I used to be interested in Gilbert and Sullivan at one time again a nerdy thing I'm just obviously a nerd yeah.

As Buchstaller (2016) points out, Fred's cautious attitudes towards innovation and changes also express themselves in his conservative stance towards modern educational policy, which he thinks has become much too lackadaisical and lenient ('I've got a fairly negative view about how education has gone'). This general conservatism might explain why Fred is the only speaker in the panel sample who has not picked up on the stative possessive *got.*

Aidan, on the other hand, the community college lecturer, adopts a much more progressive stance in the 2013 interview. As a self-professed 'left-winger', he welcomes many of the far-reaching changes British society has undergone in his lifetime, including increasingly egalitarian language ideologies (7), social mobility and diversity (8). While he portrays himself as very open-minded towards novel socio-cultural achievements, he also presents himself as an educator who strives towards an egalitarian teacher-student relationship (9).

(7) Kind of BBC accent that's changed hasn't it? And it changed from the days as well I found the old days nauseating … pretentious I will call it.

(8) I'd say people are less … polarised in the attitude than their attitude now and then what they used to be … Cockney, Geordie, Brummie what the hell does it make any difference … We've got this mobility now we have social dilution.

(9) gradually … the majority of teaching staff stopped wearing ties and wore a pullover open-necked shirt that that sort of thing. An- and things did change and the attitude you were 'Mister Fulham' in the early days 'Mister Fulham this Mister Fulham that' and then that didn't lie particularly well with me. I mean you know I'm Aidan

that'll do me. And then it towards the end it changed it became 'Aidan, Aidan this Aidan that'. There was a change a social change in the attitudes of staff and pupils and students.

(10) I'm- total time shift or whatever it was 'if the guy comes' wasn't 'guy' no- nobody said 'guy' that's an Americanism isn't it?

(11) I've got a tie I've got me wedding and funeral outfits but that's the only time it goes on.

How can we use this information to explain his enthusiastic uptake of stative possessive *got*? Note that indexical load [+young] and [+US] (Buchstaller 2016) of innovative *got* is similar to another Americanism, *guy*, which Aidan points out using himself (in 10). In contrast to other US-based innovations such as intensifier *totally* or quotative *be like*, which have triggered the wrath of language purists (Buchstaller 2015), however, the lexical item *guy* and stative possessive *got* are much safer choices for 'professionals of the language' (Sankoff et al. 1989), who want to portray themselves as au fait with modern trends but are nevertheless bound by normative expectations regarding their language use (Sankoff and Laberge 1978). Therefore, Aidan might adopt such variants as part of the egalitarian and casual persona he projects, dispelling notions of stuffiness and aloofness (see also 11). Thus, stative possessive *got* is 'available at a relatively low social cost to speakers [such as Aidan], who experience substantial [linguistic] marketplace pressures' but want to appear in touch with innovative linguistic trends (Buchstaller 2016: 17).

Conclusion

In this chapter, we have explored changes in the system of stative possession that currently affect a community in the North East of England. Our trend data reveal that the overall trajectory of the change mirrors other Northern settings (see Tagliamonte et al. 2010). When we scrutinise the individual adjustments in linguistic habitus our panel speakers make across their lifespan, we find that the community-wide trend towards increasing use of *have got* goes hand in hand with two cases of instability across the life-course. Notably, these patterns of language use are distributed according to speakers' socio-economic trajectory: while stably middle-class and upwardly mobile speakers tend to eschew the trend towards increasing ratios of *have got*, speakers whose position in the socio-economic system has remained working class embrace the change as it sweeps through the community around them. This finding adds to the growing number of panel studies that report post-critical age speakers picking up (lifespan change) or, indeed, eschewing (retrograde change) changes in community norms (Sankoff 2004; Sankoff and Wagner 2006, 2011; Wagner 2008; Bigham 2010; Prichard and Tamminga 2012; Buchstaller 2015, 2016). More specifically, our research supports Sankoff and Wagner's contention that the individuals' place in socio-economic structure can be operationalised as a determinant of their (non)adoption of ongoing linguistic trends across their lives.

The change towards the newest stative possessive variant, *got*, however, cannot be easily explained by recourse to socio-economic factors. We, therefore, rely on the thick, emic information we collected during in-depth sociolinguistic interviews (Geertz 1973) in order to explicate the individual trajectories of our panel speakers. This analysis, which remains exploratory due to the low numbers involved, suggests that socially upwardly mobile speakers who are generally open-minded towards innovation and change, as well as those individuals who maintain lifelong close contacts with young speakers, tend to embrace highly salient and rapidly incoming forms, such as *got*, while simultaneously eschewing gradual, slowly incoming variants (see also Buchstaller 2015, 2016).

Our panel sample has, thus, given us the opportunity to answer important questions about the role and impact of individual factors, such as speakers' socio-economic trajectory, their personality, network ties and the way they position themselves towards ongoing societal changes in determining the amount and direction of language change across the lifespan of the individual. Overall, our findings fully agree with Bowie and Yaeger-Dror's (2015) contention that a speaker's individual life history and their personality profile are 'more influential than would be possible if the critical period were operant' (see also Sankoff 2005). The results of our study further suggest that a combination of ethnographically collected trend and panel samples, which epitomise the socio-economic changes that have affected Tyneside, allows us to trace linguistic change across the community as well as across the life of the individual.

Notes

1. The North East region encompasses a number of other towns and cities, each with their associated varieties, such as the 'Smoggie' dialect in Middlesbrough (see Llamas 2007), the 'Mackem' dialect in Sunderland (Burbano-Elizondo 2006) and the 'Sanddancers' of South Shields (Beal et al. 2012).

2. We leave it to one of our interviewees to explain the contested geographical extent of 'Geordieland': 'People have said to me in the past and I hasten to add that this is not my own opinion that eh Geordies come from north of the river and if you're from south of the river you're not a Geordie … I used to say … "you've got to be able to piss out your back window into the Tyne before you can be classified as a Geordie". And they [people from Ashington] didn't like it'. [Aidan].

3. 'The cosmopolitan city of NewcastleGateshead was formed when Newcastle and Gateshead joined to become a single visitor destination linked by the River Tyne. [It boasts visitor magnets such as] the area's famous bridges and … the Quayside, Newcastle and Gateshead's iconic destination. A favourite English city-break destination it really has something for everybody' [http://www.visitnewcastlegateshead.co.uk/site/around-the-region/newcastlegateshead] (see Beal 2009: 153). The MSN Travel website even named Newcastle 'officially the best university city in Britain' in the years 2008–2011.

4. http://www.chroniclelive.co.uk/news/north-east-news/north-east-unemployment-figures-down-8306128

5. See also Bailey et al. (1991).

6. This is a conservative estimate since there is evidence of around 65 Newcastle and 130 Gateshead interviews. The TLS plan apparently involved interviewing approximately 250 people in Newcastle and 150 in Gateshead. How many of these interviews were indeed conducted is a matter of contention and new material keeps being unearthed (see Pellowe et al. 1972; Mearns 2015).

7. Questions included were 'Is the television always running in your house?', 'Which programmes do you watch?', 'Who do you vote for?', 'Have you ever been abroad?' and 'Do you think a woman should work once she has children?'

8. Stative *have* is distinct from dynamic *have*, which indicates events rather than states, as in *He had a swim*, from *have* expressing the meaning 'experience', as in *We had a wonderful holiday*, as well as from *have* expressing

obligation, as in *I have to mow the lawn* (see Huddleston and Pullum 2002: 111).

9. This is in contrast to North American varieties of English, where research reports increasing use *have* (Biber et al. 1999; Tagliamonte et al. 2010).

10. The percentages in Tables 9.3 and 9.5 do not add up to 100% because of rounding issues due to the small sample size.

11. We will not consider Edith since she produced very low numbers and very inconsistent patterns of stative possessives across her interview.

12. How salient is the change in the system of stative possessives? An analysis across the duration of the interview provides evidence of style-shift, the usual diagnostic adduced for socio-cognitive salience. This suggests that the variation in the system does not fully fly below the radar. Indeed, when we explored the data for signs of style shifting, we noted that Anne and Rob slightly increased their rates of *have got* across the length of the 2013 interview (from 66% to 75% for Anne and from 78% to 95% for Rob). This might suggest that the variant has achieved at least a moderate level of socio-cognitive salience amongst these two speakers, enough to allow them to modulate their linguistic system in the direction of ongoing trends (see Buchstaller 2016).

13. Already in 1971, Nelly uses two tokens of *like* in bridging contexts (Heine 2002), which do not occur in the canonical quotative frame but which, nevertheless, 'foreshadow […] a quote' (Gumperz 1982: 47). Whether these occurrences should be considered 'embryonic variants' (Gordon and Trudgill 1999) of quotative *be like* or whether they are already instances of full-blown quotation is largely a matter of interpretation (Buchstaller 2014). In any case, instances such as (a) and (b) are on the grammaticalisation path towards quotative function, and Nelly is clearly a frontrunner in their use for her generation (Edith produces one such token).

(a) Nelly_1971: Er saying things you know like 'Haway man let's away yem'.
(b) Nelly_1971: But more-or-less the way I speak and ending their words properly, like '[ɪŋ] end[ɪŋ]' you know, not saying 'end[ɪn] end[ɪn]' their words.

References

Bailey, G., Wikle, T., Tillery, J., & Sand, L. (1991). The apparent time construct. *Language Variation and Change, 3*, 241–264.

Barnfield, K., & Buchstaller, I. (2010). Intensification on Tyneside: Longitudinal developments and new trends. *English World-Wide, 31*, 252–287.

Beal, J. (2004a). English dialects in the North of England: Phonology. In B. Kortmann & E. W. Schneider (Eds.), *A handbook of varieties of English, Phonology* (Vol. 1, pp. 113–133). Berlin: Mouton de Gruyter.

Beal, J. (2004b). "Geordie Nation": Language and regional identity in the Northeast of England. *Lore and Language, 17*, 33–48.

Beal, J. (2009). Enregisterment, commodification and historical context: "Geordie" versus "Sheffieldish". *American Speech, 84*(2), 138–156.

Beal, J., Burbano-Elizondo, L., & Llamas, C. (2012). *Urban North-Eastern English. Tyneside to Teesside*. Edinburgh: Edinburgh University Press.

Biber, D., Johansson, S., Leech, G., Conrad, S., & Finegan, E. (1999). *The Longman grammar of spoken and written English*. Harlow/Essex: Longman.

Bigham, D. (2010). Mechanisms of accommodation among emerging adults in a university setting. *Journal of English Linguistics, 38*, 193–210.

Bowie, D., & Yaeger-Dror, M. (2015). Language change in real time. In P. Honeybone & J. Salmons (Eds.), *Handbook of historical phonology* (pp. 603–618). Oxford: Oxford University Press.

Buchstaller, I. (2013–2017). *Diagnostics of linguistic change: Mapping language change in real and apparent time*. FP7 Marie Curie European Research Grant.

Buchstaller, I. (2014). *Quotatives: New trends and sociolinguistic implications*. Oxford: Wiley-Blackwell.

Buchstaller, I. (2015). Exploring linguistic malleability across the life-span: Age-specific patterns in quotative use. *Language in Society, 44*(4), 457–496.

Buchstaller, I. (2016). Investigating the effect of socio-cognitive salience and speaker-based factors in morphosyntactic life-span change. *Journal of English Linguistics, 44*(3), 1–31.

Buchstaller, I., & Alvanides, S. (2013). Employing geographical principles for sampling in state of the art dialectological projects. *Journal of Linguistic Geography, 1*(2), 96–114.

Buchstaller, I., Krause, A., Auer, A., & Otte, S. (2017). Levelling across the life-span? Tracing the FACE vowel in panel data from the North East of England. *Journal of Sociolinguistics, 27*(1), 3–33.

Burbano-Elizondo, L. (2006). Regional variation and identity in Sunderland. In T. Omoniyi & G. White (Eds.), *The sociolinguistics of identity* (pp. 113–128). London: Continuum.

Chambers, J. K. (2003). *Sociolinguistic theory*. Oxford: Blackwell.

Colls, R., & Lancaster, B. (Eds.). (2001). *Newcastle upon Tyne: A modern history*. Chichester: Phillimore.

Corrigan, K. P., Moisl, H., & Beal, J. (2005). *The Newcastle Electronic Corpus of Tyneside English* (NECTE). Newcastle University. Available online: http://research.ncl.ac.uk/necte

Corrigan, K. P., Buchstaller, I., Mearns, A., & Moisl, H. (2012). *The Diachronic Electronic Corpus of Tyneside English* (DECTE). Newcastle University. Available online: http://research.ncl.ac.uk/decte

Denis, D. (2011). Innovators and innovation: Tracking the innovators of and stuff in York English. *University of Pennsylvania Working Papers in Linguistics, 17*(2), 61–70.

Geertz, C. (1973). Thick description: Toward an interpretive theory of culture. In C. Geertz (Ed.), *The interpretation of cultures: Selected essays* (pp. 3–30). New York: Basic Books.

Gordon, E., & Trudgill, P. (1999). Shades of things to come: Embryonic variants in New Zealand English sound changes. *English World-Wide, 20*, 111–124.

Gregersen, F., & Barner-Rasmussen, M. (2011). The logic of comparability: On genres and phonetic variation in a project on language change in real time. *Corpus Linguistics and Linguistic Theory, 7*, 7–36.

Gumperz, J. (1982). *Discourse strategies*. Cambridge: Cambridge University Press.

Heine, B. (2002). On the role of context in grammaticalization. In I. Wischer & G. Diewald (Eds.), *New reflections on Grammaticalization* (pp. 83–101). Amsterdam/Philadelphia: Benjamins.

Huddleston, R., & Pullum, G. (2002). *The Cambridge grammar of the English language*. Cambridge: Cambridge University Press.

Jespersen, O. (1961). *A modern English grammar on historical principles: Part IV syntax*. London: George Allen and Unwin.

Kroch, A. (1989). Reflexes of grammar in patterns of language change. *Language Variation and Change, 1*, 199–244.

Labov, W. (1994). *Principles of linguistic change, volume 1: Internal factors*. Oxford: Wiley.

Labov, W. (2001). *Principles of linguistic change, volume 2: Social factors*. Philadelphia: Benjamins.

Lenneberg, E. (1967). *Biological foundations of language*. New York: Wiley.

Llamas, C. (2007). "A place between places": Language and identities in a border town. *Language in Society, 36*(4), 579–604.

Mearns, A. (2015). Tyneside. In R. Hickey (Ed.), *Researching Northern English* (pp. 161–181). Amsterdam: John Benjamins.

Mearns, A., Corrigan, K. P., & Buchstaller, I. (2016). The Diachronic Electronic Corpus of Tyneside English and the Talk of the Toon: Issues in preservation and public engagement. In K. P. Corrigan & A. Mearns (Eds.), *Creating and digitizing language corpora, Databases for public engagement* (Vol. 3, pp. 177–210). London: Palgrave Macmillan.

Milroy, L., Milroy, J., & Docherty, G. (1997). Phonological variation and change in contemporary spoken British English. *Final Report to the ESRC, R00*, 234892.

Milroy, L., Milroy, J., Docherty, G., Foulkes, P., & Walshaw, D. (1999). Phonological variation and change in contemporary English: Evidence from Newcastle upon Tyne and derby. *Cuadernos de Filologia Inglesa, 8*(1), 35–46.

Nevalainen, T., & Raumolin-Brunberg, H. (2003). *Historical sociolinguistics: Language change in Tudor and Stuart England*. London: Longman.

OECD (Organisation for Economic Co-Operation and Development). (2006). *Territorial review: Newcastle in the North East, United Kingdom*. Paris: OECD Publishing.

Pearce, M. (2011). Exploring a perceptual dialect boundary in North East England. *Dialectologia et Geolinguistica, 19*, 3–22.

Pellowe, J., Nixon, G., Strang, B., & McNeany, V. (1972). A dynamic modelling of linguistic variation: The urban (Tyneside) linguistic survey. *Lingua, 30*, 1–30.

Prichard, H., & Tamminga, M. (2012). The impact of higher education on Philadelphia vowels. *University of Pennsylvania Working Papers in Linguistics, 18*(2), 87–95.

Rickford, J., & McNair-Knox, F. (1994). Addressee- and topic-influenced style shift: A quantitative sociolinguistic study. In D. Biber & E. Finegan (Eds.), *Perspectives on register: Situating register variation within sociolinguistics* (pp. 235–276). Oxford: Oxford University Press.

Rickford, J., & Price, M. (2013). Girlz II women: Age-grading, language change, and stylistic variation. *Journal of Sociolinguistics, 17*(2), 143–179.

Rogers, E. (2003). *Diffusion of innovations*. New York: Free Press.

Sankoff, G. (2004). Adolescents, young adults and the critical period: Two case studies from "seven up". In C. Fought (Ed.), *Sociolinguistic variation: Critical reflections* (pp. 121–139). Oxford/New York: Oxford University Press.

Sankoff, G. (2005). Cross-sectional and longitudinal studies in sociolinguistics. In U. Ammon, N. Dittmar, K. J. Mattheier, & P. Trudgill (Eds.), *Sociolinguistics: An international handbook of the science of language and society* (pp. 1003–1013). Berlin: Mouton de Gruyter.

Sankoff, G. (2006). Age: Apparent time and real time. In K. Brown (Ed.), *Encyclopedia of language and linguistics* (2nd ed., pp. 110–116). Amsterdam: Elsevier.

Sankoff, G., & Blondeau, H. (2007). Language change across the lifespan: /r/ in Montreal French. *Language, 83*(3), 560–588.

Sankoff, G., & Evans Wagner, S. (2006). Age grading in retrograde movement: The inflected future in Montréal French. *University of Pennsylvania Working Papers in Linguistics, 12*(2), 203–216.

Sankoff, G., & Evans Wagner, S. (2011). Age grading in the Montréal French future tense. *Language Variation and Change, 23*(3), 275–313.

Sankoff, D., & Laberge, S. (1978). The linguistic market and the statistical explanation of variability. In D. Sankoff (Ed.), *Linguistic variation: Models and methods* (pp. 239–250). New York: Academic Press.

Sankoff, D., Cedergren, H., Kemp, W., Thibault, P., & Vincent, D. (1989). Montreal French: Language, class, and ideology. In R. Fasold & D. Schiffrin (Eds.), *Language change and variation* (pp. 107–118). Amsterdam: John Benjamins.

Tagliamonte, S. (2012). *The roots of English*. Cambridge: Cambridge University Press.

Tagliamonte, S., D'Arcy, A., & Jankowski, B. (2010). Social work and linguistic systems: Marking possession in Canadian English. *Language Variation and Change, 22*(1), 149–173.

Thibault, P., & Daveluy, M. (1989). Quelques traces du passage du temps dans le parler des Montréalais, 1971–1984. *Language Variation and Change, 1*, 19–45.

Trudgill, P. (1988). Norwich revisited: Recent linguistic changes in an English urban dialect. *English World-Wide, 9*, 33–49.

Vall, N. (2007). *Cities in decline? A comparative history of Malmö and Newcastle after 1945*. Malmö: Malmö University Press.

Visser, F. (1963–1978). *An historical syntax of the English language*. Leiden: E.J. Brill.

Wagner, S. E. (2008). *Language change and stabilization in the transition from adolescence to adulthood*. Unpublished PhD thesis, University of Pennsylvania.

Wagner, S. E. (2012a). Age grading in sociolinguistic theory. *Language and Linguistics Compass, 6*(6), 371–382.

Wagner, S. E. (2012b). Real-time evidence for age grad(ing) in late adolescence. *Language Variation and Change, 24*(2), 179–202.

Wales, K. (2006). *Northern English*. Cambridge: Cambridge University Press.

Watt, D. (2000). Phonetic parallels between the close-mid vowels of Tyneside English: Are they internally or externally motivated? *Language Variation and Change, 12,* 69–101.

Watt, D., & Milroy, L. (1999). Patterns of variation and change in three Newcastle vowels: Is this dialect levelling? In P. Foulkes & G. Docherty (Eds.), *Urban voices: Accent studies in the British Isles* (pp. 25–46). London: Arnold.

Yaeger-Dror, M. (1994). Sound change in Montreal French. In P. Keating (Ed.), *Phonological structure and Phonetic form: Papers in laboratory Phonology 3* (pp. 267–292). Cambridge: Cambridge University Press.

Yaeger-Dror, M. (1996). Phonetic evidence for the evolution of lexical classes: The case of a Montreal French vowel shift. In G. R. Guy, C. Feagin, J. Baugh, & D. Schiffrin (Eds.), *Towards a social science of language: Papers in honor of William Labov, The linguistic structure of variation and change* (Vol. 2, pp. 263–287). Amsterdam: John Benjamins.

10

Pit Talk in the East Midlands

Natalie Braber

Introduction

Writing about North-East coalfields, Bill Griffiths (2007) stated that it is with urgency that we must collect all data held about pit language from the individuals who still have memories of it, as the time of the coalfields is over and the data will soon be lost to us forever. Mining had a unique lexicon, which changed from region to region, and from village to village, with the same word meaning different things to different people (see, e.g., Forster 1969; Douglass 1973; Griffiths 2007). Louis Fenn, writing in the coal magazine *The Miner* in 1926, said

> the typical mining village is grouped around the pit-head and has no rea-son for its existence except the requirements of the pit. It is inhabited almost entirely by miners and other grades of mineworkers […] the miners have for years been segregated from contact with other trades, and have become a specialised and peculiar folk, living their own lives and thinking

N. Braber (✉)
Nottingham Trent University, Nottingham, UK

© The Author(s) 2018
N. Braber, S. Jansen (eds.), *Sociolinguistics in England*,
DOI 10.1057/978-1-137-56288-3_10

their own thoughts […] the homogeneity of the mining village makes for an extraordinary cohesion. (cited by Griffin 1990: 7)

The use of a different language—'pit talk'—emphasised and strengthened the comradeship (which many miners during the interviews refer to as a 'brotherhood') which existed amongst mining people. This pit talk is now in danger of disappearing due to the decline of mining in Great Britain.

Much research into mining reviews specific events or memories, but does not focus on language usage (Bell 2008). This chapter aims to help rectify this oversight, and in doing so, it concentrates on the East Midlands. Although there is increased interest in language variation in the East Midlands (Flynn 2012; Braber 2015a, b; Braber and Flynn 2015; Braber and Robinson forthcoming; Ashmore is currently working on Chesterfield in Derbyshire), and there are examples of individuals who have been collecting mining vocabulary in the region (e.g. the research carried out by Bob Bradley, member of the Bilsthorpe Mining Heritage Group), there has as yet been no published research on pit talk in this area. This chapter uses the first results of a recently completed research project, entitled 'Pit Talk in the East Midlands', which was funded by the British Academy to investigate the technical jargon and mining-specific lexical terms used by these miners. This is not a comprehensive overview, but must be regarded as a provisional summary of research findings, which in itself is intended to start the discourse about pit talk in the East Midlands and contribute to a wider discussion of language use among miners in the UK and abroad.

The following pages will briefly examine the history of coal mining in the region. This is followed by a brief discussion of coal mining and cultural heritage; language of the mines (from a lexical perspective); and methodology of the pilot project and the British Academy funded project, before finally examining the vocabulary used by the region's miners in their daily lives.

Coal Mining in the East Midlands

It is, of course, impossible to give a full history of coal mining in the East Midlands within the scope of this chapter (for that history see, e.g., Griffin 1971), but it is important to understand the significance of mining in this area to realise the significance of pit talk to the miners and the region.

Coal mining historically formed the bedrock of the East Midlands' regional economy, and mining activity can be dated back to the Romans, who mined lead in Derbyshire (Mapping UK Mining Heritage; Tonge 1907: 3). There are records of small-scale coal mining in medieval Derbyshire, Leicestershire and Nottinghamshire, and some of the earliest written evidence dates back to the late middle ages (Griffin 1971: 3). However, in July 2015, the last coal mine in the East Midlands, Thoresby Colliery, closed and ended hundreds of years of coal mining in the region.

Many of the mines in Nottinghamshire had the advantage of being close to the River Trent (allowing for the transport of coal to a wider area), which was the only navigable waterway in the county until canals were cut in the late eighteenth century (Griffin 1971: 62). From the middle of the sixteenth century, the demand for coal rose rapidly, mainly because of the growing scarcity of wood. This quickening of demand stimulated technological developments and the pits in the East Midlands' counties developed in a major way in the nineteenth and twentieth centuries, with collieries increasing in size as deeper pits were sunk in more concealed coalfields rather than in the earlier-exposed, shallower seams. In the present-day UK as a whole, from 1550 to 1950, the extent of coal extraction and the number of those employed in this industry expanded at a colossal rate. In 1550, approximately 15,000 tons of coal were mined; by 1950, this had expanded to 21,600,000 tons. Those employed in the industry increased from a few hundred people to over one million persons in around 4000 mines by the time of the 1984–1985 miner strike (Keyworth and District Local History Meeting Report 2003). The importance of coal generally in the UK led to its name 'King Coal' during its heyday (Waddington et al. 2001: 9). The East Midlands coalfield was one of the most productive fields in the country (Griffin 1977: 72). The number and location of mines in the region is shown in Figs. 10.1 and 10.2.

The East Midlands led the way in the coal industry in terms of innovation and technological advances, for example, through the use of railways for transporting coal. A traditional problem of the East Midlands coalfields was that they could only supply local markets and found it difficult to compete with the sea-transported coal of the North-East. Road transport was impractical, and rivers and canals could not provide a solution. A dramatic yet cost-effective infrastructure change had to be made,

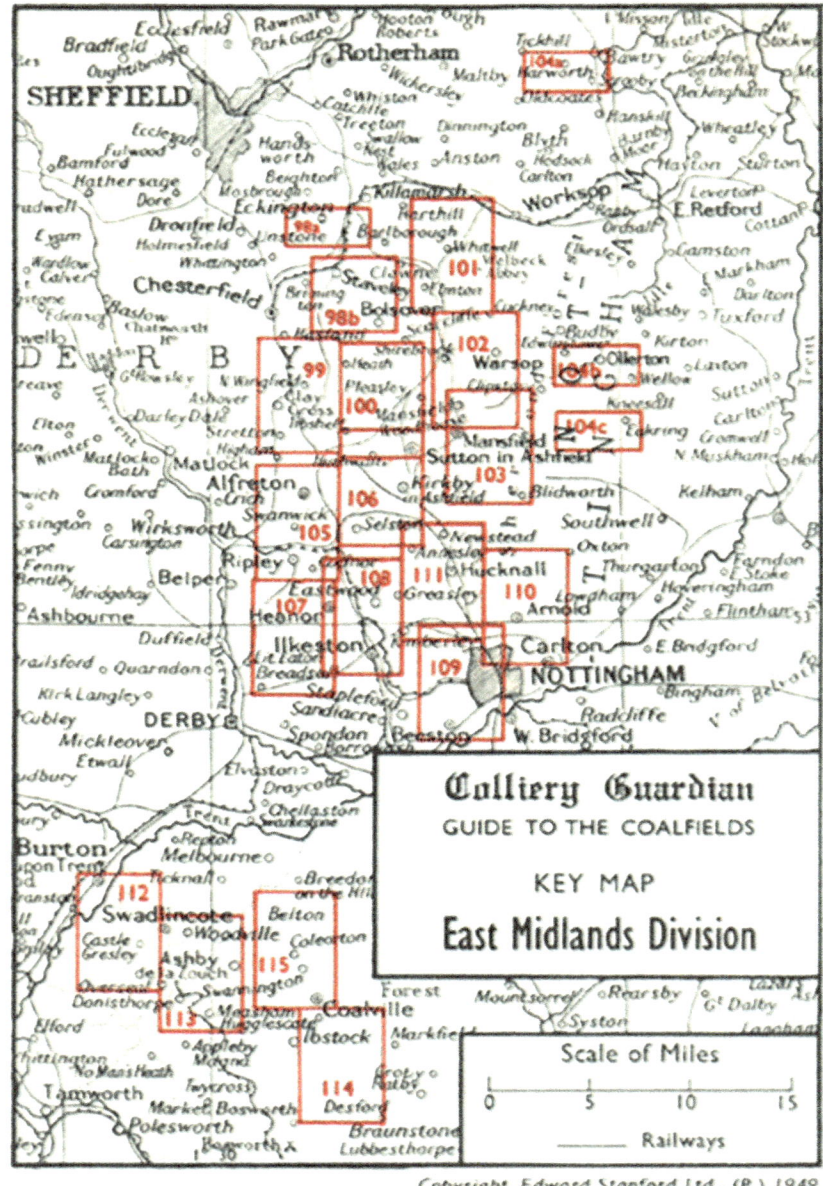

Fig. 10.1 Map showing locations of collieries in the East Midlands in the 1940 (Coalmining History Resource. http://www.cmhrc.co.uk/site/maps/em/index.html)

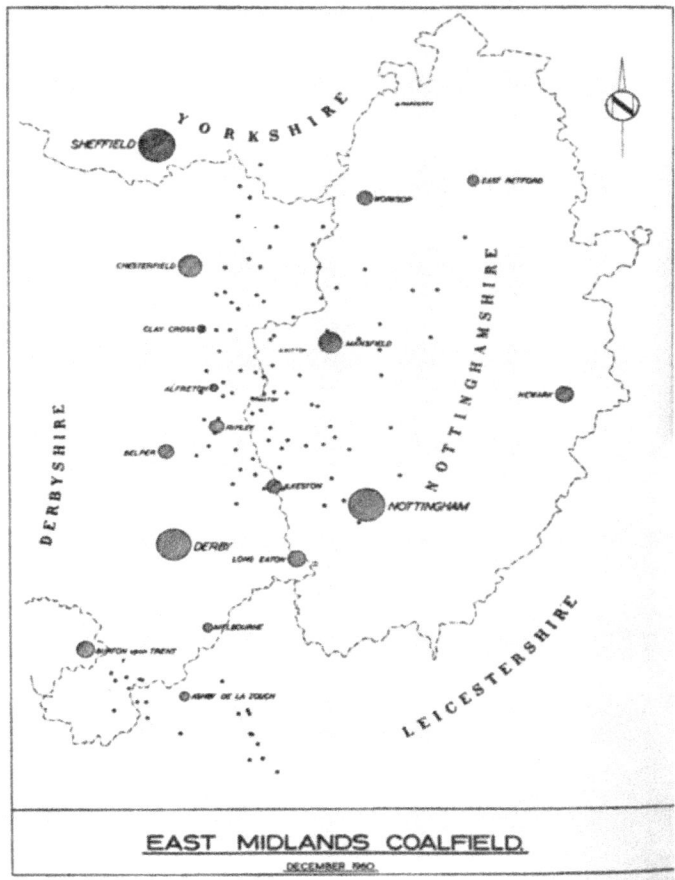

Fig. 10.2 Colliery locations in the East Midlands in the 1970s (Griffin 1971: 102)

and in this way, railways came into being to move coal from colliery to user. Canal, tramway and rail links helped the East Midlands supply more distant areas (e.g. London), and many new mining and transport settle-ments were developed to keep up with demand (Griffin 1977: 137). Coal was the bedrock on which two of the largest and most profitable railway companies—the Midland Railway and the North Eastern Railways—built their business (Griffin 1971). Also, as many of the larger collieries in the region were sunk in the late twentieth century, many of Nottinghamshire mines were leading coalfields in terms of technology. Thoresby was the earliest mine in the county to be completely powered by electricity, and it was the pioneering colliery in terms of mechanised production. It was also the first pit to turn over a million tons of coal per year and, by the late 1980s, Thoresby was producing over two million tons of coal.

The peak of the East Midlands coal output is thought to have taken place just before World War I. After World War II, over 45,000 people were employed in the industry and it is thought there were around 120 mines in the East Midlands. In Nottinghamshire alone, in 1945, there were 44 mines employing 45,587 men, of whom 34,439 worked underground (Franks 2001: 45). The increase of output from the collieries and technological advances linked to the increase in workforce had huge effects on surrounding villages as many miners moved to the East Midlands. Mining villages all around the East Midlands witnessed large population explosions and population shift as miners were frequently moved around the country. Jock Purdon—who was a miner, poet and singer from County Durham—wrote a song when he and the other miners were being transferred to the Nottinghamshire coalfield when their mine closed in 1963. It contains the words 'Leave your picks behind ye, ye'll no need them agen. And off you go to Nottingham, join Robin's merry men. Leave your cares behind ye, your future has been planned. And off ye go tae Nottingham, tae Robin's promised land' (cited by Bell 2008: 10; see also Lewis 1971: 102).

In 1947, the country's 958 pits were nationalised, and 700,000 men worked 'down the pit' across the UK. During the 1950s, well over 100 pits in the country were closed, but there was little opposition as there were plenty of jobs elsewhere (Franks 2001: 52). Six Nottinghamshire collieries closed in the 1950s, followed by a further nine in the 1960s. Already during this time, miners' wages were slipping below the average wages in other heavy industries (Franks 2001: 54). By 1970, of the 958 mines which had been nationalised, only 300 remained in operation (Franks 2001: 63–5). Between 1984 and 1989, mining jobs declined nationally from 181,000 to 66,000, and by 1992, a further 27,000 jobs had been lost. The average age of a UK miner was 34, so early retirement was not an option (Franks 2001: 83). By 1995, all remaining mines were returned to private ownership. The last mine in Derbyshire—Markham Colliery—closed in 1994. In Leicestershire, the last mine closed in 1991

(Bagworth). In Nottinghamshire, the last mine was Thoresby; it closed in 2015 (for more details see Bell 2006, 2007, 2008). As a result of the closures, many areas of the East Midlands have suffered economically, simply because some of the largest and most important employers in the region disappeared.[1]

Coal Mining and Cultural Heritage

As coal mining was such an important aspect of East Midlands culture, the sudden closure and demolition of mines and pit equipment was particularly traumatic for the region. However, many people realised that almost nothing would be left of the industry in the region unless some significant structures were listed and preserved. As a result of this awareness, structures belonging to collieries such as Pleasley Colliery in north-east Derbyshire and Coalville in Leicestershire (held by Snibston Discovery Museum) were retained and preserved, although Snibston Discovery Museum has since closed. The headstocks at Clipstone are currently in danger of being demolished, and some residents are campaigning against their demolition (this has been discussed on BBC Radio Nottingham as recently as March 2017 and the group has a Facebook page[2]).

A danger facing the preservation of coal mining heritage is that the industrial and recent nature of coal mining means that many people do not consider this *heritage*, and as a result, an important aspect of industrial heritage is at risk of being lost (Ferguson et al. 2010: 287).

Franks comments that

> [m]ost of the country's pits have vanished, and monuments are gradually appearing across the county. But their significance will soon be lost, because memories are so short-lived that all can be forgotten within the space of one generation. However, through words and pictures, the story can be saved for posterity. (Franks 2001: 4)

According to UNESCO, language plays a vital role as a vehicle for our cultural heritage and identity.[3] The language people use contains within it key information about features important to a culture's songs, sayings and legends which can help bind communities together. By focusing on their cultural traditions and language, local people can discover and appreciate the unique and shared values of their heritage and cultural identity. It allows them to explore their own language and culture and compare these with other parts of the region, empowering communities to take ownership and be proud of their heritage and culture.

However, in a similar way to oral tradition, language can be carried anywhere 'but it rarely appears in museums' (Hennessy 2012: 35). This is one of the reasons I became involved with examining the language of miners in the region. I was interested in how these symbols of industrialisation, including language, are in danger of becoming lost and how they should be preserved and can be passed onto future generations (see Kearney 2009: 210).

My work with mining communities in the East Midlands showed how frequently language was not considered a feature of preservation, as most of the focus was on memorabilia and mining objects. Many mining communities want to hold onto the last remaining aspects of their mining heritage, but as stated above, many have not considered their language and how this may be distinctive.[4] However, 'while words are ephemeral, they become things when transcribed on paper or recorded onto tape […] words are used to give meaning to objects' (Hennessy 2012: 33). I wanted to record the language of miners to preserve understanding about this way of life and allow it to be passed onto future generations. People can use heritage to help link them to a particular community and place, often in the past, and these give them greater legitimacy in the present (Harrison 2010: 243), and being able to connect to the past allows people to connect to 'cultural capital'—the ability to reconnect with the past using heritage (Harrison 2010: 245).

Language of the Mines—Pit Talk

The mining industry is one in which labour relations have not always run smoothly. Mining communities have traditionally been isolated and working-class. Furthermore, the industry has been a dangerous one to work in. Death and serious injury were a constant threat. Therefore, miners tended to develop a very powerful camaraderie and used to act as a group rather than as individuals. In this, they developed a particular sense of humour which is specific to this group (Bell 2008: 30). Douglass writes that '[t]he mine necessitates a different attitude of mind, a different temperament to that on the surface; necessarily it gives rise to a culture and language which are peculiar to that environment' (Douglass 1973: 1).

Information sheets created by curators at the National Coal Mining Museum state that there are many words that are unique to the mining industry, especially to coal miners. Not only does mining have, like any other industry, numbers of technical words or jargon, but miners working in different regions also had different dialects. For example, a person who hauled the wagons or tubs might be known as a *waggoner* in one part of the country (the information sheets do not state which part this is), a *hurrier* in Yorkshire, a *drawer* in Lancashire, a *putter* in Northumberland or a *haulage-man* in Scotland. There are also cases where the same word can mean very different things. For instance, in the East Midlands and Yorkshire, *snap* is the food a miner takes with him to eat, but to a Durham miner *snap* is an instrument used on the screens to cut waste material off coal (some of these terms can be controversial, Thomas Devlin (personal communication) notes that the miners he interviewed in the North-East did not recognise this term with this meaning, but it is given on the National Coalmining Website as meaning this). The Durham miner calls his lunch *bait*. In Scotland, it was a *piece*. Local variations in dialect and use of words can vary even between villages within one area as well as between coalfields.[5]

There are studies of mining language or *pit talk*, also known as *pitmatic* or *yakka* in the North-East coalfields, and lists of mining terminology (e.g. on the 'Coalmining History Resource Centre' website), but many of these publications are generic and not specific to a particular region. The decision was made, therefore, to focus our project on the East Midlands and interview miners from this region (see Methodology below).

All miners interviewed for this project said that there were differences in the terms and language used by different miners and that, as a result of these differences, the language in one pit was sometimes hard to understand for those who came from other pits. This confirms what other researchers have found earlier. Griffiths states that a mining dictionary of 1747 of Derbyshire contains only a few words in common with North-

East mining vocabulary and much which is 'quite alien' (Griffiths 2007: 13). It is thought that some technical terms may show regional consistency, but many familiar terms also show extensive variation (e.g. job titles, names for food and drink, and names for tools and equipment).

A 1969 survey of terms of the South Midlands has explained that miners had their own language and that the basis of this language seemed to be a mixture of local dialect and technical mining terms, but the survey has also stated that it is crucial that '[t]he language of the miner has come to express his whole culture' (Forster 1969: 1). A study on pit talk in County Durham states

> [t]he miner's "language", however strange it appears to the outsider, is an inevitable part of him. The language of the miner, regardless of what dialects it embraces, is an intricate and inseparable part of his whole culture. It is directly related to his community, his work and the way he handles it, his trade union struggles and movements, his songs and stories. (Douglass 1973: 1)

More variation is caused by migration. As stated above, there was much movement of miners around the country (as well as miners coming to the UK from abroad, e.g. Eastern Europe). However, if miners arrived in groups, they tended to retain and take pride in their own language, although they could use the 'new' language if needed (Forster 1969: 3). There were also some mines newly opened with men coming from all over the country and differences in language used could be immediately apparent. Forster comments of a situation where a Scottish miner stated that '100 yards in front of him is an old Staffordshire miner who regards him as "baiting", while behind him is a group of Warwickshire men who regard him as "dinting", he calls himself the "pavement brusher"' (Forster 1969: 3). Many miners state that, regardless of such variation, they continue to think in terms of their own terminology, as in where they first worked (Forster 1969: 3).

Finally, often the introduction of new technology meant a change in tools and methods, even though terms still referred to old tools and methods (see Forster 1969: 5). Regardless of the 'standardisation of terms', which was the policy of the National Coal Board (NCB) since nationalisation, local terms survived and were used by miners.

Methodology

As part of my research on general language variation in the East Midlands, I had been interviewing different people. Conversations arose about coal mining and I spoke to a woman who stated that her grandfather had been a miner and had his own language. I noted that although there were websites and books examining life and language of miners in north and south Wales, Scotland, Staffordshire, Canada and, particularly, in the North-East of England, there was no published research being carried out within the East Midlands.

As a result, work started on a new research project and with internal funding, I received a scholarship which would allow two students to work with me on this project which started in the summer of 2014. As one of the students working on the project was the daughter of a former miner who was very keen to talk about his life in the mine and more than happy to take part, we had access to local miners.

The interest in the project was immediately overwhelming. From 'story of the week' on the Nottingham Trent University webpage, within two weeks the story had appeared on ITV news, BBC local radio, BBC news online, teletext and all numbers of local newspapers and leaflets. As a result, we were inundated with miners who were interested in taking part, and organisations who were interested in mining and preserving mining memorabilia but had not ever considered language.

The project's aim was to bring together the words spoken by miners of the East Midlands in order to preserve a dying dialect. We wanted to examine how this vocabulary related to the wider language of the region and its literature of story and song. We had seen references elsewhere to this 'unique and bewildering terminology' (Fox 2002: 92) and wanted to investigate this from our region.

This first stage of the project consisted of interviews with 16 individual miners (mainly Nottinghamshire and Leicestershire), participation of one mining heritage group (Derbyshire) and one visit to speak to miners working in Thoresby, which was still open at that time. This stage formed a pilot study that confirmed that there was indeed a distinct mining lexicon and that this varied from pit to pit. The pilot resulted in a successful British Academy small grant, which allowed me to appoint two research assistants, Suzy Harrison and Claire Ashmore, to assist with recording

Table 10.1 Numbers of miners involved with both projects

	Pilot project	British Academy funded project
Nottinghamshire	13 (and one group interview at Thoresby)	12
Derbyshire	1 group interview with a mining heritage group	12
Leicestershire	3	6

and transcribing further interviews. In this second stage of the project, we interviewed a further 30 miners, spread among the three counties (see Table 10.1 for the overall numbers for both projects and Fig. 10.3 for the overall map with locations of all the miners we interviewed)

We interviewed miners and asked them about pit talk and what they could remember of it. All miners were interviewed in the location of their choice (for many miners, this was at home due to ill health, but some requested to be interviewed at Nottingham Trent University or at their current place of work). Most of the interviews were around an hour long and most miners were interviewed alone. We asked all miners similar questions but were also led by the miners themselves as some had more information about certain aspects, due to their experience or memories. Whilst encouraging free discussion, we also made use of predetermined questions (e.g. by using Sense Relation Networks (SRN), originally used by Llamas 1999; however, these were tailored to pit talk, see Fig. 10.4) and specific word lists to allow consistency of data capture across the geographic area so that valid comparisons can be drawn. As these miners were of different ages and worked in a range of pits, our data allowed us to look at language variation over time in a specific community.

Although we realised that the data collected and analysed as part of this project would be presented to academic audiences, an important focus of this project was to ensure accessibility to and engagement with a non-academic audience. Our final celebration event used posters and information sheets to inform those who took part in the project about our initial findings. Furthermore, our work has been published in the form of a book, *Pit Talk in the East Midlands* (Braber et al. 2017), which is suitable for non-academic readers and forms a legacy of the project, thus ensuring that the project has longevity. This book will also allow

Location of the collieries where the interviewed miners worked

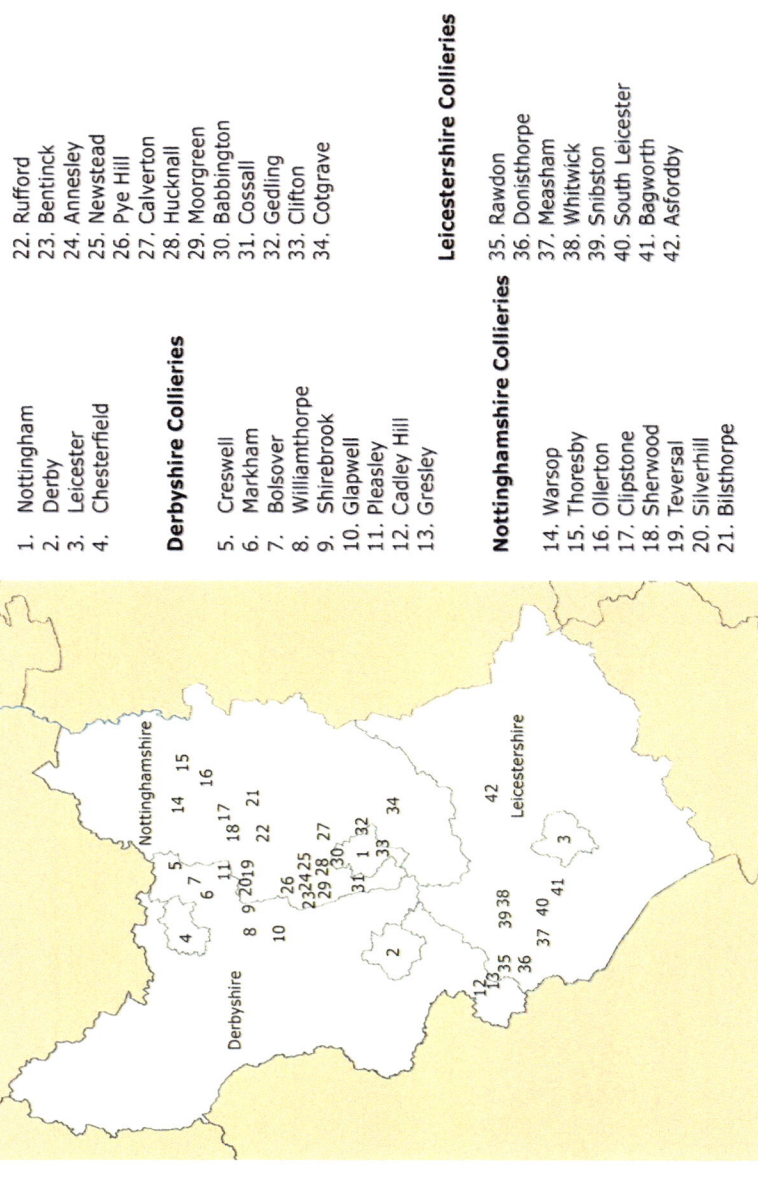

1. Nottingham
2. Derby
3. Leicester
4. Chesterfield

Derbyshire Collieries

5. Creswell
6. Markham
7. Bolsover
8. Williamthorpe
9. Shirebrook
10. Glapwell
11. Pleasley
12. Cadley Hill
13. Gresley

Nottinghamshire Collieries

14. Warsop
15. Thoresby
16. Ollerton
17. Clipstone
18. Sherwood
19. Teversal
20. Silverhill
21. Bilsthorpe

22. Rufford
23. Bentinck
24. Annesley
25. Newstead
26. Pye Hill
27. Calverton
28. Hucknall
29. Moorgreen
30. Babbington
31. Cossall
32. Gedling
33. Clifton
34. Cotgrave

Leicestershire Collieries

35. Rawdon
36. Donisthorpe
37. Measham
38. Whitwick
39. Snibston
40. South Leicester
41. Bagworth
42. Asfordby

Fig. 10.3   Map showing the locations of the miners interviewed by mine

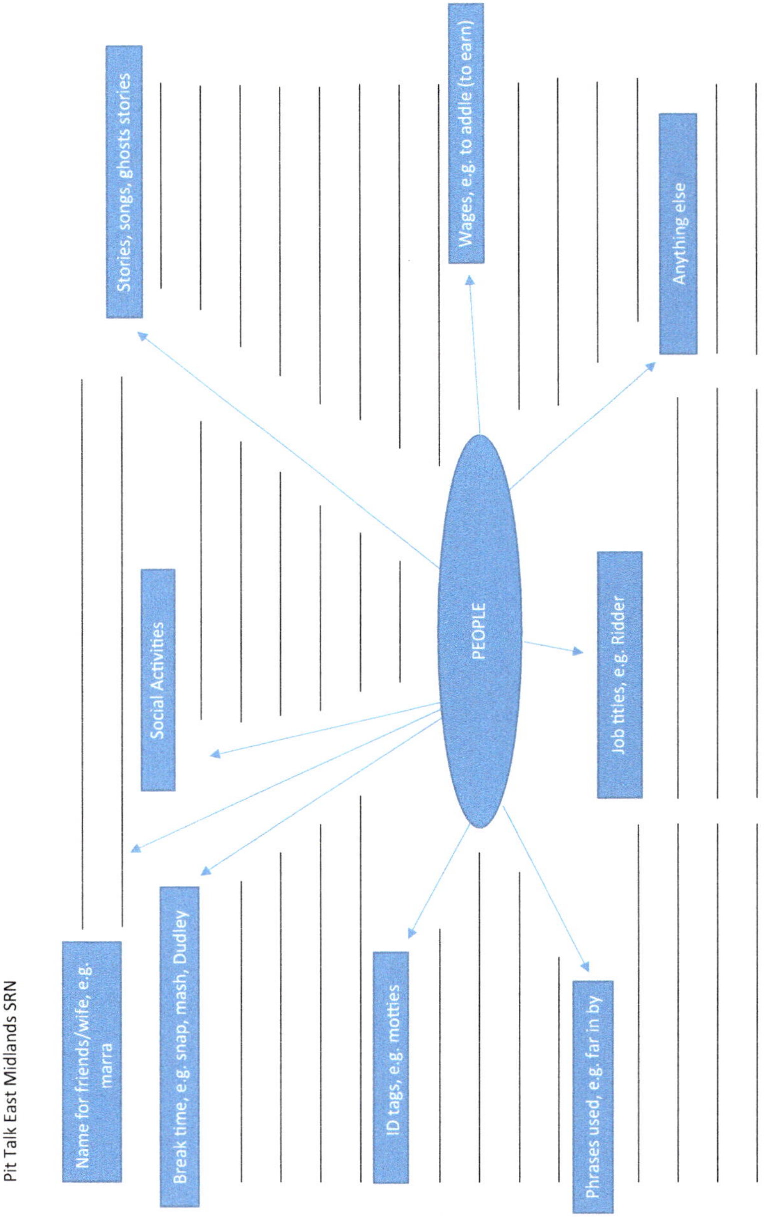

Pit Talk East Midlands SRN

Fig. 10.4 Sense Relation Networks used with the miners

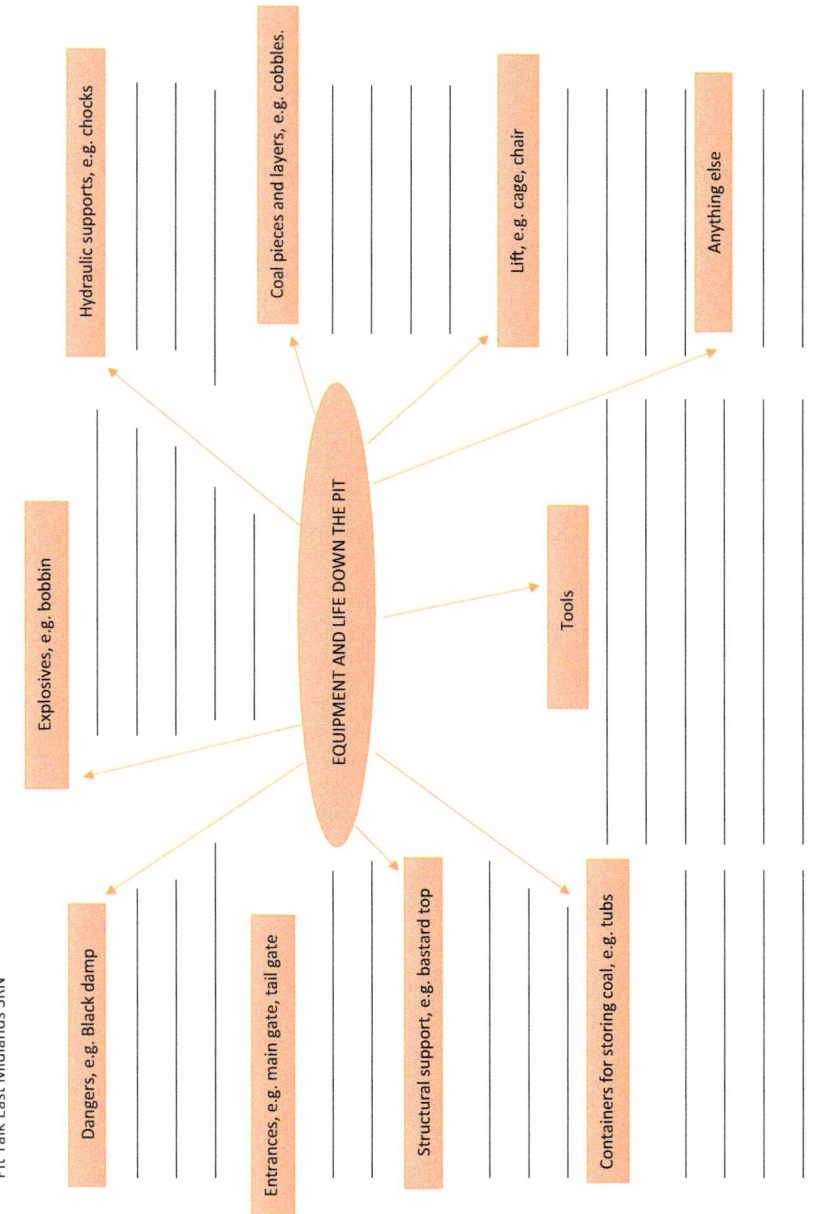

Pit Talk East Midlands SRN

Fig. 10.4 (Continued)

other researchers to compare the pit language of the East Midlands with other regions where coal mines were located.

Part of our project used social media (blogging and a Facebook page) to help involve the communities engaging with the project and to keep them updated with its progress. This aspect of the project will also create a legacy of the project, meaning other individuals and groups can engage with the work carried out on the project once it has ended. Furthermore, we are looking into the possibility of making the recordings and related transcripts available online through the East Midlands Oral History Archive (EMOHA) website, which is a well-established digital resource in the area and could potentially be shared with the British Library. Due to the sensitive nature of some of the recordings, we are still in consultation about how to best achieve this.

Results and Analysis

As stated above, this chapter focuses on lexical variation found in the interviews. More work needs to be carried out which examines phonological or morpho-syntactic variation. Additional work also needs to consider more detailed migration patterns to examine variation from other linguistic varieties, such as Scotland and the North-East, as well as miners from abroad. The employment experience of miners can also be examined in more detail.

Due to the SRNs used, we covered particular themes, which allowed comparisons to take place across the region. Before this chapter looks at specific items of pit talk, it is interesting to focus on some widespread comments made among miners. We found some overall agreements between most miners. Firstly, swearing was not acceptable in front of women. Some of the miners commented that abusive language was left behind in the pit, or washed off in the pit showers before returning home. Many of the miners acknowledged that women did swear but that the men should not use such language in front of women. There was much discussion about the use of nicknames, and most miners commented that they had nicknames, which would stay with a man throughout his working time in the mine (and beyond). These usually reflected humorous incidents which had occurred to a speaker or reflected their physical or personal attributes. Certain names would only be used in small circles (e.g. one gay miner was called *Bent Ben* by his immediate team, but they would never use this in front of other miners and they would not have accepted miners from outside their immediate group to call him by this name).

Many of the interviewed miners also commented that miners spoke differently in different mines. However, we found this comment hard to substantiate. Due to the fact that so many miners moved around and also because many mines were on the border between two areas, for example Derbyshire and Nottinghamshire, differences could be related to specific locations or to individual mines. This will be discussed in more detail later in this chapter. What we did find is that some miners used certain terms that were not used by other miners. One specific comment made by a Derbyshire miner is that Leicestershire miners call a *pick* a *peck* (they state this is a different word rather than just vowel variation) and that a *ringer* is a *crowbar* in Leicestershire and a *length* of coal was called a *stint* in Leicestershire. This could relate to the fact that the Leicestershire mines were geographically most distant from the rest of the mines of the East Midlands coalfield, and be reflected to some extent in the language. Across the project, we found it harder to get in touch with Leicestershire miners than those in Nottinghamshire and Derbyshire. This was not necessarily caused solely by distance; other factors were perhaps a relatively lower number of miners in Leicestershire and there having been less of a mining community in this region than the rest of the coalfield.

Many men moved around, so there were many influences on language use in all of the mines—local miners often commented on men coming from Scotland, Newcastle and Eastern Europe. Some of the miners said that although miners would have to adapt to their new environment, miners from other parts of the country, for example the North-East, would still use their own vocabulary where possible. At times, this led to an adoption of terms in the East Midlands, for example where the term *marra* for friend came to be used among some East Midlands miners, even though it originated in the North-East.

All miners believed that there was a 'brotherhood' between miners, even when there were problems between individual or groups of miners (especially Nottinghamshire versus Derbyshire as a result of the 1984–1985 strike which was not supported by many Nottinghamshire miners). The miners we interviewed also commented that their *banter* and humour was used extensively in order to survive and cope with the terrible working conditions. This strong camaraderie was essential to survival below ground, and often it continued above ground as many men belonged to clubs and societies run by the mines, ranging from allotment groups, football and cricket teams, brass bands, whippet and pigeon racing teams and joint-holiday organisations.

East Midlands Mining Lexicon

Food and Drink

One of the most frequently mentioned words throughout the East Midlands (without any other word given) was *snap*, meaning the food eaten at meal times in the mine. All miners were in agreement on this word and it is one that can be seen as being used frequently outside of the mines too. It can also be used as part of compound words, such as *snap time*, *snap bag/box/tin* (lunch containers), *snap cabin* (place where men could eat their snap), *snap ticket* (food sent down from the canteen for men working overtime) and *paid snap*, which was working through a meal break. The word *snap* is still frequently used by people, including those who were never miners, and it is increasingly seen as a marker of local identity (although it is also used by Yorkshire miners). This is in contrast to the word *dudley* used for the water bottle that men took with them down the mine. Although we see the use of this term by miners from all three counties, not all miners used this word. This is a good example of a word which seems to be used in some mines but not others, but this distinction is not geographical. Some Nottinghamshire miners from Thoresby commented that only underground workers would use this term and some Leicestershire miners claimed never to have heard this word being used. Many miners discussed where the term had come from. Some stated that it was because the earliest bottles were made in Dudley, others that the original manufacturers were called Dudley. However, at this time, there is not yet any concrete evidence where this term originates.

Danger

There are many terms which deal with the dangers within mining and the resulting injuries on the miners. Some examples of the health implications include words such as *beat knee* or *beat elbow* (injuries and swelling in knees and elbows due to prolonged leaning on the hard ground), *blue miner's tattoos* (scarring under the skin due to coal dust entering wounds), *deadlegs* (a miner who was not fully fit), *pinned* (to be trapped by falling coal, roof or dirt), *greenun* (pretending to be ill to get a day off work), *being on the club* (being signed off ill by a doctor), *white finger* (loss of nerve sensations in fingers due to prolonged contact with pneumatic drills) and *stag* (short for *nystagmus*, an eye disease caused by working in low-light conditions). There is also an extensive terminology for dangerous conditions within the mine itself, such as those for gasses which could be found in the mines, including *afterdamp*, *blackdamp*, *chokedamp*, *stinkdamp*, *firedamp*, *sweetdamp* and *whitedamp*, where these terms refer to carbon dioxide, methane or a mixture of carbon dioxide and carbon monoxide. Coal carts could be said to be *amain* or doing a *runner* if they had broken free and could be lethal to unsuspecting miners, or there could be an *inrush* of water flooding the mine. There were also calls to keep men safe, which included *hold down!*, *hold over!* and *hold up!* to warn pitmen to be wary of their heads, their sides and their feet.

Job Description

Many pit talk terms are concerned with job descriptions in the mining industry. These terms have changed greatly with changes in the mining industry, and job titles, for example *hostler* or *ostler*, the men who worked with the pit ponies (although these could also be referred to as *gangers*), became obsolete with changes due to the mechanisation of the mining process.[6] Sometimes, references would change due to changes within the mine. As stated above, initially *gangers* were the men who were in charge of the ponies. Their job was to take equipment along the underground roadways, which was initially carried out with ponies (as well as women and children). As many mines stopped using ponies due to mechanisation, the term *ganger* was used to describe the men moving equipment and coal along the roadways by other means—either on a conveyor or tram or by *tubs*, the name for coal containers. Other job descriptions included different levels of management, where the different levels of managers included the *gaffer* who was the boss, who could also be called an *undermanager*. Below him was the *overman*, a senior official who was in charge of an underground district, and below him the *deputy*, who was in charge of general safety measures and could also be called a *deputy overman*. These *deputies*, as well as being in charge of checking the overall safety of the men, could also enforce punishments on miners if they were seen to be neglecting their work. In the older systems, there were also *butties*; in the *big butty system*, the main *butty* was put in charge of producing all coal by the owner or manager and then paid out the rest of the workforce himself. These butties would then manage the pit with a *stover* (also called *stever*) who was the pit top boss who could control wages and labour conditions. The term *butty* was not to be confused with its alternative meeting of *friend* in some Nottinghamshire mines.

Many other job terms were descriptive in what these workers would do: the *sinkers* would be in charge of sinking new shafts (the tunnel down from the pit top); *sparkies* were electricians; *sawyers* worked in the saw mills, cutting timbers; and *fitters* were mechanics and in charge of fixing machines both above and below ground. Miners, in general, could be referred to as *colliers*, which meant the men who were driving the new *roadways* (the tunnels under ground). This sometimes had to be done with controlled explosions, and the man who carried the explosives was called the *powder monkey* and he would assist the *shot firer* with the explosive work. The men working on the actual coalface itself could also be called *hewers*, *ratchers* or *colliers*. The men who carried the drills and drilled holes were called *borers*; the men who moved up the roof supports to advance behind those creating the tunnels were called *chockers* and the men who removed old supports and set new ones as required were called *back rippers*. Floors in the mine could lift up unexpectedly, and the men whose job it was to level these back out again were called *dinters*. The coal also had to be transported back from the coalface to ground level and this included a number of workers. The *gate lad* would be in charge of opening the safety gates in the tunnels to allow the *tubs* of coal to pass through. These could be transported by horse or on a conveyor belt which was controlled by a *belt driver*. The *onsetter* (or *jigger*) would load onto the lift and the *offsetter* would take it off again. The man who worked at the pit top in charge of the lift and safety at the pit top could also be called the *banksman*. This lift was also controlled by a *bell man* who would ring a bell when it was safe to haul the coal up (or down). On ground level, the *stackers* were employed to empty the tubs of coal and to grade the coal (not all coal was of similar quality—some would be used for domestic purposes and had to be of a higher quality, whereas others could be used by power plants and could be lower-grade quality). The tunnels that were created had to be supported, not only by the *chockers* who moved along with roof supports behind the advancing conveyor, or *chock fitters* and *chock men* who were in charge of checking and repairing the chocks, but also by creating walls to hold up the ceiling by building it up with debris, and these men were called *packers*. Here, we can see that certain mines use their own terminology. One of the miners who had worked in Clipstone (in north Nottinghamshire) stated that, in that particular mine only, the term *chock man* would be used to describe the man who was in charge of the explosives to blow up walls to create coal faces. There were also the *loco drivers* who drove the underground trains for larger mines where the coalface could be a few miles away from the bottom of the shaft.

Equipment

We also found many terms, frequently to do with particular equipment, used in the East Midland mines. With these terms, we found large variation for some terms, not necessarily geographically but differing between mines and, sometimes, even within mines. One of the most frequently discussed features in the mines was the support which held up the roof and resisted the downward pressure from the roof. The actual supports were frequently called *chocks* or *props* and were initially made of wood, later to be replaced by metal hydraulic supports with either three or five legs (see Fig. 10.5). The five-legged *chock* had a *doughty prop*, which was

Fig. 10.5   Props (Reproduced with permission of Local Studies Library, Nottingham)

a beam in the middle for additional strength and support. Some miners use the term *chocks* to refer to wedges to insert in the wheels of the *tubs* (the coal containers) to stop them rolling, but these could also be referred to as *cleats, blocks, cheeseblocks, lockers, wedges* and *pinners* (this last one only if made of wood). There are also *chock nogs*, which are small pieces of wood put on top of chocks (or stated by some miners as the term used for the equipment used before hydraulic chocks were in general use), these *chock nogs* could also be referred to as *chock blocks*, with a miner in Whitick (Leicestershire) commenting that in one part of this mine these would only be referred to as *nuddies*, whereas in another shaft they could be called *chock blocks*. In some Nottinghamshire mines, the term *chocks* could also be used to describe the metal bars that ran perpendicular to the tunnel and connected the *bull bars* that ran parallel to the tunnel along the roof and gave the roof extra structure and support. Some terms would include descriptions of specific types of chock, such as the *mushroom chock* or *Desford chock*.

There are also differences in terminology for other equipment in the mine, including different names for the lift which carries men and equip-

Fig. 10.6 Men ascending in the cage (Reproduced with permission of Local Studies Library, Nottingham)

ment up and down the shaft. Most of these terms are used throughout the region, although one Derbyshire miner commented that the term *cage* is a universal term—known and used by all miners in the region (see Fig. 10.6). Other terms used to refer to the *cage* are *chair, skip, shaft, double-decker* and *manrider*. For other miners, *manrider* could only be used to refer to the underground train used in some larger mines to transport men to the coal face; this was also referred to as *paddy, paddy wagon* or *paddy's mail* (see Fig. 10.7). There are also other terms for smaller cages, used to transport material, rather than men. These include *hoppit* which could only carry one or two men, *kibble* which was more like a small bucket, *kip* which was particularly used for bulky supplies and, in very old mines, *corves* were wicker baskets used to transport material up and down the shaft. A word used around the region to describe one cage-load of men is a *bantle*, which would vary depending on the size of the cage as some would have two levels and would be capable of holding a large number of men. There is one existing research reference which mentions

Fig. 10.7 Men sitting on a manrider (Reproduced with permission of Local Studies Library, Nottingham)

that *bantle* can also be used to refer to the cage itself (Scollins and Titford 2000: 81), but this was not mentioned by any of our miners. At the end of a shift, *the last drawer* would refer to the last lift load of men to travel back up the shaft, as many larger mines would require multiple trips to be made to transport all men back to the surface after their work. Terms such as *on a flyer* and *early riders* were used to describe men who got on an early cage before the official end of their shift.

When discussing the various names for the *cage*, there was also mention of the shaft, which can describe the different entrances and exits out of the mines. Here, there is large variability between terminology and much of these are specific to individual mines. In some cases, the same word is used to describe the opposite shaft. Most mines have names for the shaft bringing men and material in and one for the shaft used to take coal and men out. Different names for the entry shaft are *number one shaft, supply gate, feeder gate, loader gate, main gate* and *mother gate*. Names for the exit shaft are: *number two shaft, supply gate, tail gate, return gate* and *loader gate*. Some of these terms were also used to describe the air flow in the mine, where clean air travels down the intake and dirty impure air by the outtake. It seems that more Nottinghamshire and Derbyshire than Leicestershire miners use *supply gate* for the shaft taking things into the mine, whereas we see this being used in the opposite way by some Leicestershire men. It is also commented that the term *feeder gate* is only used for returning materials in the Annesley mine in Nottinghamshire. Men would also talk about moving in the mine as going *inbye* or *outbye* depending on whether they were travelling away from the cage towards the coalface or back towards the shaft again.

There is much vocabulary related to tools used by miners that are regional in nature. This includes words for spanners, a *bodger* (a flat ended spanner with spiky handle) and a *shifter* (a spanner with a long, tapered end on one side which could also be used as a hammer). There are different kinds of picks—a *tadge* is a pick with a cutting edge on one side, a *radge* is used for a pick with one of the blades formed into an axe, a *tommyhawk* is a combined pick and hammer, and a *pick/peck* is a term which shows variation between Leicestershire miners who use the term *peck* where it can mean a pick or a shovel, whereas Nottinghamshire and Derbyshire men use *pick*. The term *windy pick* is used for compressed-air-operated picks. The word *banjo* refers to a round shovel. The word *ringer* is used for a crow bar, as are *pinch bars*. Hammers are often referred to as *ommers*, and there are also *nopers* which are hammers at one end and a short pick at the other end, a *mell* which is a hammer weighing up to 14 pounds and a *mortek* which can be used to refer to a variety of hammers. Some of the miners suggested that this final term had been influenced by Eastern Europeans, particularly Polish miners. Following this comment, I have noted that the Polish word for hammer is *mlotek*, so miners may have used this term following contact with Polish miners. There is also the *Monday hammer*, which is the largest hammer weighing in at 28 lbs. There are two theories about this name according to the miners we spoke to. One is that it received its name as if you used it on a Monday, you would be too tired to use it again on Tuesday. The other is that this hammer was so heavy that it was as popular as Monday. This term was not noted by Leicestershire miners.

All miners had to carry identification tags on them in case of accidents and also to record timekeeping. These tags contained each miner's individual number and there were three of them. One carried by the miner at all times, one which was kept in the main office and one which was handed to the *banksman*, so there would be a record of which men had travelled into the mine. When the miners finished their shift, they would receive this tag back and it would be a record of the shift they worked. The terms used for these tags varies (as did their shapes), with the miners referring to them as *tallies, tokens, tags, checks* and *motties*. All these terms were mentioned by miners in all three counties. Some of the miners also commented that in the newer mines, these tags were replaced with swipe cards (e.g. in Thoresby colliery in Nottinghamshire), but the men still continued to refer to them as their *motty* (or whichever word they used) (Fig. 10.8). These checks were also very important indicators of a coalminer's identity and many of the men we interviewed still had their motties, many carried them around daily (e.g. on their keyring) and all could remember their individual numbers.

Fig. 10.8   Image of motties (Taken by Suzy Harrison)

Links to Above Ground

Other words reflect local language variations also found outside the mines. For example, a very large shovel is called an *elephant's tab*, where *tab* is an East Midlands word for *ear*. Many of the miners also referred to *Are you mashing?* when enquiring about making a cup of tea. Outside the mine, this can be particularly heard in the Leicestershire area, although for the miners this has a more widespread usage as it is mentioned by miners from mines in Derbyshire and Nottinghamshire. Personal communication with Dave Douglass, author of *Pit Talk in County Durham* (1973), suggested that many words found in the mines reflect the older language of the region. He states that dialect words which may have been disappearing above ground remained below ground to be used by miners who were working in their separate world. Many men commented on the word *duck*, which can be used for men and women and is used frequently in the mines. This word is particularly symbolic for people from the East Midlands and is frequently used to symbolise local identity (including messages on mugs, pencils, t-shirts and advertising billboards). However, this sense of local identity does not include mining identity specifically, as it does in areas such as the North-East, for example (see Fig. 10.9), for a cushion on sale in Northumberland.

Other terms of address included *lad*, which was used for all young miners. *Youth*, on the other hand, could be used for men of all ages. Other terms of address included *mi owd, mucka* and the term *serry* which appears to have multiple spellings, possibly referring to different pronunciations by the miners (including *sirree, sithee, sorry* and *surry*). Some miners mentioned the word *marra*, which is a North-East miner's term for a friend, and they said that this usage had spread to some part of the East Midlands. Some miners commented they would only use it when speaking to miners from the North-East while others commented they would use it more widely. Other local vocabulary terms mentioned by miners included *snicket*, which describes a small alleyway connecting two main tunnels in the mine but can also be used to refer to the alleyways between terraced houses. Many men commented on pronunciation of words, which reflects local pronunciation, including *dot* (dirt), *ot* (hurt), *os* (horse), *watter* (water), *faither* (father) and *owd* (old).

Fig. 10.9 Image of commodified mining language in the North-East (Taken by Natalie Braber)

Conclusion

Our research project has attempted to record mining language used in the East Midlands in order to preserve this heritage for future generations. We found clear examples of a distinct mining lexicon used by formers miners of the East Midlands. Due to the specific nature of this work, specialised words were needed to describe the processes of work. We found attitudes surrounding pit talk, which included swearing and taboo words, but these should not be used outside the mine. We discussed words relating to food and drink, particularly *snap*, which appears to be a universal word among East Midlands' miners. Many words which illustrate the dangerous nature of the work carried out were found, relating both to the physical nature of the work and the injuries that could result from such work. The many different jobs in the mines were represented by specific job descriptions, some of which changed over time as mines modernised and mechanised. These different jobs necessitated the use of different tools, and many words were used throughout the mines to describe the hammers, spanners and other equipment needed for the miners to carry out their job.

A tangible product of this project is a provisional East Midlands mining lexicon. Much more work needs to be done, but, in this chapter, we have listed different words under the subheadings: food and drink; danger; job description and equipment although others are also evident and are discussed in the *Pit Talk in the East Midlands* book. It is interesting to examine to what extent such language has moved outside the mines and also how it is affected by the local dialects found in the East Midlands. We can see the influence of local variation in the ways words are pronounced, and that some terms used in the mines, such as *snicket*, may also have other meanings outside the mines. We could also see that some words used in the mine, such as *snap*, had spread outside the immediate mining communities.

Future work will include closer examination of migration patterns of miners and how this could relate to specific lexical patterns. It will also be interesting to examine how many miners worked across the region in different mines to investigate whether this led to changing language practices. More work is also needed to examine the extent of differences between the East Midlands coal regions and other coal-mining regions in the UK. Some of the words in this lexicon may also be found in other regions, and that is to be expected, as we know many miners and their families moved around the country following work. However, there are many terms which are distinctive to the East Midlands, and these words add to the distinct identity of 'miner' held by many who formerly worked in the pits.

Acknowledgements Images in this chapter have been reproduced with permission of the Local Studies Library, Nottingham. This is not the case for all images—there is also the image of the motties, which was taken by Suzy Harrison.

I would like to thank Suzy Harrison and Claire Ashmore for their work on the Pit Talk in the East Midlands research project, funded by the British Academy. They carried out many of the interviews and completed many of the transcriptions. Thanks are also due to John Towler of the Local Studies Library at Nottingham Library for helping with the images, and the Local Studies Library for allowing me to use these images. I would also like to thank the two reviewers of this chapter.

Notes

1. For example, see documents produced by local authorities, such as the North Nottinghamshire Local Development Strategy: http://www.nottinghamshire.gov.uk/media/109973/localdevstrategynorthnotts.pdf which discusses unemployment, low incomes and other issues resulting from mine closures.
2. https://www.facebook.com/Save-Clipstone-Colliery-Headstocks-106659108993/
3. See, for example, UNESCO's website and details on intangible heritage: http://www.unesco.org/culture/ich/en/oral-traditions-and-expressions-00053
4. Following a presentation to local heritage groups about 'pit talk', the treasurer of the South Derbyshire Mining Association commented that his society had not considered language as part of their heritage, but realised that it was actually an important resource.
5. See 'mining words' on the National Coalmining Museum resources, https://www.ncm.org.uk/downloads/42/Mining_Words.pdf
6. Recent research has uncovered signing on books of one Nottinghamshire mine which lists job descriptions over an extended period of time. Future research will allow the examination of changing job titles and how they changed over time following mechanisation and changing work conditions.

References

Bell, D. (2006). *Memories of the Derbyshire coalfield*. Newbury: Countryside Books.

Bell, D. (2007). *Memories of the Leicestershire coalfield*. Newbury: Countryside Books.

Bell, D. (2008). *Memories of the Nottinghamshire coalfield*. Newbury: Countryside Books.

Braber, N. (2015a). *Nottinghamshire dialect*. Sheffield: Bradwell Books.

Braber, N. (2015b). Language perception in the East Midlands. *English Today, 31*(1), 16–26.

Braber, N., Ashmore, C., & Harrison, S. (2017). *Pit talk of the East Midlands*. Sheffield: Bradwell Books.

Braber, N., & Flynn, N. (2015). The East Midlands: Nottingham. In R. Hickey (Ed.), *Researching Northern Englishes* (pp. 369–392). Amsterdam: John Benjamins.

Braber, N., & Robinson, J. (Forthcoming). *East Midlands English*. Berlin: Mouton de Gruyter.

Douglass, D. (1973). *Pit talk in county Durham*. Oxford: TruExpress.

Ferguson, R., Harrison, R., & Weinbren, D. (2010). Heritage and the recent and contemporary past. In T. Benton (Ed.), *Understanding heritage and memory* (pp. 277–315). Manchester: Manchester University Press.

Flynn, N. (2012). *A sociophonetic study of Nottingham speakers*. Unpublished PhD Thesis, University of York, UK.

Forster, W. (1969). *Pit-talk: A survey of terms used by miners in the South Midlands*. Leicester: Vaughan Papers in Adult Education.

Fox, A. (2002). *Oral and literate culture in England 1500–1700*. Oxford: Oxford University Press.

Franks, A. (2001). *Nottinghamshire miners' tales*. Nottingham: Adlard Print.

Griffin, A. R. (1971). *Mining in the East Midlands 1550–1947*. Plymouth: Frank Cass and Company.

Griffin, A. R. (1977). *The British coalmining industry. Retrospect and prospect*. Ashbourne: Moorland Publishing.

Griffin, C. P. (1990). *The Nottinghamshire miners' industrial union. 'Spencer Union'. Rufford branch minutes 1926–1936*. Nottingham: The Thoroton Society of Nottinghamshire.

Griffiths, B. (2007). *Pitmatic: The talk of the North East coalfield*. Newcastle: Northumbria University Press.

Harrison, R. (2010). Heritage as social action. In S. West (Ed.), *Understanding heritage in practice* (pp. 240–276). Manchester: Manchester University Press.

Hennessy, K. (2012). From intangible expression to digital cultural heritage. In M. L. Stefano, P. Davis, & G. Corsane (Eds.), *Safeguarding intangible cultural heritage* (pp. 33–45). Woodbridge: Boydell Press.

Kearney, A. (2009). Intangible cultural heritage. Global awareness and local interest. In L. Smith & N. Akagawa (Eds.), *Intangible heritage* (pp. 209–225). London: Routledge.

Keyworth and Local History Meeting Report. (2003). Available online: http://keyworth-history.org.uk/about/reports/0310.htm

Lewis, B. (1971). *Coal mining in the eighteenth and nineteenth centuries*. London: Longman.

Llamas, C. (1999). A new methodology: Data elicitation for social and regional language variation studies. *Leeds Working Papers in Linguistics and Phonetics, 7*, 95–118.

Mapping UK Mining Heritage. Available online: http://mininghistorythehumanjourney.net/edu/EastMidlandsIntro.shtml

National Coalmining Museum. Mining for words. Available online: https://www.ncm.org.uk/downloads/42/Mining_Words.pdf

Scollins, R., & Titford, J. (2000). *Ey up mi duck! Dialect of Derbyshire and the East Midlands*. Newbury: Countryside Books.

Tonge, J. (1907). *Coal*. London: Archibald Constable.

Waddington, D., Critcher, C., Dicks, B., & Parry, D. (2001). *Out of the ashes? The social impact of industrial contraction and regeneration on Britain's mining communities*. London: The Stationery Office.

11

Studying Intonation in Varieties of English: Gender and Individual Variation in Liverpool

Claire Nance, Sam Kirkham, and Eve Groarke

Introduction

Much of the previous sociophonetic research in the UK has considered variation at the segmental level, but with lesser focus on prosodic variation (Foulkes et al. 2010). In this chapter, we provide an overview of sociophonetic treatments of intonation and identify directions for future research in this area. We then present results from a small-scale study of intonational variation in Liverpool English, which is widely recognised as a highly distinctive variety of British English. In his phonetic description of this variety, Watson (2007: 358) remarks that work on Liverpool

This research was funded by a Lancaster University Linguistics and English Language Undergraduate Internship (SPRINT). We would like to thank our participants for lending their time and expertise. We would also like to thank the anonymous reviewers and the editors of this book for their feedback.

C. Nance (✉) • S. Kirkham
Lancaster University, Lancaster, UK

E. Groarke
NHS, Sheffield, UK

© The Author(s) 2018
N. Braber, S. Jansen (eds.), *Sociolinguistics in England*,
DOI 10.1057/978-1-137-56288-3_11

275

English intonation is 'minimal' and that 'more systematic investigation is required'. This chapter aims to contribute towards plugging this gap in the literature and providing a better understanding of sociolinguistic variation in the UK. In the following sections, we review previous socio-linguistic intonational work in the UK, different analysis frameworks and some suggestions for best practices. We further present the results of our analysis of Liverpool intonation, before suggesting directions and methods that could be used in future work.

Phrase-Final Rises and the 'Urban Northern British' Group

The intonational feature that has perhaps received most attention in UK studies is the extensive use of phrase-final rises in declaratives in the north of the country, while falls would be more common in the south (e.g. Cruttenden 1994: 133; Ladd 2008). In such instances, a sentence such as 'They like eating cake' might be produced with the pitch rising on or just after the final accented syllable of the phrase, which then stays at a high plateau until the end of the phrase. Another common pattern is for pitch to drift slightly downwards at the end of the phrase. In Cruttenden's (1997) terminology, these are referred to as a 'rise-plateau' and 'rise-plateau-slump', respectively. Additionally, Cruttenden refers to a contour known simply as 'rise', where pitch slowly glides upwards to the end of the phrase.

The use of phrase-final rises in declaratives appears to be a dialectal feature, which is common in several urban dialects, such as Glasgow (Mayo 1996; Mayo et al. 1997; Vizcaino-Ortega 2002; Cruttenden 2007; Sullivan 2010; Nance 2013, 2015), Belfast (Jarman and Cruttenden 1976; Wells and Peppé 1996; Rahilly 1997; Grabe et al. 2000; Grabe and Post 2002; Lowry 2002; Grabe 2004; Sullivan 2010), Birmingham, Newcastle (Pellowe and Jones 1978; Local et al. 1986) and Liverpool (Knowles 1973, 1978). The broad intonational similarity between these dialects in declaratives has led Cruttenden (1997) to refer to this group of dialects as the 'Urban Northern British' (UNB) group.

Specific to the Liverpool context, Knowles (1973: 175) notes that Liverpool speakers employ a narrower pitch range than other dialects and also states that middle class speakers are less likely to use the traditional Liverpool rising contours compared to working class speakers. Knowles (1973) states that the rising contour in Liverpool is most likely to be of Irish origin due to the substantial numbers of Irish immigrants to the city in the nineteenth century. However, this seems unlikely for several reasons. First, as Cruttenden (1994: 133) notes, Irish immigration cannot explain all of the rising contours in the UNB group: Newcastle did not have substantial numbers of Irish immigrants until well after the first commentaries on the city's distinctive intonation. Second, there is extensive variation in Irish and Irish English intonation (Dalton and NíChasaide 2003, 2005; Dorn et al. 2011). Many dialects of Irish and Irish English do not use rising contours in the way that the UNB group do. Therefore, even if UNB rises are the result of Irish immigration, this is not a straightforward relationship and is likely to be indirect and multifaceted.

Uptalk

The rises discussed above, which are traditional dialect features of the UNB group, are qualitatively and sociolinguistically different from another kind of rise which has been widely studied in the sociophonetic literature: High Rising Terminal (HRT). Also referred to as 'Uptalk', or 'Australian Question Intonation' (AQI), HRT is an apparently recent addition to the UK intonational inventory (Bradford 1997; Shobbrock and House 2003; House 2006; Barry 2007; Levon 2015). This contour is distinguished by a contour that rises and then keeps on rising until the end of the phrase to the uppermost reaches of a speaker's commonly used pitch range (Ladd 2008: 125). Previously, HRT was thought not to occur in the UNB dialects (Fletcher and Harrington 2001; Fletcher et al. 2002, 2005; Ladd 2008), though recent work suggests that it is beginning to be used in these dialects as well (Cruttenden 2007; Sullivan 2010; Nance 2015). In terms of the sociolinguistic distribution of these two kinds of rise, the UNB rise is a feature of the traditional dialects of the cities in which it occurs. HRT, however, is an innovative feature and has been

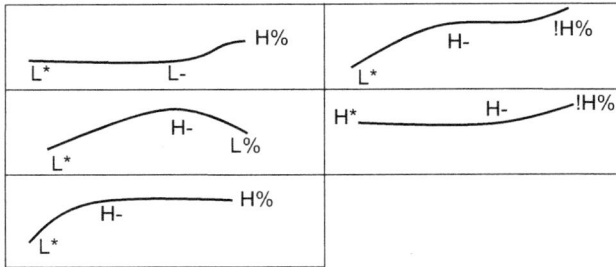

Fig. 11.1 Comparison of different kinds of rising contour in our notation. UNB rises are shown on the left and HRT rises on the right

observed as occurring most frequently in upper middle class and female speakers (Bradford 1997; Barry 2007; Levon 2015; Warren 2016). A schematic diagram showing the comparison between contours considered as UNB rises and contours considered as HRT is shown in Fig. 11.1.

Sociophonetics of Intonation

The most commonly investigated intonational feature with reference to sociolinguistic variation is the use of HRT. Previous studies have found that the use of HRT tends to be more prevalent among young females; however, it is still used by male speakers (Guy and Vonwiller 1984; Guy et al. 1986; Fletcher et al. 2005; Ritchart and Arvaniti 2014). There is also evidence of the relation of variation to ethnicity, such as the use of greater HRT amongst ethnically Maori people in New Zealand (Britain 1992). Warren (2005) notes gender and age differences in the phonetic realisation of HRT, with young females starting their rises later in the phrase. Studies not focusing on the use of HRT also note sociolinguistic differences in pitch and intonation more generally; for example, Daly and Warren's (2001) study of New Zealand English find that women may use a greater pitch range and dynamism than men.

A parameter along which intonation has been found to vary is speech context, or *style* in the Labovian sense. For example, Cruttenden (2007) finds intonational *diglossia* in the speech of a young Glaswegian woman: in conversational speech, she uses the rise-plateau and rise-plateau-slump contours typical of Glaswegian, but in read speech she uses more falls which are typical of southern British English. Similarly, Lowry (2011) describes differences between males and females and finds that females are likely to style-shift, using different proportions of rising and falling contours across read sentences, story-telling and an interactive task. Taking a slightly different approach, Podesva (2011) demonstrates how the frequency of specific intonation patterns and their phonetic realisation are used by three gay professionals to construct different personae in different social contexts.

A complicating factor in a sociolinguistic treatment of intonation is that this prosodic feature is often used to convey subtle pragmatic meanings (see House 2006 for a review), which must be accounted for before a sociolinguistic analysis of the data can be put forward (Milroy and Gordon 2003: 185; Foulkes et al. 2010: 721). It is for this reason that many of the studies cited here (as well as our own) choose to investigate intonation using carefully controlled read sentences or map tasks rather than sociolinguistic interviews or more naturally occurring data.

If data have been collected in the form of read sentences, then the pragmatic function of the sentence can be predefined and different functions easily compared. This is the approach taken in recent surveys of British English and Irish Gaelic dialects (e.g. Grabe et al. 2000; Grabe and Post 2002; Dalton and NíChasaide 2003; Grabe 2004; Dalton and NíChasaide 2005; Dorn et al. 2011). Another possible way of accounting for pragmatic function is to code for it within existing data and use this coding information in statistical modelling to account for any pragmatic effects. For example, Stirling et al. (2001) developed a framework for coding discourse events, which was then used in later studies (Fletcher and Harrington 2001; Fletcher et al. 2002, 2005; McGregor and Palethorpe 2008). Similarly, Ritchart and Arvaniti (2014) classified each sentence type as one of the following: question, statement, holding the floor and confirmation request. Using a coding scheme developed for analysing different discourse events in sociolinguistic interviews (Gregersen et al. 2009), Nance (2013, 2015) and Jespersen (2015) chose to compare a subset of discourse functions within interview and conversational data.

Analysing Intonation

Two main approaches are used in sociolinguistic approaches to intonational variation. The first uses an Autosegmental Metrical (AM) framework (e.g. Pierrehumbert 1980; Ladd 2008) to transcribe contours into phonological units. The second compares the phonetic realisation of contours that are phonologically identical or similar (e.g. the timing of the start of a rise, or the pitch range used a rise; see Warren 2005). Some studies use a combination of both, identifying phonological differences between speakers and sentence types, but also analysing phonetic differences within phonological categories. AM approaches to intonation claim that an intonational contour can be broken down into a series of significant pitch events, which are the phonological building blocks of intonational meaning. For example, *pitch accents* are contrastive pitch events, which occur on stressed syllables, but not every stressed syllable receives the extra prominence associated with a pitch accent. Pitch accents are usually notated by * in AM notation. A pitch accent associated with low pitch is shown as L*, and a pitch accent associated with high pitch is notated as H*. Breaking down a continuous intonational contour into phonological units is analytically useful for a variety of reasons. We have found this approach convenient for sociophonetic analysis as it allows us to make meaningful comparisons of similar elements, such as pitch accents or how phrases are ended.

The most commonly used AM framework is ToBI (Tones and Break Indices), which was originally developed to transcribe American English intonation (Beckman and Elam 1997; Beckman et al. 2006). Early studies conducted using ToBI quickly realised that it was often necessary to adapt transcription systems such as ToBI for the language or dialect under study (for applications of this principle see Jun 2005, 2014). Using ToBI, or another widely used AM framework such as IViE (Grabe et al. 2001), the proportion of different contour types can be compared across sociolinguistic categories or discourse functions and sentence types.

In ToBI, the final pitch accent in the phrase is known as the *nuclear accent*, while in IViE *nuclear accent* refers to the most prominent pitch accent in the phrase. Generally speaking, the most prominent pitch accent is also the last one and seems to be an important location for intonational meaning (Ladd 2008: 131). The accent preceding the nuclear accent is known as the *pre-nuclear accent*. In AM approaches, intonational contours can be divided into large units known as Intonation Phrases (IPs). A boundary tone occurs at the end of an IP and is notated with the '%' symbol. Pierrehumbert (1980: 19) states that IP boundaries can be found where a speaker makes a non-hesitation pause, or at a point where they could pause without disrupting the flow of discourse. However, as pointed out by Cruttenden (1997: 29) and Nolan (2008: 440), there may be little or no pause between IPs in spontaneous speech. Instead, these authors suggest looking at a combination of prosodic features, which taken together may be indicative of an IP boundary. Such prosodic features can include lengthening of the final syllable, a large pitch excursion (up or down), a change in loudness (usually quieter at the end of an IP) and a general slowing down of speech rate (Cruttenden 1997: 29–37). Phrase accents mark the boundary of smaller prosodic units, known as 'intermediate phrases' (ips). Phrase accents are usually notated with a '-', i.e. a low phrase accent would be 'L-' and a high phrase accent would be 'H-'. Some AM approaches, such as IViE, do not recognise the existence of ips; see Grabe (1998) for discussion on this topic.

Similar to sociophonetic studies of segmental variation, the phonetic influence of surrounding material must also be accounted for in intonational analysis. The majority of intonation studies measure f0 as an estimate of pitch, yet f0 can only be measured in voiced sounds. For this reason, many studies choose to compare read sentences where the material can be closely controlled in order to include mainly voiced sounds. The amount of unaccented material preceding and following pitch accents may also affect their realisation: first, nuclear accents are susceptible to *truncation* (Erikson and Alstermark 1972) and/or 'compression' (Bannert and Bredvad 1975). These terms refer to strategies adopted by speakers when there are not enough syllables after the nuclear accent to fully realise a boundary tone contour. Speakers can adopt two strategies: either end their contour abruptly and not produce a full rise or fall, *truncation*, or compress the full contour into a short space of time, *compression*. In order to allow for potential compression or truncation effects, sociolinguistic studies of uncontrolled material should account for the number of syllables after the nuclear accent (see Warren 2005; Nance 2015). Secondly, pitch accents are also susceptible to the effects of *tonal crowding* (e.g. Arvaniti et al. 2006), which refers to a process by which pitch accents occurring in close succession are affected by the proximity of other pitch accents. In order to account for this possibility, studies of uncontrolled materials could avoid IPs where there is no unaccented material between pitch accents and label the number of syllables between each pitch accent to include in the modelling.

In this section, we have spent some time reviewing the AM approach to intonation in the hope that it will be more widely used in sociophonetic research.

Summary and Research Questions

To summarise the relevance of this previous work to the current study, Liverpool is claimed to belong to the UNB group of dialects where phrase-final rising intonation contours are common, but this dialect has been subject to little modern intonational study. The most detailed description was conducted in Knowles (1973) before the advent of widespread digital speech recording and analysis. Although data from Liverpool were collected in the Intonational Variation in English project (e.g. Grabe 2004), this was not fully analysed or compared to the other dialects. In this chapter, we aim to provide a descriptive account of Liverpool intonation to fill this gap in our understanding of variation in one of the UK's major urban centres. We also aim to investigate how intonation varies along two social dimensions in Liverpool: speaker gender and individual variation. The research questions investigated here are as follows:

1. What are the characteristic features of Liverpool intonation?
2. Is there evidence to suggest sociolinguistic variation in Liverpool intonation?

Method

The participants for this study were five male speakers and four female speakers aged 20–22 years. All were born and raised in Liverpool and had spent the majority of their lives in the city and its suburbs. Four participants had spent some time away at university in Lancaster and one had attended university in Leeds. The speakers were all of lower middle class or upper working class background. Participants were recorded by the third author in their own home, or in a quiet room at the University of Liverpool or Lancaster University. Recordings were made on laptops using a Beyerdynamic Opus 55 headset microphone, and a Sound Devices USBPre2 preamplifier and audio interface.

The data collection consisted of (1) read sentences and (2) a task designed to elicit more natural speech within a structured context. The sentences were presented to each participant twice on the computer screen in random order, interspersed with 12 distracter sentences. The sentences included eight declaratives (e.g. They are drawing the library), four questions without morphosyntactic markers (e.g. He's running the relay?), four inversion questions (e.g. Will you live near the building?), four wh-questions (e.g. Why are we drawing?) and four coordination questions (e.g. Did you say yellow or mellow?). These particular contexts were chosen to reflect the data collection method used in the IViE project for later comparison with other varieties (see Appendix for a list of sentences). We changed the lexical content of the sentences from the IViE materials to make them more relevant to a northern speech community; for example, we altered sentences referring to London suburbs. The second speech task required participants to watch a silent two-minute cartoon featuring the well-known British fictional character *Mr. Bean*. They were then asked to watch the video again and provide a commentary on the events as they unfolded. In this study, we only analysed data from the sentences part of the experiment and did not report any further information on the video description task. In total, we analysed 419 nuclear pitch accents and boundary tones. Sixteen utterances were excluded as unsuitable for analysis, mainly due to the presence of substantial creaky voice among some female speakers. The data presented represent the first stage in a wider project, comparing intonational variation in Liverpool with that of Manchester, a city around 50 miles away from Liverpool that is not reported as part of the UNB intonation group.

In this chapter, we concentrate on the pitch events at the end of IPs: nuclear pitch accents, phrase accents and boundary tones. Our analysis has two aspects: a categorical phonological analysis using ToBI labelling and a phonetic analysis of pitch height and range within phonologically similar contours. In order to conduct this analysis we used a version of ToBI adapted for Glaswegian English—GlaToBI (Mayo 1996; Mayo et al. 1997). We selected this labelling system as Glasgow English, similar to Liverpool English, is reportedly part of the UNB group of dialects. GlaToBI removes the intrinsic up-step cuing property of an H phrase accent such that H-L% represents a falling pitch, rather than a level pitch in conventional ToBI. Additionally, contra Mayo (1996), we have retained the more conventional L* and L*+H labels rather than their suggested L*H. Figure 11.2 shows a schematic representation of each contour, its GlaToBI label and a description of the contour. In this initial description we combined some tonal categories for clarity: Down stepped !H* accents were combined with H*; H+L* accents were combined with L*. We also allowed for the possibility of no discernable pitch movement.

Previous descriptive work on Liverpool suggests that speakers exploit a small pitch range in their intonation, leading to the perception that they are somewhat monotone (Knowles 1973: 175). In order to investigate this phonetic aspect of intonation, we obtained measures of f0 at the turning points in pitch, which were manually identified during the ToBI labelling. The pitch range for each speaker was calculated as the median f0 of their L*, L- and L% values subtracted from the median of their H*, H- and H% values. Values were reported in semitones using the formula

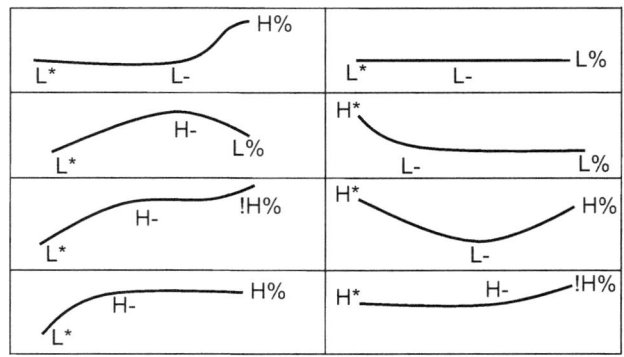

Fig. 11.2 Schematic representation of each contour and its GlaToBI labelling

$12 * \log2(f/127.09)$, where f refers to the frequency in Hertz (Traunmüller and Eriksson 1995), in order to compare pitch excursions in a perceptually meaningful way.

Results and Discussion

Characteristics of Liverpool Intonation

This section shows the results of the ToBI labelling of different sentence types (discourse functions) according to each speaker's productions. The contours used by each speaker in each discourse function are shown in Fig. 11.3.

Overall, the most commonly occurring contour was L* L-H% (shown in purple in the figure), which in Knowles' (1973) terminology is a *rise*. In these contours, f0 rose gradually from the final pitch accent onwards and reached an H target right at the end of the IP. This H was not especially high in pitch, so we did not consider these as related to the HRT phenomenon. The widespread use of the *rise* is somewhat in contrast to the previous literature on the UNB group of dialects. Studies of Belfast

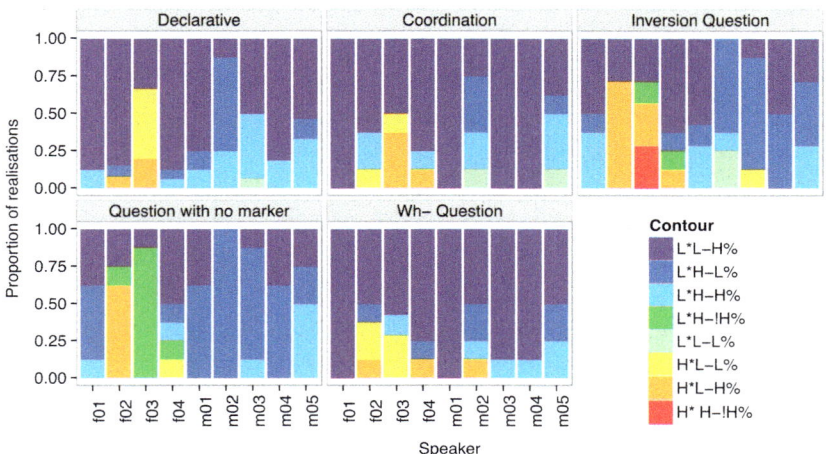

Fig. 11.3 Contours used in each sentence type by each speaker

and Glasgow report widespread use of the *rise-plateau*, which Knowles refers to as a *step* (e.g. Mayo 1996; Grabe 2004; Cruttenden 2007; Sullivan 2010; Lowry 2011). In these contours, pitch rises to its final high target on the accented syllable and remains there on a plateau. These contours, represented here as L* H-H% (light blue in the figure), were fairly common in our data, but not as widespread as L* L-H% (purple in the figure; 12.6% and 55.3% of the data, respectively). High rises were only used by one speaker in one context: inversion questions. This suggests that HRT is not used in declaratives by our speakers and we have no evidence suggesting that it is used by speakers in Liverpool.

Since Liverpool speakers use rising contours in declaratives, an interesting question is how they distinguish questions and statements. In the case of inversion questions (e.g. Will you live near the building?) and wh-questions (e.g. Why are we drawing?), there are clear lexical or syntactic cues to the phrase being a question. However, in the case of questions without morphosyntactic markers (e.g. He's running the relay?), cues must come from elsewhere. In Liverpool, there appears to be a clear intonational difference between these questions and declarative statements: our speakers use mainly *rises* (L* L-H%) for declaratives (62.59%, 87/139 tokens) and L* H-L% for questions without markers (43.06%, 31/72 tokens). In these L* H-L% contours, pitch dropped markedly at the end of the phrase, almost to the speaker's minimum pitch. The difference between the use of these two different contours was significant ($\beta = -3.68$, $p < .001$; logistic mixed effects regression model with contour variant as outcome variable, sentence type and gender as fixed effects, and speaker and accented word as random intercepts).

Our analysis also considers the pitch range used by speakers. The pitch range of each speaker in semitones is shown in Fig. 11.4 (absolute values). This was calculated as the difference between each speaker's value for H tones and each speaker's value for L tones. Liverpool speakers do indeed appear to exploit a fairly narrow pitch range. For some speakers, the range used is between 1 and 2 semitones. The range that humans can distinguish is typically around 1 Hz—less than 1 semitone (Kollmeier et al. 2008). In comparison to the values, which are just perceivable, the ranges employed by our speakers are not vastly different; thus, we would agree with Knowles' (1973) observation that small pitch ranges are used in Liverpool.

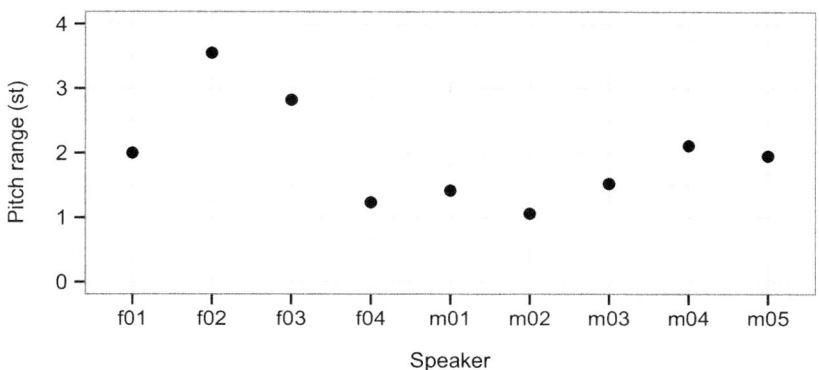

Fig. 11.4 Median pitch range used by each speaker (absolute values; semitones)

Variation in Liverpool Intonation

In this section, we consider differences across the dataset in order to suggest avenues for future sociolinguistic work on intonation in Liverpool. There are two possible sociolinguistic parameters along which our data might vary: gender and across individuals. In terms of gender-based variation, we found significant differences between male and female speakers in the proportion of L* H-L% contours (β = −2.58, SE = 1.12, p = .02; logistic mixed effects regression model with contour variant as outcome variable, sentence type and gender as fixed effects, and speaker and accented word as random intercepts). We also considered the possibility of gender variation in the pitch range data. In this case, there were no significant differences between the male and female speakers in our sample (*t*-test, ns.).

Although there were no significant gender differences in the pitch range exploited, Fig. 11.4 clearly depicts that f02 and f03 behave somewhat differently from the other two female speakers and the male speakers in the sample: f02 and f03 use a much larger pitch range than the other speakers. Similarly, data in Fig. 11.3 show that f02 and f03 again behave differently from the rest of the dataset, using more falling contours (H* L-L% and H* L-H%). In particular, f03 used a large number of H* L-L% contours in declaratives, which would be more typical of southern British English than

Liverpool English. We collected data about the social background of our speakers through their postcode, which was used to evaluate the level of social deprivation in their area, and we also collected information as to whether they had moved house or city, but found no substantial differences in the backgrounds of f02 and f03 when compared with the other speakers. Our study is small scale, but these data provide insight into future possibilities for research in sociolinguistic variation in Liverpool. It appears that there may be some influences from other varieties in the speech of two female speakers, which may hint at change in Liverpool and/or gender-based variation within the community.

Conclusions

This chapter has presented some of the methods used and common parameters analysed in sociolinguistic treatments of intonation. Foulkes et al. (2010: 721) state that the paucity of sociophonetic studies on prosody may be due to the difficulties surrounding controlling for pragmatic function. Recent research initiatives attempt to address this, especially in the area of intonation (e.g. Warren 2016). Our own analysis also aims to show how controlled materials can be used to produce interesting and sociolinguistically meaningful data, especially as a starting point for conducting an initial dialect description and sociolinguistic investigation.

Our study has provided some initial analysis of Liverpool intonation within a modern phonological framework: AM phonology (Pierrehumbert 1980; Ladd 2008). We have demonstrated that Liverpool is a member of the UNB group, commonly employing rising contours in declaratives as claimed in previous literature, such as Cruttenden (1997) and Ladd (2008), but now explicitly investigated. These contours are similar to other UNB dialects, such as Glasgow and Belfast, in the sense that the rise takes place over a narrow pitch range and starts from low in the speaker's range, unlike HRT contours (Ladd 2008). However, Liverpool is slightly different from previous descriptions of Belfast and Glasgow, as the most common kind of declarative rise is a very gradual drift upwards in pitch until the end of the IP, unlike the step up in pitch and plateau of Belfast and Glasgow.

Although our study so far is small scale in nature, we have provided some possible insight into variation in the community: two female speakers behaved somewhat differently from the rest of the sample and used a wider pitch range overall as well as fewer rising contours in declaratives. Also, they produced some declaratives that were more typical of non-UNB varieties. There are several possible explanations for this finding: first, as a result of dialect contact, young women in Liverpool no longer use the intonation which is distinctive of their dialect. Secondly, these young women were reacting to the fairly formal context of reading sentences from a computer screen. It is also possible that their behaviour was speaker-specific and not reflective of any kind of wider trend. Out of these three explanations, we find the second one most convincing. Research on Liverpool English suggests that the city's dialect is resisting some of the changes sweeping across other British varieties, such as /t/-glottalling (Watson 2006, 2007; Clark and Watson 2016). We therefore find it unlikely that intonation is changing in such a radical fashion. However, it seems probable that these young women may have been able to style-shift and produce sentences in a formal southern-influenced manner for the purposes of our experiment. Our ongoing analysis of the video retelling data will allow us to better answer this question.

Future research could consider these possibilities in more detail. Liverpool is an interesting context because of Watson's (2006) claim that the city is resisting many diffusing features and because the dialect of the area is so distinctive. We plan to continue this analysis in more detail with a larger dataset and also compare Liverpool to a non-UNB area, Manchester, which is a geographically proximal but linguistically distinct city. This raises an interesting question regarding where an isogloss between a UNB variety such as Liverpool and a non-UNB variety such as Manchester might lie. Is there a sudden divide? Or is there a border zone, which is intonationally varied? In addition to this, our data suggest some possibility of gender variation in intonation. But how widespread is such variation in the community? Are there differences according to social class? Questions such as these have been addressed through sociophonetic treatments of segmental features, but greater analysis of prosodic features is necessary in order to provide more comprehensive accounts of sociophonetic variation and change. We hope to inspire future research in this area.

Appendix

List of sentences used for eliciting contours:

1. Simple statements:

    1. He was bringing some dinner.
    2. You were stirring the pudding.
    3. We were driving in a limo.
    4. They are drawing the library.
    5. We were wearing some goggles.
    6. He was running in the relay.
    7. She was drowning in the river.
    8. We were living near the building.

2. Questions without morphosyntactic markers:

    1. He's running the relay?
    2. You were stirring the pudding?
    3. She's drowning in the river?
    4. They're drawing the library?

3. Inversion questions:

    1. Can I drive in a limo?
    2. Were you drawing the library?
    3. Will you live near the building?
    4. Are they wearing some goggles?

4. Wh-Questions:

    1. Where is my dinner?
    2. When are you running?
    3. Why are we drawing?
    4. Who'll be the driver?

5. Coordinations:

1. Are you growing limes or lemons?
2. Did you say mellow or yellow?
3. Are we going bowling or running?
4. Did he say lino or lilo?

References

Arvaniti, A., Ladd, R., & Mennen, I. (2006). Phonetic effects of focus and 'tonal crowding' in intonation: Evidence from Greek polar questions. *Speech Communication, 48*, 667–696.

Bannert, R., & Bredvad, A. (1975). Temporal organisation of Swedish tonal accent: The effect of vowel duration. *Working Papers in Phonetics, 10*, 1–36. Lund University.

Barry, A. (2007). *The Form, function, and distribution of high rising intonation in Southern Californian and Southern British English*. Unpublished PhD thesis, University of Sheffield.

Beckman, M., & Elam, G. A. (1997). *Guidelines for ToBI labelling*. Ohio: The Ohio State University Research Foundation.

Beckman, M., Hirschberg, J., & Shattuck-Hufnagel, S. (2006). The original ToBI system and the evolution of the ToBI framework. In S.-A. Jun (Ed.), *Prosodic models and transcription: Towards prosodic typology* (pp. 9–54). Oxford: Oxford University Press.

Bradford, B. (1997). Upspeak in English. *English Today, 13*(3), 29–36.

Britain, D. (1992). Linguistic change in intonation: The use of high rising terminals in New Zealand English. *Language Variation and Change, 4*, 77–104.

Clark, L., & Watson, K. (2016). Phonological leveling, diffusion, and divergence: /t/ lenition in Liverpool and its hinterland. *Language Variation and Change, 28*(1), 31–62.

Cruttenden, A. (1994). Rises in English. In J. Windsor-Lewis (Ed.), *Studies in general and English phonetics* (pp. 155–173). London: Routledge.

Cruttenden, A. (1997). *Intonation* (2nd ed.). Cambridge: Cambridge University Press.

Cruttenden, A. (2007). Intonational diglossia: A case study of Glasgow. *Journal of the International Phonetic Association, 37*(3), 257–274.

Dalton, M., & Chasaide, A. N. (2003). Modelling intonation in three Irish dialects. In *Proceedings of the 15th international congress of phonetic sciences*, Barcelona.

Dalton, M., & Ní Chasaide, A. (2005). Tonal alignment in Irish dialects. *Language and Speech, 48*(4), 441–464.

Daly, N., & Warren, P. (2001). Pitching it differently in New Zealand English: Speaker sex and intonation patterns. *Journal of SocioLinguistics, 5*(1), 85–96.

Dorn, A., O'Reilly, M., & Ní Chasaide, A. (2011). Prosodic signalling of sentence mode in two varieties of Irish (Gaelic). In *Proceedings of the 17th international congress of the phonetic sciences*. Hong Kong: City University Hong Kong.

Erikson, Y., & Alstermark, M. (1972). Fundamental frequency correlates of the grave word accent in Swedish: The effect of vowel duration. In *Speech transmission laboratory KTH. Quarterly progress and status report* (pp. 2–3). Stockholm: KTH Royal Institute of Technology.

Fletcher, J., & Harrington, J. (2001). High-rising terminals and fall-rise tunes in Australian English. *Phonetica, 58*, 215–229.

Fletcher, J., Storling, L., Mushin, I., & Wales, R. (2002). Intonational rises and dialogue acts in the Australian English map task. *Language and Speech, 45*(3), 229–253.

Fletcher, J., Grabe, E., & Warren, P. (2005). Intonational variation in four dialects of English: The high rising tune. In S.-A. Jun (Ed.), *Prosodic typology: The phonology of intonation and phrasing* (pp. 390–409). Oxford: Oxford University Press.

Foulkes, P., Scobbie, J., & Watt, D. (2010). Sociophonetics. In W. Hardcastle, J. Laver, & F. Gibbon (Eds.), *Handbook of the phonetic sciences* (pp. 703–754). Oxford: Blackwell.

Grabe, E. (1998). *Comparative intonational phonology: English and German*. Unpublished PhD thesis, Max Planck Institut für Psycholinguistik.

Grabe, E. (2004). Intonational variation in urban dialects of English spoken in the British Isles. In P. Gilles & J. Peters (Eds.), *Regional variation in intonation* (pp. 9–31). Tübingen: Linguistische Arbeiten.

Grabe, E., & Post, B. (2002). Intonational variation in English. In B. Bel & I. Marlin (Eds.), *Proceedings of speech prosody* (pp. 343–346). Aix-en-Provence: Laboratoire Parole et. Langage.

Grabe, E., Post, B., Nolan, F., & Farrar, K. (2000). Pitch accent realization in four varieties of British English. *Journal of Phonetics, 28*, 161–185.

Grabe, E., Post, B., & Nolan, F. (2001). Modelling intonational variation in English. In *Proceedings of prosody 2000* (pp. 51–57). Poznan: Adam Mickiewitz University.

Gregersen, F., Nielsen, S. B., & Thøgersen, J. (2009). Stepping into the same river twice on the discourse context analysis in the LANCHART project. *Acta Linguistica Hafniensia, 41*, 30–63.

Guy, G., & Vonwiller, J. (1984). The meaning of an intonation in Australian English. *Australian Journal of Linguistics, 4*, 1–17.

Guy, G., Horvarth, B., Vonwiller, J., Daisley, E., & Rogers, I. (1986). An intonational change in progress in Australian English. *Language in Society, 15*, 23–52.

House, J. (2006). Constructing a context with intonation. *Journal of Pragmatics, 38*, 1542–1558.

Jarman, E., & Cruttenden, A. (1976). Belfast intonation and the myth of the fall. *Journal of the International Phonetic Association, 6*, 4–12.

Jespersen, A. (2015). Intonational rises and interaction structure in Sydney Aboriginal English. In *Proceedings of the 18th international congress of the phonetic sciences*, Glasgow.

Jun, S.-A. (Ed.). (2005). *Prosodic typology: The phonology of intonation and phrasing*. Oxford: Oxford University Press.

Jun, S.-A. (Ed.). (2014). *Prosodic typology II: The phonology of intonation and phrasing*. Oxford: Oxford University Press.

Knowles, G. (1973). *Scouse: The urban dialect of Liverpool*. Unpublished PhD thesis, University of Leeds.

Knowles, G. (1978). The nature of phonological variables in scouse. In P. Trudgill (Ed.), *Sociolinguistic patterns in British English* (pp. 80–90). London: Arnold.

Kollmeier, B., Brand, T., & Meyer, B. (2008). Perception of speech and sound. In J. Benesty, M. M. Sondhi, & Y. Huang (Eds.), *Springer handbook of speech processing* (pp. 61–83). Berlin: Springer.

Ladd, D. R. (2008). *Intonational phonology* (2nd ed.). Cambridge: Cambridge University Press.

Levon, E. (2015). Gender and interactional meaning: High Rising Terminals in London. Oral presentation at *international conference on language variation in Europe conference*, Leipzig.

Local, J., Kelly, J., & Wells, B. (1986). Towards a phonology of conversation: Turn-taking in urban Tyneside speech. *Journal of Linguistics, 22*, 411–437.

Lowry, O. (2002). The stylistic variation of nuclear patterns in Belfast English. *Journal of the International Phonetic Association, 32*(1), 33–42.

Lowry, O. (2011). Belfast intonation and speaker gender. *Journal of English Linguistics, 39*(3), 209–232.

Mayo, C. (1996). *Prosodic transcription of Glasgow English: An evaluation of GlaToBI*. Unpublished Master's thesis, University of Edinburgh.

Mayo, C., Aylett, M., & Ladd, D. R. (1997). Prosodic transcription of Glasgow English: An evaluation study of GlaToBI. In G. Kouroupetroglou & G. Carayiannis (Eds.), *Proceedings of an ESCA workshop: Intonation: Theory, models and applications* (pp. 231–234).

McGregor, J., & Palethorpe, S. (2008). High rising tunes in Australian English: The communicative function of L* and H* pitch accent onsets. *Australian Journal of Linguistics, 28*(2), 171–193.

Milroy, L., & Gordon, M. (2003). *Sociolinguistics: Method and interpretation.* Oxford: Blackwell.

Nance, C. (2013). *Phonetic variation, sound change, and identity in Scottish Gaelic.* Unpublished PhD thesis, University of Glasgow.

Nance, C. (2015). Intonational variation and change in Scottish Gaelic. *Lingua, 160,* 1–19.

Nolan, F. (2008). Intonation. In B. Aarts & A. McMahon (Eds.), *Handbook of English linguistics* (pp. 433–459). Malden: Blackwell.

Pellowe, J., & Jones, V. (1978). On intonational variability in Tyneside speech. In P. Trudgill (Ed.), *Sociolinguistic patterns in British English* (pp. 101–121). London: Arnold.

Pierrehumbert, J. (1980). *The phonology and phonetics of English intonation.* Unpublished PhD thesis, Massachusetts Institute of Technology.

Podesva, R. (2011). Salience and the social meaning of declarative contours: Three case studies of gay professionals. *Journal of English Linguistics, 39*(3), 233–264.

Rahilly, J. (1997). Aspects of prosody in Hiberno-English: The case of Belfast. In J. Kallen (Ed.), *Focus on Ireland* (pp. 109–132). Amsterdam: John Benjamins.

Ritchart, A., & Arvaniti, A. (2014). The form and use of uptalk in southern California English. In *Proceedings of speech prosody*, Dublin.

Shobbrock, K., & House, J. (2003). High rising tones in southern British English. In *Proceedings of the 15th international congress of phonetic sciences* (pp. 1273–1276), Barcelona.

Stirling, L., Fletcher, J., Mushin, I., & Wales, R. (2001). Representational issues in annotation: Using the Australian map task corpus to relate prosody and discourse structure. *Speech Communication, 33,* 113–134.

Sullivan, J. (2010). *Approaching intonational distance and change.* Unpublished PhD thesis, University of Edinburgh.

Traunmüller, H., & Eriksson, A. (1995). The perceptual evaluation of F0-excursions in speech as evidenced in liveliness estimations. *Journal of the Acoustical Society of America, 97,* 1905–1915.

Vizcaino Ortega, F. (2002). A preliminary analysis of yes/no questions in Glasgow English. In *Proceedings of speech prosody* (pp. 683–686), Aix-en-Provence.

Warren, P. (2005). Patterns of late rising in New Zealand English: Intonational variation or intonational change? *Language Variation and Change, 17*, 209–230.

Warren, P. (2016). *Uptalk: The phenomenon of rising intonation.* Cambridge: Cambridge University Press.

Watson, K. (2006). Phonological resistance and innovation in the North West of England. *English Today, 22*(2), 55–61.

Watson, K. (2007). Liverpool English. *Journal of the International Phonetic Association, 37*(3), 351–360.

Wells, B., & Peppé, S. (1996). Ending up in Ulster: Prosody and turn taking in English dialects. In E. Couper-Kuhlen & M. Selting (Eds.), *Prosody in conversation: Interactional studies* (pp. 101–131). Cambridge: Cambridge University Press.

12

Peripheral Communities and Innovation: Changes in the GOOSE Vowel in a West Cumbrian Town

Sandra Jansen

Introduction

GOOSE-fronting describes the gradual shift of the place of production of the GOOSE vowel towards the front of the oral cavity across apparent time. Figures 12.1 and 12.2 provide examples of such a shift in Carlisle English (cf. Jansen 2017). John is a 60-year-old middle-class (MC) male speaker whose GOOSE vowel occupies a back position even though the standard deviation is quite high on the F2 dimension, which also means we see a lot of intraspeaker variation (Fig. 12.1). John still has a more traditional realisation of the GOOSE vowel. The vowel plot in Fig. 12.2 shows the vowel space of Jen, a 23-year-old MC female speaker. Her GOOSE vowel

This research was supported by the Rising Star Grant from the University of Brighton. I would like to thank the two reviewers for their valuable comments which greatly improved this chapter. I would also like to thank Laurel Mackenzie and Anne Fabricius for their patience when helping me to understand FAVE and Daniel Ezra Johnson for his help with statistics. Of course, I am responsible for any shortcomings.

S. Jansen (✉)
University of Paderborn, Paderborn, Germany

© The Author(s) 2018
N. Braber, S. Jansen (eds.), *Sociolinguistics in England*,
DOI 10.1057/978-1-137-56288-3_12

60–year–old male

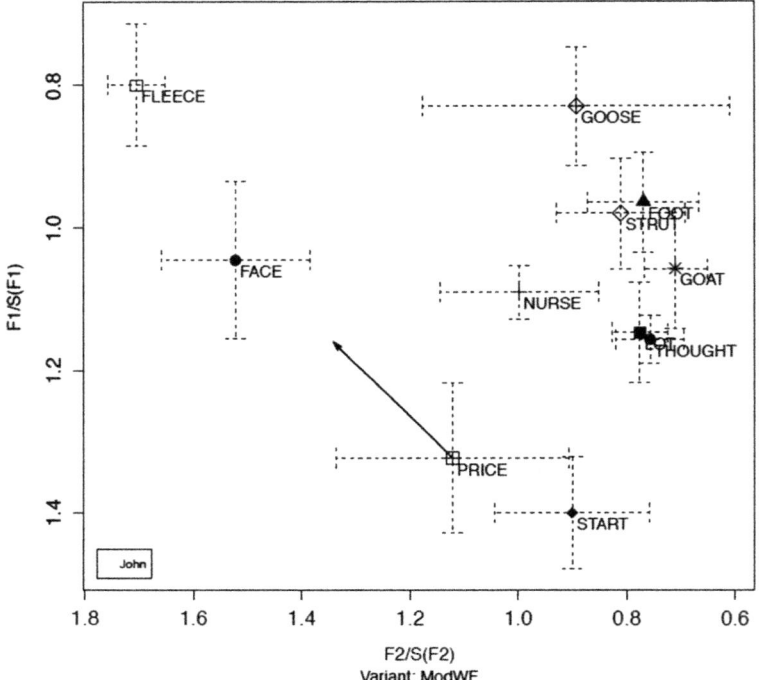

Fig. 12.1   Vowel plot of John, a 60-year-old MC male speaker from Carlisle

is found in a very front position. Across apparent time, we find this change towards a fronter GOOSE vowel in Carlisle.

Studies conducted in North America (e.g. Ash 1996; Fought 1999; Fridland and Bartlett 2006; Labov et al. 2006; Baranowski 2007, 2008; Fridland 2008; Hall-Lew 2009; Hinrichs et al. 2013), South Africa (e.g. Mesthrie 2010), New Zealand (e.g. Hay et al. 2008; Maclagan et al. 2009) and the UK (e.g. Bauer 1985; Torgersen 1997; Torgersen and Kerswill 2004; Scobbie et al. 2012; Stuart-Smith 2013) show that fronting of GOOSE is under way. In England, the fronting of /uː/ has been described for a number of varieties, e.g. Henton (1983), Hawkins and Midgley (2005), Harrington et al. (2008) for Received Pronunciation (RP)/Standard Southern British English; Flynn (2012) for Nottingham;

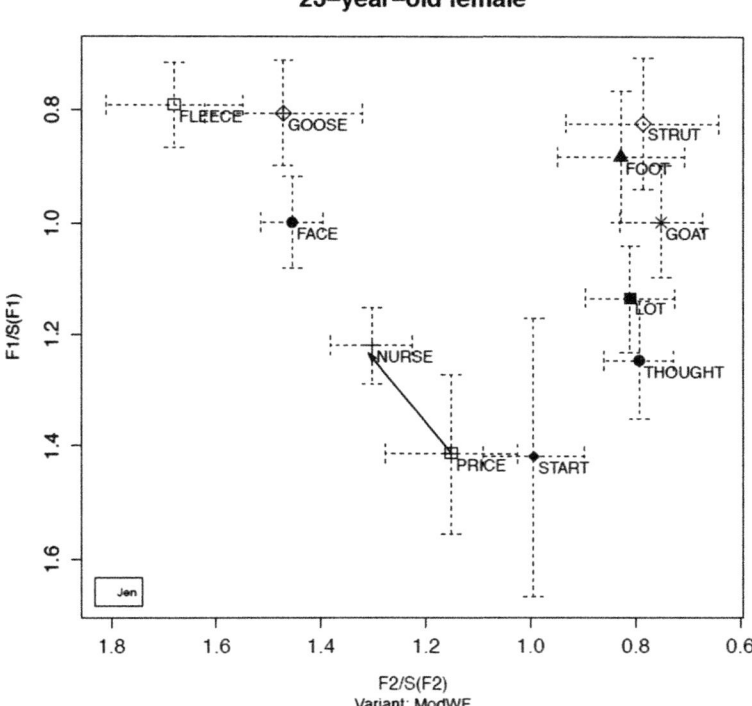

Fig. 12.2 Vowel plot of Jen, a 23-year-old MC female speaker

Jansen (2012a, b, 2017) for Carlisle; Haddican et al. (2013) for York; Holmes-Elliott (2015) for Hastings; Sóskuthy et al. (2015) for Derby; and Baranowski (2017) for Manchester. In fact, GOOSE-fronting can be seen as the most studied synchronic vowel change in varieties of English to date.

The majority of studies which have investigated this change have focused on urban vernaculars. Yet a wealth of evidence shows that more peripheral dialects can diverge from developments which are observed in more urban areas (cf. Smith and Holmes-Elliott 2017). The study reported in this chapter contributes to our understanding of the propagation of change and underscores how important it is to consider a range of different communities when building models of sound change.

Previous Research

Structural regularity seems to be a main characteristic of GOOSE-fronting according to Fridland (2008: 449):

> back vowel fronting is very regular, differing mainly in the degree of advancement overall. This regularity in diffusion makes it a good candidate for an internally motivated shift, driven by instability in the American vowel system more generally, rather than any regional or social association.

This instability which leads to GOOSE-fronting has been found in varieties of English in the UK as well, and the studies mentioned above show that GOOSE-fronting is in many cases an internally motivated change. So far, studies on GOOSE have found a strong consistency in the structural constraints in the fronting process: words with a preceding palatal /j/ are consistently produced with fronter GOOSE vowels than words with preceding anterior coronals which are fronter than preceding velars and bilabials (cf. Baranowski 2007, 2008; Hall-Lew 2009; Flynn 2012; Holmes-Elliott 2015; Jansen 2017).

There are different explanatory strands for the fronting of GOOSE, including phonological and phonetic reasons. One of the most often stated explanations is the occurrence of parallel shifts (cf. Labov 1994; Durian and Joseph 2011; Fruehwald 2013). Ash (1996: 23) discusses fronting and the stability of GOOSE in some areas of the American Midwest:

> In the case of /uw/; there is no pressure for it to move front, as there is no back vowel which is moving in its direction and threatening the merger. There is also no pressure for it to stay high and back, since there are no other high central or high nonperipheral front vowels. Its movement forward is not opening a hole in the back, since the allophones before /l/ are remaining in place.

Stockwell and Minkova (1997), on the other hand, suggest that the crowding of the back space could be a reason for the fronting of GOOSE.

On the phonetic level, Flynn (2012: 389) proposes that the high F2 of /j/ might be maintained in the transition between /j/ and /uː/, which then causes the high proportion of fronted values in this environment. Ohala (1981) discusses how sound changes triggered by coarticulation can arise, acknowledging the role of the hearer in language change. Harrington et al. (2011) pick up this point and suggest that coarticulation is highly likely to be the cause for vowel changes that occur across languages.

Coda /l/ is frequently identified as the strongest phonetic constraint which resists fronting. The inhibition of change has resulted in the GOOSE/GHOUL split in many varieties (cf. Wells 1982; Labov 1994; Holmes-Elliott 2015).

Milroy (2007) discusses back vowel fronting as a global phenomenon in English, which can easily be adopted in a speech community because of structural readiness and the fact that very little social meaning is attached to these forms in the different varieties. However, studies such as Hall-Lew (2005), Koops (2010) and Mesthrie (2010) reveal that social meaning can be a significant factor in the progression of this change.

In Carlisle, the closest city to Maryport (45 km away), Jansen (2017) also finds GOOSE-fronting. All groups participate in the change towards a fronted variant across apparent time, conditioned by the strong internal constraints also found in other varieties. However, social stratification exists as well, with women and middle-class speakers using more fronted variants than working-class and male speakers. Similarly, studies such as Flynn (2012) and Holmes-Elliott (2015) find strong linguistic factors combined with socially stratified results for this change.

Research on language variation and change processes in peripheral areas of the UK exist but are sparser than studies in urban areas, e.g. studies such as Tagliamonte and Smith (2002), Smith and Durham (2011), Tagliamonte (2013) and Maguire (2014) focus on peripheral areas. Studies have shown that developments in peripheral areas can diverge from changes in urban areas (e.g. Smith and Holmes-Elliott 2017), and so far, the GOOSE vowel has not been investigated in peripheral areas in the UK. However, in order to understand the details of language change, communities such as Maryport need to be included in the pool of communities which are investigated. On the one hand, we can expect more conservative forms of English to be retained in peripheral communities and on the other hand, social structures in peripheral communities are more likely to differ from communities in urban spaces, which could have an effect on linguistic choices. Above all, the interplay of conservative and innovative forms at an early stage of a change can provide us with more information about changes which are already quite advanced in other communities. The following section discusses aspects of the historical background of the GOOSE vowel and the sociolinguistic background of Maryport.

Historical Background of GOOSE-Fronting

From a diachronic perspective, GOOSE-fronting is a process which has been in progress for at least a century in the south of England. In the revised version of *An Outline of English Phonetics*, Jones (1932: 32) reported the fronting of /uː/ in palatal preceding environments:

> The most important subsidiary long uː is an 'advanced' variety. It is used when j precedes, as in *music* **ˈmjuːzik**, *tube* **ˈtjuːb**, *deluge* **ˈdeljuːdʒ**. By calling it 'advanced' we mean that the part of the tongue which is highest is the central part – a part more forward than the 'back'.

This statement suggests that the place of articulation of the GOOSE vowel has moved towards the front of the oral cavity. Roach and Hartman (1997) describe the fronting of GOOSE as a radical shift in RP, which had been ongoing for 20–30 years. However, Jones's (1932) description mentioned above points to an earlier initiation of this change and also to a constraint which is repeatedly confirmed in sociolinguistic studies in England—words with a preceding palatal /j/ are leading the change.

In the north-west, a fronted variant was described in the twentieth century as well. For Manchester, Wells (1982) transcribes the GOOSE vowel as [ʏ] and Baranowski (2017) finds a front of centre /u/. In West Cumbria, this kind of fronting of GOOSE has not been described but Wright (1979: 31; see also Wells 1982: 184ff) reports a historically diphthongal variant with offglide for GOOSE:

Middle English o, which occurred in words now spelt with oo such as *noon*, *moon*, *boots* and *tooth*, has normally given rise to threefold development, namely

	Phonetic representation	Example
1. Traditional **ee-er**	ɪə	**mee-ern** (moon)
2. Intermediate **i-u**	ɪʊ	In West Cumbria **mi-un**
3. Approximated standard English **oo**	uː	Especially in South Cumbria **moon**

Fronted onsets of a particular group of words are reported in conservative versions of West Cumbrian dialect speech. Residuals of this intermediate form can be found in words like *school* [skɪʊl]/[skɪʊɫ][1], but this variant is becoming very infrequent now. The main variant found in Maryport now is a monophthongal [uː] with a slight offglide, while Haddican et al. (2013) and Jansen (2017) report an increase in the diphthongisation of GOOSE by a raised onset.

Sociolinguistic Background of Maryport

Maryport is a peripheral town with a population of 11,000 in the Allerdale borough on the West Cumbrian coast (see Fig. 12.3). The next biggest city is Carlisle, which is located 45 km north-west of Maryport. Direct access to a motorway does not exist; people either need to pass through the Lake District or go to Carlisle to get on the M6. London is about 530 km away, with Maryport being one of the furthest places from London in England. Maryport is classed as a tourist town, but 'unlike some areas in Cumbria, Maryport did not benefit from the tourist boom of the last century' (Tagliamonte 2013: 30).

A profile description produced by Allerdale Borough Council provides information on the strengths and weaknesses of the community. Major concerns are the high level of deprivation, high unemployment and the isolation from the M6 and hence the rest of the country, while the strengths include good local public transport and the fact that houses are affordable (Allerdale Borough Council 2014).

Fig. 12.3   Geographical position of Maryport in Cumbria (d-maps.com)

The two towns of Whitehaven and Workington are situated south of Maryport. Both are about twice as big as Maryport. Several main employers are found in the area, the biggest employer probably being the nuclear power station Sellafield with over 10,000 employees

(Sellafield Ltd. 2017). A large number of people from Maryport commute to Workington and Whitehaven for work and go to college or school there. Workington is the place for nights out and for running errands. There is a train connection and frequent buses to Workington.

At present, Maryport must be categorised as an exocentric open[2] community. Even though the community is situated in a peripheral area and people from Maryport are still identified as members of this community by people from surrounding areas, the (younger) speakers do not seem to be protective of local norms anymore. Traditional dialect features such as [aʊ] in words like *thought* and centralising diphthongs [ɪə] in *face* are more and more frequently being replaced by pan-northern features.

It is not realistic to classify Maryport as an endocentric closed community at any point in the twentieth century, but compared to other communities along the west coast of Cumbria, face-to-face contact with speakers from other communities was for a long time restricted, and up to this point in time, the number of contact situations has been limited due to the geographically peripheral position.

Nevertheless, several people in my dataset had served in the armed forces for some time. This might partly have to do with the fact that there are not many job opportunities in the area. Of course, this has repercussions on the dialect, and the influence of people joining the armed forces for a while and then coming back to their home town has not been investigated very much.[3]

Anecdotal linguistic impressions are that the dialects of the other two towns on the west coast—Workington and Whitehaven—are distinct but less broad than in Maryport. In the town and along the west coast we can observe *micro-localism* (MacRaild p.c.), i.e. people's orientation towards and concentration on their own town or a specific area within the town or village.

Research Questions

The chapter aims to discuss innovation and change in the GOOSE vowel in Maryport English by investigating the following research questions:

1. Can linguistic innovation be attested for the GOOSE vowel in Maryport English?
2. Do we find similar constraints for this innovation in Maryport as in other communities?
3. What are the reasons for these changes?

Sample, Interviews and Transcription

The data for this study stem from sociolinguistic interviews which were conducted by myself in Maryport in July/August 2014 for the project *Mergers, Splits and Traditional Forms: Variation and Change in Vowels in Peripheral Cumbria*. The participants were people who had grown up in Maryport and had lived in the town for most of their life, i.e. they had not been subject to many outside influences due to dialect contact. Table 12.1 provides information about the sample in the study. Overall, the data of 18 participants divided into three age groups were analysed: old speakers (born 1918–1950), middle-aged speakers (born 1952–1972) and young speakers (born 1983–1994).

Sociolinguistic interviews (30–60 minutes in length) were chosen as the method of data collection (cf. Labov 1984). To explore the nature of the variation in this vowel, a Labovian approach to style is used, investigating variation in interview and sentence-list style (cf. Labov 1972).

For the interviews, I used a Zoom H-4 N recorder at a sampling rate of 44.1 kHz and a Beyerdynamic Opus 55 headset. The recordings were orthographically transcribed and time-aligned using ELAN (Sloetjes and Wittenburg 2008). Following transcription, all files were checked for accuracy of both content and alignment.

Table 12.1 Sample overview

Age group	Old (1918–1948)		Middle-aged (1952–1972)		Young (1983–1994)		Total
Sex	M	F	M	F	M	F	
	2	3	3	4	4	2	
Total	5		7		6		18

Vowel Extraction, Lexical Coding and Normalisation

The sound files were subjected to forced alignment of segments with FAVEalign (Rosenfelder et al. 2011), an automatic alignment tool adapted for sociolinguistic interviews. The programme facilitates the automatic conversion of an orthographic transcription into phonemes by looking up words and their transcriptions in a pronunciation dictionary.[4] Following the alignment, FAVEextract (Rosenfelder et al. 2011), a programme which allows the automatic extraction of formant measurements for a given speaker in an aligned sound file, was used to extract all vowel tokens[5] in the interview and sentence list which had a duration of at least 50 ms, and these were measured at the midpoint and included in the analysis.

In a following manual step, I identified GOOSE, TRAP, KIT, FOOT and GOAT[6] tokens from the extraction file for the purposes of normalisation, which resulted in a total sample of 7,898 tokens. In a third step, lexical items with certain phonetic characteristics were excluded from the analysis in order to avoid environmental influences:

1. Preceding or following liquids or clusters (*truck, fleece, dress, strut, hill, bard*)
2. Following nasals (*ban, bin, ben, hand, ham, hang*)
3. Following velars in the case of /æ/ (*hag, hack*)
4. Preceding or following vowel (Di Paolo et al. 2010: 88)

In addition, words such as *do, too* and *you* were deleted from the list of tokens because they tend to be unstressed in connected speech. The final sample contained 1,392 GOOSE tokens, which is an average of 77 tokens per speaker. In order to compare the data across speakers, i.e. to neutralise the physiological differences between speakers, the data were normalised using the modified Watt and Fabricius method (Fabricius et al. 2009)[7] in the *Vowel Normalization Suite* (Thomas and Kendall 2007). This is a vowel-extrinsic normalisation method which bases the calculation of normalised values on points that represent the corners of the vowel space.

Table 12.2 provides a list of the independent variables used for the statistical modelling in this study. The list is partly adapted from Jansen (2012b, 2017) and Hinrichs et al. (2013). Jansen's distinction between preceding phonetic environments is based on studies such as Mesthrie (2010), Baranowski (2007, 2008) and Hall-Lew (2009) in which the preceding environments /j/ and anterior coronals were of special interest as well as following /l/. Hinrichs et al. (2013) used a more fine-grained distinction for preceding and following environments but did not single out preceding /j/, preceding anterior coronals and following /l/. In the present study, both approaches are combined.

Statistical Analysis

I examined the effect of linguistic and social factors on changes in the GOOSE vowel by fitting a series of linear mixed-effects regression models in Rbrul (Johnson 2009). In the present chapter, I focus on the diachronic development of F1 and F2 in the GOOSE vowel, which indicates the place of articulation in the height dimension (F1) and the front-back dimension (F2) of the oral cavity.

The initial plan was to investigate fronting by analysing changes in F2. However, the statistical analysis of this variable showed that the relevant changes are happening in terms of height. Hence, a separate statistical model using normalised F1 as a dependent variable was conducted. Higher F2 values represent a more fronted variant, while lower F1 values mean that the vowel is raising. The fixed social predictors which were tested were speaker sex, age group and style. Speaker sex and style were binary distinctions: male and female, and interview and sentence-list style. Three age groups were investigated: young, middle-aged and old (see Table 12.2). The linguistic factors were preceding and following environment and duration. Speaker and word were included as random factors in the model.

Table 12.2 Independent variables used for modelling GOOSE-fronting in Rbrul

Categorical variable	Factor level
preceding phonetic environment	labial, anterior coronal, postalveolar/velar, palatal /j/
following phonetic environment	labial, coronal, dorsal, /l/, pause
sex	male, female
age group	young, middle-aged, old
style	interview, sentence list
duration	ms
speaker	random
word	random

Turton (p.c.) points out that many English people have variable realisations of /j/ in this environment. However, yod-dropping does not seem to be common in Maryport yet; hence, variation of this environment does not have to be accounted for. Palatalisation in words like *Tuesday* is also not very common yet

Findings

Multivariate Analysis

Table 12.3 presents the statistical results of the mixed-effect model in this sample. Coefficients provide us with information on how strong the constraints are. They range from positive infinity to negative infinity, and the larger the difference between coefficients in a constraint, the stronger is the effect size. The model already shows that age is not a significant factor, while sex, preceding and following environment, and duration are predictors for variation. In addition, the interaction between sex and preceding environment is significant. In the following, I will discuss the different constraints and which patterns we can observe.

Change in Apparent Time

As discussed in the "Previous Research" section, in studies where data from different generations exist, almost all show an increase in the use of a fronted GOOSE vowel (e.g. Ash 1996; Labov et al. 2006; Baranowski

Table 12.3 Rbrul output for F2 values in GOOSE

Factor	Coefficient	Tokens	Mean
Sex			
F	.074	672	1.309
M	−.074	720	1.150
Preceding environment			
anterior coronal	.061	350	1.236
postalveolar/velar	.003	416	1.199
palatal /j/	.000	482	1.253
labial	−.063	144	1.196
Following environment			
coronal	.095	370	1.348
labial	.014	156	1.203
/l/	−.009	274	1.215
dorsal	−.039	22	1.156
#	−.060	570	1.162
Duration			
+1	−.702		
Interactions			
Sex*preceding environment $p < 0.001$			
Speaker mean	1.227		
Log.likelihood	558.695		
df	16		
R^2	.5		

2007, 2008, 2017; Maclagan et al. 2009; Flynn 2012; Jansen 2012a, b, 2017; Haddican et al. 2013; Stuart-Smith 2013; Holmes-Elliot 2015). Figure 12.4 displays the distribution of F2 across the three different age cohorts in Maryport. However, a continuous increase in F2 across apparent time, which would indicate a change in progress, is not observable. Instead, we notice a curvilinear distribution of the median between the age groups. Old and young speakers are using higher average F2 values than the middle-aged group. The lack of continuous progression of fronting is indeed a rather surprising finding given that this scenario has only been described for very few varieties of English before.[8] At the same time, the variation between minimum and maximum F2 values in each age group decreases across apparent time.

The above results indicate that speakers in Maryport are not taking part in GOOSE-fronting, a change which has reached a global dimension in varieties of English. As other studies have shown (e.g. Smith and

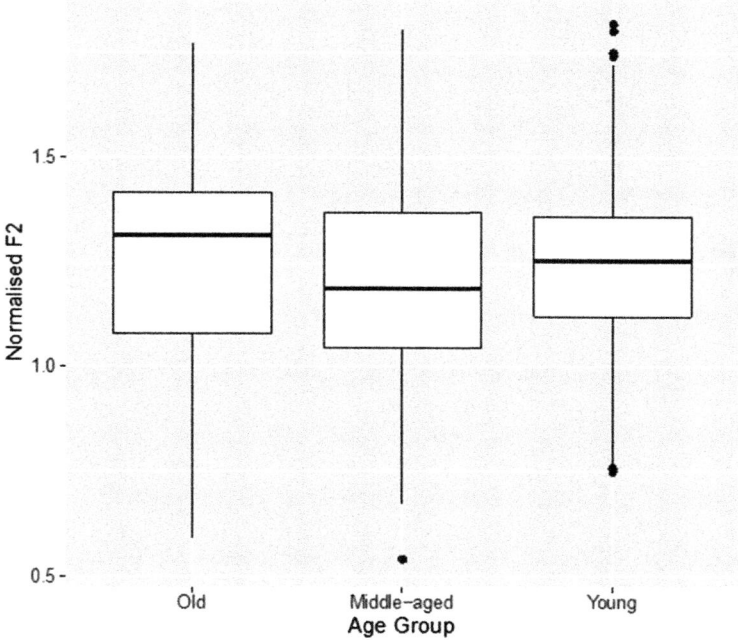

Fig. 12.4 Overall distribution of normalised F2 by age group

Holmes-Elliott 2017), varieties in more peripheral areas might diverge from more general trends, which seems to be the case here. Even though stratification according to age does not exist, in the following, I investigate the linguistic and social factors in order to find out if patterns in the variation of GOOSE occur, which might provide indications for an initiating stage of change.

Linguistic Factors

As detailed above, the linguistic patterning of GOOSE-fronting is remarkably consistent across varieties. In particular, preceding contexts have been shown to play a strong role in governing the variation (e.g. Baranowski 2007, 2008; Hall-Lew 2009; Flynn 2012; Holmes-Elliott

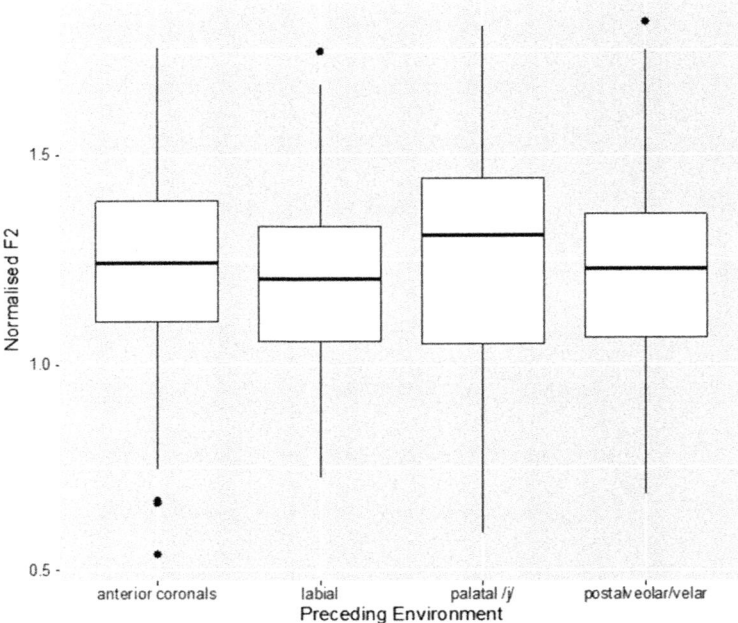

Fig. 12.5 Overall distribution of normalised F2 by preceding environment

2015; Jansen 2017). Rudiments of this pattern are also observable in the Maryport data. Figure 12.5 presents the distribution of normalised F2 by the preceding environment, showing that the palatal /j/ environment has the highest average values and the largest deviation while the other preceding environments display lower average F2 values. Even though a change in progress is not observable, variation does occur and the observable order of factors in this constraint is similar to the constraint orders in other varieties where we observe change in progress: palatal /j/ > anterior coronal > other environments (postalveolar/velar and labial) (e.g. Labov 1980, 1994; Ash 1996; Baranowski 2008; Hall-Lew 2009; Flynn 2012; Jansen 2012b, 2017). However, the variation of F2 between anterior coronals, postalveolar/velar and labial environments is comparatively low.

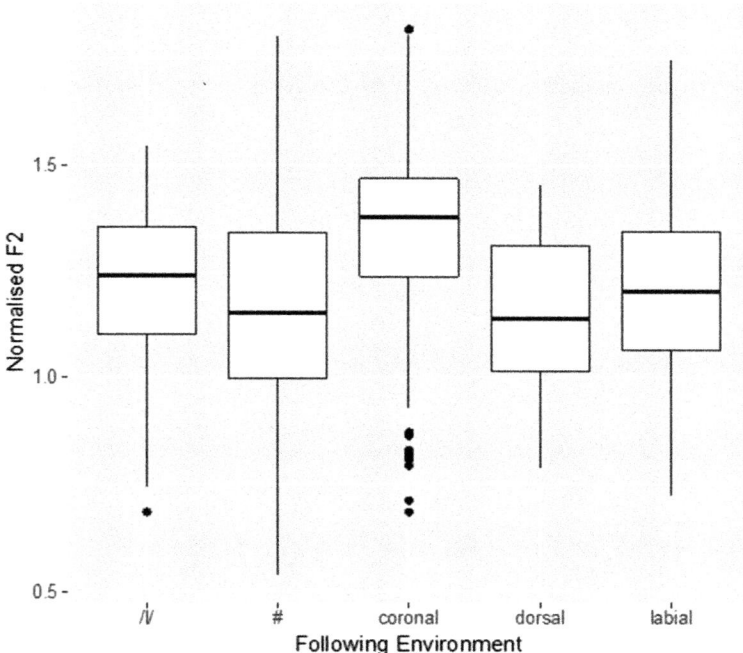

Fig. 12.6 Overall distribution of normalised F2 by following environment

Figure 12.6 illustrates the distribution of F2 according to the following environment. As discussed above, because coda /l/ has an inhibiting nature (cf. Hall-Lew 2009; Flynn 2012; Holmes-Elliott 2015), we would expect the F2 values for GOOSE in this environment to be lower than in other environments. However, Fig. 12.5 shows that the F2 values for coda /l/ overlap with other following environments, i.e. tokens of GOOSE which are followed by coda /l/ are not produced distinctively further back than in the other following environments. Hence, a GOOSE/GHOUL split which is attested for other varieties (cf., e.g., Holmes-Elliott 2015) does not exist in Maryport English. However, there is a clear trend that the vowel followed by anterior coronals has higher F2 values than when it is followed by segments from other environments. The results described here are another indicator that processes which we observe in more mainstream varieties are not necessarily found in peripheral areas.

Social Factors

Turning to the social factors, style is the first factor to be investigated. Although GOOSE-fronting is often categorised as a change below the level of awareness (cf. Holmes-Elliott 2015: 188), studies such as Mesthrie (2010) and Flynn (2012) find style to be a significant factor in the change. The boxplots in Fig. 12.7 indicate that F2 is slightly lower for sentence-list style than for interview style in Maryport. However, this difference is not statistically significant (see Table 12.3).

In contrast to the findings for style, a very clear distinction for the social factor of sex is observable in Maryport (see Fig. 12.8), which is also statistically significant (cf. Table 12.3). Women have far higher F2 values than men, i.e. they produce the GOOSE vowel further front than men.

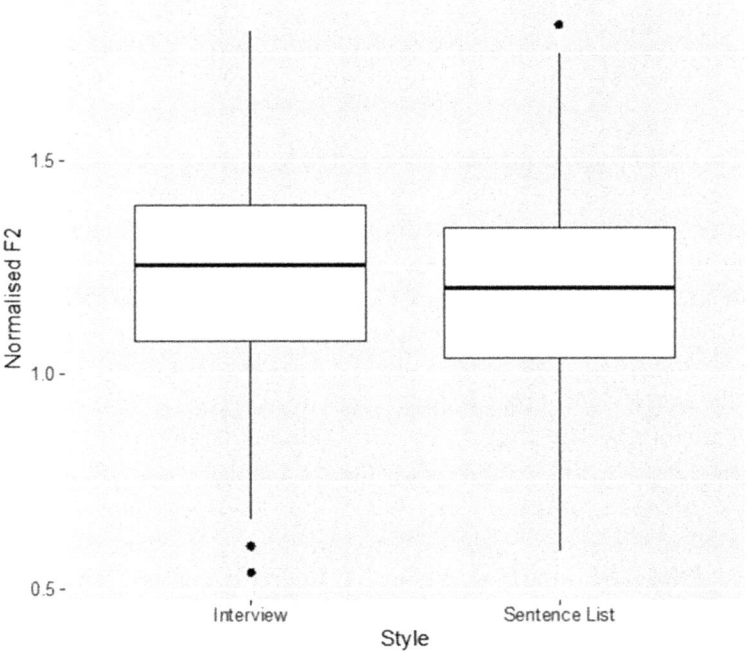

Fig. 12.7 Overall distribution of F2 by style

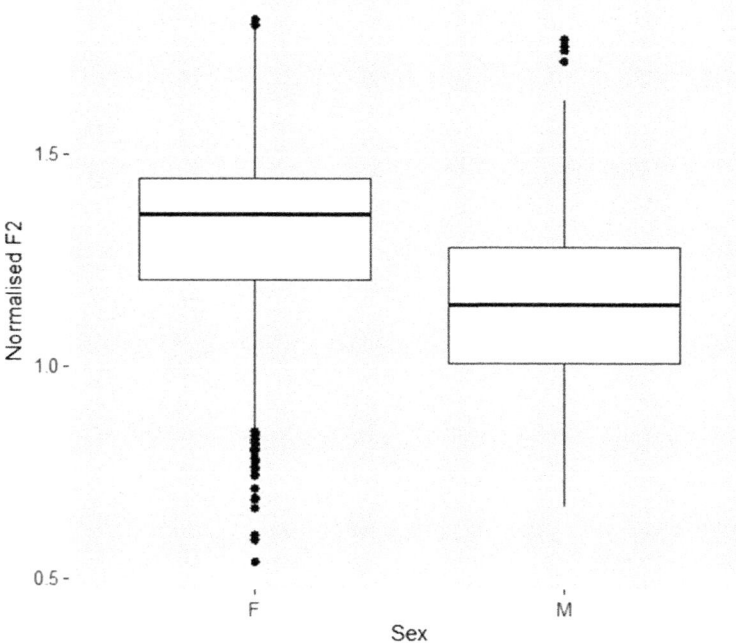

Fig. 12.8 Overall distribution of F2 by sex

This is a very strong difference in sex distribution which has rarely been found in other studies (cf., e.g., Flynn 2012).

Taking a closer look at the arrangement of GOOSE in the vowel systems of female and male speakers in the community, the two vowel plots in Figs. 12.8 and 12.9 provide information about the distribution of GOOSE in the vowel space according to sex and age. Even though an interaction between sex and age does not exist, i.e. fronting across apparent time is not expected, the visualisation of those vowel plots provides us with information about differences in the distribution of the vowel in the different age groups.

The vowel plot for female speakers (Fig. 12.9) reveals that the GOOSE vowel is produced in a fairly central position by women while the male speakers have a more retracted GOOSE vowel. The vowel plot for male speakers (Fig. 12.10) shows a different clustering. In general, men have

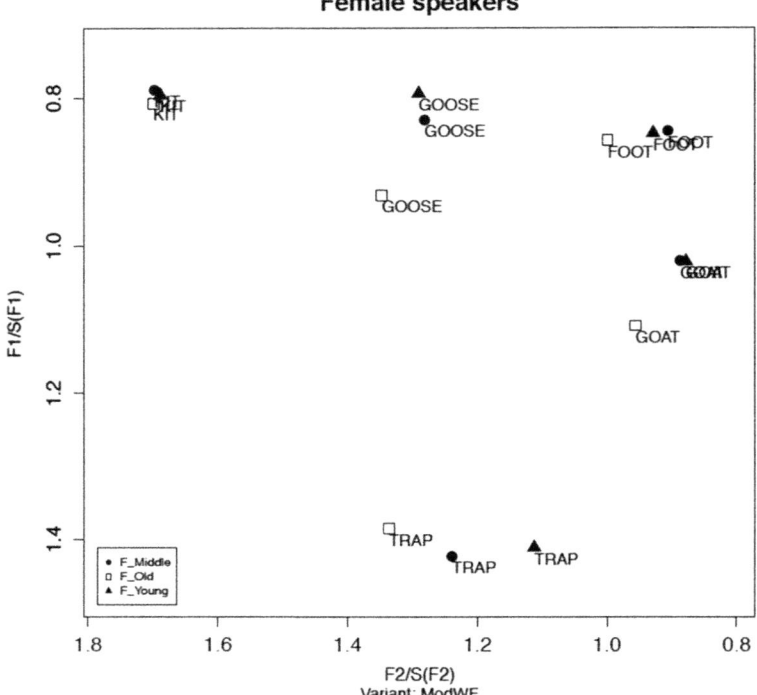

Fig. 12.9 Vowel plots for female speakers across apparent time

lower F2 values than women (cf. Fig. 12.8), which means that the GOOSE vowel is produced further back in the vowel space by male speakers. The difference in place of production between the two sex groups is quite striking, and it is retained between the two groups across apparent time.

The results show that the GOOSE vowel is quite stable on the front-back dimension across apparent time. In contrast, in Figs. 12.9 and 12.10, we can observe changes for this vowel in the height dimension. While the GOOSE vowel is raising for female speakers across apparent time, male speakers show a reverse distribution, i.e. old speakers have the lowest F1 values and the young speakers have the highest F1 values, which means the latter group produces a lower realisation of the GOOSE vowel than the old and middle-aged speakers. In the following, the changes observed in

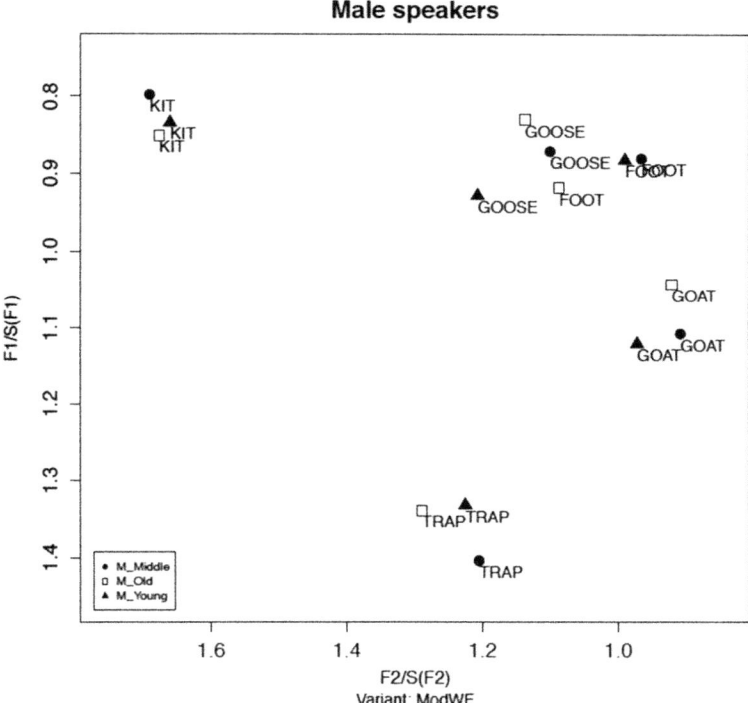

Fig. 12.10 Vowel plots for male speakers across apparent time

the height dimension are investigated in more detail. While a lot of literature exists on the fronting of GOOSE, changes in the height dimension have hardly been discussed in the literature.

Variation and Change in F1

Multivariate Analysis

Table 12.4 provides the statistical results of the mixed-effect model with F1 as the application value. The same constraints which were tested in the statistical model for F2 were tested in this model. The variables of age as

Table 12.4 Rbrul output for F1 as the application value

Factor	Coefficient	Tokens	Mean
Sex			
M	.008	720	.879
F	−.008	672	.866
Age group			
old	.021	473	.888
middle-aged	−.007	545	.853
young	−.013	374	.883
Style			
interview	.001	1261	.873
sentence list	−.001	131	.871
Preceding environment			
anterior coronal	.015	35	.881
labial	.013	144	.882
postalveolar/velar	−.006	416	.903
palatal /j/	−.022	416	.838
Following environment			
/l/	.074	274	.941
labial	−.015	156	.861
#	−.016	570	.863
dorsal	−.017	22	.870
coronal	−.026	370	.843
Duration			
+1	−.272		
Interactions			
Sex*age group			
Age group*preceding environment			
Sex*preceding environment			
Age group*style			
Speaker mean	.873		
Log.likelihood	1527.843		
df	29		
R^2	.515		

well as sex, style, preceding and following environment are significant factors in the model. In addition, the interactions between sex and age group, age group and preceding environment, sex and preceding environment, and age group and style are significant. In the following, I will discuss the different constraints and which patterns we can observe.

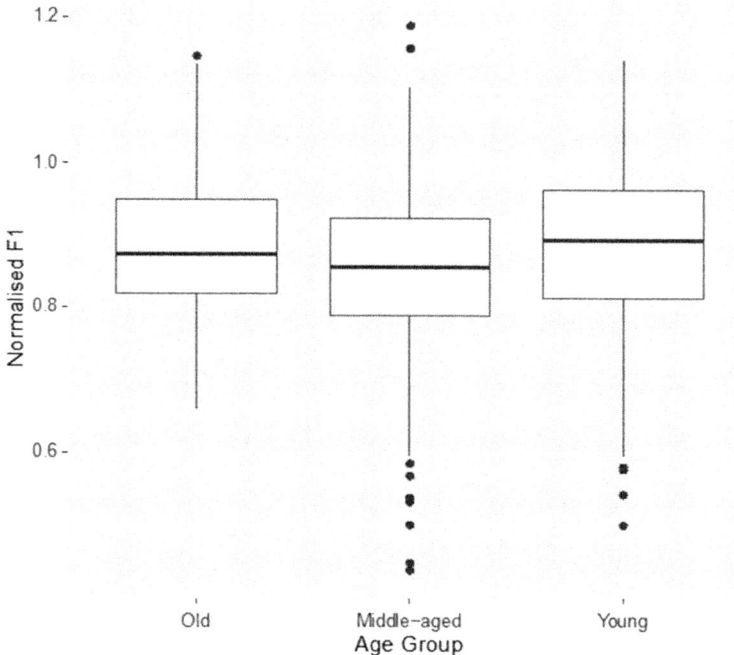

Fig. 12.11   Overall distribution of F1 according to age group

Change in Apparent Time

Figure 12.11 displays the distribution of F1 across the three different age cohorts in Maryport. As with the results for F2, we see that a continuous increase of F1 across apparent time, which would indicate a change in progress, is not observable. However, the statistical model in Table 12.4 reveals that age is indeed a significant factor, which means that we are likely to observe a change of some sort.

Figure 12.12 presents the interaction between age group and sex. Both sex groups are involved in a change across apparent time. However, the changes we see for both sex groups are moving in opposite directions, or in other words, male and female speakers are diverging in their choice of linguistic forms. Across apparent time, the F1 values for women decrease, which means that the vowel is raised, while

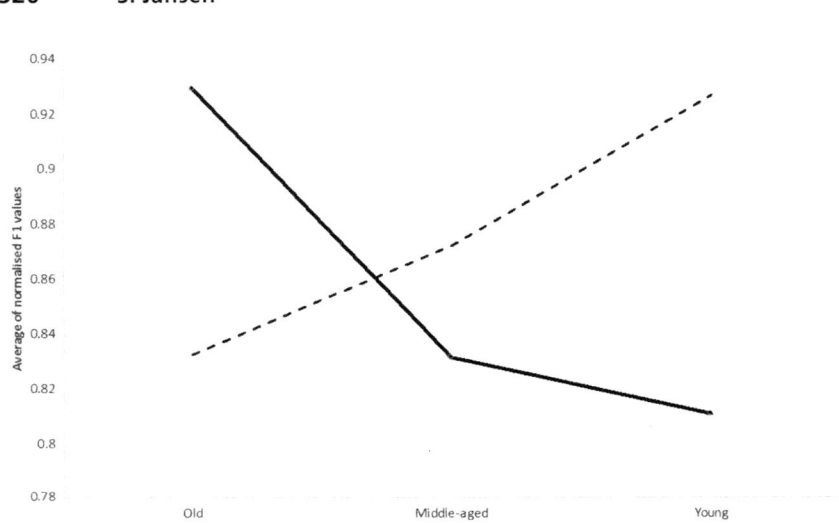

Fig. 12.12   F1 by sex across apparent time

the F1 values increase for male speakers, i.e. they produce the GOOSE vowel continuously lower in the vowel space.

Internal Factors

Turning to the language-internal factors, the results for preceding environment are set out in Fig. 12.13, while Fig. 12.14 illustrates the distribution of F1 according to following environment. The distribution of F1 in Fig. 12.13 shows that the median value for preceding labials, anterior coronals and postalveolar/velar environments are similar. However, the distribution of F1 for palatal /j/ is somewhat lower than for the other environments.

The distribution of F1 according to the following environment (Fig. 12.14) reveals that the median for following pause, coronal, dorsal and labial is quite similar. The distribution of /l/ as following environment, however, sticks out as it displays higher F1 values than the other environment, i.e. the realisation of GOOSE is lower when followed by /l/ than in other following environments.

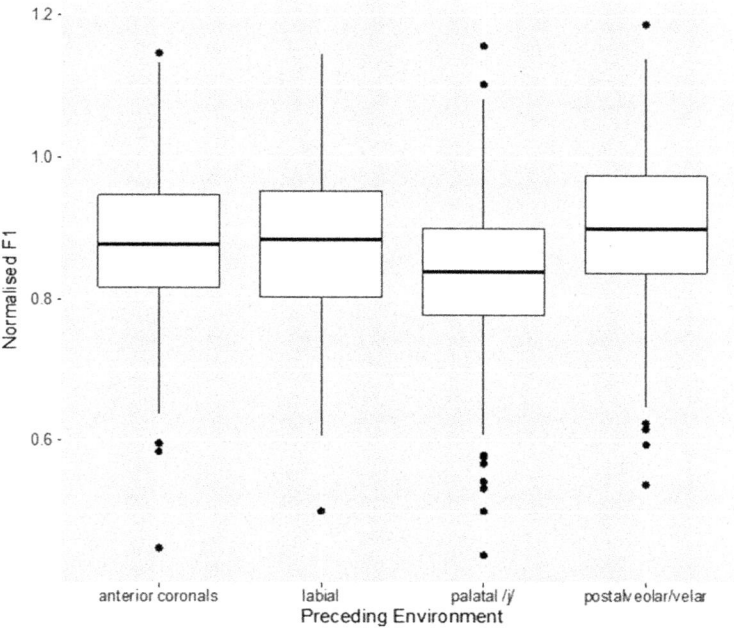

Fig. 12.13 Overall distribution of F1 according to preceding environment

The results for the variation and change of the GOOSE vowel in Maryport set out in this chapter reveal a stable situation for the front-back dimension in the oral cavity, but we observe change in the height dimension. We now turn to the discussion of the results.

Discussion

In the introduction, I suggested that investigating GOOSE-fronting as innovation in a peripheral area would add to our knowledge about this often globally perceived change. In order to do so, I analysed social and linguistic constraints on the front-back dimension to shed light on the variation in this vowel in Maryport. The findings for F2 suggest that even though we see some social and structural stratification, a fronting

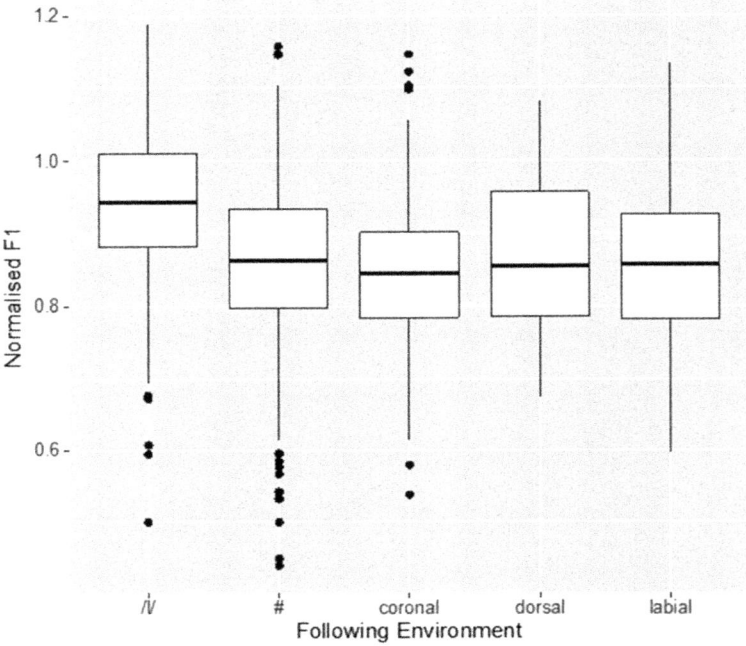

Fig. 12.14 Overall distribution of F1 according to following environment

process is not observable across apparent time. This result challenges the assumption that we are observing a general trend of GOOSE-fronting in varieties of English.

The majority of studies on GOOSE-fronting are based in urban areas, while this study provides evidence that studying communities in more peripheral areas can shed more light on the propagation of this change. As outlined above, various studies find that the strongest constraint in the fronting process is the preceding environment. The constraint order is also quite consistent across varieties in the UK (e.g. Flynn 2012; Jansen 2012a, b, 2017; Scobbie et al. 2012; Stuart-Smith 2013; Turton and Baranowski 2014; Holmes-Elliot 2015) but also in North America (e.g. Fought 1999; Hall-Lew 2005, 2009; Fridland and Bartlett 2006; Labov et al. 2006; Baranowski 2008; Hinrichs et al. 2013; Wing-mei Wong 2014) and other varieties of English: palatal /j/ > anterior coronals >

other environments. And indeed, the descriptive analysis of the data in this study provides the same order. However, while structural stratification similar to other varieties seems to exist to some extent, a change towards a fronter GOOSE vowel is not apparent.

A lack of fronting has only been described for very few varieties, e.g. Newcastle English (Beal et al. 2012)[9] and Singapore English (Deterding 2003). The argumentation for the lack of this change in the former variety is that a traditional fronted vowel blocks the fronting of GOOSE. For the latter, the GOOSE vowel seems to be very stable while in Maryport English GOOSE is produced further front than FOOT, in Singapore English GOOSE is produced further back than FOOT. A fronted variant which blocks the fronting, as we find in Newcastle English, does not seem to exist in the speech of the people in this sample.

While we cannot observe GOOSE-fronting as innovation in Maryport, changes are evident on the height dimension. A few studies have mentioned the raising of GOOSE (e.g. Hall-Lew 2009) but systematic observations have not taken place. However, in this study, there is no clear direction of change, but male and female speakers are diverging in their linguistic choices.

The stark difference in the realisation of this vowel between the sex groups might have to do with the social roles both sexes occupy in the community. Even though very traditional roles of men and women in the community are starting to erode, conservative values such as having a family, having a partner (as a woman), the man as breadwinner and the woman taking care of the children are still very strong. However, women seem to be becoming more independent, e.g. the youngest female is the only person in the sample who goes to university, but overall, it is still a male-dominated community. This lack of parity between the sexes might be reflected by the linguistic choices made by the speakers of the different groups in the community.

As shown in other studies (e.g. Labov 2001; Watt 2002; Durham 2011; Jansen 2012b), women seem to adopt more prestigious, less local forms. If we assume this is the case in Maryport, where women are moving to a more raised GOOSE vowel, this higher vowel realisation might be seen as more prestigious, and the women are using the less local, raised form, while middle-aged and younger men are moving in the opposite direction. Other studies have shown that young men seem to reorientate themselves towards local norms when a variety is under threat of levelling (e.g. Labov 1963; Dubois and Horvath 1999; Durham 2011), but this does not seem to be the reason for the lowering of GOOSE in Maryport as they are diverging from the linguistic choices older male speakers are making.

If we compare the results of this study to the findings in Carlisle (Jansen 2012b, 2017), the outcome could not be more different. While speakers of all ages and sex groups participate in the GOOSE-fronting change in Carlisle, in Maryport—a mere 45 km away from Carlisle—we find a very different linguistic situation. Studies of American English have shown that GOOSE-fronting diffused geographically (e.g. Ash 1996). While studies of this kind are lacking for the UK, it is surprising that GOOSE-fronting has not made inroads into Maryport English. Given that we find extensive GOOSE-fronting in Carlisle and given that people frequently commute to Carlisle for work and leisure, we could expect some fronting in Maryport. However, in conversations, speakers in Carlisle always point out that West Cumbria is a very different dialect area and this study shows that different high back vowel systems operate in Maryport to Carlisle English. In her comparative sociolinguistic study—which included Maryport as a research site—Tagliamonte (2013: 195) states that 'the communities exhibit a profile that is consistent with an earlier stage in the ongoing development of that system in English more generally'. It is certainly true that the present study provides another view on the changes in the GOOSE vowel to that described in other—less peripheral—areas. In order to establish the linguistic situation fully, a study of the high back vowel in Workington as a neighbouring community would provide more information about motivations for change and stability in this vowel in West Cumbria.

Conclusion

The phonological system of Maryport English is undergoing a vast number of changes at the moment (Jansen in preparation). However, the most widely reported vowel change in English, the fronting of the GOOSE vowel, is not attested in this variety yet, though the structural constraints found in other studies are rudimentarily attested, and most importantly, a change towards fronting of this vowel is not observable in Maryport (yet).

On the other hand, we do observe a change in progress for F1, which seems to be driven by external factors, and I have—tentatively—suggested that women are striving for a less local form. In order to understand the mechanisms behind this lack of fronting and the early stages of fronting, more peripheral varieties on the West Cumbrian coast need to be investigated.

Notes

1. Variation between dark and light /l/ exists.
2. Kerswill (2015; based on Andersen and Røyneland) discusses four types of communities: Type 1 are *endocentric closed* communities, i.e. they are geographically peripheral and self-contained. Type 2 are *endocentric open* communities, which are urban and innovative. Because of their openness due to high external contact, features may diffuse outwards. However, they are resistant to outside features. Type 3 are *exocentric closed* communities, where linguistic norms are pervious to outside influence, but contact is slight. Type 4 are *exocentric open* communities, which are often rural, and unlike Type 1, they are not protective of local norms. Instead, they are strongly affected by incoming features, diffusing from local urban centres.
3. All four participants who had joined the armed forces for a while told me that they had to 'tone down' their accent, otherwise the others in their battalion would not have been able to understand them; this could become a crucial detail in life-threatening situations. This clearly has repercussions on their long-term use of dialect but also on the dialect contact situation in the town.
4. A modified version of the BEEP dictionary for British English (FAVEalign, Rosenfelder et al. 2011) was used.
5. Stop words are function words which are most likely to have reduced vowels. A list of stop words was automatically excluded from the measurements by FAVEalign.

6. FLEECE was deliberately not chosen as one of the 'corner vowels' as it has a strong diphthongal quality.
7. Flynn (2011) shows that for northern English varieties, the Watt and Fabricius normalisation method (Fabricius et al. 2009) is preferable.
8. Cf. Beal et al. (2012) and Ferragne and Pellegrino (2010) for Newcastle and Deterding (2003) for Singapore.
9. Though Jasmine Warburton (Turton p.c.) finds that GOOSE is somewhat fronting in Newcastle.

References

Allerdale Borough Council. (2014). Locality profile: Maryport. Available online: http://www.allerdale.gov.uk/downloads/MARYPORT_LOCALITY_PROFILE.pdf

Ash, S. (1996). Freedom of movement: /uw/-fronting in the Midwest. In J. Arnold, R. Blake, B. Davidson, S. Schwenter, & J. Solomon (Eds.), *Sociolinguistic variation: Data, theory and analysis: Selected papers from NWAV 23 at Stanford* (pp. 3–25). Stanford: CSLI Publications.

Baranowski, M. (2007). *Phonological variation and change in the dialect of Charleston, South Carolina*. Durham: Duke University Press.

Baranowski, M. (2008). The fronting of the back upgliding vowels in Charleston, South Carolina. *Language Variation and Change, 20*(3), 527–551.

Baranowski, M. (2017). Class matters: The sociolinguistics of GOOSE and GOAT in Manchester English. *Language Variation and Change*.

Bauer, L. (1985). Tracing phonetic change in the received pronunciation of British English. *Journal of Phonetics, 13*, 61–81.

Beal, J., Burbano-Elizondo, L., & Llamas, C. (2012). *English from Tyne to Tees: Urban varieties of the North-East of England*. Edinburgh: Edinburgh University Press.

d-maps.com. Cumbria. Available online: http://d-maps.com/m/europa/uk/cumbria/cumbria29.pdf

Deterding, D. (2003). An instrumental study of the monophthong vowels in Singapore English. *English World-Wide, 24*(1), 1–16.

Di Paolo, M., Yaeger-Dror, M., & Beckford Wassink, A. (2010). Analyzing vowels. In M. Di Paolo & M. Yaeger-Dror (Eds.), *Sociophonetics: A student's guide* (pp. 87–106). Oxon/New York: Routledge.

Dubois, S., & Horvath, B. (1999). When the music changes, you change too: Gender and language change in Cajun English. *Language Variation and Change, 11*(3), 287–313.

Durham, M. (2011). Right dislocation in northern England: Frequency and use – Perception meets reality. *English World-Wide, 32*(3), 257–279.

Durian, D., & Joseph, B. D. (2011, October). Making sense of shifty changes: The role of phonetic analogy in vowel shifts. Presented at *New Ways of Analysing Variation (NWAV)* 40, Georgetown University, 27–30.

ELAN. Max Planck Institute for Psycholinguistics, The Language Archive, Nijmegen, The Netherlands. Available online: http://tla.mpi.nl/tools/tla-tools/elan/

Fabricius, A., Watt, D., & Johnson, D. E. (2009). A comparison of three speaker-intrinsic vowel formant frequency normalization algorithms for sociophonetics. *Language Variation and Change, 21*(3), 413–435.

Ferragne, E., & Pellegrino, F. (2010). Formant frequencies of vowels in 13 accents of the British Isles. *Journal of the International Phonetic Association, 40*(1), 1–34.

Flynn, N. (2011). Comparing vowel formant normalisation procedures. *York Papers in Linguistics, 11*, 1–28.

Flynn, N. (2012). *A sociophonetic study of Nottingham speakers*. Unpublished PhD thesis, University of York.

Fought, C. (1999). A majority sound change in a minority community: /u/-fronting in Chicano English. *Journal of SocioLinguistics, 3*(1), 5–23.

Fridland, V. (2008). Patterns of /uw/, /ʊ/ and /ow/ fronting in Reno, Nevada. *American Speech, 83*(4), 432–454.

Fridland, V., & Bartlett, K. (2006). The social and linguistic conditioning of back vowel fronting across ethnic groups in Memphis, Tennessee. *English Language and Linguistics, 10*(1), 1–22.

Fruehwald, J. 2013. *Phonological involvement in phonetic change*. Unpublished PhD thesis, University of Pennsylvania.

Haddican, W., Foulkes, P., Hughes, V., & Richards, H. (2013). Interaction of social and linguistic constraints on two changes in northern England. *Language Variation and Change, 25*, 371–403.

Hall-Lew, L. (2005). One shift, two groups: When fronting alone is not enough. *University of Philadelphia working papers in linguistics 10.2: Selected papers from NWAVE 32*.

Hall-Lew, L. (2009). *Ethnicity and phonetic variation in a San Francisco neighborhood*. Unpublished PhD thesis, Stanford University.

Harrington, J., Kleber, F., & Reubold, U. (2008). Compensation for coarticulation, /u/-fronting, and sound change in Standard Southern British: An acoustic and perceptual study. *Journal of the Acoustical Society of America, 123*, 2825–2835.

Harrington, J., Kleber, F., & Reubold, U. (2011). The contributions of the lips and the tongue to the diachronic fronting of high back vowels in Standard Southern British English. *Journal of the International Phonetic Association, 41*(2), 137–156.

Hawkins, S., & Midgley, J. (2005). Formant frequencies of RP monophthongs in four age groups of speakers. *Journal of the International Phonetic Association, 35*(2), 183–199.

Hay, J., Maclagan, M., & Gordon, E. (2008). *New Zealand English*. Edinburgh: Edinburgh University Press.

Henton, C. (1983). Changes in the vowels of received pronunciation. *Journal of Phonetics, 11*, 353–371.

Hinrichs, L., Bohmann, A., & Gorman, K. (2013). Real-time trends in the Texas English vowel system: F2 trajectory in GOOSE as an index of a variety's ongoing delocalization. *Rice Working Papers in Linguistics, 4*, 1–12.

Holmes-Elliott, S. (2015). *London calling: Assessing the spread of metropolitan features in the southeast*. Unpublished PhD thesis, University of Glasgow.

Jansen, S. (2012a). High back vowel fronting in the north-west of England. In S. Calamai, C. Celata, & L. Ciucci (Eds.), *Proceedings of 'sociophonetics' at the crossroads of speech variation, processing and communication* (pp. 29–32). Pisa: Edizioni della Normale.

Jansen, S. (2012b). *Variation and change in the Cumbrian city dialect of Carlisle*. Unpublished PhD thesis, University of Duisburg-Essen.

Jansen, S. (2017). Change and stability in GOOSE, GOAT and FOOT: Back vowel dynamics in Carlisle English. *English Language and Linguistics*.

Jansen, S. (in preparation). From an endonormative close to an exonormative open community: Social changes and phonological levelling in a peripheral Cumbrian town.

Johnson, D. E. (2009). Getting off the GoldVarb standard: Introducing Rbrul for mixed effects variable rule analysis. *Language and Linguistics Compass, 3*(1), 359–383.

Jones, D. (1932). *An outline of English phonetics* (3rd ed.). Leipzig: Teubner.

Kerswill, P. (2015, September). Sociolinguistic typology, dialect formation and dialect levelling in industrial and post-industrial Britain: Vernacular speech since 1800. Presentation at the *10th UK Language variation and change conference*, York University.

Koops, C. (2010). /u/-fronting is not monolithic: Two types of fronted /u/ in Houston Anglos. *University of Pennsylvania Working Papers in Linguistics, 16*(2), Article 14.

Labov, W. (1963). The social motivation of a sound change. *Word, 19*, 273–309.

Labov, W. (1972). *Sociolinguistic patterns*. Philadelphia: University of Pennsylvania Press.

Labov, W. (1980). The social origins of sound change. In W. Labov (Ed.), *Locating language in time and space* (pp. 251–266). New York: Academic Press.

Labov, W. (1984). Field methods of the project on linguistic change and variation. In J. Baugh & J. Sherzer (Eds.), *Language in use* (pp. 28–66). Englewood Cliffs: Prentice Hall.

Labov, W. (1994). *Principles of linguistic change. Volume I: Internal factors*. Oxford: Blackwell.

Labov, W. (2001). *Principles of linguistic change. Volume II: Social factors*. Oxford: Blackwell.

Labov, W. (2010). *Principles of linguistic change. Volume III: Cognitive and cultural factors*. Oxford: Wiley-Blackwell.

Labov, W., Ash, S., & Boberg, C. (2006). *Atlas of North American English: Phonetics, phonology and sound change*. Berlin: Mouton de Gruyter.

Maclagan, M., Watson, C. I., Harlow, R., King, J., & Keegan, P. (2009). /u/ fronting and /t/ aspiration in Māori and New Zealand English. *Language Variation and Change, 21*(2), 175–192.

Maguire, W. (2014, April). Variation and change in a traditional northern English rural dialect. Presentation at the *6th Northern Englishes Workshop*, Lancaster University.

Mesthrie, R. (2010). Socio-phonetics and social change: Deracialisation of the GOOSE vowel in South African English. *Journal of SocioLinguistics, 14*(1), 3–33.

Milroy, L. (2007). Off the shelf or over the counter? On the social dynamics of sound changes. In C. Cain & G. Russom (Eds.), *Studies in the history of the English language* (Vol. 3, pp. 149–172). Berlin/New York: Mouton de Gruyter.

Ohala, J. (1981). The listener as a source of sound change. In C. S. Masek, R. A. Hendrick, & M. F. Miller (Eds.), *Parasession on language and behavior* (pp. 178–203). Chicago: Chicago Linguistic Society.

Roach, P., & Hartman, J. (1997). *English pronunciation dictionary* (15th ed.). Cambridge: Cambridge University Press.

Rosenfelder, I., Fruehwald, J., Evanini, K., & Yuan, J. (2011). FAVE (Forced Alignment and Vowel Extraction) program suite. Available online: http://fave.ling.upenn.edu

Scobbie, J. M., Stuart-Smith, J., & Lawson, E. (2012). Back to front: A socially-stratified ultrasound tongue imaging study of Scottish English /u/. *Rivista di Linguistica/Italian Journal of Linguistics, 24*(1), 103–148.

Sellafield Ltd. (2017). *Facts*. Available online: http://www.sellafieldsites.com/press-office/facts/

Sloetjes, H., & Wittenburg, P. (2008). Annotation by category – ELAN and ISO DCR. *Proceedings of the 6th International Conference on Language Resources and Evaluation.* Marrakesh

Smith, J., & Durham, M. (2011). A tipping point in dialect obsolescence? Change across the generations in Lerwick, Shetland. *Journal of SocioLinguistics, 15*(2), 197–225.

Smith, J., & Holmes-Elliott, S. (2017). The unstoppable glottal: Tracking the development of an iconic British variable. *English Language and Linguistics, 21*, 1–33.

Sóskuthy, M., Foulkes, P., Haddican, W., Hay, J., & Hughes, V. (2015). Word-level distributions and structural factors codetermine GOOSE fronting. *Proceedings of the 18th International Congress of Phonetic Sciences.* Glasgow.

Stockwell, R., & Minkova, D. (1997). On drifts and shifts. *Studia Anglica Posnaniensia, XXXI*, 283–303.

Stuart-Smith, J. (2013, September). In the aftermath of /u/ leaving. Glaswegian vowels through real and apparent time. Presentation at the *9th UK Language Variation and Change conference*, University of Sheffield.

Tagliamonte, S. (2013). *The roots of English*. Cambridge: Cambridge University Press.

Tagliamonte, S., & Smith, J. (2002). "Either it isn't or it's not": Neg/aux contraction in British dialects. *English World-Wide, 23*(2), 251–281.

Thomas, E. R., & Kendall, T. (2007). NORM: The vowel normalization and plotting suite. Available online: http://lingtools.uoregon.edu/norm/index.php

Torgersen, E. (1997). *Some phonological innovations in south-east British English*. Unpublished MA thesis, University of Bergen.

Torgersen, E., & Kerswill, P. (2004). Internal and external motivation in phonetic change: Dialect levelling outcomes for an English vowel shift. *Journal of SocioLinguistics, 8*(1), 23–53.

Turton, D., & Baranowski, M. (2014, October). T[ʉ] c[ʉɫ] for sch [ʉɫ]: The interaction of /l/ -darkening and /u/-fronting in Manchester. Presentation at *NWAV 43*, University of Chicago.

Watt, D. (2002). 'I don't speak with a Geordie accent, I speak, like, the northern accent': Contact-induced levelling in the Tyneside vowel system. *Journal of SocioLinguistics, 6*(1), 44–63.

Wells, J. C. (1982). *Accents of English. Volume I.* Cambridge: Cambridge University Press.

Wing-mei Wong, A. (2014). GOOSE-fronting among Chinese Americans in New York City. *University of Pennsylvania Working Papers in Linguistics, 20*(2), Article 23.

Wright, P. (1979). *Cumbrian Dialect.* Clapham: Daleman Books.

13

'Doing Cornishness' in the English Periphery: Embodying Ideology Through Anglo-Cornish Dialect Lexis

Rhys J. Sandow and Justyna A. Robinson

Introduction

Historically, the relationship between Cornwall and the rest of England has been 'bitter and sometimes violent' (Ferdinand 2013: 207). In this relationship, there exists an asymmetric distribution of power that has invariably disfavoured Cornwall. This situation has impacted upon and shaped the identity of Cornish people. More specifically, many Cornish people position themselves in opposition to England and the English. This opposition is manifested at many levels of everyday life and social structure, including eating habits, music and iconography, as well as language.

The current study focuses specifically on the social meaning of linguistic variation in Cornwall. Although there remains little sociolinguistic research on mainland Cornwall,[1] Celtic scholars have noticed that many Cornish people have used their linguistic distinctiveness as an expression of their autonomy, as a point of departure from 'Englishness' (Jenner

R.J. Sandow (✉) • J.A. Robinson
University of Sussex, Brighton, UK

© The Author(s) 2018
N. Braber, S. Jansen (eds.), *Sociolinguistics in England*,
DOI 10.1057/978-1-137-56288-3_13

333

1904; Kennedy 2016). This linguistic distinctiveness comes in many forms, ranging from fluent use of the Cornish language,[2] to the use of the Anglo-Cornish dialect,[3] with the latter being the focus of the study presented here. Despite sharing many features with Standard English, Anglo-Cornish has a variety of non-standard dialect features at the levels of phonology and grammar, such as the presence of rhoticity and periphrastic *do*. Also, the Anglo-Cornish dialect is recognisable by its lexis, for example, *croust* ≈ 'lunch', *stank* ≈ 'walk' and *emmett* ≈ 'tourist'. Among the people of Cornwall, there is noticeable variation in the use of the Anglo-Cornish dialect, particularly with respect to vocabulary. Yet, it is not entirely clear which factors explain this variation. Considering the historical links between Cornish identity and local language, one may suspect that the use of traditional Anglo-Cornish lexis is related to regional identity (cf. Beal and Burbano-Elizondo 2012). In the current chapter, we explore this idea by investigating the extent to which the use of Anglo-Cornish lexis reflects a Cornish-oriented worldview. In order to do this, we investigate the lexical variation of the concept LUNCH BOX, among male speakers in the mainland Cornish town of Redruth.

Previous Research

Before we consider the relationship between lexis and social identity, we briefly look at the larger picture of lexis and society. Historical linguists (e.g. Hughes 2000) show that broad sociocultural and political contexts affect lexical variation and change. When it comes to specific social dimensions, lexical variation can correlate with the age of speakers (Boberg 2004; Beeching 2011) and gender (Johnson 1993; McColl Millar et al. 2014).

The parameter that is most frequently employed by linguists to explain lexical variation is space. Projects such as the *Survey of English Dialects* (Orton and Dieth 1962–1971) and *BBC Voices* (Wieling et al. 2014) show that individual words can be reliable diagnostics of the geographical space occupied by social groups. Recent studies of dialects consider the relationship between space-related usage and regional identity. They show that hearers and/or readers attribute regional or social characteristics to the users of particular lexical items (see Beaton and Washington 2015; Cooper 2017). For example, Beal and Burbano-Elizondo (2012) show that, in Tyneside, the use of *lad* can index local identity and serve to reinforce in-group solidarity. Moreover, sociolinguistic studies acknowledge the role of lexis in the processes of indexicality (e.g. Bucholtz 1999; Silverstein 2003). However, studies of regional identity as expressed via lexical usage are rather infrequent. This is surprising as vocabulary is, arguably, the level of language which is most accessible to conscious modification and manipulation through which speaker's affiliation can be projected and recognised.

The aim of the current study is to identify and explain patterns of socio-demographic usage and indexical meanings associated with dialect lexis. More specifically, we explore the distribution of dialect lexis in relation to socio-demographic categories, as well as the ideological stances that they reflect and reconstruct. In order to explore these questions, we focus on the words used to express the concept LUNCH BOX among male speakers in Redruth, Cornwall. In this community, the concept LUNCH BOX can be expressed by using, primarily, four variants. These four variants are the supra-local forms *lunch box* and, *sandwich box*, as well as the Anglo-Cornish terms *crib box* and *croust tin*. We investigate lexical usage by employing a lexis-oriented methodological framework, which consists of spot-the-difference tasks, a picture-naming task, an identity questionnaire and interviews.

Cornwall and Redruth

Situated on the South-West peninsula, Cornwall contains both the most southerly (The Lizard) and westerly points (Land's End) in England, boasting over 250 miles of coastline and 12 areas of outstanding natural beauty. The conventional iconography of Cornwall can be largely attributed to authors such as Daphne du Maurier [e.g. *Jamaica Inn* (1935) and *Rebecca* (1938)] and Winston Graham (*Poldark* 1945–2002). As a result, many non-Cornish people hold perceptions of Cornwall which Kennedy (2016: 40) describes as the 3 Rs; '*romantic, rural,* and *remote*'.

However, the lived-in experiences of people from the mainland Cornish town of Redruth are very different. Until the eighteenth century, Redruth was a small market town. In the nineteenth century, the town saw huge population growth to satisfy the fast-developing mining industry (Clegg 2005: 94). As a result, during Cornwall's boom years in the nineteenth century, Redruth was known as 'the richest square mile in the … world' (Wigmore 2016) and was at the forefront of all things new and modern. However, today the town is 'characterised by pockets of intense deprivation', in parts of which up to a third of working-age residents receive out-of-work benefits (Mumford 2014). In December 2015, the food bank in Redruth, a town of 14,000 people, was used 2095 times (Wigmore 2016). Since the collapse of Cornwall's traditional industries,[4] which has been seen in Redruth and across the region, the negative financial impact has been, to some extent, offset by the tourism/hospitality sector which has become a vital economic asset for the Cornish economy as a whole. But Redruth seldom attracts tourists. Consequently, the financial benefits of the tourism industry are largely inaccessible to the town and its people. As a result, Redruth typifies the economic hardship which has, in many ways, defined much of post-industrial Cornwall.

These historical and socio-economic contexts have shaped the thinking of Redruth's people about their place in the world and, therefore, their identity. Conceptualisations of Cornish identity, which traditionally centred on extractive industries, are being replaced by new interpretations of what constitutes Cornishness (Deacon 2007). Among members of the community in Redruth, and in Cornwall more broadly, the social value of Cornish identity has become a 'fundamental tension' within the community (Deacon 2007: 2). For many, being Cornish provides a genuine and profound sense of belonging, whereby one's sense of self can largely be attributed to where one is from and the collective identity of place found at the level of the community. To other native Cornish people, Cornish identity is indicative of 'navel-gazing parochialism' (Willett 2016: 583), which reinforces the backward stereotype of Cornwall. Some believe that this parochial outlook inhibits the county's ability to progress, economically, as well as socially (see Willett 2016). The current study investigates how such outlooks on Cornwall and Cornishness are reflected on the level of lexical usage in Redruth.

LUNCH BOX in Redruth

The current study focuses on the production and perception of a single lexical variable, LUNCH BOX, in the mid-Cornwall town of Redruth. More specifically, this is a study of onomasiological[5] variation, whereby we investigate the different ways in which a concept—that is, LUNCH BOX— is lexicalised. From prior knowledge of the community and of the way that language is used therein (Sandow was born and raised in Cornwall), as well as from an exploratory use of Sense Relation Networks [(SRNs) see Llamas 1999; Braber this volume], we identified four variants which we know to be in use in Redruth—that is, *lunch box, sandwich box, crib box* and *croust tin.*[6] *Crib box* and *croust tin*[7] are Anglo-Cornish dialect forms used for the concept LUNCH BOX.[8] These terms exist in competition with supra-local variants *sandwich box* and *lunch box*. It is a common feature of dialect typology that regional varieties of language tend to reflect a distinct local flavour through the use of regional words in the semantic field of FOOD (Braber this volume).

The Framework

In order to investigate the production and perception of Anglo-Cornish lexis, we have devised a methodological framework which consists of four complementary methods of data collection. These are spot-the-difference tasks, a picture-naming task, an identity questionnaire and interviews. Even though, individually, none of these methodologies are unique, together, they form a lexis-oriented methodological framework. This framework allows for controlling lexical variation as well as modelling intra-speaker variation, inter-speaker variation and implicit and explicit attitudes to language and society.

In order to control for lexical variation and maintain semantic equivalence between variants, we adopt task-oriented methodologies (cf. Anderson et al. 1991; Nagy 2011). More specifically, building on Diapix tasks (see Van Engen et al. 2010; Baker and Hazan 2011; Stamp et al. 2016), we employed spot-the-difference games as our task-based vernacular-oriented methodology. Diapix tasks are an innovative application of spot-the-difference games which were initially developed in order to elicit spontaneous speech while controlling for context (see Van Engen et al. 2010). With their origins in laboratory phonetics (see Van Engen et al. 2010), these tasks have consistently been shown to elicit a natural speech style in contrast to traditional reading passages. Previous applications of Diapix methodologies have focused on key words (e.g. Baker and Hazan 2011). However, the repurposed spot-the-difference tasks used in the current study require a subtle shift of attention, away from key words and towards key concepts (see also Stamp et al. 2016).[9]

Not only does this methodology target the vernacular, it enables the researcher to control and manipulate the context. For example, we identified the concept LUNCH BOX to be onomasiologically interesting. As a result, two sets of spot-the-difference scenes were designed[10] to include this concept. Having met with individual participants, Sandow presented a speaker with a printed copy of the *table* scene (see Fig. 13.1) and the *living room* scene (see Fig. 13.2)—each of which contained a drawing of a typical lunch box found in England. In both of these scenes, the lunch boxes varied in colour between the two frames. The main advantage of such an approach is that all participants are exposed to the same experimental conditions. By controlling the target concepts, the conceptual input is identical across all speakers; yet, as we show in the next section, the linguistic output varied. This ensures that the semantic dimension of meaning is held constant, allowing us to isolate, and ultimately investigate, the social meaning carried by lexical items.

Fig. 13.1 Spot-the-difference task: The *table* scene

Fig. 13.2 Spot-the-difference task: The *living room* scene

After being presented with the spot-the-difference scenes, the researcher (Sandow) asked each participant to identify a pre-determined number of differences, having warned them that they were doing so 'against the clock'. This was done in order to achieve the elicitation of a relatively natural style of speech by increasing cognitive pressure. We did this to fully engage the speaker's attention in completing the task and, thus, limit the attention that a speaker paid to their use of language. The task was considered complete when all of the pre-determined differences were named.

While the spot-the-difference tasks are designed to elicit a casual speech style, we employed a picture-naming task in order to elicit variants of the concept LUNCH BOX in a careful speech style. The picture-naming task involved speakers being shown an image and being asked 'what do you call this?'. For example, speakers were shown an image of a typical example of the concept LUNCH BOX[11] and asked to name it.

Next, participants were asked to complete an oral identity questionnaire [(henceforth IDq) cf. Llamas 1999; Burbano-Elizondo 2008] which consisted of ten statements such as '[b]eing Cornish is a big part of who I am' (see Appendix). Participants were asked to rate the extent to which they agreed with statements on a scale from one to five, with five indicating total agreement and one representing total disagreement. The participants' scores (between one and five) for each statement were added together to form an individual aggregate score. The purpose of this procedure is to elicit data that allow for quantitative categorisation of speakers' Cornish identity.

The last part of data collection was an interview. The interviews broadly followed conversational modules (see Labov 1984), which included topics such as Cornish identity, the (past, present and future) local community and culture. Here, we sought to elicit social and metalinguistic comments. Those who self-reported being familiar with *crib/croust* were asked, 'if you were to hear and not see a person that you didn't know using the word *crib* or *croust*, what kind of person would you think you're talking to?'. Participants' answers were often the catalyst for further dialogue, where they explained their answers in more detail. Since Sandow,[12] who carried out each of the interviews, is from Redruth, these conversations reinforced the insider–insider relationship between interlocutors. Localised narratives, such as those about the local rugby team, local jokes and mutual friends, were important to legitimise the insider status of the interviewer.

The Speakers

Twenty-one male participants, aged 22–80, who lived and/or worked in Redruth, took part in the current study. We recruited participants through friend-of-a-friend/snowball sampling. Some of the participants knew each other. We focus on male rather than female speakers due to their well-documented higher use of traditional dialect forms (e.g. Chambers and Trudgill 1998). We made note of participants' occupation and age. Participants come from a range of social backgrounds, such as mechanics, an author, a postal worker, a care worker and students. Participants were split into *blue-collar* (n = 10) and *white-collar* (n = 11) occupational categories. Moreover, we categorised the speakers according to age into *younger* [(than 25) n = 8] and *older* [(than 35) n = 13] groups. Our age categorisation was based on bottom-up analysis of data (see Analysis). Not all of these speakers have lived the entirety of their lives in Cornwall. These loose criteria were necessary to balance the sample as, until very recently, there were no higher education institutions in Cornwall. If the sample were limited to speakers who had always lived in Cornwall, this would necessarily exclude those with a university education. Interviews were conducted in locations identified as convenient for the informants. These included cafés, universities and places of work, such as the staff-room of a mechanical workshop. Sandow met individual participants for one-to-one interviews, each of these were conducted with Sandow and the participants sat opposite one another at a table.

Analysis

Spot-the-difference and naming tasks elicited 63 variants of the concept LUNCH BOX across the investigated sample (three variants per speaker). Only three variants of the concept LUNCH BOX turned out to be used by speakers from Redruth. These are the Anglo-Cornish dialect terms *crib box* (9/63) and *croust tin* (1/63) and the supra-local variant *lunch box* (53/63). The following analysis is based around the Anglo-Cornish terms only, that is, *crib box*/*croust tin*. *Lunch box* is not discussed here because our interests lie in unpacking the social meaning of traditional Anglo-Cornish dialect lexis. Also, due to the low frequency of *croust tin* in our data, we collapse the two local terms—*crib box* and *croust tin*—into the category Anglo-Cornish terms.[13] This is common practice in descriptions of the Anglo-Cornish dialect (e.g. Merton 2003).

The linguistic data is operationalised by categorising speakers in relation to whether or not they used the dialect terms *crib box*/*croust tin*.[14] These categories are then unpacked in order to present a more detailed analysis of the production and perception of Anglo-Cornish dialect lexis. Speakers who used the Anglo-Cornish dialect terms are coded in two ways. Either they used the dialect terms categorically, that is, in both casual and careful speech styles, or they used local terms in only one style. Those speakers who used the dialect terms non-categorically are split into two groups, that is, whether *crib box*/*croust tin* was present in casual speech (used only in spot-the-difference tasks) or careful speech (used only in the naming task). Speakers who did not produce any examples of Anglo-Cornish dialect lexis were categorised on the basis of their awareness of the terms *crib box*/*croust tin* through the use of metalinguistic questions. Those who are aware of dialect lexis but did not use it were coded separately from those who did not recognise *crib box*/*croust tin*.

In order to find out if language is explained by socio-demographic factors, we correlate speakers' age and type of work with use of Anglo-Cornish dialect lexis (Fig. 13.3). This Figure shows that the only group that does not use the Anglo-Cornish dialect variants at all are the younger white-collar speakers. Although all older speakers are aware of the Anglo-Cornish dialect terms, most did not use *crib box/croust tin*. Only two individuals—one younger and one older blue-collar—speakers used dialect lexis categorically, that is, in both careful and casual style. In the careful speech style elicited from naming tasks, six participants used Anglo-Cornish terms, as opposed to only two in the casual speech style, that is, the spot-the-difference tasks.

Figure 13.3 shows that, when only age is considered, all older speakers recognise the dialect terms, whereas, most younger speakers do not. This

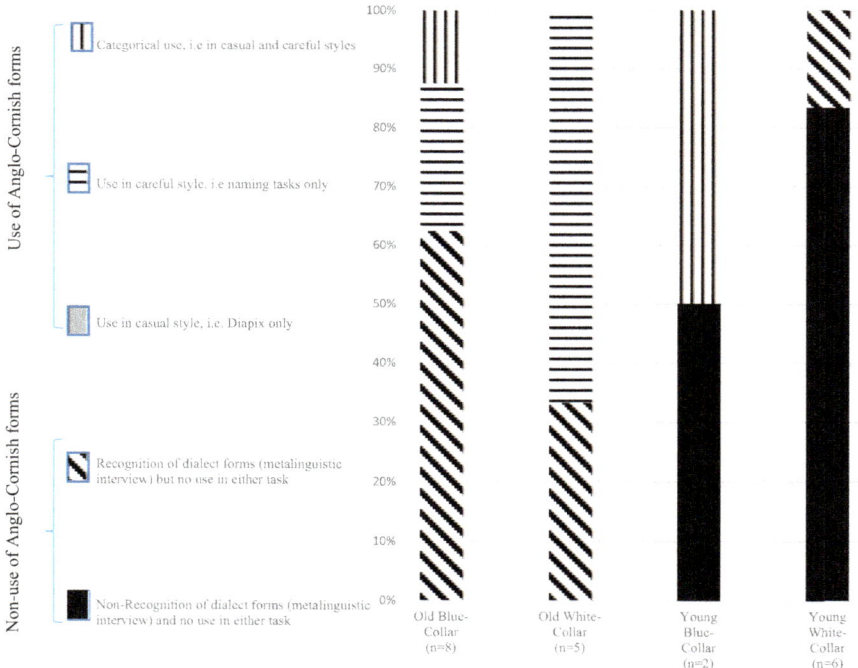

Fig. 13.3 Age and type of work in relation to use of the dialect form *crib box/croust tin*

could be explained by the trajectories of linguistic change in progress (e.g. Labov 1972), where traditional terms are maintained in the speech of older speakers. What is surprising is that although we would expect to find declining dialectal terms to linger in casual—rather than careful—speech (e.g. Robinson 2012a), our data suggest that traditional Anglo-Cornish dialect lexis appears more frequently in the careful style of older speakers. It is possible that *crib box/croust tin* carry an indexical load, which is in some way desirable for many older speakers and accessed by them when they pay attention to their language. One of the contexts in which this might happen is when speakers want to signal their affiliation to a region. In fact, the positive relationship between dialectal use and place identity is well evidenced in sociolinguistic literature (Watt and Milroy 1999; Watt 2002; Johnstone 2011). In light of this, we next consider whether speakers' perceived regional identity explains the observed variation in the use of LUNCH BOX terms.

A bottom-up exploration of the identity questionnaires reveals that the usage of Anglo-Cornish terms form two clusters, with an IDq score of 35/50 being the point at which rates of recognition and use of the local dialect terms change dramatically. Although the possible range of scores on the IDq was between 10 and 50, actual scores were between 17 and 49, with a mean score of 34.95. An IDq score above 35 indicates a strong sense of Cornish identity, whereas a score below 35 reflects a weak sense of Cornish identity. Those speakers who scored above 35 on the IDq were far more likely to use and recognise the dialect terms *crib box/croust tin*. Those who scored below 35 did not exhibit any use of local dialect lexis and were much less likely to recognise the terms *crib box/croust tin*.

Figure 13.4 maps the frequency of usage of *crib box/croust tin* onto participants' age and scores from the identity questionnaire.

When we combine age and identity, as presented in Fig. 13.4, a clearer picture of lexical variation emerges in comparison to the one presented in Fig. 13.3. The older speakers with a high IDq score all recognised the Anglo-Cornish terms, which were used in at least one context by five of the ten individuals in this category—that is, older speakers with a high IDq score. Likewise, the three older speakers with an IDq score below 35 were aware of the terms. However, none of these speakers with a weak sense of Cornish identity actually used the Anglo-Cornish terms. Similarly

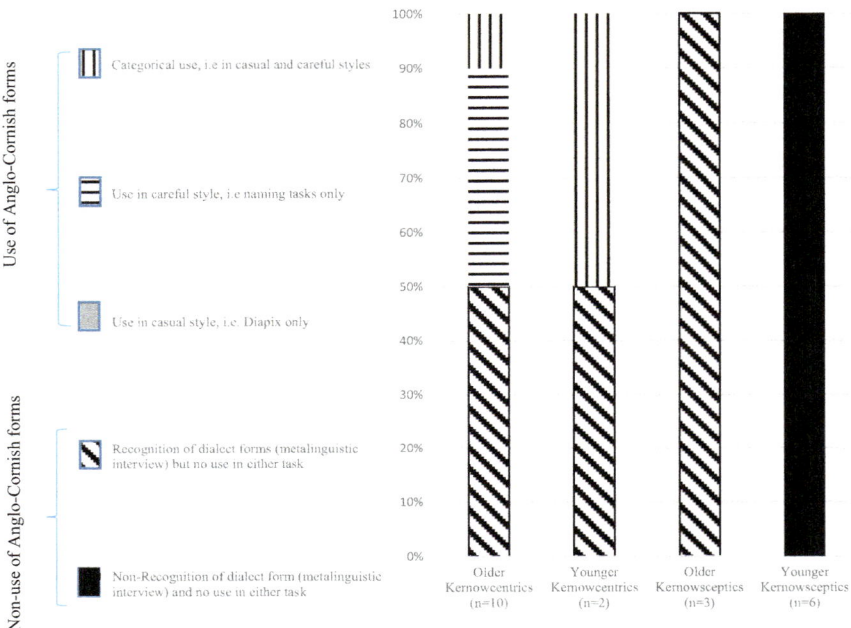

Fig. 13.4 Age and identity in relation to use of the dialect form *crib box/croust tin*

as their older low IDq scoring counterparts, none of the younger speakers with a low IDq score used local dialect terms. Unlike all older speakers, none of the six younger speakers with a low IDq score were familiar with the dialect variants. Both younger speakers with a strong sense of Cornish identity recognised the dialect terms, one of whom did not use the Anglo-Cornish terms at all and the other used *crib box* categorically. Potential disadvantages of the small sample of younger with high IDq scores are offset by presenting a detailed qualitative analysis of the speakers, which is presented in the discussion section.

The most interesting finding in our attempt to square identity, age and usage, refers to the way that older speakers with high IDq scores use their lexical repertoire of the concept LUNCH BOX in different stylistic contexts. In the discussion of Fig. 13.3, we find an unexpected pattern of stylistic variation where Anglo-Cornish terms are maintained in the careful speech style of older speakers. Reanalysing the data through the prism of regional identity (Fig. 13.4), we see that the use of Anglo-Cornish dialect lexis in the careful style is only found among those participants with high IDq scores. Each of the speakers who style-shifted were older and scored highly ($\geq$35) on the IDq. No speakers used the dialect form in the casual elicitation procedure, that is, spot-the-difference tasks, and not in the careful elicitation procedure, that is, naming task. This means that the direction of style-shifting, for those who did so, was unidirectional. For six out of eight younger speakers, style-shifting was not possible because they were unfamiliar with the dialect form.

When older speakers pay more attention to what they say, many use Anglo-Cornish lexis. Previous sociolinguistic studies observe the opposite pattern—that is, that standard forms are more likely to be found in formal speech styles (e.g. Trudgill 1974). Here, we argue that, for our participants, the value of indexing affiliation to local region through the use of local lexis is greater than the value that can be gained from showing a belonging to England through the use of standard language. This is explained by a desire among those speakers to retain a local identity. This complements Dann (2016), who observed that younger speakers use more Anglo-Cornish tokens of the BATH vowel in formal speech. Our study, shows that this process also happens at the level of lexis, not only phonology. In comparison to Dann (ibid.), our study additionally elicits data from across generations, which enables us to draw conclusions regarding how dialectal language change happens from the point of view of style. Language change of salient dialect lexis is mostly resisted in formal styles.

Discussion

For many participants, when they are highly aware that their language is being observed, they use local dialect words in order to project their strong sense of Cornish identity. This is evident in our usage data, as Anglo-Cornish dialect lexis is most frequently found in careful speech styles. This is additionally supported with metalinguistic comments gathered from informants in this study. Participants consistently spoke about the link between the use of the Anglo-Cornish dialect and Cornish identity. For example, one older speaker with a low IDq score stated that 'there has been a dialect renaissance' due to the function of the 'Cornish dialect as an identity marker'. He went on to say that 'it may not be as natural for [Cornish] people to use the [variety of] language that they might have and that has been diluted over time… [Cornish] people are perhaps making a choice to conspicuously use [the Anglo-Cornish dialect]'. To a large extent, these observations are reflected in our usage data, particularly in relation to style-shifting, whereby the dialect terms were more frequently found in the careful speech style. This suggests that the Anglo-Cornish dialect has a performative function. Performativity refers to the process whereby speakers elect to foreground an aspect of their identity—Cornishness—by using available semiotic resources such as their sociolinguistic repertoire (see Coupland 2007). Our observation, that speakers use the Anglo-Cornish dialect in a performative manner, is consistent with comments from our informants. For example, an older speaker with a high IDq score claimed that '[the Anglo-Cornish dialect] is a performance, a deliberate performance'. The next issue to consider is precisely what is being performed through the use of Anglo-Cornish dialect lexis.

Our data reveal that one of the persona traits that is performed through the use of local vocabulary is a defiant, conservative attitude towards change in Cornwall, particularly exogenous change. Many older speakers articulated their frustration at a perceived loss of Cornish autonomy. For example, an older white-collar speaker with a high IDq score commented that 'there are people moving down from up-country [*up-country* 'the rest of England'] trying to take charge and tell you what to do' (our insertion). A concrete example of this is that Cornwall qualified for the European Union's largest economic grant, *Objective One* funding in 1999 as its gross value added (GVA) per head was below 75% of the European average. Despite this, it was the only region in Britain that qualified for this money that did not administer the aid internally (Deacon 2007: 226). There is a growing frustration that decisions regarding Cornwall's future are not being made by those with a lived-in understanding of Cornwall. Willett (2009: 5) suggests that 'Cornwall is poor because policy is based on what some people *expect it to be* rather than what the overall experience of life in Cornwall is' (original emphasis). Similarly, centralising institutions has led many Cornish people to become more insular and parochial by refusing to identify with or be defined by a bureaucratic elite whom they feel does not understand or represent their concerns. As Hall (1991: 33) notes, '[t]he return to the local is often a response to globalisation' as a backlash against a world which they perceive to be becoming anonymous, impersonal and homogenised.

We argue that this 'return to the local' can be reflected on the level of lexis. An example of this pattern can be found in our data. The sole younger speaker who used an Anglo-Cornish dialect term, Tim,[15] scored very highly on the IDq (45/50). This speaker consistently engaged in nostalgic narratives regarding the Cornwall that his grandparents so fondly remembered from their childhood and made clear his strong belief that modern Cornwall had changed for the worse. This speaker, among many others in our sample, talked about members of 'the silent generation', that is, those born in 1920–1940, using the dialect forms *crib box/ croust tin* as part of their vernacular speech variety. Not only did Tim use the local dialect form, he did so categorically. Throughout his narratives, Tim revives traditional conceptualisations of Cornwall and Cornishness. By engaging in narratives which reveal his Cornwall-oriented worldview and by using Anglo-Cornish dialect features, Tim uses language as a part of a semiotic performance which legitimises and reinforces his strong Cornish identity.

The other younger speaker who recognised the dialect terms, Mark, is a typical example of a 'broker' (see Eckert 2000). Mark is a member of the local rugby and cricket clubs, he surfs, is involved in the local music scene, attends a top London university and usually spends his summers doing labour-intensive/manual work. He is engaged in a variety of communities of practice, which means that he is exposed to a broad spectrum of linguistic and social norms. As a result, it is unsurprising to observe that Mark varies in his use of language at multiple levels.[16] Mark's connections with the local region are also reflected in his awareness of the investigated Anglo-Cornish terms. During the interview, Mark did use Anglo-Cornish lexis, such as *emmet* for 'tourist'. However, our data, and Mark's metalinguistic commentary, suggest that, though he is aware of *crib box/croust tin*, these are not forms that he uses himself.

The two speakers described earlier, Tim and Mark, were not typical of the younger speakers in our sample. The majority of younger speakers

(6/8) were not aware of the dialect terms and received a low IDq score. Many of these younger speakers criticised the 'othering' of 'the English'. In particular, one white-collar younger speaker with a low IDq score said 'there's being proud of where you're from and then there's being blinkered and I've always felt like the attitude down here [in Cornwall] has been blinkered… maybe I've attached negative connotations to being proper Cornish'. Another younger white-collar speaker with a low IDq score noted that 'it's hard to imagine a world outside Cornwall when you're in Cornwall'. These commentaries suggest that some speakers perceive a distinct Cornish way of life to be parochial and insular.

There are tensions observed within the community, where contrasting worldviews exist among speakers sharing the same space and the same time—that is, Redruth in the twenty-first century. The coexistence of conflicting perspectives has led to an ideological division within the Redruth community, which is reflected in our sample. The evaluations of local orientations, in respect to Cornish identity, as outlined earlier were summarised by an older white-collar worker with a high IDq score, 'Alan':

Alan:	I hope that people are still proud of [being Cornish]… some people are very *very* Cornish, aren't they?
RS:	Yeah
Alan:	You know 'I'm Cornish and that's it, I'm not English, I'm Cornish'
RS:	Yeah, yeah, yeah
Alan:	And there's others who say 'yeah we're Cornish but we're also English as well'
RS:	Yeah
Alan:	You know, we're not, we're not just our own little county down here, we are a part of England even though we're Cornish. [We] should be proud of that

Based on participant observation and data analysis, we suggest that Cornish people represent one of at least two ideological stances—Kernowcentrism or Kernowscepticism (*Kernow* is the Cornish language word for Cornwall). Deacon (2007) argues that one can split Cornish historians into two historiographic camps, that is, the Kernowcentrics and the Kernowsceptics. Here, we argue that it is appropriate to expand this idea to the people of Cornwall. We suggest that the label *Kernowcentric* signifies people who believe that Cornwall should have greater autonomy and perceive sociopolitical encroachment from outside of the county to be unwelcome. These speakers are a conduit for 'narratives of historic victimhood' (Kennedy 2016: 15) that can form the basis of ideologies which can form and be assimilated into the worldview of successive generations, or as Kennedy (2016) argues, a Cornish *habitus*. This contrasts with the Kernowsceptics, who believe that such narratives are self-perpetuating. In their view, economic and cultural assemblages in Cornwall should be more closely wedded to those systems on a national scale. For these individuals, the extent to which Cornwall is similar to England is greater than the extent to which it is different; yet, for Kernowcentrics, this situation is the reverse. Although many Kernowsceptics are proud to be Cornish, their outlook is much more global.

Kernowcentric and Kernowsceptic ideological stances were reflected in participants' answers to the identity questionnaire. It was at the 35/50 IDq score that reflected not only a division in usage of dialect terms, but of ideology, too. When interview data are compared with the identity questionnaire, there is a correlation between in speakers' attitude towards Cornwall and IDq scores. Analysis of qualitative data from interviews and speakers' IDq scores indicate that those who scored ≥35/50 can be considered Kernowcentrics and an aggregate score of <35/50 reflects a Kernowsceptic outlook. Although typically, older speakers are Kernowcentrics and younger speakers are Kernowsceptics, there are speakers who do not fit this general pattern. Of the older speakers, 69% are Kernowcentrics, whereas only 25% (2/8) of younger speakers appear to be Kernowcentrics. Similarly, there is not a consistent relationship between socio-economic class and identity. For example, considering education and (parents') occupation, out of all speakers in our sample, the two younger Kernowcentrics are positioned highest and lowest on the socio-economic class continuum. Although identity and class often correlate, identity and an individual's sense of belonging to a place often transcend traditional class divisions.

The data presented in the current study demonstrate that many individuals index their Kernowcentric worldview through the use of Anglo-Cornish lexical forms *crib box/croust tin*, whereas Kernowsceptic speakers exclusively employ supra-local variants. All uses of local dialect lexis in this study took the form of *crib box*—with the exception of one older individual with a high IDq score who used the *croust tin* form in the careful speech style. During the interview, this person commented that he is a fluent speaker of Cornish. Therefore, we can interpret his use of *croust tin* in careful speech to be a process of identity marking, whereby the Anglo-Cornish form is used to showcase his bilingualism. This suggests that there is a hierarchy—from the most Cornish variant, *croust tin*, to *crib box*, to the least Cornish form *lunch box*.

The Social Function of *crib box/croust tin*

Though we have analysed the intra- and inter-speaker distribution of the dialect lexical terms, we are yet to investigate how they are used to position oneself within the local social matrix pertaining to the Kernowcentric/sceptic ideologies. By exploring the indexical value of the dialect terms *crib box/croust tin,* we can also explain why such distributional patterns as seen in Figs. 13.3. and 13.4. exist. Speakers' metalinguistic comments reveal that the Anglo-Cornish dialect lexis carry a variety of social indices. A number of connotations were highly variable among our participants. For example, many white-collar workers associated the dialect form with older blue-collar workers; yet, by and large, blue-collar workers made no such association. These metalinguistic commentaries, coupled with interview data and the fieldworker's participant observations of the speech community, facilitate the exploration of the social function of the dialect terms *crib box/croust tin* in relation to the concept LUNCH BOX, which we discuss next.

Participants in our study consistently remarked that the Anglo-Cornish terms were used by manual workers as an in-group marker. For example, an older Kernowcentric speaker, Gerald, observed that 'when the apprentice comes in and you've got twelve other people who are calling it a *crib break*, it's going to be a *crib break*, isn't it?'. Thus, in interactions between speakers of the Anglo-Cornish dialect, the local form can function as a shibboleth of in-group membership. Yet, on the community level, in the interests of intelligibility, supra-local variants are often the more conducive option, particularly when one considers that up to two-thirds of the community are non-Cornish (Bewnans Kernow 2014: 5).[17] If one were to use the dialectal variant with a non-Cornish interlocutor, it would be detrimental to the overall cooperative function of a conversation. Informants suggested that the dialect form was used to reinforce an insider versus outsider dichotomy, almost akin to code-switching. For example, Piran, an older Kernowcentric speaker, commented that 'people will deliberately use Cornish words to confuse [non-Cornish] people... and exclude them'. Thus, depending on one's audience, Anglo-Cornish dialect lexis can exclude the out-group while developing solidarity with the in-group.

Over a period of time spanning approximately three generations, there appears to have been a revalorisation of the Cornish dialect. Its usage has shifted from being subconscious, habitual, and vernacular to being vestigial, and strongly indexical. Lexical attrition (see McColl Millar et al. 2014) has led to such a severe reduction in usage that it is not only absent from the vocabulary that many younger speakers use, but the vocabulary that they know, too. This is because, not only do many younger speakers not use the terms *crib box/croust tin*, they are not aware of their meaning, or even aware of their existence. The older speakers grew up in a time when some Cornish mines remained operational, albeit in terminal decline.[18] Thus, the traditional communities in which the use of this dialectal variant was commonplace was an active part of the culture in which the older speakers grew up. As the younger speakers did not grow up in a community with functioning mines, they lack this lived-in experience. To some extent, this accounts for why many younger speakers were not aware of the dialect terms; yet, all older speakers at least recognised the regional forms. As a result of this apparent diachronic change, we suggest that the Anglo-Cornish lexical items investigated here may be becoming post-vernacular, or deregistered (cf. Cooper 2017). Indeed, some speakers spoke of the form in the past tense, for example, 'it *was* associated with manual male labour' (our emphasis). This statement also reinforces our observation that the Anglo-Cornish terms are associated with traditional working-class males. However, although this perceived association is apparent in our interviews, our analysis of usage data have not supported this.

Both the Kernowcentrics and the Kernowsceptics are united in their desire to see Cornwall thrive once again. However, although there is consensus on the overarching goal—that is, to increase living standards—the way in which this can best be achieved is a point of conflict and division within the community. Although all speakers cited positive and negative aspects of Cornwall and Cornishness, for some, the positives outweigh the negatives and, for others, the opposite is true. The use of *crib box/croust tin* allow one to be socially locatable with respect to this parameter of social identity—that is, Kernowcentrism/scepticism. By contrast, the supra-local variants *lunch box* does not make the speaker socially locatable, that is, from the use of a Standard English form one cannot reliably predict the speaker's ideological stance in relation to local orientation. This is because supra-local variants have a much higher relative frequency of usage and are used across the ideological spectrum. Therefore, the social function of *lunch box* is less marked. The use of Anglo-Cornish dialect terms, in opposition to supra-local ones, were used exclusively by Kernowcentric individuals. For many speakers, the use of the dialect form can function as a semiotic embodiment of their stance in relation to the value of Cornish identity. These observations, supplemented by the social and stylistic variation evidenced above, indicate that a process of attrition has relegated the dialect terms to a performative semiotic embodiment of regional identity, as opposed to comprising part of the vernacular speech variety.

Informed by both quantitative and qualitative data analysis, we introduce an 'indexical field' (see Eckert 2008) for the Anglo-Cornish dialect terms *crib box/croust tin* (Fig. 13.5). This visualisation technique allows us to present 'a constellation of ideologically linked meanings' (Eckert 2008: 94), which are possible social meanings attached by individuals to *crib box/croust tin*. Each of these social meanings are possible meanings attributed to the Anglo-Cornish terms once the variants have been filtered through an individual's 'ideological lens' (Moore and Podesva 2009: 479). Moreover, each indexical meaning is situated within the context of a multidimensional semiotic system, such as the sartorial choices of the speaker. The labels in the indexical field are characteristics, values, stances or ideologies that we have observed to be associated with the use of *crib box/croust tin*. Each of these labels is discussed in the current analysis. Primarily, we have observed an indexical link between

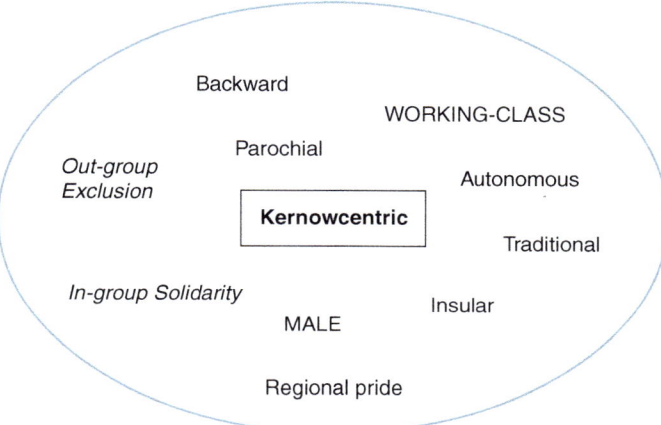

Fig. 13.5 Indexical field for the dialect forms *crib box/croust tin*. Bold and bordered = ideological orientation, capitals = first-order indexicalities, regular lowercase = second, third, and higher order indexicalities, italics = audience-based considerations (We do not claim the indexical field to be exhaustive, merely illustrative)

using Anglo-Cornish dialect lexis and a particular ideological stance, that is, Kernowcentrism (Fig. 13.5). However, other perceived attributes are also indexed by the use of *crib box/croust tin*. Consistently reinforced associations between male-oriented manual labour and the Anglo-Cornish forms *crib box/croust tin* have developed an association with the working class, more specifically, working-class males. Thus 'working-class' and 'male' are first-order indexicalities (see Silverstein 2003) for the Anglo-Cornish terms. Next, we further unpack the social meaning of *crib box/croust tin* to reveal second, third, and higher order indexical values. These indexical values exist on a broad evaluative spectrum, some of which are, arguably, negatively valenced and others are, arguably, positively valenced. These are *backward, parochial, insular, traditional, autonomous* and *regional pride*. As well as this, *crib box/croust tin* have pragmatic functions, which can serve to exclude members of the out-group, who do not understand Anglo-Cornish dialect lexis, and simultaneously develop solidarity with the other members of the in-group—that is, other Kernowcentrics.

Conclusion

By employing the proposed combination of methodological techniques, the current study demonstrates that methodological innovation can facilitate the elicitation and exploration of onomasiological data. Typically, the way in which the socially conditioned nature of the lexicon is understood is inhibited by the shallow sociological analysis afforded by the dialectological framework. The current study shows that, in order to accurately report on the usage of lexical variants, one must consider variation in the social, as well as the regional, dimension. Participant observation methods allow us to not only better explain the distribution of lexical items, but also to explain why these patterns appear to exist. If third-wave variation theory is concerned with linguistic aspects of identity construction, then the lexicon can be a highly informative level of analysis. By adding an identity vector to the analysis, the current study further showcases the value of considering emic social categories (cf. Eckert 2000; Moore and Podesva 2009).

In the current study, we demonstrate that some lexical variants are conditioned by social categories which reinforce and reconstruct social meanings.[19] More specifically we showcase the value of considering the role of identity in language variation and change in relation to onomasiological variation of the nominal concept LUNCH BOX in Redruth, Cornwall. IDq scores can work in conjunction with elicitation procedures in order to complement macro-level ideologies with micro-level linguistic variation. We show that lexical items can be strategically employed in order to index an ideological stance—that is, Kernowcentrism or Kernowscepticism. Just as one can, arguably, *do* gender (see West and Zimmerman 1987), it appears that one can also *do being Cornish* by employing lexical forms with Kernowcentric indices.

Speakers' use and evaluations of the dialect forms *crib box/croust tin* suggest that its usage is highly indexical. The current study shows the extent to which words carry socio-semantic meanings. These social meanings can be consciously or subconsciously employed to identify individuals within—or in opposition to—larger social structures. More specifically, in Redruth, we have seen that dialect lexis can function to broadcast one's identity in relation to Kernowcentrism, in opposition to Englishness, via a semiotic performance. Thus, in contrast to the typically negative perceptions of the Cornish dialect, such as 'farmer' and 'weird' (Montgomery 2007: 248), many Kernowsceptics have reappropriated their difference as a badge of honour by employing Cornwall's unique dialect as an 'emblem of difference' (Vernon 1998: 154). Kent (2013: 55) has observed that learning the Cornish language is the 'ultimate ideological commitment' to presenting a distinct, non-English, Cornish way of being. Although dialect lexis is a less extreme manifestation of an ideological commitment to Kernowcentrism, this study demonstrates that *crib box*/*croust tin* are being employed in order to embody a Cornwall-oriented worldview.

Notes

1. Moore and Carter (2015) present an account of sociophonetic variation and change in the Isles of Scilly, Cornwall. Dann (2016) has conducted preliminary sociophonetic research on in-migrants in West Cornwall.
2. The Cornish language is a member of the Brythonic branch of the Celtic language family.
3. The Anglo-Cornish dialect is a variety of English spoken in Cornwall. It is also known by a range of alternative labels, including Cornish English and Cornu-English.
4. Other than mining, Cornwall's traditional industries include farming and fishing. However, in Redruth, mining was the most prominent industry, and the only one of these three to collapse entirely.
5. This contrasts with semasiological variation, where the object of study is a single lexical item with variable semantic meanings, such as *gay* 'happy' and *gay* 'homosexual' (see Robinson 2012b).
6. Although these were the variants that we identified as likely to appear in our data, the methodologies that we employed made it possible that a range of other variants could have occurred, such as *crib bag* or *sandwich tin*.
7. Alternative combinations, that is, *crib tin* and *croust box*, are not attested in the investigated community. This was verified by informal discussions with Anglo-Cornish speakers.
8. Etymologically, *croust* originates in Latin, *crusta*, and has been used in England since Middle English time as *crust*, 'the hard, dry outside of

bread' (see Oxford English Dictionary (OED) online). It was borrowed into the Cornish language, and remains in use in the Anglo-Cornish dialect. In Cornwall, through metonymic extension, *croust* developed into 'the entire meal, usually taken during mid-morning or midday'. This meaning is evidenced to be characteristic of Cornish lexis (Wakelin 1984). *Crib* is a Germanic term for 'a feeding trough'. Its usage as an Anglo-Cornish term for 'food provisions' has been documented since the nineteenth century through glossaries of Cornish words and through narratives centred on Cornish life (OED online).

9. Another key difference between this study and previous applications of Diapix methodology is that they have typically been dialogic, involving interactions between two participants, yet we use a monologic format (see also Boyd et al. 2015). In order to make this possible, participants were asked to 'think out loud'.

10. The spot-the-difference scenes described here were designed to meet our specifications by Tyler Crewes—an independent graphic designer from Camborne, Cornwall.

11. Image was taken from http://brecon.fyinetwork.co.uk/my,8972-tradesman-lunch-boxes

12. It was important to establish this link through narratives as Sandow has a perceptually pan-southern English accent.

13. The analysis of the socio-semantic relationship between *crib box* and *croust tin* is an issue that remains to be explored in future research.

14. We consider the spot-the-difference scenes as a single context, which is analysed categorically—that is, use or non-use of Anglo-Cornish terms. There was no intra-speaker variation between responses to the 'table' and 'living room' spot-the-difference scenes.

15. All names used in this study are pseudonyms.

16. Mark varies between rhoticity and non-rhoticity and at times loses his TRAP/BATH split.

17. In Cornish studies, there is very little consensus on what constitutes a native Cornish person (Deacon personal communication). Therefore, if one were to use a different metric, this figure would undoubtedly change.

18. The last operational tin mine in Cornwall, which was located on the periphery of Redruth, 'South Crofty', closed in 1998.

19. We suggest that future research may be best served by additionally considering a third category which occupies the ideological middle-ground, the Kernowsympathisers.

Appendix

Identity Questionnaire

To what extent (1–5) do you agree with the following statements?

1- Completely disagree
2- Mostly disagree
3- Neither agree nor disagree
4- Mostly agree
5- Completely agree

1. Being Cornish is a big part of who I am.
2. I am proud to be Cornish.
3. A distinct Cornish identity, in contrast to the rest of England, is a good thing.
4. Cornwall council should be given more control over the county and, therefore, Westminster should have less control of Cornwall.
5. Cornish life is independent of 'English' life.
6. I would like to live in Cornwall for the rest of my life.
7. I would be more likely to vote for a performer on a talent show if they were from Cornwall.
8. Funding for the Cornish language should be increased.
9. Using the Cornish dialect is a big part of what makes me, me.
10. I think that the Cornish dialect is an important marker of Cornishness.

References

Anderson, A. H., Bader, M., Bard, E. G., Boyle, E., Doherty, G., Garrod, S., Isard, S., Kowtko, J., McAllister, J., Miller, J., Sotillo, C., Thompson, H. S., & Weinert, R. (1991). The HCRC map task corpus. *Language and Speech, 34*(4), 351–366.

Baker, R., & Hazan, V. (2011). DiapixUK: Task materials for the elicitation of multiple spontaneous speech dialogs. *Behaviour Research Methods, 43*(3), 761–770.

Beal, J., & Burbano-Elizondo, L. (2012). 'All the lads and lasses': Lexical variation in Tyne and Wear. *English Today, 28*(4), 10–22.

Beaton, M. E., & Washington, H. B. (2015). Slurs and the indexical field: The pejoration and reclaiming of *faveldo* 'slum-dweller'. *Language Sciences, 52*, 12–21.

Beeching, K. (2011). The sociolinguistics of lexical variation in standard French: A diachronic perspective. In T. Pooley & D. Lagorgette (Eds.), *On linguistic change in French: Sociohistorical approaches* (pp. 37–53). Chambéry: University of Savoy Press.

Bewnans Kernow. (2014). *Report on the Cornwall council Cornwall local plan strategic policies – Proposed submission document 2010–2030*. Available online: http://www.bewnanskernow.org/uploads/2/3/1/8/23183698/bk_local_plan_april_2014.pdf

Boberg, C. (2004). Real and apparent time: Late adoption of changes in Montreal English. *American Speech, 79*(3), 250–269.

Boyd, Z., Elliot, Z., Fruehwald, J., Hall-Lew, L., & Lawrence, D. (2015, April). An evaluation of sociolinguistic elicitation methods. Paper presented at *the 18th international conference of the phonetic sciences*, Glasgow, UK, 10–14 April.

Bucholtz, M. (1999). "Why be normal?": Language and identity practices in a community of nerd girls. *Language in Society, 28*(2), 203–223.

Burbano-Elizondo, L. (2008). *Language variation and identity in Sunderland*. Unpublished PhD thesis. University of Sheffield.

Chambers, J. K., & Trudgill, P. (1998). *Dialectology* (2nd ed.). Cambridge: Cambridge University Press.

Clegg, D. (2005). *Cornwall & the Isles of Scilly: The complete guide*. Trowbridge: Cromwell Press.

Cooper, P. (2017). 'Deregisterment' and 'fossil forms': The cases of *gan* and *mun* in 'Yorkshire' dialect: The changes in what features constitute 'Yorkshire' dialect from the 19th century to the 21st. *English Today, 33*(1), 43–52.

Coupland, N. (2007). *Style: Language variation and identity*. Cambridge: Cambridge University Press.

Dann, H. (2016). *Language, identity and indexicality: A sociophonetic study of first generation in-migrants in Cornwall*. Unpublished MA thesis, University of Sheffield.

Deacon, B. (2007). *Cornwall: A concise history*. Cardiff: University of Wales Press.

Du Maurier, D. (1935). *Jamaica Inn*. London: Little, Brown and Company. reprinted in 2013.

Du Maurier, D. (1938). *Rebecca*. London: Virago Press. reprinted in 2007.

Eckert, P. (2000). *Linguistic variation as social practice*. Oxford: Blackwell.

Eckert, P. (2008). Variation and the indexical field. *Journal of Sociolinguistics, 12*(4), 453–476.

Van Engen, K. J., Baese-Berk, M., Baker, R. E., Choi, A., Kim, M., & Bradlow, A. R. (2010). The wildcat corpus of native and foreign-accented English: Communicative efficiency across conversational dyads with varying language alignment profiles. *Language and Speech, 53*(4), 510–540.

Ferdinand, S. (2013). A brief history of the Cornish language, its revival and its current status. *E-Keltoi: Journal of Interdisciplinary Celtic Studies, 2*, 199–227.

Graham, W. (1945–2002). *The Poldark novels* (Vols. 1–12). London: Pan Macmillan. Reprinted in 2015.

Hall, S. (1991). The local and the global: Globalization and ethnicity. In A. King (Ed.), *Culture, globalization, and the world-system* (pp. 19–40). Minneapolis: University of Minnesota Press.

Hughes, G. (2000). *A history of English words*. Oxford: Blackwell.

Jenner, H. (1904). Preface to 'A handbook of the Cornish language'. In D. R. Williams (Ed.), *Henry and Katherine Jenner: A celebration of Cornwall's culture, language, and identity* (pp. 49–55). London: Francis Boutle (2004).

Johnson, E. (1993). The relationship between lexical variation and lexical change. *Language Variation and Change, 5*(3), 285–303.

Johnstone, B. (2011). Making Pittsburghese: Communication technology, expertise, and the discursive construction of a regional dialect. *Language & Communication, 31*(1), 3–15.

Kennedy, N. (2016). *Cornish solidarity: Using culture to strengthen communities*. Port Laoise: Evertype.

Kent, A. M. (2013). *Towards a Cornish philosophy: Values, thought, and language for the West Britons in the twenty-first century*. Port Laoise: Evertype.

Labov, W. (1972). *Sociolinguistic patterns*. Philadelphia: University of Pennsylvania Press.

Labov, W. (1984). Field methods of the project on linguistic change and variation. In J. Baugh & J. Sherzer (Eds.), *Language in use: Readings in sociolinguistics* (pp. 28–54). Englewood Cliffs: Prentice Hall.

Llamas, C. (1999). A new methodology: Data elicitation for social and regional language variation studies. *Leeds Working Papers in Linguistics and Phonetics, 7*, 95–118.

McColl Millar, R., Barras, W., & Bonnici, L. M. (2014). *Lexical variation and attrition in the Scottish fishing communities*. Edinburgh: Edinburgh University Press.

Merton, L. (2003). *Oall rite me ansum: A salute to Cornish dialect*. Newbury: Countryside Books.

Montgomery, C. (2007). *Northern English dialects: A perceptual approach*. Unpublished PhD thesis, University of Sheffield.

Moore, E., & Carter, P. (2015). Dialect contact and distinctiveness: The social meaning of language variation in an island community. *Journal of Sociolinguistics, 19*(1), 3–36.

Moore, E., & Podesva, R. (2009). Style, indexicality, and the social meaning of tag questions. *Language in Society, 38*(4), 447–485.

Mumford, J. (2014). Hidden Cornwall: Not beaches and ice-cream but poverty and violence. In *The Guardian* [online]. Available online: https://www.the-guardian.com/society/2014/jan/04/hidden-cornwall-beaches-poverty-domestic-violence

Nagy, N. (2011). Lexical change and language contact: Faetar in Italy and Canada. *Journal of Sociolinguistics, 15*(3), 366–382.

Orton, H., & Dieth, E. (1962–71). *Survey of English dialects*. Leeds: E. J. Arnold.

Oxford English Dictionary (OED) Online. Available at http://www.oed.com/

Robinson, J. A. (2012a). A sociolinguistic perspective on semantic change. In K. Allan & J. A. Robinson (Eds.), *Current methods in historical semantics* (pp. 199–230). Berlin: Mouton.

Robinson, J. A. (2012b). A gay paper: Why should sociolinguistics bother with semantics? *English Today, 28*(4), 38–54.

Silverstein, M. (2003). Indexical order and the dialectics of sociolinguistic life. *Language & Communication, 23*(3), 193–229.

Stamp, R., Schembri, A., Evans, B., & Cormier, K. (2016). Regional sign language varieties in contact: Investigating patterns of accommodation. *Journal of Deaf Studies and Deaf Education, 21*(1), 70–82.

Trudgill, P. (1974). *The social differentiation of English in Norwich*. Cambridge: Cambridge University Press.

Vernon, J. (1998). Cornwall and the English imagi(nation). In G. Cubitt (Ed.), *Imagining nations* (pp. 153–172). Manchester: Manchester University Press.

Wakelin, M. (1984). Cornish English. In P. Trudgill (Ed.), *Language in the British Isles* (pp. 195–198). Cambridge: Cambridge University Press.

Watt, D. (2002). 'I don't speak with a Geordie accent, I speak, like, the Northern accent': Contact induced levelling in the Tyneside vowel system. *Journal of Sociolinguistics, 6*(1), 44–63.

Watt, D., & Milroy, L. (1999). Patterns of variation and change in three Newcastle vowels: Is this dialect levelling? In P. Foulkes & G. Docherty (Eds.), *Urban voices: Accent studies in the British Isles* (pp. 25–46). London: Arnold.

West, C., & Zimmerman, D. H. (1987). Doing gender. *Gender and Society, 1*(2), 125–151.

Wieling, M., Upton, C., & Thompson, A. (2014). Analyzing the BBC voices data: Contemporary English dialect area and their characteristic lexical variants. *Literary and Linguistic Computing, 29*(1), 107–117.

Wigmore, T. (2016). The real Cornwall: A county poorer than Lithuania and Hungary. In *New Statesman* [online]. Available online: http://www.newstatesman.com/politics/welfare/2016/02/real-cornwall-county-poorer-lithuania-and-hungary

Willett, J. (2009). *Why is Cornwall so poor? Narrative, perception and identity.* Unpublished PhD thesis, University of Exeter.

Willett, J. (2016). Cornwall's devolution deal: Towards a more sustainable governance. *The Political Quarterly, 87*(4), 582–589.

14

Residual Rhoticity and Emergent *r*-sandhi in the North West and South West of England: Different Approaches to Hiatus-Resolution?

William Barras

Introduction

This chapter focuses on the distribution of *r*-sandhi in the speech encountered in two areas of England: East Lancashire and Oxfordshire. The East Lancashire data were collected in 2009 as part of a project reported in Barras (2011) comparing levels of rhoticity with levels of *r*-sandhi. This sought to account for some typologically unusual patterns by considering socially constructed notions of *place* and *space* as well as the predictions made by more strictly phonological accounts of the relationship between these two *r*-related phenomena. The Oxfordshire data were collected in 2011 and 2012 by Caroline Piercy as part of a broader survey designed to address the question of whether Oxfordshire speech should be regarded as a south-western variety of the English of England. Data collection methods included adapted versions of the tasks that the East Lancashire speakers were asked to complete; therefore, the two datasets include comparable material on levels of *r*-sandhi in various phonological contexts.

W. Barras (✉)
University of Aberdeen, Aberdeen, UK

© The Author(s) 2018
N. Braber, S. Jansen (eds.), *Sociolinguistics in England*,
DOI 10.1057/978-1-137-56288-3_14

Rates of production of *r*-sandhi are compared in recordings of speech from two dialect areas: East Lancashire, which is still variably rhotic, and Oxfordshire, which is now non-rhotic but which was a rhotic area in the *Survey of English Dialects*. Some East Lancashire speakers appear to have simultaneous rhoticity and *r*-sandhi, possibly as some form of *last gasp* stage before eventual loss of rhoticity. The Oxfordshire speakers conform to a more typical pattern of non-rhoticity and presence of *r*-sandhi, but, particularly for younger speakers, rates of both intrusive-*r* and linking-*r* are variable, with vowel hiatus alternatively resolved with a glottal stop. This could reflect the spread of a levelled hiatus resolution system, affecting high vowels as well as the non-high vowels associated with *r*-sandhi.

Dialectological Overview

The two geographical areas in question have been associated with rhoticity in traditional dialectological surveys. The *Survey of English Dialects* (Orton and Dieth 1962, henceforth SED) and works derived from it, such as Orton et al. (1978), indicate that, in the speech of older, mainly male, participants recorded in the mid-twentieth century, the county of Lancashire was marked by rhoticity. Across county boundaries to Westmorland (now part of Cumbria) to the north, or to Yorkshire to the east, this was largely not the case. Indeed, the correspondence between the isoglosses for rhoticity generated from SED material and the pre-1974 county boundary of Lancashire is very noticeable. Furthermore, this rhoticity has been observed to be a socially salient stereotype of Lancashire speech: referring to the rose emblems of Yorkshire and Lancashire. Wells (1982: 367) identifies this as 'white rose /ˈfaːmə/, red rose /ˈfaːrmər/'; Ellis (1968: 20) notes that the *r* in '*yard, hear, turn* and so on' is 'sounded heavily by actors or comedians wanting to emphasise the Lancashire connection'. However, in the latter half of the twentieth century, multiple sources of evidence have shown that the geographical reach of rhoticity has receded in Lancashire. The two largest urban regions of traditional Lancashire, centred on the cities of Manchester and

Liverpool, are essentially non-rhotic (Wells 1982: 368), although these urban areas were not surveyed by the SED, which focused on rural varieties. The north of the county around Lancaster and that part of traditional Lancashire 'across the sands' that is now part of Cumbria are also non-rhotic. Despite this change, parts of East Lancashire maintain rhoticity consistently.

Britain (2009) refers to 'an island of rhoticity' centred on Accrington; Austin (2007) documents very robust levels of rhoticity in Rossendale; Barras (2011) found variable but clearly evident levels of rhoticity in both of those locations, but a marked decline in rhoticity in Ramsbottom, Bury and Prestwich, which are progressively closer to urban (and non-rhotic) Manchester. Figure 14.1 shows these locations, together with the SED isogloss for rhoticity in *third*.[1]

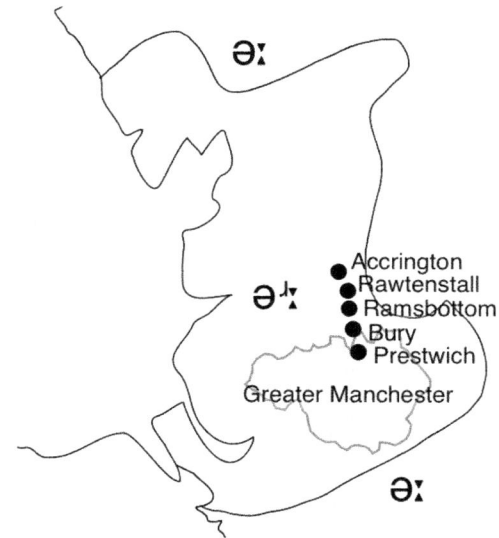

Fig. 14.1 East Lancashire localities superimposed on the *Survey of English Dialects* isogloss for rhoticity, based on the *Linguistic Atlas of England* map for *third* (Orton et al. 1978: Ph30). Outline map source http://www.d-maps.com/carte. php?num_car=2555&lang=en

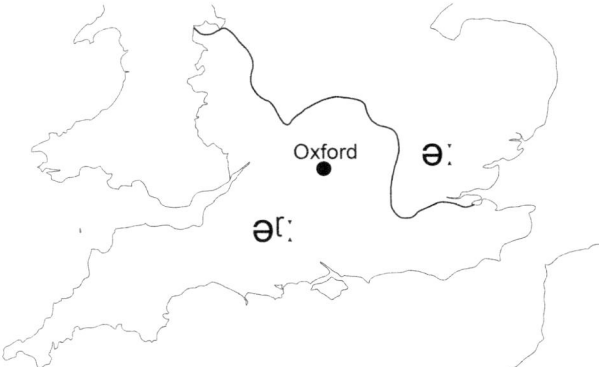

Fig. 14.2 Oxford superimposed on the *Survey of English Dialects* isogloss for rhoticity, based on the *Linguistic Atlas of England* map for *third* (Orton et al. 1978: Ph30). Outline map source http://www.d-maps.com/carte.php?num_car=2555&lang=en

The SED shows rhoticity in a wide area of the south west of England, including Oxfordshire, as shown in Fig. 14.2.

However, rhoticity in the south west has also become more restricted geographically. In his map of modern dialect areas, Trudgill (2000: 65) suggests that Oxfordshire is now in a *Central Southwest* dialect area—one of the features that distinguishes this area from the *Lower Southwest* of Devon and Cornwall is the presence of rhoticity in the lower south west. Younger speakers in a study of Dorset speech (Piercy 2006) show a very rapid decline in production of coda /r/ compared to older speakers in the same area. Trudgill goes on to propose a set of possible future dialect areas (2000: 83), most of which are focused on a large city. On this map, areas labelled *London* and *Bristol* intersect Oxfordshire, meaning that there is a question of whether future dialect developments in the county will be influenced by London to the east or Bristol to the west. While rhoticity is by no means the only dialect feature of significance here, it does have a prominent role in accent perceptions and language attitudes (see, for example, Foulkes and Docherty 2006: 411 on the indexicality of /r/ in different varieties of English). In addition to sociolinguistic implications, rhoticity has consequences for the rest of the phonological system of a dialect.

Phonological Overview

The focus of this chapter is not on rhoticity in itself, but on variation in *r*-sandhi—a phenomenon that has been argued to be in complementary distribution with rhoticity (e.g. Giegerich 1999: 196). The typical argument is that there has been a diachronic change in English varieties of English entailing a loss of coda /r/ and a corresponding increase in surface homophony. The examples in Table 14.1 demonstrate this shift.

In connected speech, [ɹ] is maintained when it could fill the onset of the following syllable; therefore, phrases such as *spar is* or *fetter it* would continue to contain a surface [ɹ], even in the case of speakers who no longer pronounce an [ɹ] in words such as *spar* or *fetter* when they occur pre-pausally or pre-consonantally. This process is typically labelled 'linking-*r*'; in terms of the development of, for example, Received Pronunciation English, the continued presence of an orthographic <r> in the spelling of such words means it is viewed as standard. It is often claimed to be categorical for many speakers of non-rhotic accents (Foulkes 1997: 76). The extension of this use of [ɹ] to fill a potential hiatus between syllables (after exactly the same vowels as linking-*r*) to include examples such as *spa is* or *feta is* is labelled 'intrusive-*r*' because there is no etymological /r/ in the words, and no <r> in the spelling, so that a surface [ɹ] can be viewed as *intruding* in speech. This phenomenon attracts overt and unfavourable comment (Cruttenden 2001: 289), and some speakers actively suppress intrusive-*r* in their speech. Given the homophony involved in pairs such as *spa* and *spar*, Giegerich (1999: 194) argues that such suppression of intrusive-*r* relies on knowledge of the orthography, rather than on purely phonological factors.

Table 14.1 Increased homophony in non-rhotic accents

Word	Possible rhotic realisation	Possible non-rhotic realisation
fetter	[fɛtəɹ]	[fɛtə]
feta	[fɛtə]	[fɛtə]
spar	[spɑɹ]	[spɑ]
spa	[spɑ]	[spɑ]
lore	[lɔɹ]	[lɔː]
law	[lɔː]	[lɔː]

There has been extensive debate about the phonological status of hiatus-filling sandhi-*r*. Some questions focus on whether non-rhotic speakers have an underlying coda /r/ (which would be deleted in non-sandhi contexts), or have no such underlying coda /r/, but rather a process of insertion which is triggered by sandhi contexts (see, for example, Foulkes 1997: 76 for a summary of this debate). Other phonologists have sought to draw parallels between the behaviour of /r/ in these examples and the formation of hiatus-filling glides after high vowels in similar contexts, suggesting that the relationship between non-high vowels and /r/ mirrors that between high vowels and [j] or [w] (Broadbent 1991, 1999). Still further debate has focused on developments in Optimality Theory in order to address the question of why /r/ would be the optimal candidate for hiatus-filling work after non-high vowels, rather than say /t/ or a glottal stop (for a summary of these arguments, see Uffmann 2007: 453–4).

One feature that many of these analyses share is the assumption that, by definition, only non-rhotic speakers will have productive processes of *r*-sandhi leading to intrusive-*r*. Without non-rhotic homophony of (historically) /r/-final and non-/r/-final words, the process of analogy will not have led to the use of [ɹ] as a hiatus filler in non-etymological contexts. An interesting alternative model is outlined in Britton (2007), in which there is a degree of *r*-ful homophony, entailing hyper-rhotic pronunciations of words without etymological /r/. However, some models, such as that proposed by Uffmann (2007), do not actually rule out the possibility that rhotic speakers could have the same hiatus-filling strategy as non-rhotic speakers. Indeed, the model's failure to do this is discussed as a potential objection to it: Uffmann goes on to argue that, perhaps, there is no *a priori* reason why rhotic speakers could not also have productive intrusive-*r* systems, but it is just that such a variety happens not to be attested. Other phonologists also suggest that there is no systemic ban on rhotic speakers producing intrusive-*r* (for instance, Harris 1994: 253; Carr 1999: 127). However, such predictions are qualified by the fact that, even if such a pattern is possible, it has not been observed.

Some researchers have sought to shed light on the extent to which rhotic and non-rhotic speakers have linking and intrusive-*r*, using extensive samples of recorded speech. These include historical data based on a corpus of old recordings, as reported in Hay and Sudbury (2005), and present-day data including the use of specially designed reading tasks, as in Foulkes (1997), Hay and Maclagan (2010) and Barras (2011). These projects have found evidence that, while taking a historical long view of the loss of rhoticity and development of intrusive-*r* can support neat phonological models such as the rule-inversion hypothesis proposed by Vennemann (1972), when more granular data is considered, involving individual speakers and, in the case of the New Zealand data considered by Hay and Sudbury (2005), spanning the time during which rhoticity was lost, it is evident that an individual speaker can be rhotic to a greater or lesser degree of consistency and also produce intrusive-*r* variably. While Hay and Sudbury show that there is a robust correlation between declining production of coda /r/ and increasing use of intrusive-*r*, individual speakers can have phonological systems that permit both phenomena.

Research focusing on present-day data continues this enquiry. Hay and Maclagan (2010) show that, even in the speech of present-day non-rhotic speakers, production of intrusive-*r* is very variable and could be conditioned by various factors, from the nature of the preceding vowel to the frequency of the collocation providing the hiatus context for intrusive-*r*.

Methodology

One feature of intrusive-*r* that potentially makes it difficult to investigate is its comparative infrequency in everyday conversational speech. Foulkes (1997: 83) explains that 13 hours of conversational recordings yielded seven tokens of intrusive-*r*. This infrequency poses a problem, particularly if various conditioning factors are to be investigated. With this in mind, researchers who wish to collect tokens of intrusive-*r* have used various types of reading task in order to generate sufficient tokens and to control the phonological contexts of these tokens. Hay and Maclagan (2010) use a set of sentences which they describe as 'a bit weird': while constructions such as *Oprah-ise* or *bra-ify* are plausible in the sentence frames the participants were given, it is also very likely that these words have not been encountered before in the participants' day-to-day lives.

Nonetheless, such an approach does allow for a full range of preceding vowels and other contexts to be included in the data set. Barras (2011) used a similar approach, in that participants were asked, at the end of a sociolinguistic interview lasting an hour or more, to read a set of sentences containing examples of (potential) linking and intrusive-*r*, as well as filler sentences. They were then asked to participate in a further elicitation task which involved adding suffixes to place names in order to form longer words. The data from these tasks carried out in East Lancashire, and adapted versions of them carried out in Oxfordshire, form the basis of the discussion in this chapter.

The Sentences Task

The sentences, given in Table 14.2, attempt to cover a range of preceding vowels and following segments. In practice, several of the prompts are marginally lexical, such as the attempt to represent an extended central vowel [ɜː] as a hesitation particle <uhhhh>. Others relied on the use of a hyphen to indicate a syllable boundary, as in <vanilla-y>, in order to avoid orthographic sequences such as <ay>, which may well cause speakers to utter a vowel [eɪ] instead of the hiatus context. Participants varied in their responses to prompts such as this, so not every speaker produced all the possible tokens of potential *r*-sandhi included in the sentences. The Oxfordshire data were recorded using a subset of the 35 of the sentences in Table 14.2, in order to reduce the length of the activity for participants. Twenty-five potential intrusive-*r* sentences were used.

The Elicitation Task

The prompts for this task were presented on a laptop screen, and participants could press an arrow on the keyboard to move to the next prompt. Some sample screens are shown in Fig. 14.3.

The idea here was to highlight the word-formation process and to avoid some of the orthographic problems that can occur when presenting prompts as in the sentences task mentioned earlier. While this task emphasised the morphological process of word-formation and could be

Table 14.2 Reading prompts for the sentences task

Word boundary linking-*r*	Word boundary intrusive-*r*	Morpheme boundary linking-*r*	Morpheme boundary intrusive-*r*	Intrusive-*r* (reduced vowel)
ɔ The radio tuner always goes on the bottom shelf A metal ruler always comes in handy when you're doing DIY I sent a letter and a postcard when I was on holiday	There's a difference between a comma and a full stop How do Angela and Becky cope with the stress? The tuna always sells out quickly I'm going to India and China next year Did you see Big Brother? Rula always complains about the tasks	There's some fancy lettering on it, so it might be valuable That bird has very feathery wings I suppose it was quite a humorous story, but I didn't find it very funny	When I have to write a letter, I'm no good at punctuation. All that fullstopping and comma-ing gives me a headache The ice-cream has a kind of vanilla-y taste That vase is quite China-esque, but I don't think it's an antique	He shoulda eaten something before he set off I think Emma'll be here soon There's a lotta apples and oranges on sale today I said I was gonna and I did, so there! You hafta investigate the situation before you start accusing people Do ya always talk so loudly?
ɔ The birds soar up in the sky but you can still hear them singing I adore all dogs, especially collies It's got a more intense flavour if you like spicy food	Dogs like to gnaw on bones Guess what? I saw an elephant in town today The field is covered in straw and hay	The price of petrol keeps soaring up higher and higher these days She thought the kitten was adorable This cake is really moreish – I can't stop eating it!	I'm going to make a withdrawal from the bank You need to teach your cat that climbing and clawing are only allowed on her scratching post, not on your furniture I was sawing up some logs in the back garden	–

(continued)

Table 14.2 (continued)

	Word boundary linking-r	Word boundary intrusive-r	Morpheme boundary linking-r	Morpheme boundary intrusive-r	Intrusive-r (reduced vowel)
ɑ	Look at that car over there: it's bright yellow. He had a big scar on his cheek If you need to go to a shop there's a Spar in the village	When we went on holiday there was a spa in the village We're flying to Panama on Tuesday from Manchester Airport My grandma always likes a cup of tea	The gate was barring our way so we climbed over it It's a starry night tonight so there'll be frost The workmen are tarring the road today, so there'll be delays	When we went to the Lake District it was so peaceful; the only sound was the sheep baa-ing We were um-ing and ah-ing for ages That jacket is Eddie Stobart-ish but the other one is definitely Eddie Shah-ish	–
ɛ	I stare every time I see a Rolls Royce go by, in case someone famous is in it That pesky bear always steals picnic baskets They swear all the time while they're at work	He uses a lot of slang. He says yeah instead of yes	She thinks there's too much swearing on TV They were just staring at it in disbelief That apple crumble tastes a bit pearish	I say yes, she says yeah. We're always yessing and yeah-ing at each other	–

(continued)

Table 14.2 (continued)

	Word boundary linking-*r*	Word boundary intrusive-*r*	Morpheme boundary linking-*r*	Morpheme boundary intrusive-*r*	Intrusive-*r* (reduced vowel)
3	The cat left fur everywhere. Everyone makes mistakes: To err is human You need to stir everything together thoroughly	When he can't think of the answer he just goes 'Uhhh' until someone else says it	I got a referral to see a specialist next week I was stirring the mixture just like the recipe told me to That's an incredibly furry cat	She kept making these long drawn out 'ummmm' and 'uhhhh' noises. It was so annoying that I said, 'Stop umm-ing and uhhh-ing and get on with it!'	–

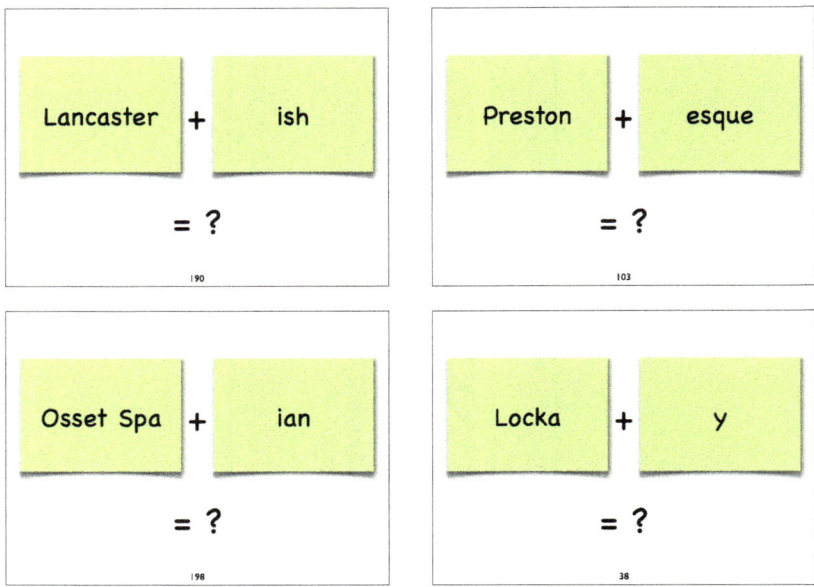

Fig. 14.3 Four sample screens from the elicitation task

seen as somewhat removed from natural speech, it avoided the use of hyphens or other respellings which were used in the sentences task. Furthermore, in the case of the Lancashire data, there was an attempt to provide some context for the task: all the place names were more or less local to the north west of England, and a map was available to show their location (and in the case of little-known place names such as *Locka*, to show that they did exist). The Oxfordshire data were collected using an adapted version of the task, again to reduce its duration and also to include some more locally significant examples such as *Bicester*.

The Participants

There are some differences in the sample populations in the two areas. As explained above, the East Lancashire project sought to consider fine-grained geographical variation through the use of five neighbouring localities. The Oxfordshire data were collected in and around Oxford and do not have the same degree of structured geographical distribution. On the other hand, while the East Lancashire participants were in two distinct age groups (60+ and 18–22), the Oxfordshire participants covered a range of ages from 22 to 66, and while in some analyses I split the sample into younger and older speakers to mirror the approach in the East Lancashire survey, it was also possible to consider speaker age as a continuous variable. All 30 of the East Lancashire participants were female, while the Oxford sample contained seven male and ten female participants.

Transcription Procedure

The Lancashire and Oxfordshire recordings were orthographically transcribed in ELAN (Max Planck Institute for Psycholinguistics 2008) before a second pass in which potential tokens of rhoticity, linking-*r* and intrusive-*r* were coded. The coding was conducted on an auditory basis, with additional reference to the formant tracks on a spectrogram for unclear or ambiguous tokens. ELAN's *Clip to Praat* function (Boersma and Weenink 2015) allowed instant visualisation of individual tokens; as the realisation of /r/ for all speakers in both datasets was almost entirely consistent as [ɹ], a lowering of F3 was considered to be evidence of a consonantal /r/. Rather than a binary r-0 alternation, a three-label scheme was used. Tokens labelled – contained no trace of consonantal constriction; tokens labelled ++ had a strongly consonantal [ɹ]; an intermediate + category was used for tokens which sounded somewhat *r*-ful, and for which there was some movement of F3 on the spectrogram, but which were less constricted than the clear ++ tokens. While this approach was still essentially auditory, it allowed for the fact that some tokens of *r* are more consonantal than others (as investigated in detail by Hay and Maclagan 2010). In the multivariate analyses reported below, a binary r-0 opposition was considered by collapsing the ++ and + categories to 'r', in contrast to – as '0'; in other analyses, the three-way coding scheme was used.

The tokens were coded for a range of potential influencing factors: the preceding segment, the following segment, the nature of the sandhi environment as a word boundary or a word-internal morpheme boundary, the degree of stress on the preceding syllable. In the East Lancashire dataset, place and age group were included as potential factors; for the Oxfordshire dataset, age was included, but place was not: all the participants were from the city of Oxford or its outlying areas. Both sets of results were then subject to a mixed-effects logistic regression analysis using the step up/step down scheme in Rbrul (Johnson 2008, 2009), which gave an indication of which linguistic or social factors were involved in conditioning the production of *r* in the different contexts. In all analyses, individual speaker was included as a random intercept.

Results and Discussion

Rhoticity (Tables 14.3 and 14.4)

The Oxfordshire speakers have very low levels of coda-*r* production, while the East Lancashire data indicate much higher rates of rhoticity, particularly in Rossendale and Accrington. The social factors of Place and Age Group were retained in the models, with the older speakers favouring *r*-realisation and the younger speakers disfavouring it. These patterns are straightforwardly in-line with predictions about the likely declining state of rhoticity in East Lancashire and Oxfordshire. Of more interest are the data on *r*-sandhi and the potential for links between rhoticity and *r*-sandhi.

Linking-*r* (Tables 14.5 and 14.6)

Overall rates of production of linking-*r* are high in both localities, and especially so in East Lancashire. The models retain linguistic factors such as the nature of the preceding segment or the morphological boundary providing the sandhi context; in both localities, the age of speakers was also a significant factor, with older speakers favouring production of linking-*r*. The situation in East Lancashire raises the question of the speakers' phonological status: if some speakers are consistently rhotic, realisation of /r/ in the sandhi contexts generated in the tasks would be expected regardless of whether there was a vowel hiatus to fill. The results for intrusive-*r*, however, are more surprising.

Table 14.3 Multivariate analysis of coda /r/ in East Lancashire

	East Lancashire coda /r/		
Input probability	0.134		
Total *N*	12,831		
Deviance		8894.66	
	Log odds	%	*N*
Preceding segment category	*p*. < 1.18e-154		
Back	0.668	35	3729
Non-back	−0.668	17	9642
Following segment	*p*. < 4.56e-63		
Pause	0.642	30	2822
Consonant	−0.642	20	10,549
Morphological boundary	*p*. < 2.88e-20		
None	0.405	26	4410
Morpheme	0.303	18	1359
Word	−0.002	21	7207
Clitic	−0.706	8	395
Place	*p*. < 1.77e-09		
Rossendale	2.524	53	2781
Accrington	1.589	35	2786
Ramsbottom	−0.322	15	2317
Bury	−1.400	5	2376
Prestwich	−2.391	2	2751
Stress	*p*. < 7.82e-07		
Stressed	0.177	27	7089
Unstressed	−0.177	16	6282
Age group	*p*. < 0.000142		
Older	0.588	26	6938
Younger	−0.588	18	6433
SpeakerID	Random		

Table 14.4 Multivariate analysis of Oxfordshire coda /r/

	Oxfordshire coda /r/		
Input probability	0.00		
Total *N*	802		
Deviance		104.485	
	Log odds	%	*N*
Age group	*p*. < 1.3e-06		
Older	9.169	4	310
Younger	−9.169	0	492
Stress	*p*. < 5.76e-118		
Stressed	0.433.	2	330
Unstressed	−0.433	1	472
Preceding segment category	*p*. < 0.000169		
Back	0.388	3	202
Non-back	−0.388	1	600
SpeakerID	Random		

Table 14.5 Multivariate analysis of linking-*r* in East Lancashire

	East Lancashire linking-*r*		
Input probability	0.957		
Total *N*	6018		
Deviance		2644.486	
	Log odds	%	*N*
Morphological boundary	*p*. < 2.54e-45		
Morpheme	1.543	98	2993
Word	−1.543	87	3025
Task style	*p*. < 2.87e-45		
Conversation	1.254	93	2558
Sentences	−0.450	81	1083
Elicitation	−0.804	98	2377
Preceding segment category	*p*. < 1.73e-07		
Back	0.415	96	2277
Non-back	−0.415	90	3741
Stress	*p*. < 0.00372		
Unstressed	0.184	91	2910
Stressed	−0.184	93	3108
Age group	*p*. < 0.00409		
Older	0.279	94	2910
Younger	−0.279	91	3108
Place	*p*. < 0.00724		
Rossendale	0.556	96	1144
Bury	0.275	94	1254
Accrington	0.003	93	1254
Ramsbottom	−0.306	91	1069
Prestwich	−0.528	89	1297
SpeakerID	Random		

Table 14.6 Multivariate analysis of linking-*r* in Oxfordshire

	Oxfordshire linking-*r*		
Input probability	0.775		
Total *N*	1132		
Deviance		795.225	
	Log odds	%	*N*
Morphological boundary	*p*. < 6.11e-89		
Morpheme	1.637	94	790
Word	−1.637	39	342
Age group	*p*. < 0.0104		
Older	0.24	83	480
Younger	−0.24	73	652
SpeakerID	Random		

Intrusive-*r* (Tables 14.7 and 14.8)

In the case of East Lancashire, task style was significant, with the conversation and elicitation tasks favouring production of intrusive-*r*, and the sentences task disfavouring its production. It is unsurprising that a careful, reading speech style should disfavour a sandhi phenomenon such as intrusive-*r*, and that spontaneous casual conversational connected speech should favour intrusive-*r*. The fact that the elicitation task favours production of intrusive-*r* suggests that this task caused some speakers to produce intrusive-*r* more frequently than they do when asked to read full sentences.

Table 14.7 Multivariate analysis of intrusive-*r* in East Lancashire

	East Lancashire intrusive-*r*		
Input probability	0.427		
Total *N*	3229		
Deviance		3094.282	
	Log odds	%	*N*
Task style	*p.* < 5.78e-16		
Conversation	0.628	33	198
Elicitation	0.167	52	2311
Sentences	−0.795	27	720
Preceding segment	*p.* < 5.19e-14		
ɑ	1.057	56	730
ɔ	0.393	45	974
ɜ	−0.027	31	16
ə	−0.331	42	1382
ɛ	−1.092	16	127
Morphological boundary	*p.* < 4.11e-11		
Clitic	1.472	63	24
Morpheme	−0.177	51	2609
Word	−1.295	23	596
Place	*p.* < 0.0197		
Prestwich	1.484	69	674
Bury	0.991	60	702
Accrington	−0.633	31	676
Ramsbottom	−0.644	32	536
Rossendale	−1.198	31	641
Stress	*p.* < 0.04		
Unstressed	0.346	44	1424
Stressed	−0.346	47	1805
SpeakerID	Random		

Table 14.8 Multivariate analysis of intrusive-*r* in Oxfordshire

	Oxfordshire intrusive-*r*		
Input probability	0.671		
Total *N*	1068		
Deviance		1057.597	
	Log odds	%	*N*
Preceding Seg.	*p.* < 2.17e-10		
ɜ	0.525	60	15
ɑ	0.494	67	320
ɔ	0.355	64	305
ə	−0.663	45	400
ɛ	−0.711	32	28
Morphological boundary	*p.* < 5.47e-10		
Clitic	1.794	67	9
Morpheme	−0.158	63	881
Word	−1.636	25	178
Task style	*p.* < 0.000221		
Elicitation	0.393	65	714
Sentences	−0.393	40	354
SpeakerID	Random		

The preceding segment was significant. Preceding [ɑ] and [ɔ] favour realisation of intrusive-*r*, whereas preceding [ɜ], [ə] and [ɛ] disfavour its production: the analysis has effectively distinguished between back and non-back preceding vowels. Morphological boundary was added next, and the model suggests that clitics favour the production of intrusive-*r*, whereas other boundary positions disfavour its production. However, this finding should be approached with some caution: there are vastly fewer tokens in the clitic category than in the other categories, and the category consists of one repeated example in the sentences task: *Emma'll be here soon*.

Place was added next, with Prestwich and Bury favouring production of intrusive-*r*, while Accrington, Ramsbottom and Rossendale disfavour its production. If the hypothesis that there is a correlation between level of rhoticity and level of intrusive-*r* is correct, then this finding is logical, because the Prestwich and Bury speakers are consistently non-rhotic, while the speakers in the other localities are rhotic to varying degrees. Finally, stress was added to the model: unstressed positions favour production of intrusive-*r* while stressed positions disfavour its production.

The Oxfordshire data for intrusive-*r* from the sentences and elicitation tasks are coded for the same linguistic factors as the East Lancashire data, but given the nature of the Oxfordshire sample population, there are differences in the social factors: place is not included in this analysis and age is treated as a continuous variable. After individual speaker is added to the model, preceding segment, morphological boundary, and task style are all retained as significant. In the case of task style, it again seems that the elicitation task favours production of intrusive-*r* while the sentences task disfavours its production. The morphological boundary result shows that the clitic contexts favour intrusive-*r* production while the other morpheme and word boundary contexts disfavour its production. Preceding [ɑ,ɔ,ɜ] favour production of intrusive-*r* while preceding [ə,ɛ] disfavour its production. While there are several potential lines of enquiry suggested by these analyses, the following discussion will focus on the relation between speakers' level of rhoticity and their likelihood of producing intrusive-*r*.

Rhoticity and Intrusive-*r*

In the East Lancashire data, levels of rhoticity across the participants range from 74% for one older Accrington speaker down to 0% for three Prestwich speakers. By grouping the participants according to their location, a striking difference in levels of rhoticity is observed across the localities that are progressively further north from Manchester, as shown in the map in Fig. 14.1. These by-location results are shown in Fig. 14.4, which splits the data according to the two age groups in the sample.

The younger group of speakers show a different pattern from the older speakers, in which Rossendale is the most consistently rhotic locality, with Accrington speakers having a reduced rate of rhoticity compared to their older counterparts, and younger speakers in the other three localities having very little evidence of rhoticity, with only sporadic *r*-ful tokens.

These results suggest that there are two groups of speakers in the Lancashire data: those who are variably rhotic, and who could be argued to have coda /r/ as part of their underlying phonemic system with varying levels of consistency in whether it is realised as a surface [ɹ] segment, and

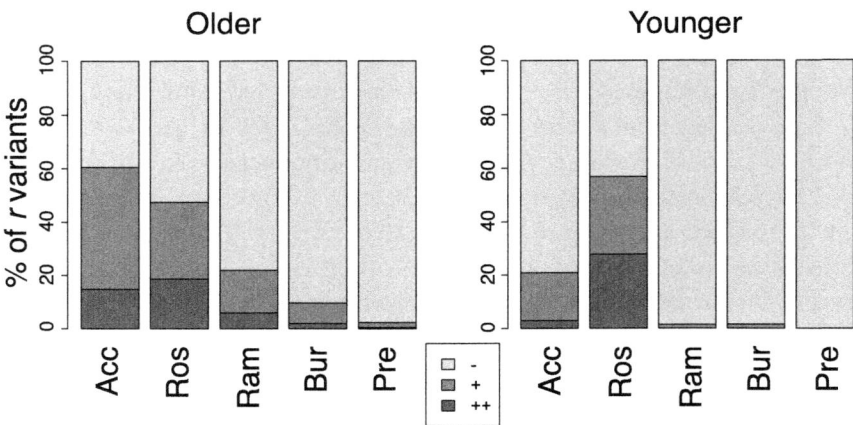

Fig. 14.4 Levels of rhoticity across the five East Lancashire localities. The shading represents −, + and ++ tokens of *r*

those who are non-rhotic and could be argued to have a consistent /r/ deletion rule, or no underlying coda /r/. If they have different underlying systems, these two groups would be predicted to behave differently with respect to *r*-sandhi: the clearly non-rhotic speakers would be expected to be able to use intrusive-*r* to fill vowel hiatus; the rhotic speakers would not. In practice, and matching the research conducted on archive New Zealand recordings by Hay and Sudbury (2005), it is seen that the rhotic speakers do produce intrusive-*r* to varying degrees.

Figure 14.5 shows the relation between levels of rhoticity and production of word-internal intrusive-*r* in the East Lancashire sentences task; four speakers who were consistently non-rhotic and six speakers who were consistently non-*r*-intruding are not included here. Across the East Lancashire speakers as a group, there is a negative correlation between levels of rhoticity and production of word-internal intrusive-*r*. However, the scatterplot suggests that there are two groups of speakers: many of the Prestwich, Bury and Ramsbottom speakers have very sporadic incidence of rhoticity, while the Rossendale and Accrington speakers have more frequent rhotic utterances. Within this second group, some individual speakers have surprisingly high levels of *r*-intrusion given their level of rhoticity: 11Ros (a younger Rossendale speaker) and 2Acc (an older Accrington speaker).

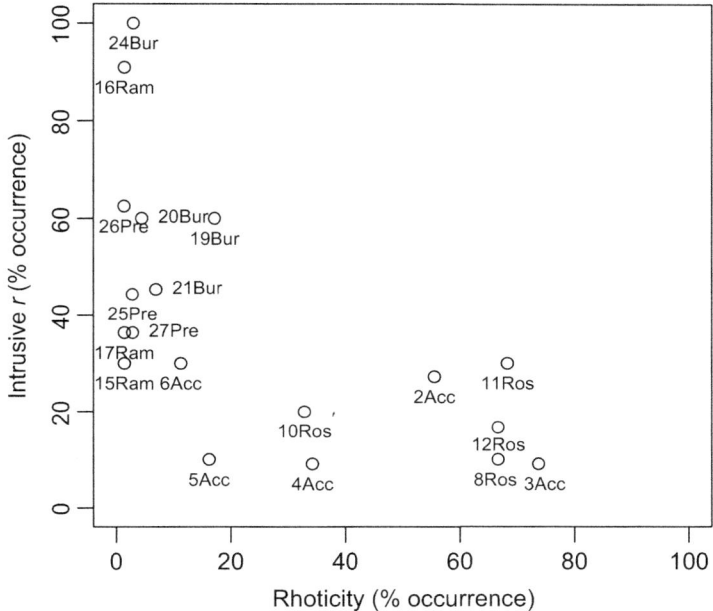

Fig. 14.5 Relation between rhoticity and word-internal intrusive-*r* in the Lancashire sentences task data. Spearman's rho = −0.71, *p* = 0.001

One potential way of accounting for this pattern is to suggest that, for some speakers, the non-high vowels associated with *r*-intrusion have effectively been re-specified, with *r*-colouring affecting their realisation even in non-sandhi environments. Hyper-dialectal or hyper-rhotic *r* is non-etymological *r* that can occur in non-sandhi environments, such as utterance finally or in coda consonant clusters. It is mentioned by Wells (1982) and Trudgill (1986) as a feature of traditionally rhotic dialects in contact with non-rhotic incoming varieties, for example, in parts of the south west of England, leading to citation forms such as *comma* [kɒmɚ]. It has also been reported in East Lancashire varieties by Vivian (2000) and Austin (2007). In the East Lancashire data, hyper-dialectal *r* is very rare: there are 12 tokens in the entire dataset, and looking at the individual examples allows several of them to be accounted for as artefacts of hesitant speech in which an intrusive-*r* was triggered but the speaker stumbled or paused before uttering the following syllable. Leaving aside these potentially hyper-rhotic examples, for which plausible alternative explanations are possible, the remaining tokens are very sporadic and do not reflect the hyper-dialectal *r* noted in some varieties of English.

The presence of both coda /r/ and intrusive-*r* in the speech of some Rossendale and Accrington speakers is clearly unusual. Barras (2011) argues that the younger Rossendale speakers, in particular, seem to be resisting the spreading influence of Manchester-influenced speech, despite the fact that contact between speakers from the rhotic and non-rhotic areas is an everyday occurrence. The younger Rossendale speakers' level of coda /r/ realisation remains high, while younger speakers in neighbouring Ramsbottom have essentially lost rhoticity and match the speakers recorded in Bury and in Prestwich. This could be evidence of a strengthening isogloss between non-rhotic Manchester-influenced speech and (variably) rhotic traditional Lancashire-influenced speech. Such a development would not be unique: where a local vernacular is under threat from a supra-local variety, there is sometimes evidence of a fight-back, such that certain features of the local variety are emphasised as being particularly significant locally (Britain 2009: §2.6). This resistance leads to hyper-dialectalisms, which can result in an increased frequency of use of the traditional features and an extension of these features into other phonological environments. These behaviours are typically argued to be a *last gasp* before the local variety gives way to a levelled supra-local variety. What is more surprising is that, along with high levels of coda-*r* production, intrusive-*r* increases in the speech of younger Rossendale speakers. Previous arguments have been made that, in dialect contact situations, such as the rhotic/non-rhotic border in parts of the south west of England, *r* in general becomes a sort of local identity symbol (Trudgill 1986: 75), and it seems to be produced wherever it is feasible to do so, leading to the production of examples such as *sauce* [sɔɹs]. This can be understood as a reaction against the encroachment of non-rhoticity from surrounding varieties.

However, the Rossendale situation is not like this. Younger Rossendale speakers do not show increased levels of hyper-dialectal *r*. They show an increase in intrusive-*r* in sandhi contexts, and only in these contexts. This pattern is difficult to reconcile with a reaction against incoming non-rhoticity. If anything, these speakers seem to have accurately adopted a feature of the incoming varieties; *accurately* in that the precise conditioning context is adopted (after [ɑ, n ə] in sandhi environments), as well as the linguistic outcome (production of non-etymological *r*). So, contact with the non-rhotic majority of speakers has apparently led not only to maintenance of one part of the traditional system (rhoticity) but also to accurate adoption of part of the incoming supra-local system (intrusive-*r* in sandhi contexts). However, the direction of travel appears to be towards a general levelling to a non-rhotic and *r*-intruding variety.

The Oxfordshire data provide some supporting evidence for such a conclusion. While the sampling strategy used here did not have the same geographical basis as the East Lancashire study, with most participants living in Oxford suburbs or in smaller towns in Oxfordshire, it was possible to carry out some apparent-time analysis of the data. Participants ranged from 22 to 66 years of age at the time of the recordings, meaning that there were no speakers quite as old as the oldest Lancashire speakers (the oldest of whom was 90). The decline in rhoticity appears to be further advanced in Oxfordshire than it is in East Lancashire: the isogloss for rhoticity is presumably further west than Oxford now.[2] The combination of the age of participants and the general decline in rhoticity means that the Oxfordshire participants were all essentially non-rhotic, with four speakers having some instances of coda /r/ production as weakly consonantal + tokens, some of which were perhaps artefacts of a performance style in the reading task: the surname *Stobart* seemed to attract a rhotic pronunciation for two of the speakers who produced no other coda /r/ tokens. While Oxfordshire was shown to be rhotic in earlier dialectological surveys, it is no longer, and the use of intrusive-*r* by the participants in this sample might reflect a more stable system of non-rhoticity than is yet evident in the East Lancashire locations of Rossendale and Accrington.

The results for intrusive-*r* for the Oxfordshire participants show that these vary considerably by individual speaker as seen in Fig. 14.6.

This individual speaker variation matches the regression model in Table 14.8 in which speaker age did not play a part. However, the model

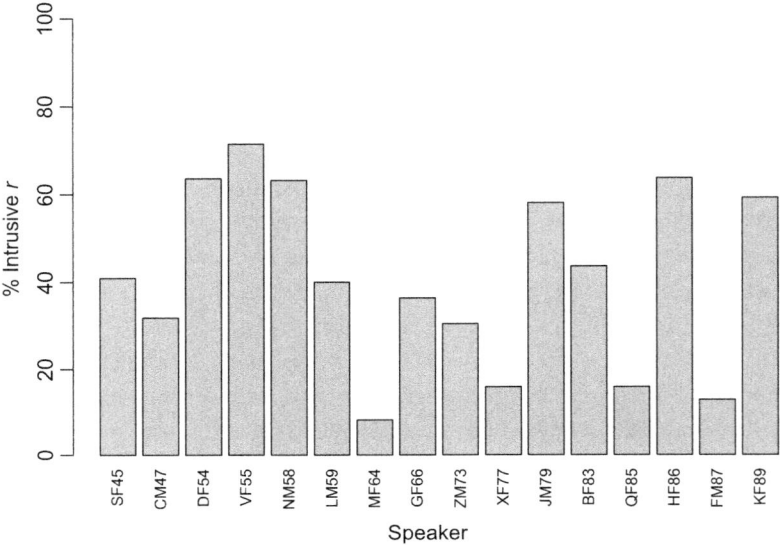

Fig. 14.6 Levels of intrusive-*r* for individual speakers in the Oxfordshire sentence task data. Speaker codes include the year of birth

for linking-*r* did retain age group, with younger speakers disfavouring its production.

It is, of course, possible that the nature of the reading tasks led to an unnatural style of delivery which might have affected the likelihood of speakers producing *r*-sandhi. However, the coding of the data for linking and intrusive-*r* took account of clear pauses and intonation breaks, which would not be expected to trigger *r*-sandhi; these were excluded from frequency counts of linking and intrusive-*r*. The sentences did, however, contain some fairly unusual constructions and, in some cases, participants seemed to produce intrusive-*r* in response to particular prompts which were somewhat less outlandish. For example, the prompts *vanilla-y* and *clawing*, both of which could conceivably occur in natural conversation, were often read very fluently and with a strong intrusive-*r*, while other prompts which are potentially less frequent in natural speech (e.g. *comma-ing* or *Shah-ish*) sometimes did not result in an intrusive-*r* even though the word or phrase was read with no intonation break. However, this was subject to a great deal of variation both within the speech of an individual and across participants, and some speakers did produce an intrusive-*r* when reading words they were unlikely to have come across before, such as *comma-ing*, while avoiding them in words such as *clawing*. Arguments could be made both ways in order to explain this difference: words such as *clawing* might be subject to semi-conscious modification in pronunciation, such that a stigmatised intrusive-*r* is avoided, while previously unattested examples such as *comma-ing* might reflect the unmodified output of a phonological hiatus resolution process. On the other hand, it could be that, as per some predictions of usage-based models involving frequency (e.g. Bybee 2006: 10), relatively frequently occurring examples such as *clawing* might be stored and accessed complete with a hiatus-filling *r*, while unfamiliar tokens might be subject to a phonological process of *r*-intrusion which is very variable in its application.

Furthermore, there were often individual inconsistencies between the production of linking-*r* and intrusive-*r*. Some speakers would produce intrusive-*r* regularly in unusual examples such as *yeah-ing* but in the same sentence would use a glottal stop or a form of glide in linking contexts such as *we're always*. It is sometimes claimed that linking-*r* is more or less obligatory and consistent, while intrusive-*r* is variable and also subject to conscious modification of speech in order either to avoid it (see Cruttenden 2001) or, unusually, to shift towards it in formal speech (see Foulkes 1997). The Oxford speakers suggest that linking-*r* can be inconsistent in its production.

Phonological accounts of *r*-sandhi often address the 'why *r*?' question. Answers have included proposals for *r* to be the default consonant which is inserted when no other consonant is specified; spreading accounts in which properties of the preceding vowel spread to a syllable onset position; the idea that *r* is the least marked option available for filling a hiatus; or the idea that an underlying /r/ is present even in words where historically there was no coda /r/. In the case of the younger Rossendale speakers from East Lancashire, a sociophonological explanation may be that *r* is a default hiatus filler because it has a dual socio-and-phonological function: it meets the need to fill the hiatus and is also a possible local identity marker (Trudgill 1986: 75). This argument is somewhat complex: these speakers have apparently taken intrusive-*r* as a hiatus filler 'off the shelf' (Milroy 2008) from what happens elsewhere, but have adapted it to have a local significance in terms of 'being Rossendale'. In a discussion following a pilot of the elicitation task, one young, rhotic Rossendale speaker stated: 'we would say "a bit Gretnarish" and we'd put an *r* in', a suggestion which met with agreement from other Rossendale speakers in the room. Of course, speakers' self-awareness of specific phonological features is not always a reliable guide, and such comments should clearly be viewed with caution.

Nonetheless, these results suggest that some Rossendale speakers are diverging from the typical phonological patterns of being either *rhotic-and-non-r-intruding* or *non-rhotic-and-r-intruding*. This phenomenon illustrates Horvarth and Horvarth's point that 'place effects can mask the universal phonological patterns' (2001: 54). While intrusive-*r* is generally linked to loss of rhoticity, in the specific local circumstances of Rossendale, it can coexist with rhoticity. The idea that a particular hiatus-filling segment can be socially significant and can entail a reshaping of the phonological system has been reported for London English. Britain (2009: 147) notes the use of [ʔ] as a hiatus filler, something also noted in Tyneside English (Foulkes 1997: 78), both in the specific cases of prevocalic instances of *the* and *a*, and in V#V hiatus positions more generally, and explains how this could be a marker of 'non-Anglo' status because of its use by various ethnic minority groups. Furthermore, this feature seems to have spread outside London: it is reported in the speech of young third-generation members of an Italian minority in Bedford (Britain and Fox 2009). This finding hints that a 'supralocal ethnolect' (Britain 2009: 147) may be emerging. A particular feature of the hiatus-filling strategy noted in non-Anglo London and Bedford speech is that it involves a levelling of the phonological system: where many varieties employ a range of hiatus-filling segments ([j] after high-front vowels, [w] after high and back vowels and [ɹ] after non-high vowels), this developing non-Anglo variety of English has [ʔ] in all contexts. Therefore, the new development is not just the adoption of a particular segment to fill a particular category of hiatus, but involves a reshaping of the phonological system. In the light of this, it is quite plausible for young Rossendale speakers to have reshaped their phonological system in terms of methods for filling hiatus. This change has apparently occurred even though they have not undergone a loss of rhoticity and the resulting series of processes of loss of contrast and then reanalysis of the underlying structure of sets of words that are argued to have caused intrusive-*r* to have emerged in the first place.

In the case of the younger Oxfordshire speakers, it might well be that their next stage is a shift towards the sort of levelled hiatus-filling system noted above. Certainly, they are much less consistent in using *r* in linking contexts than the East Lancashire speakers are, and it is also the case that, during the process of coding tokens of *r*, I noted a tendency for some of the Oxfordshire speakers to use a glottal stop in hiatus positions after high vowels and to have levelled systems of definite article allomorphy so that *the other* was [ðəʔʌðə].

Conclusion

This discussion of elicited tokens of *r*-sandhi has shown that there is variation in the frequency with which linking and intrusive-*r* are produced and in the factors that contribute to this variation. This variation is apparent across the two dialect areas I have discussed, and between individual speakers in each area. It is also evident that speakers sometimes behaved differently in response to the two tasks, with the place-name-based elicitation task triggering increased levels of intrusive-*r* compared to the classic reading task. This raises questions about which task is a better match for speakers' natural spontaneous speech. Bluntly, it could be the case that the repeated exposure to potential *r*-sandhi contexts in the elicitation task causes participants to produce a higher frequency of intrusive-*r* than they otherwise would. As Foulkes (1997) notes, intrusive-*r* is rare, and this is the reason for devising reading and elicitation tasks to push participants to demonstrate what they do when they are confronted with *r*-sandhi contexts in the speech they are being prompted to produce. Ideally, truly spontaneous, natural speech would sidestep possible task-related effects, if only a sufficient number of tokens could be obtained. Developments in the creation of large spoken-word corpora might represent the next step in investigating patterning in use of *r*-sandhi. However, for investigation of *r*-sandhi, accurate lexical identification (rather than just vowel identification) is important in order to appropriately categorise each token of surface *r* and this is something that requires refinement, even in state-of-the-art, automated systems such as DARLA (Reddy and Stanford 2015). Nonetheless, the ability to process very large sets of recorded data would offer a way forward, both from the constraints on using spontaneous speech pointed out by Foulkes (1997: 83) and from questions about the representativeness of elicited tokens of *r*-sandhi that arise given the different behaviour of speakers in the sentences and elicitation tasks reported on in this chapter.

Acknowledgements Map data from this chapter was drawn with outlines from http://www.d-maps.com/carte.php?num_car=2555&lang=en.

Notes

1. A reviewer notes that rhoticity might be more prevalent in the SED after NURSE vowels than after other vowels; *third* was chosen for this map for clarity, as there is a consistent [ɜ̯ː] vowel across the region shown on the map. The maps for *arm* or *darning* (START) still have rhoticity closely following the traditional Lancashire border, but with a range of vowels involved ([aˑ̯ː], [æˑ̯ː], [ɜ̯ː]); therefore, the maps are less clear. The same is true for *hare* (SQUARE) with [ɜ̯ː] and [ɛɜ̯] variants.
2. A reviewer notes that a feature such as rhoticity might have undergone a general decline simultaneously across the southwest outside of certain centres; Piercy's (2006) study of rhoticity in Dorset certainly seems compatible with this view, showing a very rapid decline in production of coda /r/ by younger speakers compared to older speakers.

References

Austin, S. (2007). *The decline of rhoticity in East Lancashire*. Unpublished BA dissertation, Lancaster University.

Barras, W. (2011). *The sociophonology of rhoticity and r-sandhi in East Lancashire English*. Unpublished PhD thesis, University of Edinburgh.

Boersma, P., & Weenink, D. (2015). *Praat: Doing phonetics by computer* [Computer program]. Version 5.4.08. Available online: http://www.praat.org/

Britain, D. (2009). One foot in the grave? Dialect death, dialect contact, and dialect birth in England. *International Journal of the Sociology of Language, 196*(197), 121–155.

Britain, D., & Fox, S. (2009). The regularisation of the hiatus resolution system in British English: A contact-induced 'vernacular universal'? In M. Filppula, J. Klemola, & H. Paulasto (Eds.), *Vernacular universals and language contacts: Evidence from varieties of English and beyond* (pp. 177–205). London: Routledge.

Britton, D. (2007). A history of hyper-rhoticity in English. *English Language and Linguistics, 11*, 525–536.

Broadbent, J. (1991). Linking and intrusive *r* in English. *UCL Working Papers in Linguistics, 3*, 281–301.

Broadbent, J. (1999). A new approach to the representation of coronal segments. In S. J. Hannahs & M. Davenport (Eds.), *Issues in phonological structure* (pp. 1–25). Amsterdam: John Benjamins.

Bybee, J. (2006). *Frequency of use and the organization of language.* Oxford: Oxford University Press.

Carr, P. (1999). *English phonetics and phonology.* Oxford: Blackwell.

Cruttenden, A. (2001). *Gimson's pronunciation of English.* London: Arnold.

Ellis, S. (1968). Lancashire dialect and its Yorkshire subsidiary. *Journal of the Lancashire Dialect Society, 17*, 18–21.

Foulkes, P. (1997). English [r]-sandhi – A sociolinguistic perspective. *Histoire, Epistémologie, Langage, 19*, 73–96.

Foulkes, P., & Docherty, G. J. (2006). The social life of phonetics and phonology. *Journal of Phonetics, 34*, 409–438.

Giegerich, H. J. (1999). *Lexical strata in English: Morphological causes, phonological effects.* Cambridge: Cambridge University Press.

Harris, J. (1994). *English sound structure.* Oxford: Blackwell.

Hay, J., & Maclagan, M. (2010). Social and phonetic conditioners on the frequency and degree of "intrusive /r/" in New Zealand English. In D. Preston & N. Niedzielski (Eds.), *Methods in sociophonetics* (pp. 41–70). New York: Walter de Gruyter.

Hay, J., & Sudbury, A. (2005). How rhoticity became /r/–sandhi. *Language, 81*, 799–823.

Horvarth, B., & Horvarth, R. (2001). A multilocality study of a sound change in progress: The case of /l/ vocalization in New Zealand and Australian English. *Language Variation and Change, 13*(1), 37–57.

Johnson, D. E. (2008). *Rbrul.* Available online: http://www.danielezrajohnson.com/rbrul.html

Johnson, D. E. (2009). Getting off the GoldVarb standard: Introducing Rbrul for mixed-effects variable rule analysis. *Language and Linguistics Compass, 3*(1), 359–383.

Max Planck Institute for Psycholinguistics. (2008). *Language archiving technology: ELAN*. Available online: http://www.lat-mpi.eu/tools/elan

Milroy, L. (2008). Off the shelf or under the counter? On the social dynamics of sound changes. In C. Cain & G. Russom (Eds.), *Studies in English historical linguistics III – Managing chaos: Strategies for identifying change in English* (pp. 149–172). Berlin: Mouton de Gruyter.

Orton, H., & Dieth, E. (1962). *Survey of English dialects (introduction and basic material)*. Leeds: Published for the University of Leeds by E.J. Arnold.

Orton, H., Sanderson, S., & Widdowson, J. (1978). *The linguistic atlas of English*. London: Croom Helm.

Piercy, C. (2006). *'Mixed with others it sounds different doesn't it': A quantitative analysis of rhoticity from four locations in Dorset*. Unpublished MA dissertation, University of Essex.

Reddy, S., & Stanford, J. (2015). Toward completely automated vowel extraction: Introducing DARLA. *Linguistics Vanguard, 1*, 15–28.

Trudgill, P. (1986). *Dialects in contact*. Oxford: Blackwell.

Trudgill, P. (2000). *The dialects of England* (2nd ed.). Oxford: Blackwell.

Uffmann, C. (2007). Intrusive [r] and optimal epenthetic consonants. *Language Sciences, 29*, 451–476.

Vennemann, T. (1972). Rule inversion. *Lingua, 29*, 209–242.

Vivian, L. (2000). */r/ in Accrington: An analysis of rhoticity and hyperdialectal /r/ in East Lancashire*. Unpublished BA thesis, University of Essex.

Wells, J. C. (1982). *Accents of English*. Cambridge: Cambridge University Press.

Index[1]

[1]Note: Page numbers followed by 'n' refers to notes.

© The Author(s) 2018
N. Braber, S. Jansen (eds.), *Sociolinguistics in England*,
DOI 10.1057/978-1-137-56288-3

CPSIA information can be obtained
at www.ICGtesting.com
Printed in the USA
LVOW05*1939020218
565058LV00021B/254/P